Algebra II

Grades 5-8

by
Chad Helgeson
and
Margaret Thomas

Published by Instructional Fair
an imprint of
Frank Schaffer Publications®

Instructional Fair

Authors: Chad Helgeson, Margaret Thomas
Editor: Jerry Aten

Frank Schaffer Publications®

Instructional Fair is an imprint of Frank Schaffer Publications.

Send all inquiries to:
Frank Schaffer Publications
3195 Wilson Drive NW
Grand Rapids, Michigan 49534

Algebra II—grades 5-8

ISBN: 0-7424-1789-1

5 6 7 8 9 10 11 MAZ 11 10 09 08 07 06

NCTM Standards of Math for Grades 5–8

Note to Teacher: Each activity in this book has been linked to the related NCTM Standard listed below. The numbers of the related standards for each activity are indicated in the Table of Contents.

1. Number and Operations – Understand numbers, ways of representing numbers, relationships among numbers, and number systems. Understand meanings of operations and how they relate to one another. Compute fluently and make reasonable estimates.

2. Algebra – Understand patterns, relations, and functions. Represent and analyze mathematical situations and structures using algebraic symbols. Use mathematical models to represent and understand quantitative relationships. Analyze change in various contexts.

3. Geometry – Analyze characteristics and properties of two- and three-dimensional geometric shapes and develop mathematical arguments about geometric relationships. Specify locations and describe spatial relationships using coordinate geometry and other representational systems. Apply transformations and use symmetry to analyze mathematical situations. Use visualization, spatial reasoning, and geometric modeling to solve problems.

4. Measurement – Understand measurable attributes of objects and the units, systems, and processes of measurement. Apply appropriate techniques, tools, and formulas to determine measurements.

5. Data Analysis and Probability – Formulate questions that can be addressed with data and collect, organize, and display relevant data to answer them. Select and use appropriate statistical methods to analyze data. Develop and evaluate inferences and predictions that are based on data. Understand and apply basic concepts of probability.

6. Problem Solving – Build new mathematical knowledge through problem solving. Solve problems that arise in mathematics and in other contexts. Apply and adapt a variety of appropriate strategies to solve problems. Monitor and reflect on the process of mathematical problem solving.

7. Reasoning and Proof – Recognize reasoning and proof as fundamental aspects of mathematics. Make and investigate mathematical conjectures. Develop and evaluate mathematical arguments and proofs. Select and use various types of reasoning and methods of proof.

8. Communication – Organize and consolidate their mathematical thinking through communication. Communicate their mathematical thinking coherently and clearly to peers, teachers, and others. Analyze and evaluate the mathematical thinking and strategies of others. Use the language of mathematics to express mathematical ideas precisely.

9. Connections – Recognize and use connections among mathematical ideas. Understand how mathematical ideas interconnect and build on one another to produce a coherent whole. Recognize and apply mathematics in contexts outside of mathematics.

10. Representation – Create and use representations to organize, record, and communicate mathematical ideas. Select, apply, and translate among mathematical representations to solve problems. Use representations to model and interpret physical, social, and mathematical phenomena.

Table of Contents

0-7424-1789-1 *Algebra*

Name ______________________ Date ______________________

Graphing Using a Table of Values

Complete the chart for each equation and graph. Charts may vary.

Example: $y = 2x$

x	y
$^-2$	$^-4$
0	0
2	4

1. $y = {}^-3x + 6$

x	y

2. $y = x - 2$

x	y

3. $y + 2x = {}^-2$

x	y

4. $2y + 6x = 5$

x	y

5. $y = \frac{1}{3}x + \frac{3}{2}$

x	y

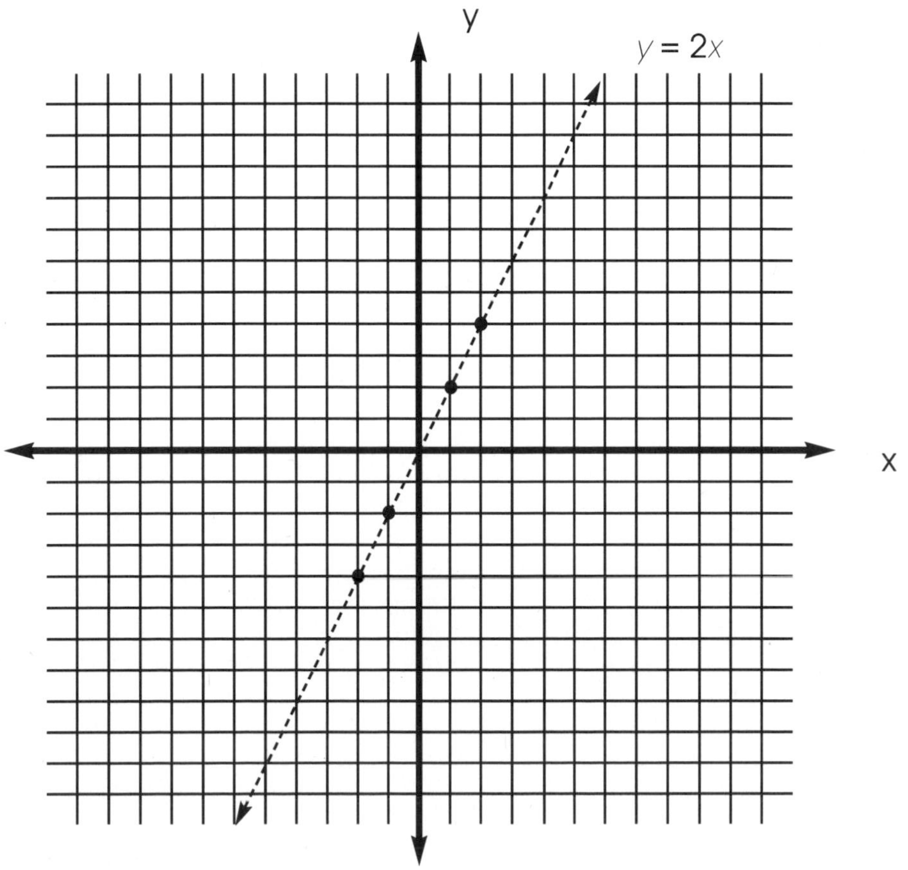

Name ______________________ Date ______________________

Slope

Find the slope of the line passing through two points using the formula:

slope = $m = \frac{(y_2 - y_1)}{(x_2 - x_1)}$.

Example: (1, 1) (4, 2)

(x_1, y_1) (x_2, y_2)

$m = \frac{(2 - 1)}{4 - 1} = \frac{1}{3}$

1. (15, ⁻12) (10, ⁻2)
2. (5, ⁻12) (15, ⁻2)
3. (⁻3, 14) (⁻1, 28)
4. (9, 6) (4, 6)
5. (8, 14) (22, ⁻9)
6. (33, 59) (0, 0)
7. (14, 21) (14, 6)
8. (5, 17) (⁻18, 9)
9. (16, ⁻1) (8, 9)
10. (⁻4, 2) (6, 9)
11. (8, 4) (7, ⁻3)
12. (⁻1, ⁻19) (⁻15, 4)
13. (⁻8, ⁻1) (6, 6)

Parallel lines have equal slopes. Two pairs of the lines indicated by the given points are parallel. Give the problem numbers of the parallel lines:

________ & ________ . ________ & ________ .

Perpendicular lines intersect to form right angles. (If they are not vertical or horizontal, then the product of the slopes equals ⁻1.) Two pairs of the lines indicated by the given points are perpendicular. Give the problem numbers of the perpendicular lines:

________ & ________ ; ________ & ________ .

What can be said about the relationship of any vertical line to any horizontal line?

____

0-7424-1789-1 *Algebra*

Name ______________________ Date ______________________

Slope and *Y*-Intercept

Find the slope and y-intercept from each graph.

$$\text{Slope} = \frac{\text{rise}}{\text{run}} = \frac{(y_2 - y_1)}{(x_2 - x_1)}$$

Hint: Think of rise as "ryse" to remind you that the y's go on top.

Example:

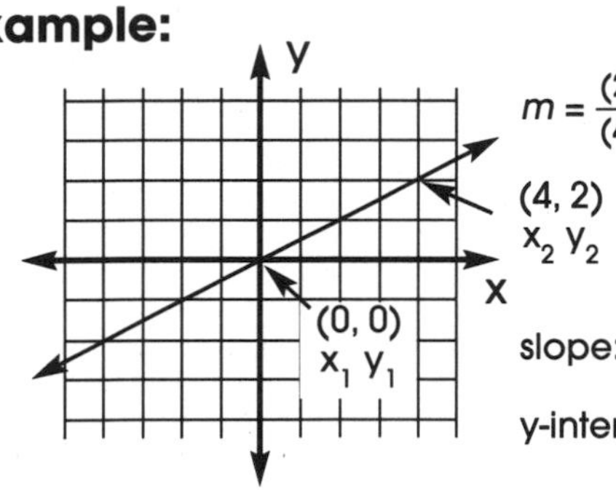

$m = \frac{(2 - 0)}{(4 - 0)} = \frac{2}{4} = \frac{1}{2}$

slope: $\frac{1}{2}$

y-intercept: (0, 0)

1.

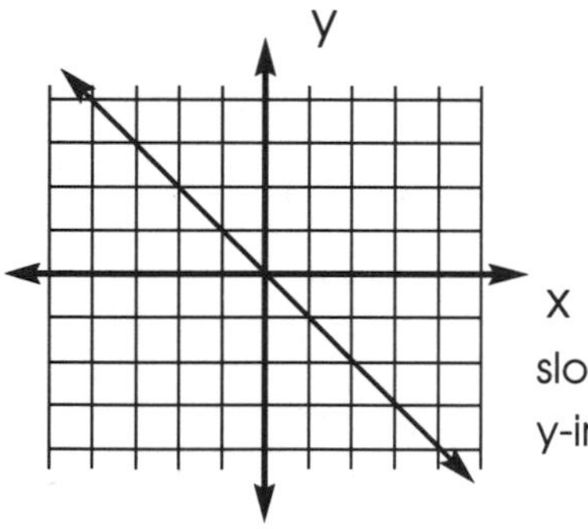

slope:
y-intercept:

2.

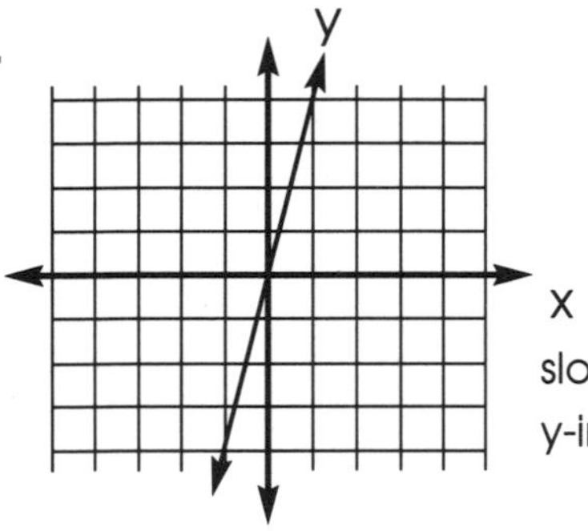

slope:
y-intercept:

3.

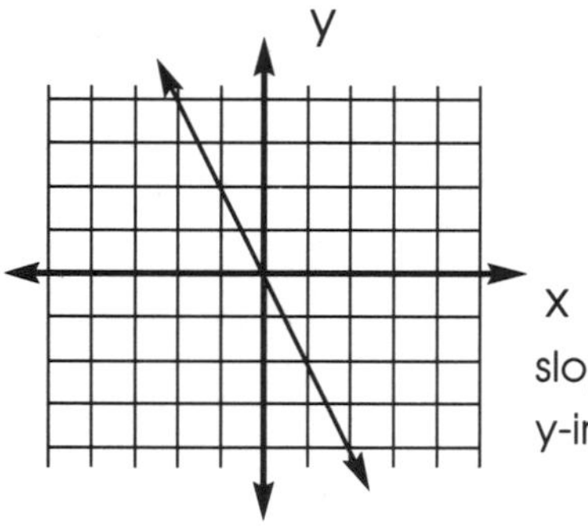

slope:
y-intercept:

4.

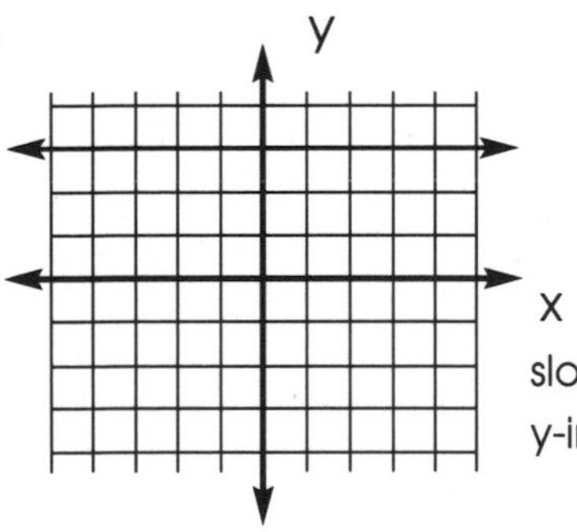

slope:
y-intercept:

5.

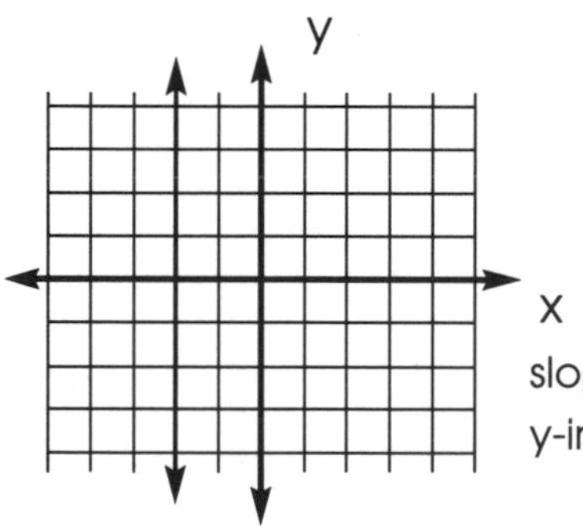

slope:
y-intercept:

6.

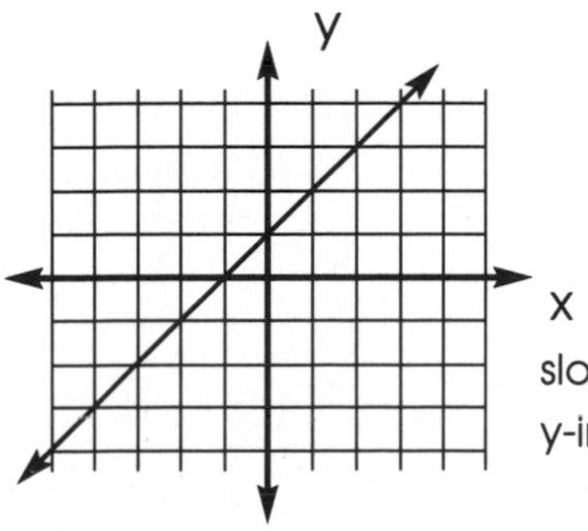

slope:
y-intercept:

7.

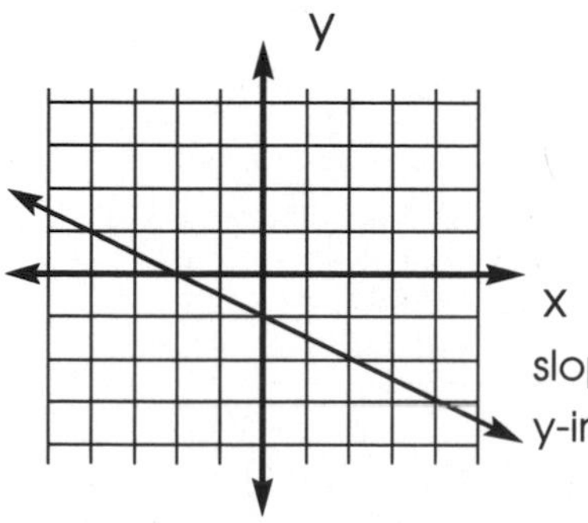

slope:
y-intercept:

0-7424-1789-1 *Algebra II*

Name ______________________________ Date ______________________________

X- and Y-Intercepts

Graph each linear equation using the x- and y-intercepts. Add units to both axes.

Example: $2x + 4y = 8$

x	y
0	2
4	0

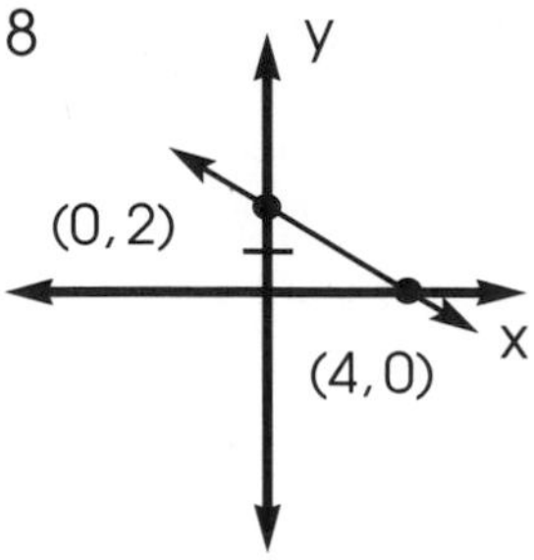

1. $3x - 2y = 12$

x	y
0	
	0

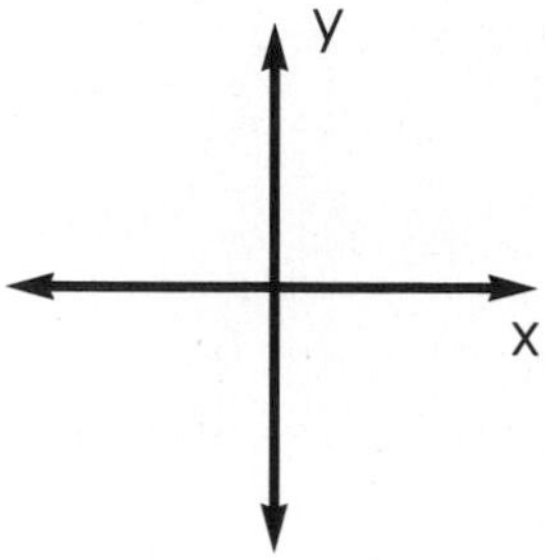

2. $-x + y = 5$

x	y
0	
	0

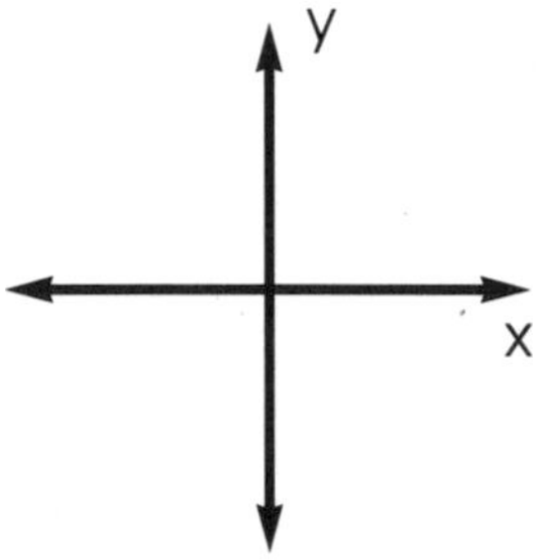

3. $5x - y = 10$

x	y
0	
	0

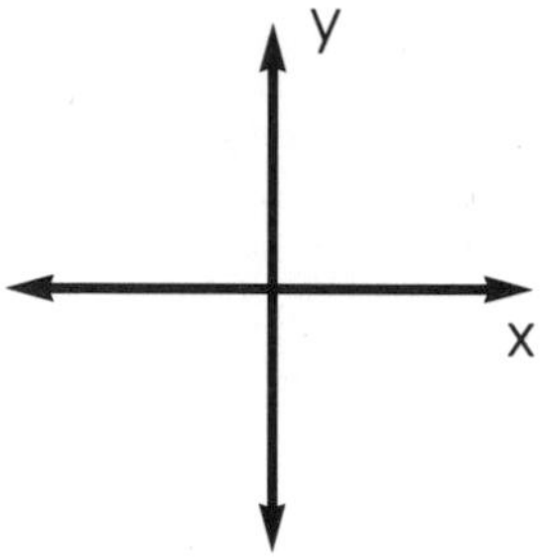

4. $\frac{1}{2}x + y = 5$

x	y
0	
	0

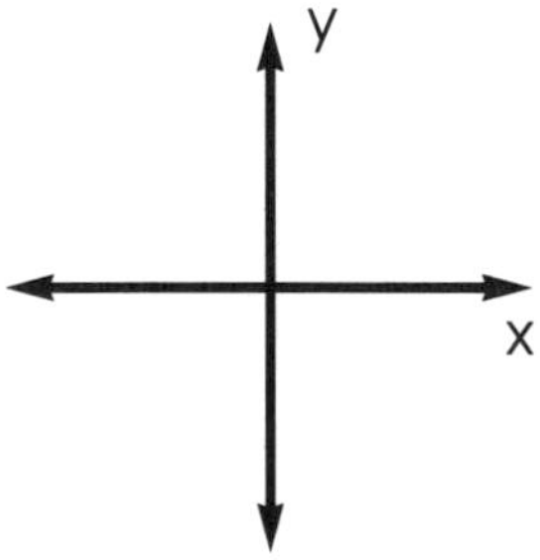

5. $10x - 2y = {}^{-}10$

x	y
0	
	0

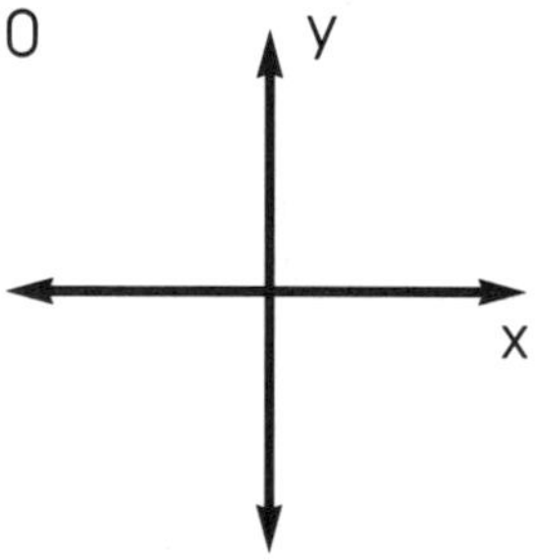

6. $x - \frac{1}{3}y = 2$

x	y
0	
	0

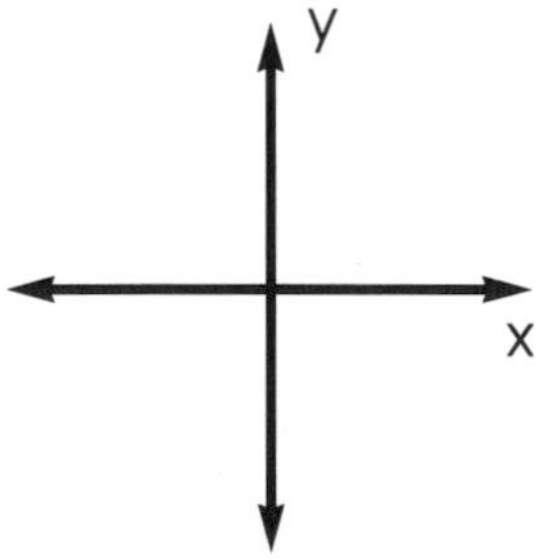

7. $\frac{1}{3}x + \frac{1}{2}y = {}^{-}1$

x	y
0	
	0

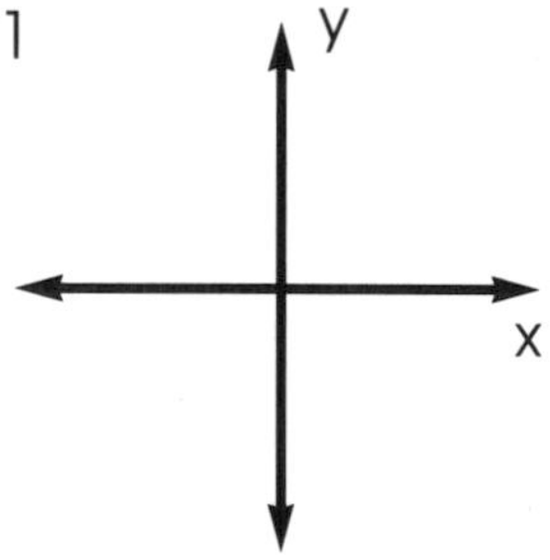

8. $8x - \frac{1}{2}y = 4$

x	y
0	
	0

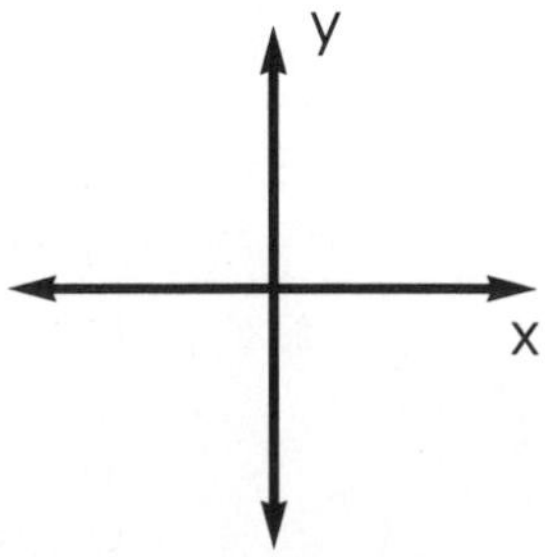

9. $\frac{2}{3}x + \frac{1}{2}y = 6$

x	y
0	
	0

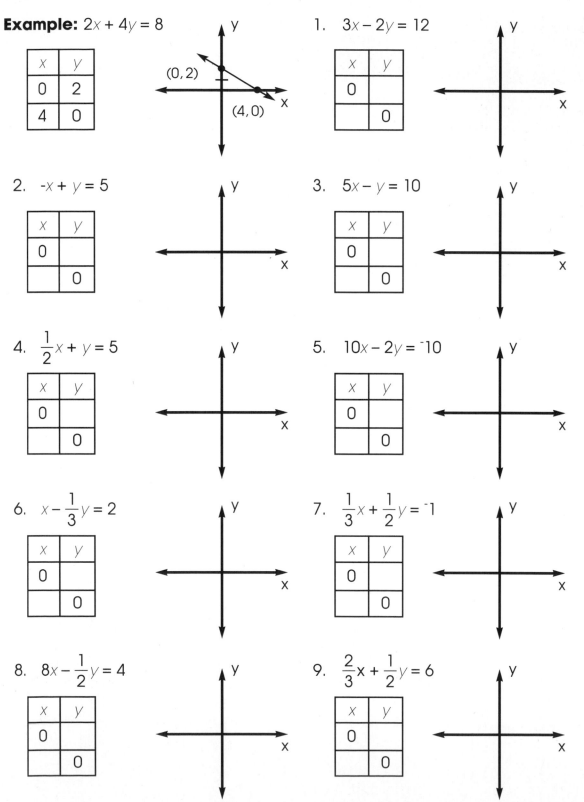

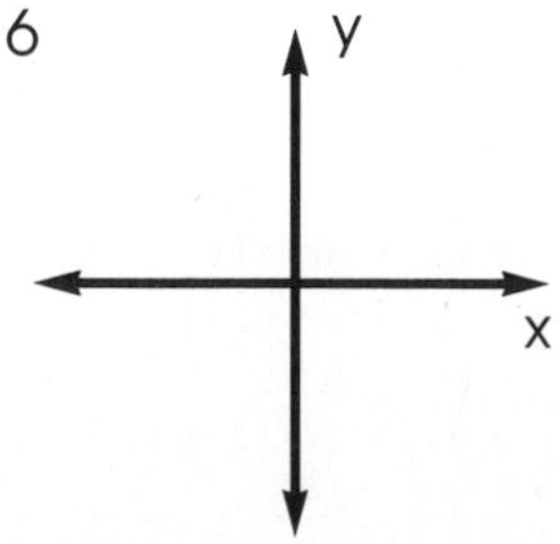

0-7424-1789-1 *Algebra*

Name ______________________________ Date ______________________________

Slope and *Y*-Intercept

Graph each linear equation using the slope and y-intercept. Add units to both axes. $y = mx + b$, where m = slope and b = y-intercept.

Example: $y = 2x + 1$

y – int (0, 1)

$m = \frac{2}{1} = \frac{\text{up 2}}{\text{right 1}}$

Note: Move up 2 and over one from y-intercept.

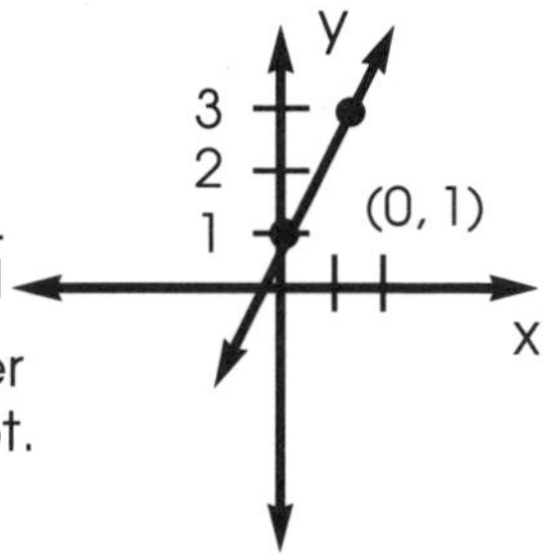

1. $y = -x + 6$

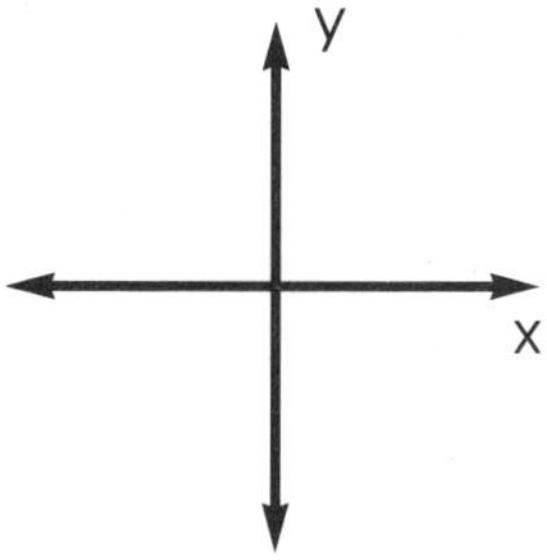

2. $y = \frac{^-2}{3}x - 1$

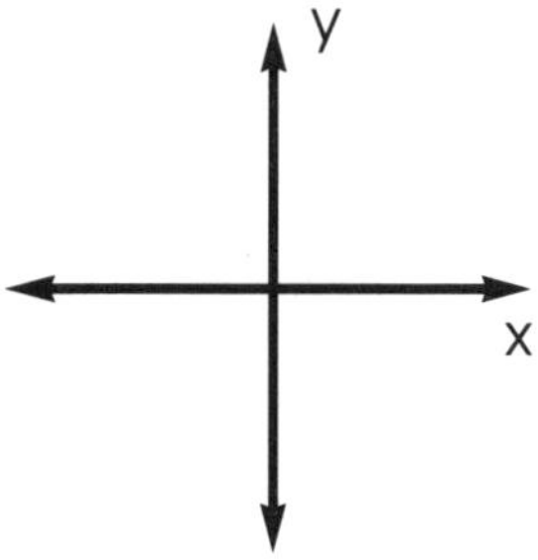

3. $y = 5x + 5$

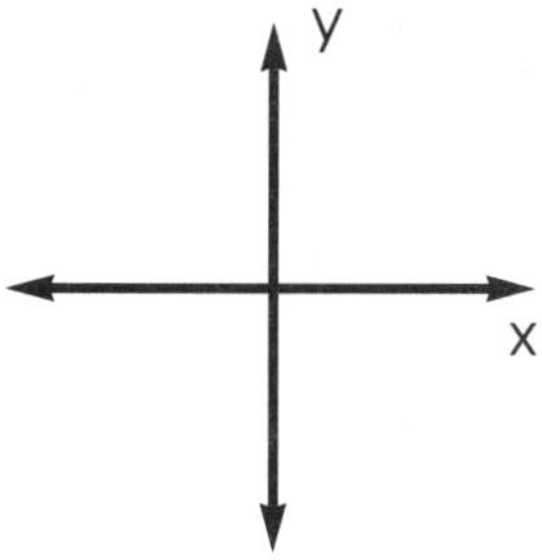

4. $y = 4x$

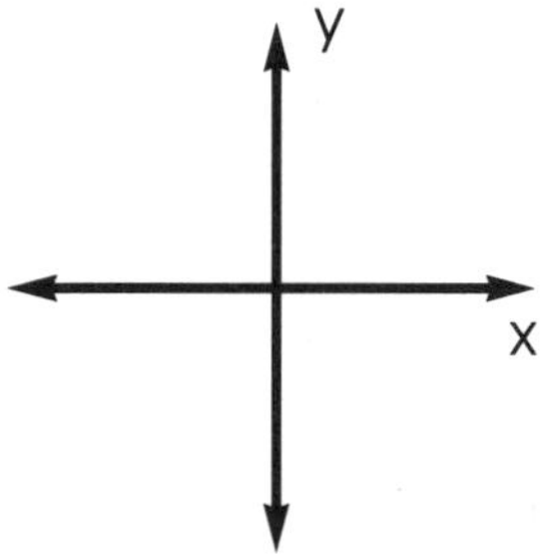

5. $y = 4$

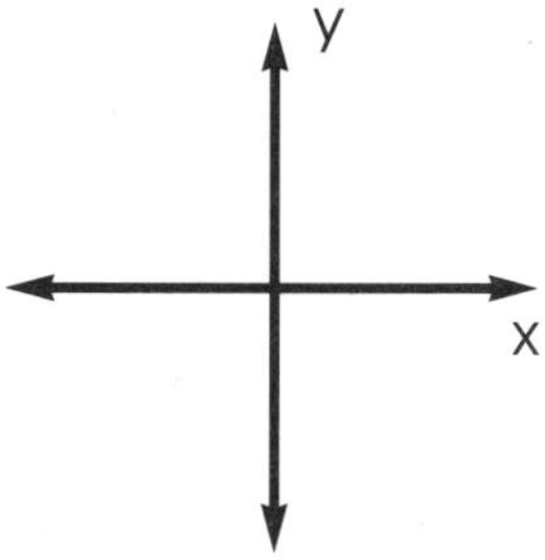

6. $x = {^-9}$

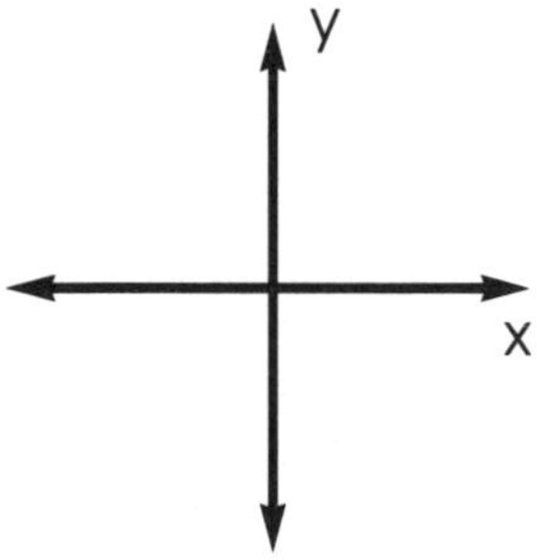

7. $y = {^-2}x - 4$

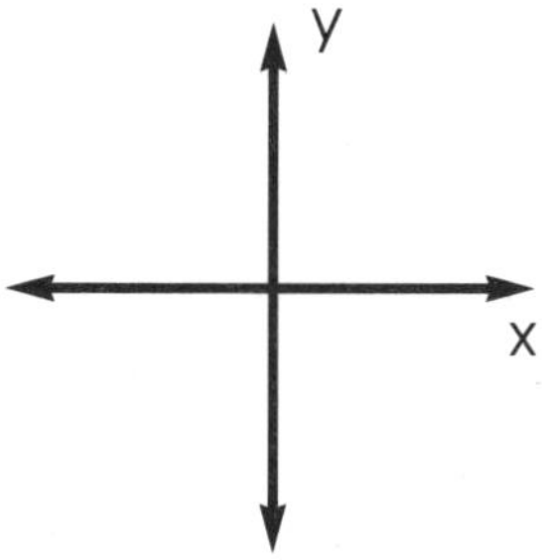

8. $y = \frac{3}{5}x$

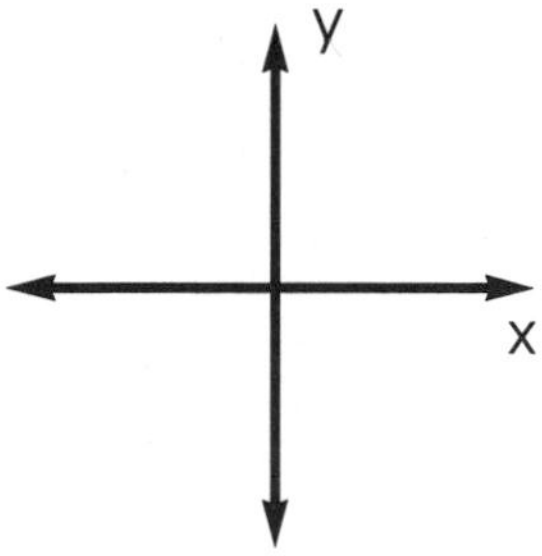

9. $y = \frac{^-1}{2}x + 3$

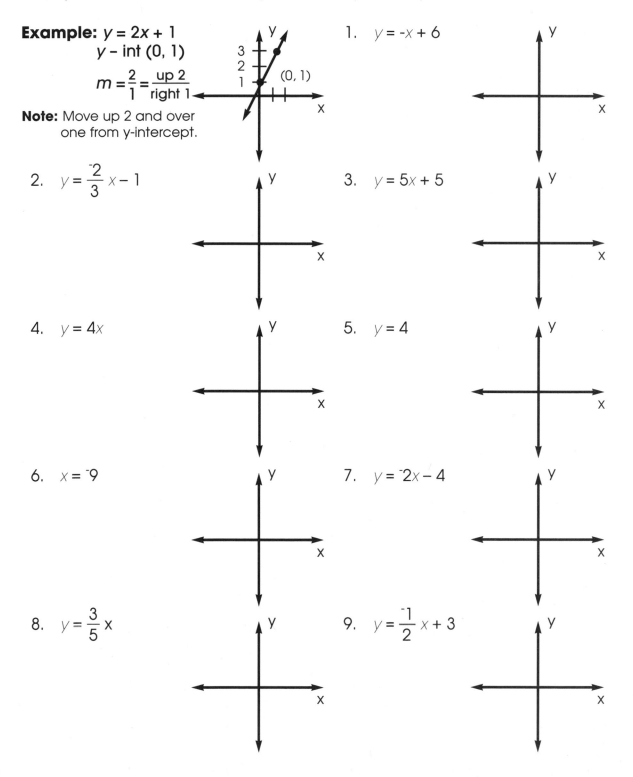

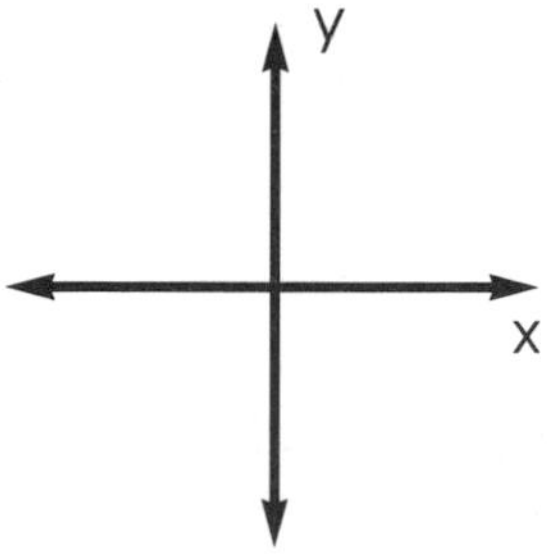

Name ______________________ Date ______________________

Graphing Linear Inequalities

Graph each inequality, recalling that $\le$ and $\ge$ require a solid line which includes the values on the line, while $<$ and $>$ require a dashed line, excluding the values on the line.

Example 1: $2x + 6y \ge 12$

x	y
0	2
6	0

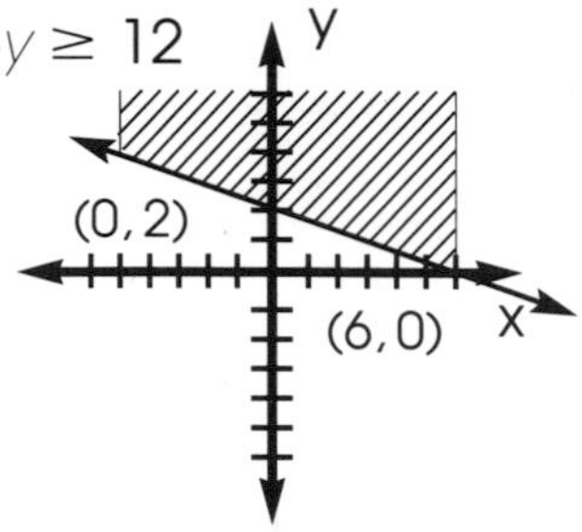

Example 2: $y > {}^{-}2x$

$m = \frac{{}^{-}2}{1}$ $\frac{\text{Down 2}}{\text{Right 1}}$

y – int (0, 0)

Note: Dashed line

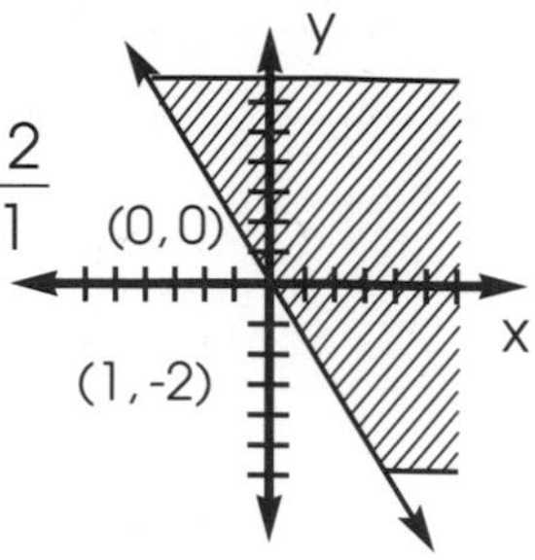

1. $y > x + 1$

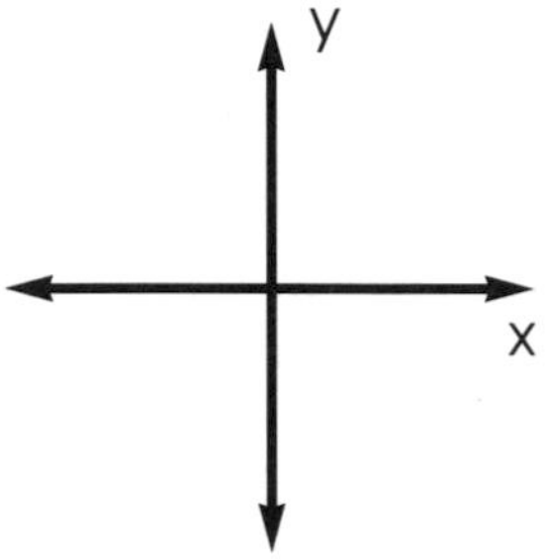

2. $3x - y \le 6$

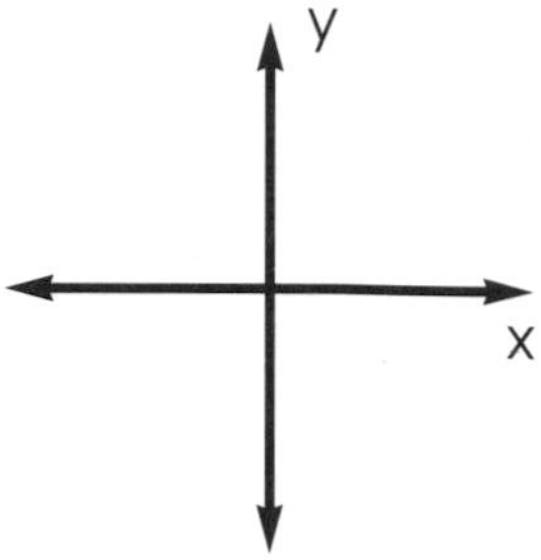

3. $y + 5 \le 0$

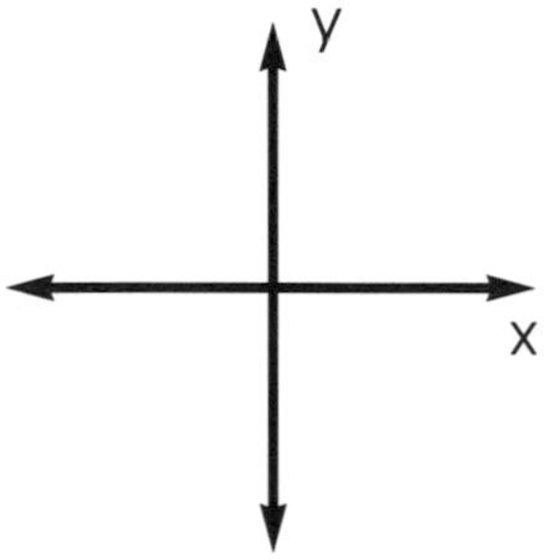

4. $y \ge 2x - 3$

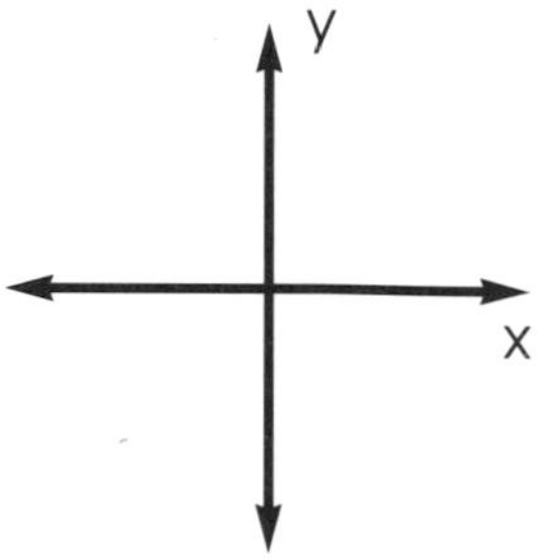

5. $x + y < 3$

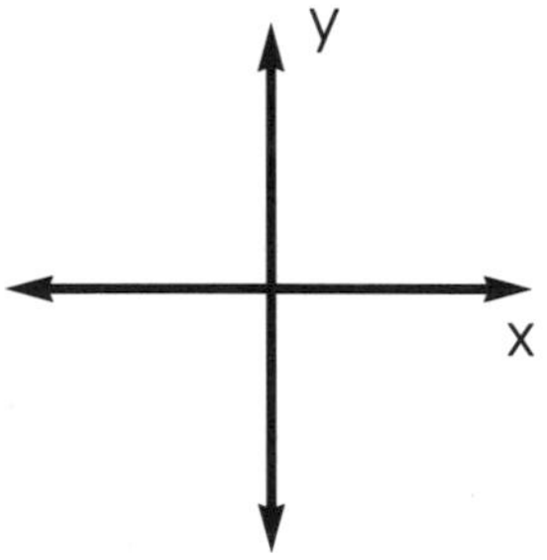

6. $2x + y > {}^{-}8$

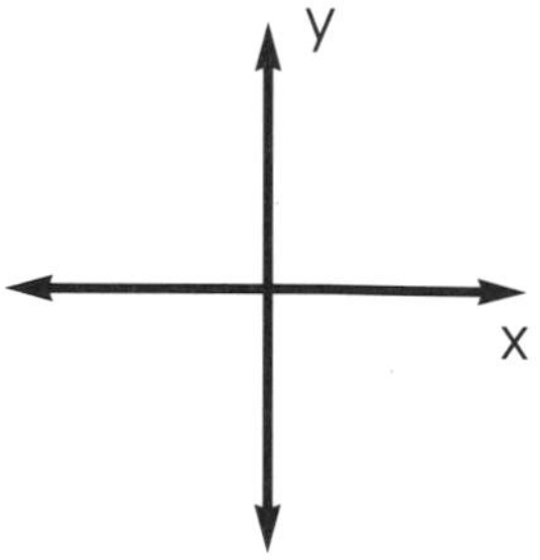

7. $y < -\frac{1}{2}x + 1$

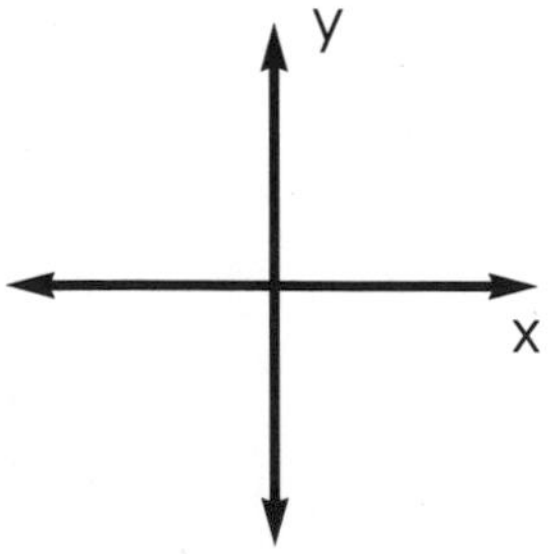

8. $3x - 4y \le 12$

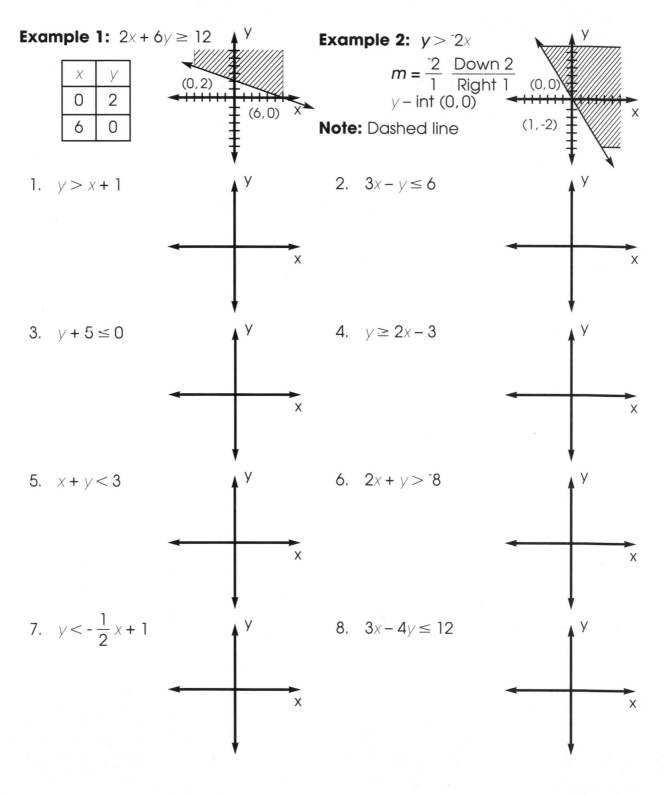

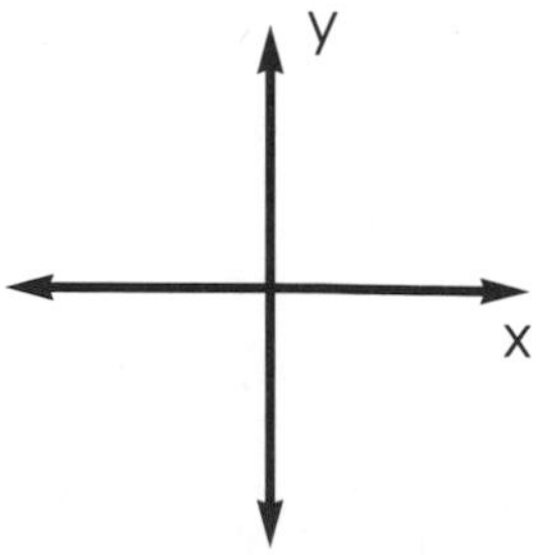

0-7424-1789-1 *Algebr*

Name ______________________________ Date ______________________________

Solving Systems by Graphing

Estimate the solution of the system by graphing.

Example: $\begin{cases} x - y = 6 \\ 2x + y = 0 \end{cases}$

x	y
0	$^{-}6$
6	0

x	y
0	0
1	$^{-}2$

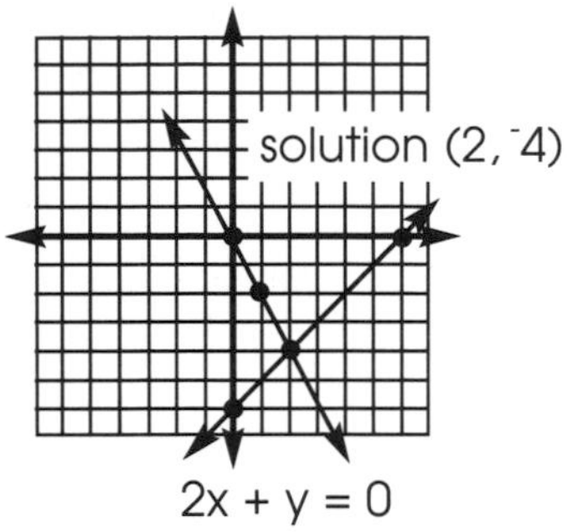

1. $\begin{cases} y = 6 \\ 2x - 2y = {}^{-}4 \end{cases}$

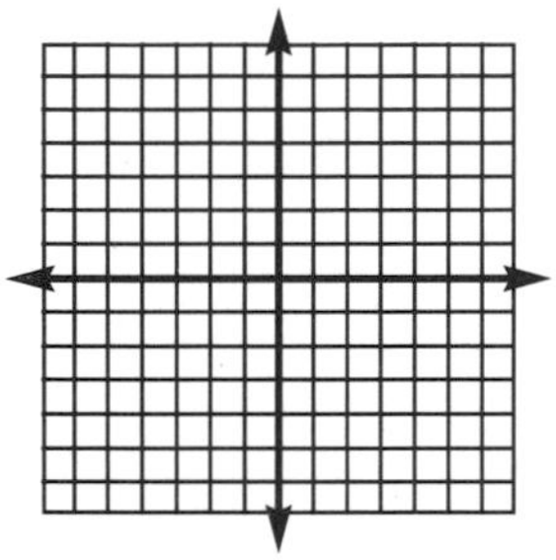

2. $\begin{cases} x = 4 \\ y = 2x \end{cases}$

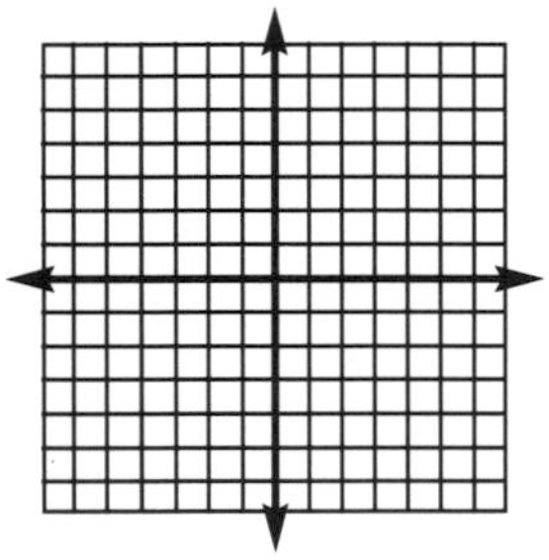

3. $\begin{cases} 2x - y = 1 \\ 3x + y = {}^{-}6 \end{cases}$

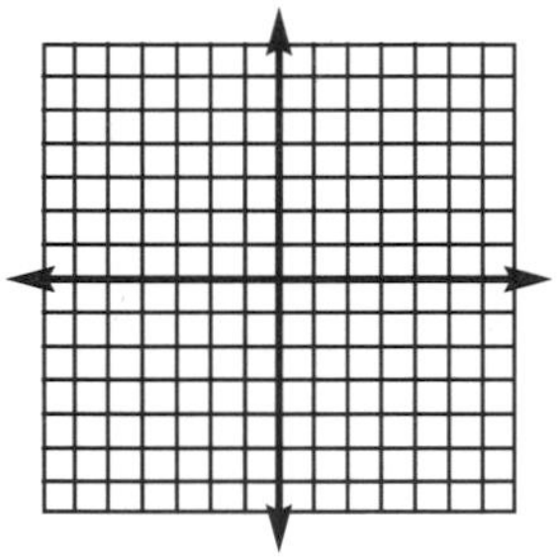

4. $\begin{cases} 2x - y = 5 \\ x - y = 1 \end{cases}$

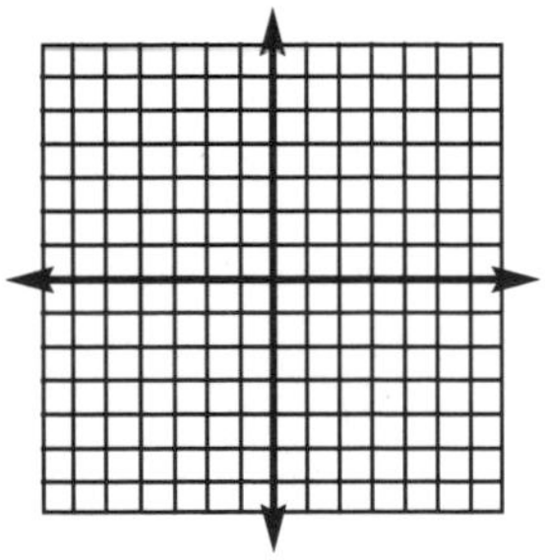

5. $\begin{cases} x = 2 \\ y = {}^{-}6 \end{cases}$

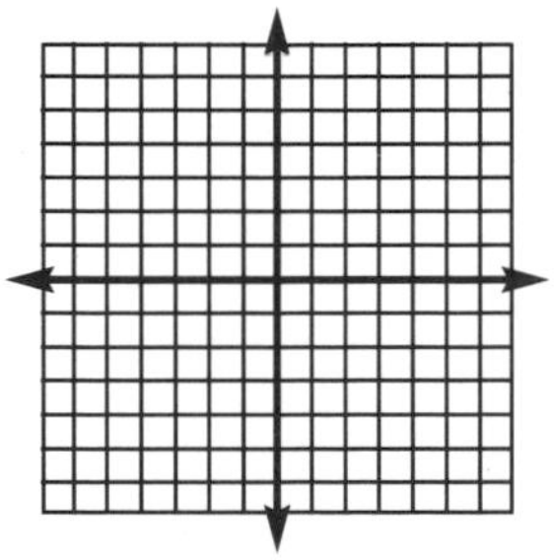

6. $\begin{cases} 2x + y = {}^{-}6 \\ 3x + y = {}^{-}10 \end{cases}$

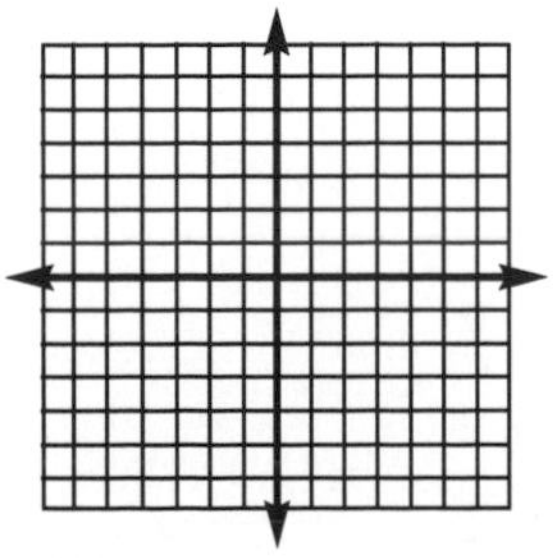

7. $\begin{cases} 7y + 15 = 3x \\ 15 = 3x + 2y \end{cases}$

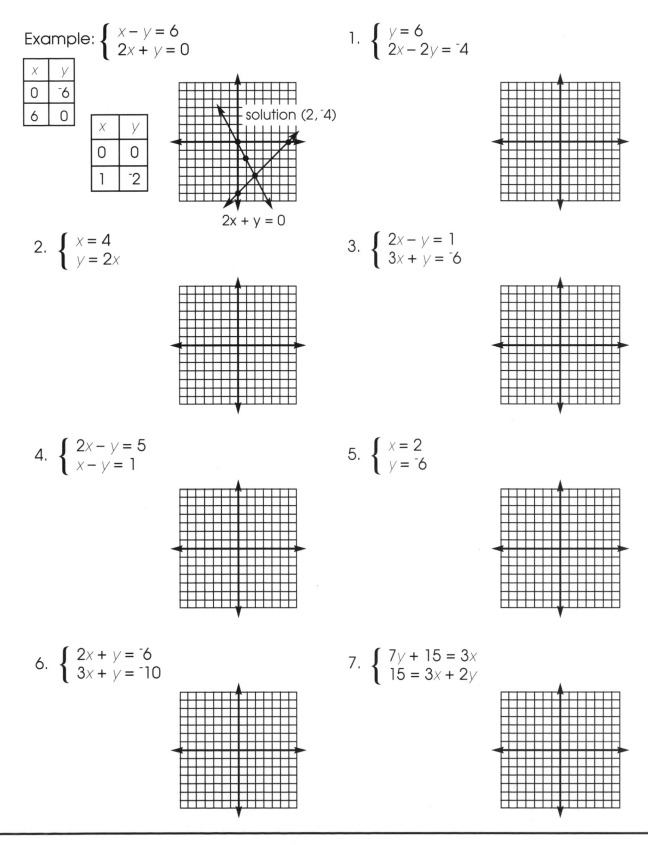

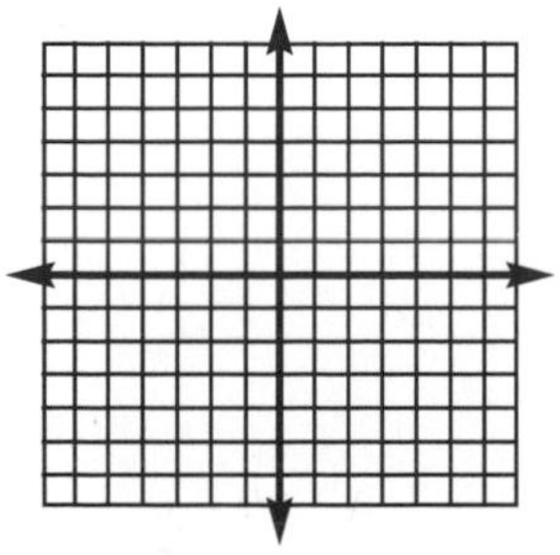

Name ______________________ Date ______________________

Solving Systems by Elimination

Create a quick graph and solve the system by elimination.

Hint: Rewrite one or both of the equations so that adding "eliminates" a variable.

Example: $\left\{ 3x - 4y = {}^{-}15 \right.$

x	y
0	$\frac{15}{4} \approx 3.75$
$^{-}5$	0

x	y
0	$^{-}2$
$-\frac{2}{5}$	0

$3x - 4y = {}^{-}15$
$4(5x + y = {}^{-}2)$

$3x - 4y = {}^{-}15$
$\underline{20x + 4y = {}^{-}8}$
$23x = {}^{-}23$
$x = {}^{-}1$

$5x + y = {}^{-}2$
$y = {}^{-}5\,({}^{-}1) - 2$
$y = 3$

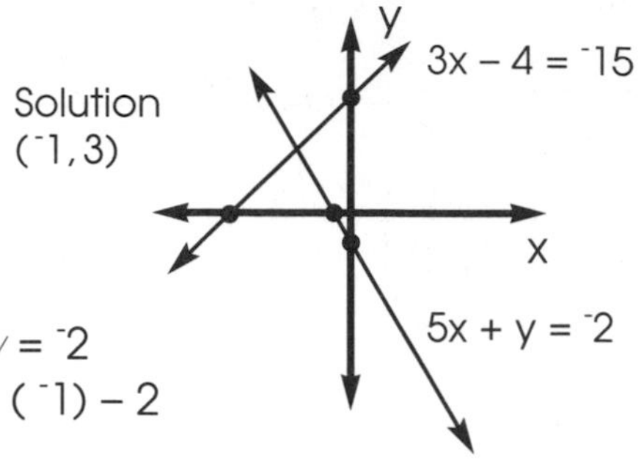

1. $\begin{cases} 2x + y = 0 \\ {}^{-}2x + 3y = 8 \end{cases}$

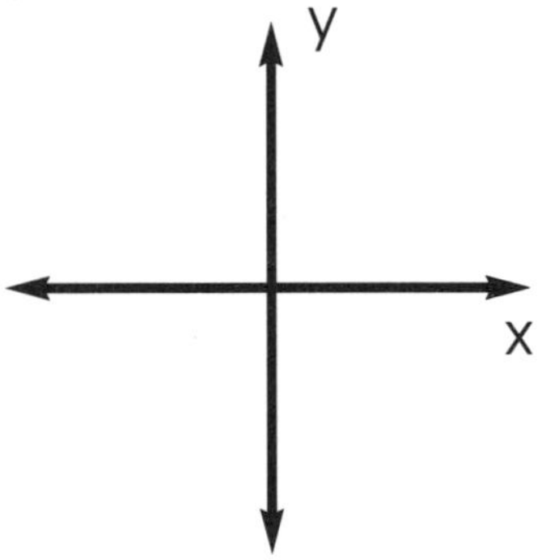

2. $\begin{cases} 5x - 6y = 16 \\ 5x + y = 2 \end{cases}$

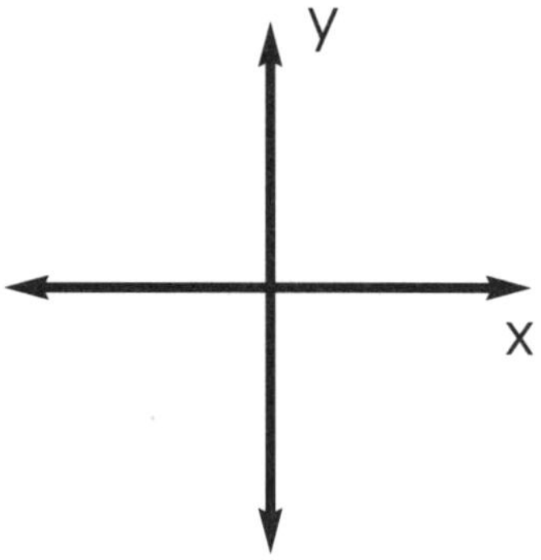

3. $\begin{cases} 4x - 2y = {}^{-}2 \\ 4x + 3y = {}^{-}12 \end{cases}$

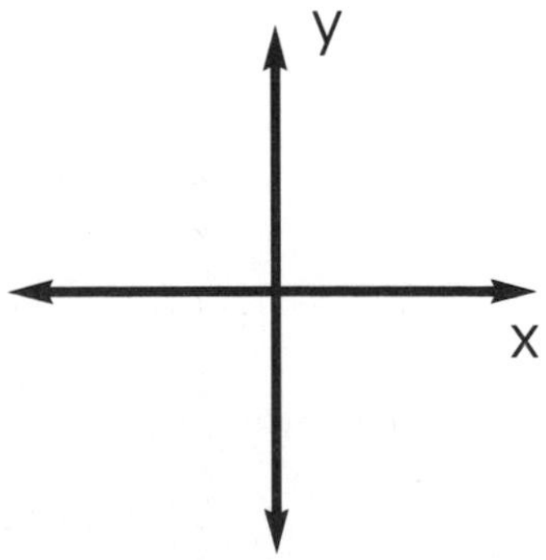

4. $\begin{cases} x - 2y = {}^{-}8 \\ 3x + y = 4 \end{cases}$

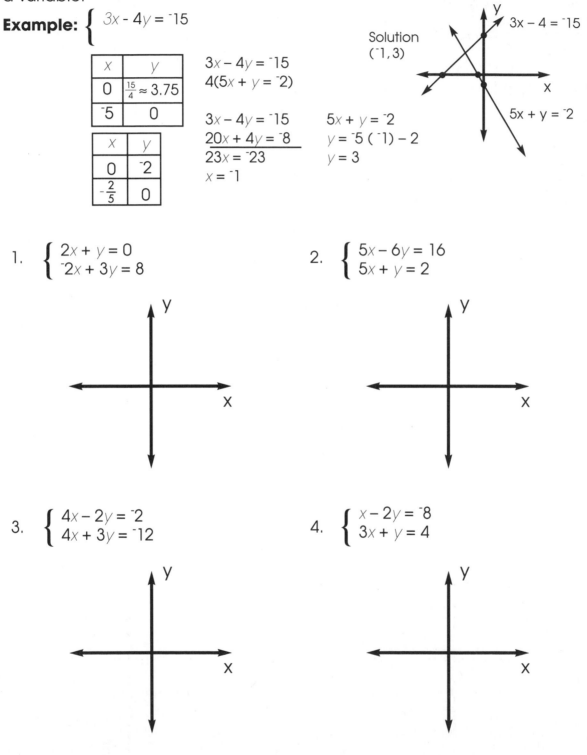

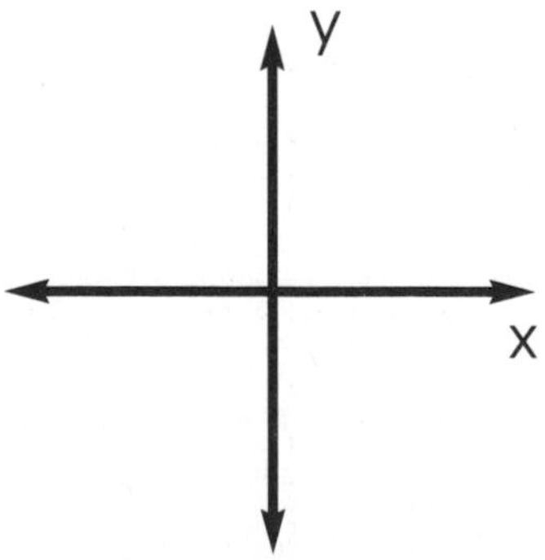

0-7424-1789-1 Algebra

Name ______________________________ Date ______________________________

Solving Systems by Substitution

Create a quick graph and solve the system by substitution.

Example: $\begin{cases} y = -x + 6 \\ x - 2y = {}^{-}6 \end{cases}$

x	y
0	3
$^{-}6$	0

graph: y – int (0, 6)

$m = \frac{^{-}1}{1}$ $\quad \frac{\text{down one}}{\text{right one}}$

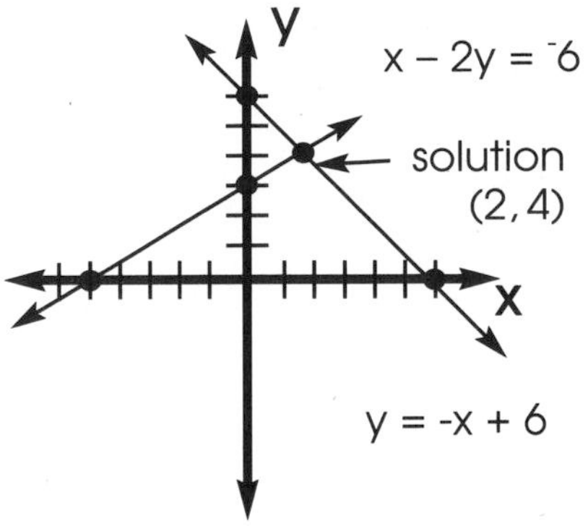

solve: $x - 2(-x + 6) = {}^{-}6$

$x + 2x - 12 = {}^{-}6$ $\qquad y = -x - 6$

$3x = 6$ $\qquad y = {}^{-}2 + 6$

$x = 2$ $\qquad y = 4$

1. $\begin{cases} y = 3x \\ x + y = 8 \end{cases}$

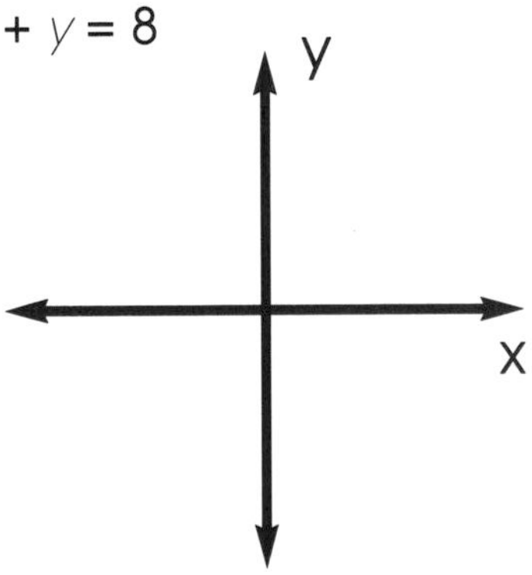

2. $\begin{cases} 2x = 3y \\ x = 3y - 3 \end{cases}$

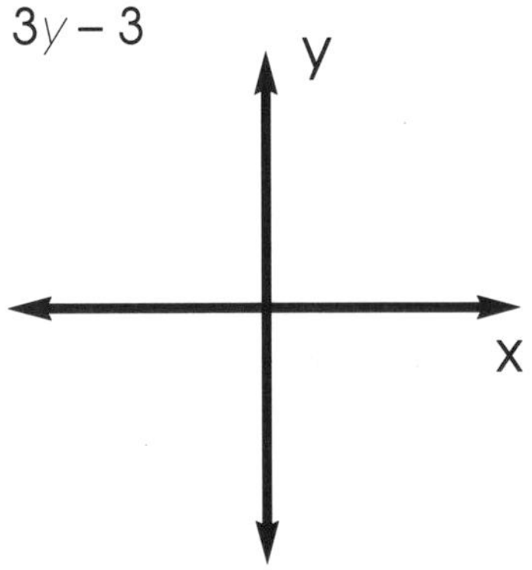

3. $\begin{cases} y = x - 2 \\ x + y = 0 \end{cases}$

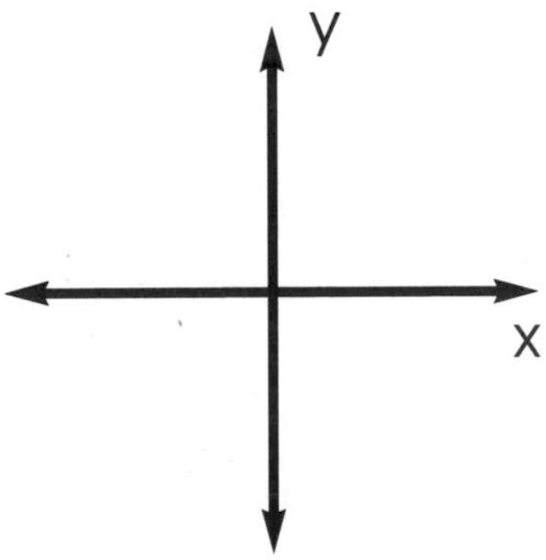

4. $\begin{cases} \frac{3}{2}x - 2y = 20 \\ y = \frac{^{-}5}{4}x \end{cases}$

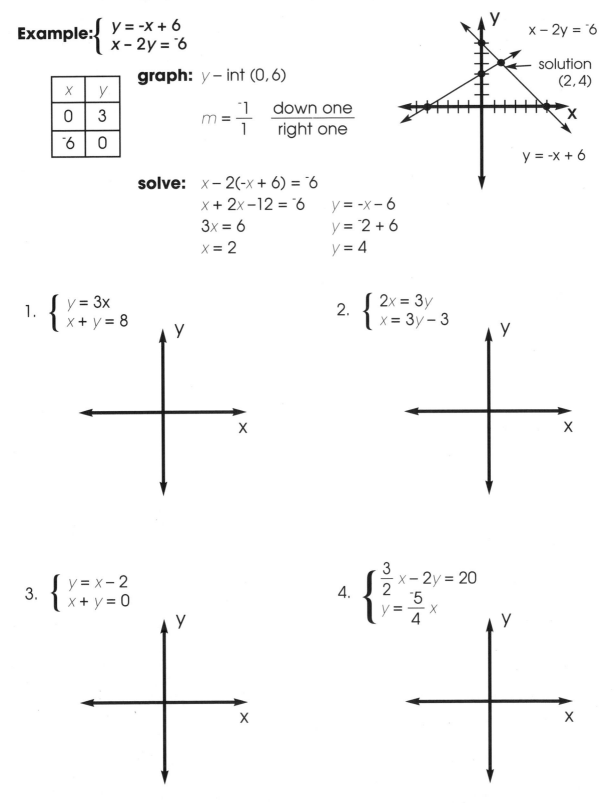

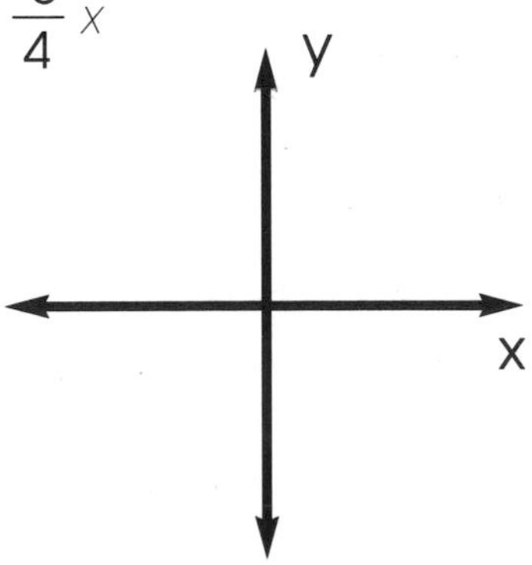

Name ______________________________ Date ______________________________

Graphing Systems of Linear Inequalities

Graph the system of linear inequalities.

Example: $\begin{cases} y \geq x - 1 \\ y \leq {}^-2x + 1 \end{cases}$

Note: < or > = dashed lines

≤ or ≥ = solid lines

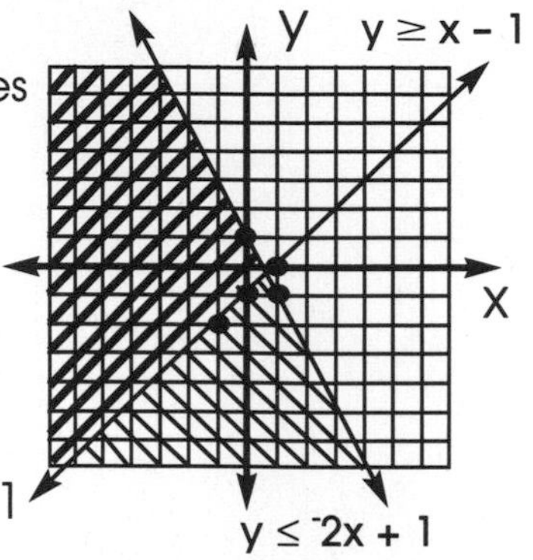

1. $\begin{cases} x - 2y < {}^-8 \\ 3x + y > 4 \end{cases}$

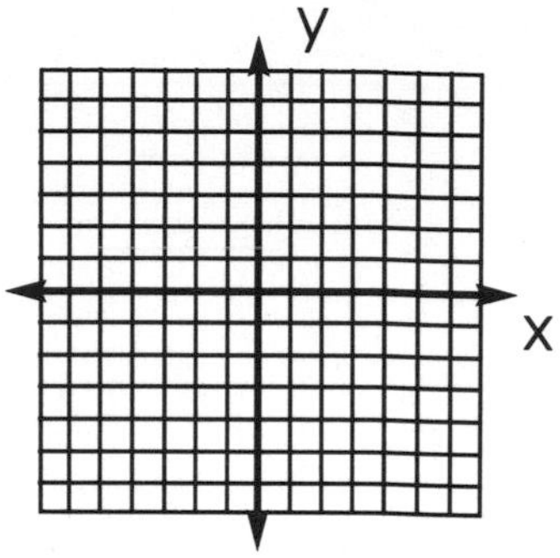

2. $\begin{cases} 3x - 5y > 11 \\ 4x - 3y \geq 5 \end{cases}$

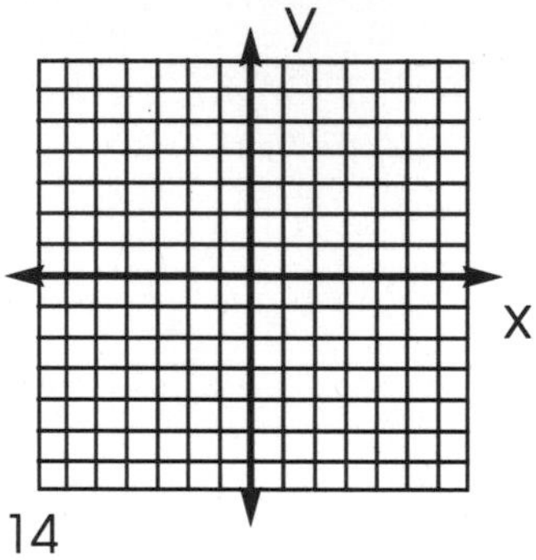

3. $\begin{cases} y > \frac{1}{2}x + 3 \\ y > 3 \end{cases}$

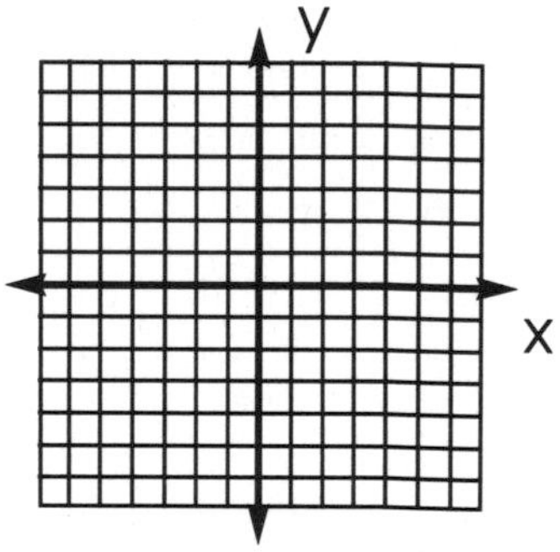

4. $\begin{cases} 2x + 3y \leq 14 \\ 3x - 2y < {}^-5 \end{cases}$

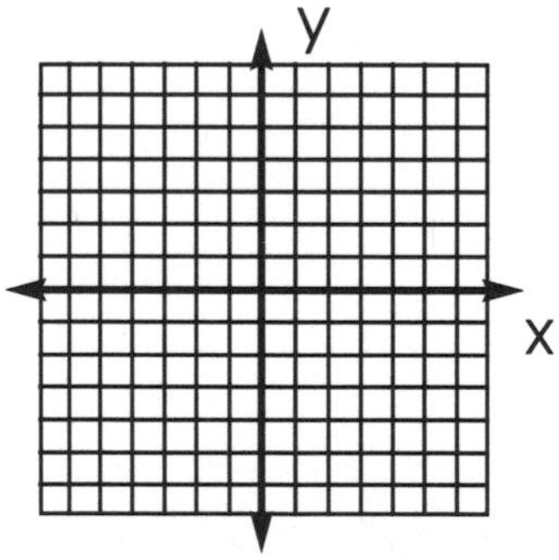

5. $\begin{cases} 5x + 2y > {}^-8 \\ 2x - 5y \leq {}^-9 \end{cases}$

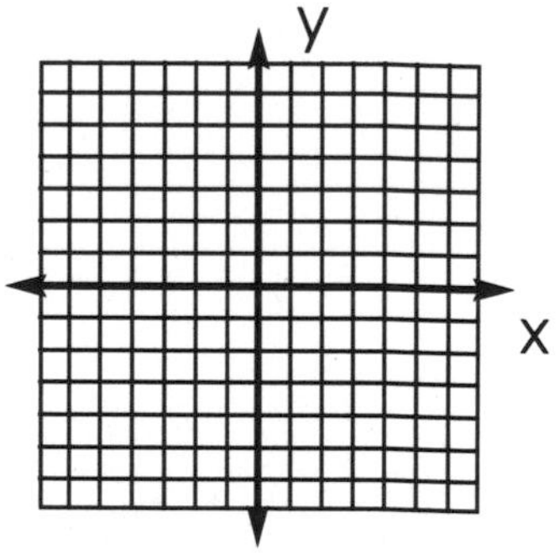

6. $\begin{cases} x \geq 6 \\ y \leq 2x - 6 \end{cases}$

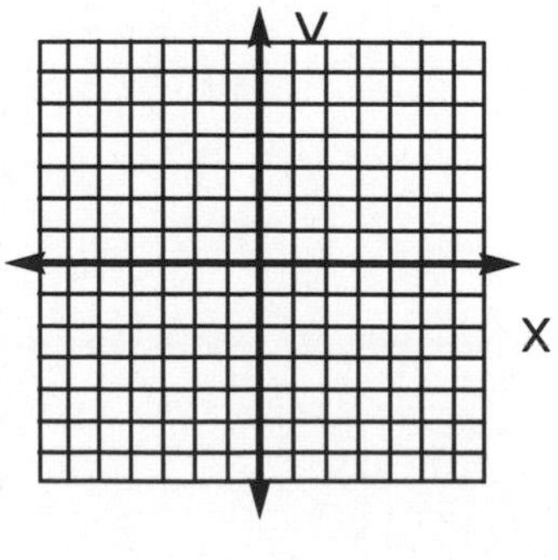

7. $\begin{cases} y > {}^-2x + 4 \\ y \leq 6x - 3 \end{cases}$

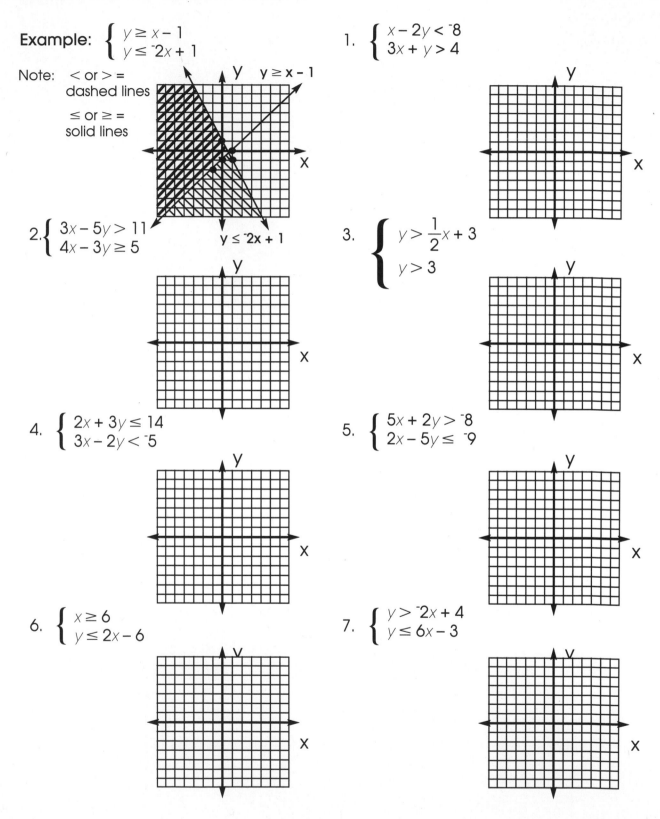

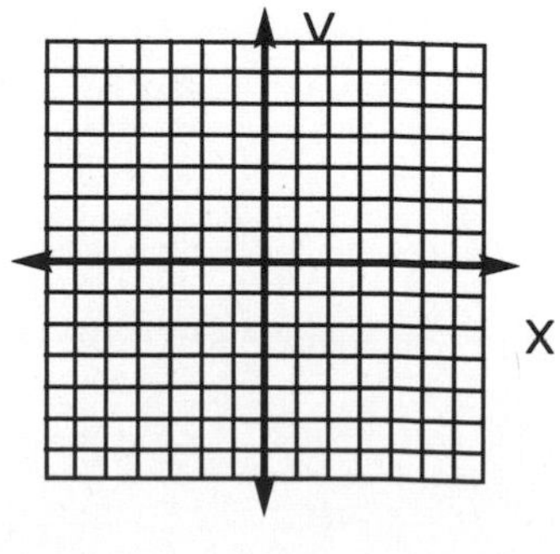

Name ______________________ Date ______________________

Review: Solving Linear Systems

Create a quick graph and solve using elimination or substitution.

1. $\begin{cases} 2x - 4y = 18 \\ 3x - y = 22 \end{cases}$

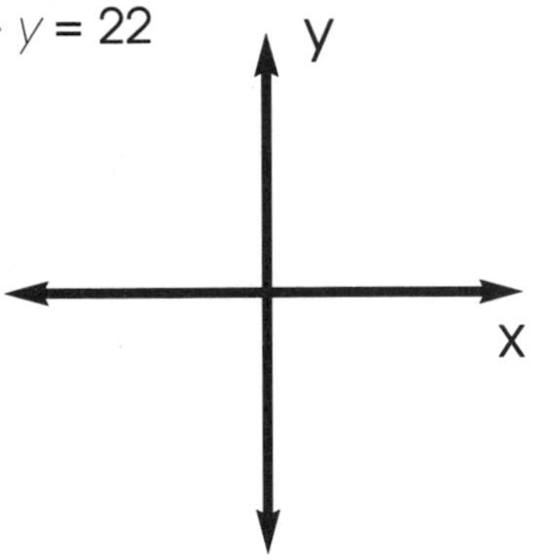

2. $\begin{cases} 3x + 10y = 16 \\ x = {}^{-}6y \end{cases}$

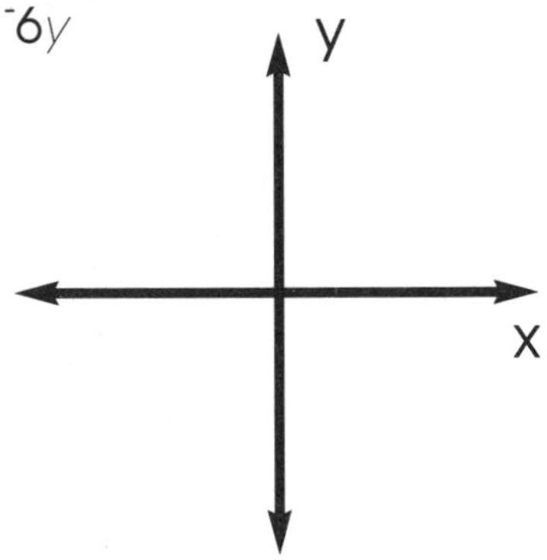

3. $\begin{cases} y = 5x \\ {}^{-}3x + 2y = {}^{-}28 \end{cases}$

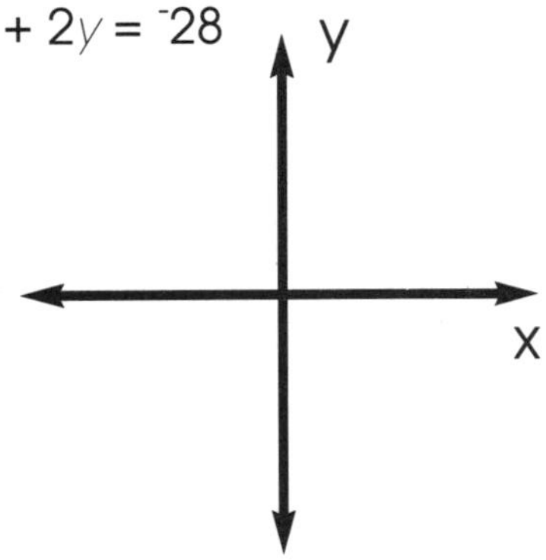

4. $\begin{cases} 4x - 5y = {}^{-}19 \\ 3x + 7y = 18 \end{cases}$

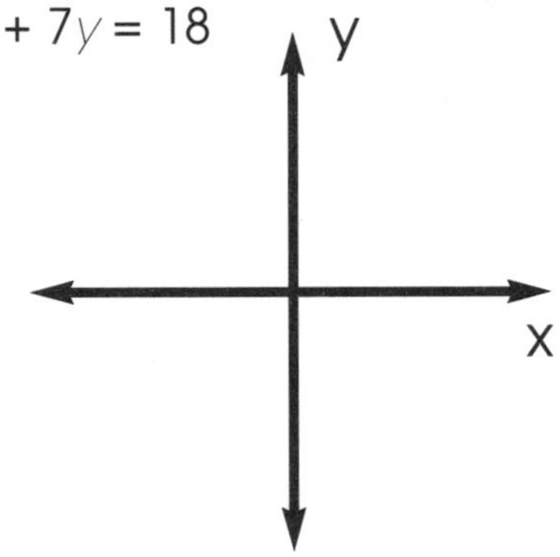

5. $\begin{cases} y = 4 \\ 5x - 6y = 11 \end{cases}$

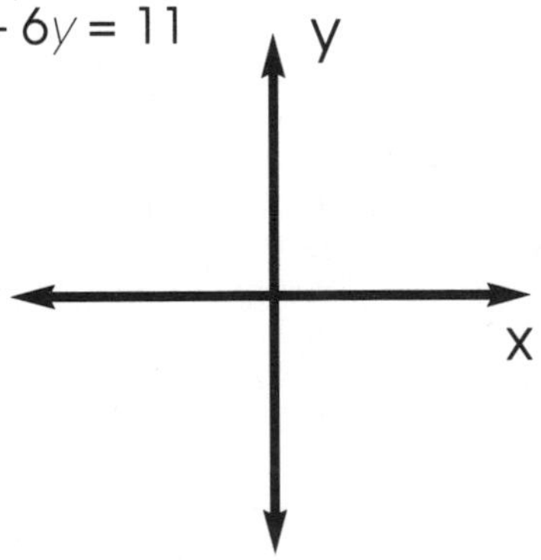

6. $\begin{cases} y = x - 4 \\ 2x - y = {}^{-}2.5 \end{cases}$

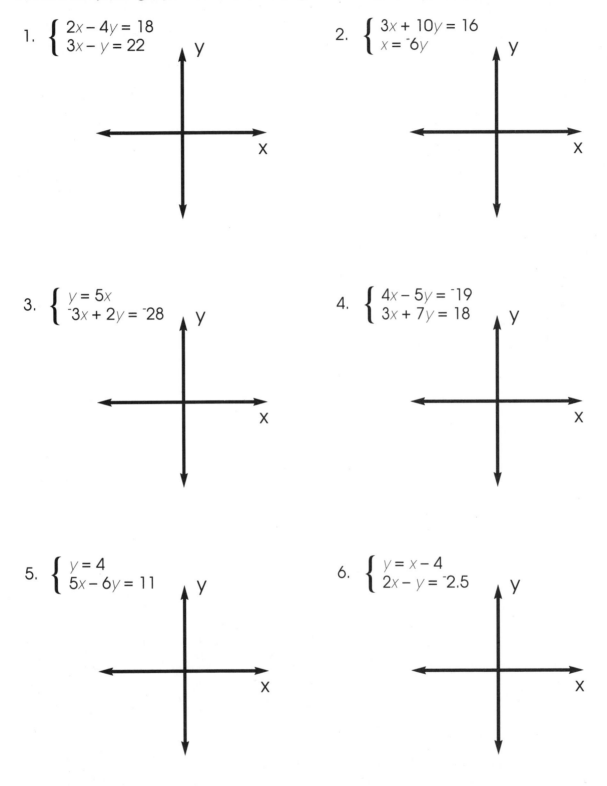

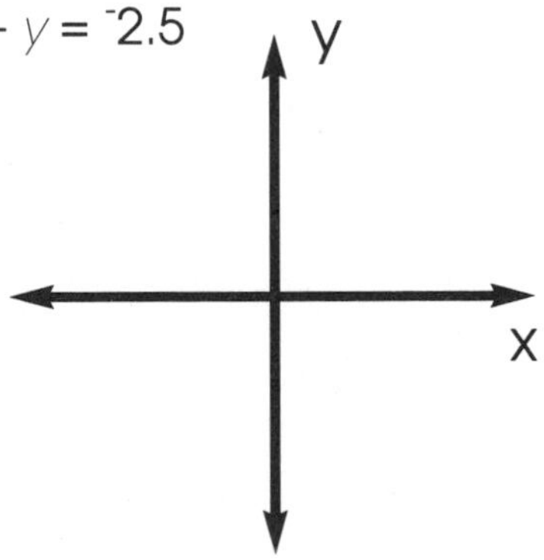

0-7424-1789-1 *Algebra II*

Name ______________________ Date ______________________

Graphing Quadratics: $y = ax^2$

Graph each quadratic equation using a table of values. Charts may vary.

Example: $y = x^2$

x	y
-2	4
-1	1
0	0
1	1
2	4

1. $y = 2x^2$

x	y

2. $y = -x^2$

x	y

3. $y = {}^{-}3x^2$

x	y

4. $y = \frac{1}{3}x^2$

x	y

5. $y = \frac{-1}{2}x^2$

x	y

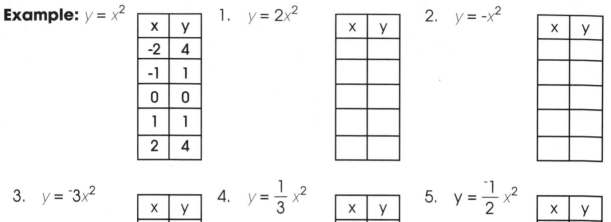

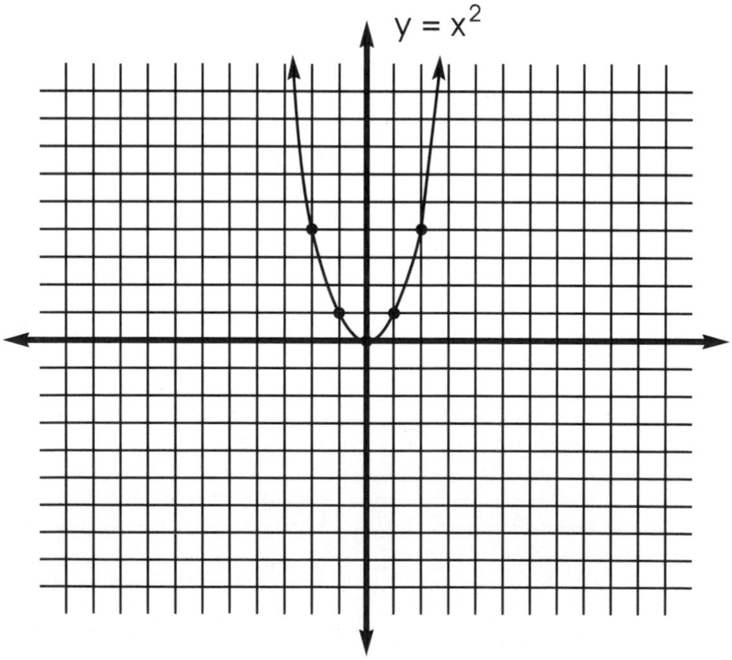

How do the constants *a* and *-a* alter the graph?

Name ____________________ Date ____________________

Graphing Quadratics: $y = ax^2 + c$

Graph each quadratic equation.

Example: $y = x^2 + 1$

x	y
-2	5
-1	2
0	1
1	2
2	5

1. $y = x^2 - 2$

x	y

2. $y = 2x^2$

x	y

3. $y = \frac{1}{2}x^2 - 9$

x	y

4. $y = {}^{-}3x^2 + 6$

x	y

5. $y = \frac{2}{3}x^2 - 3$

x	y

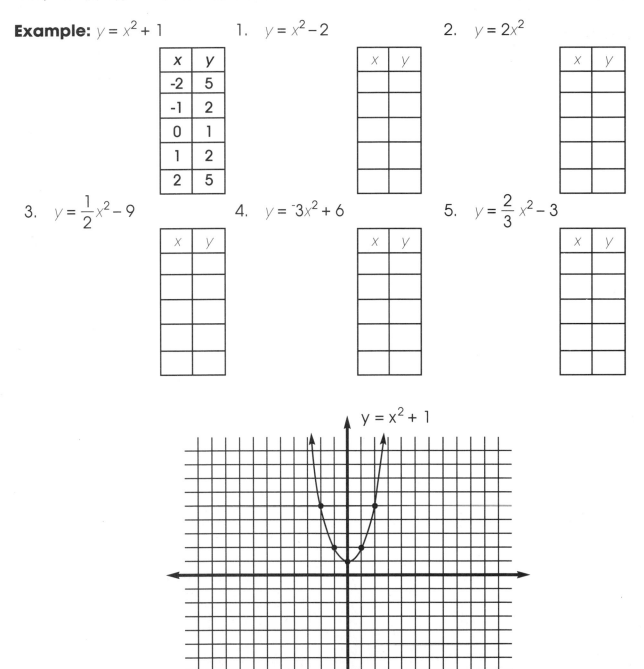

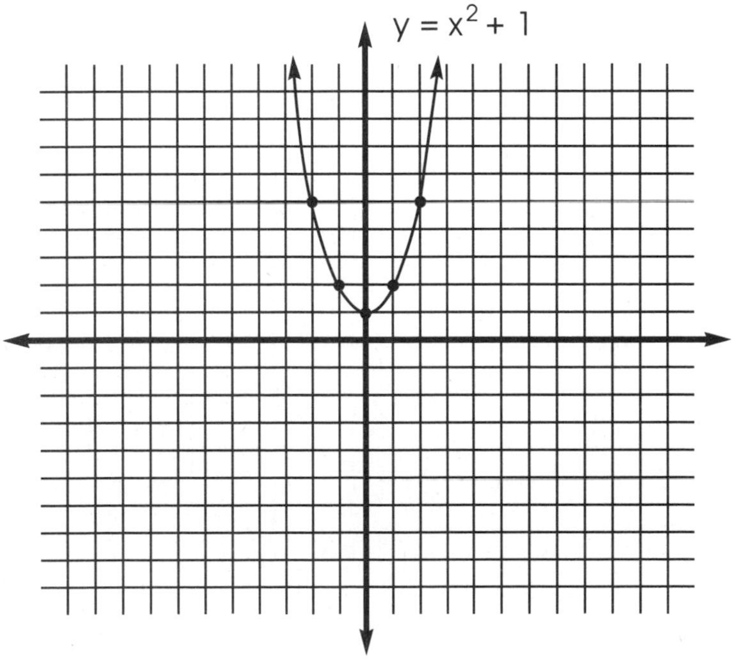

How do the constants *c* and -*c* alter the graph?

Name ______________________________ Date ______________________________

Graphing Quadratics: $y = a(x - b)^2 + c$

Graph each quadratic equation. Chart may vary.

Example: $y = (x - 2)^2$

x	y
0	4
1	1
2	0
3	1
4	4

1. $y = 2(x + 3)^2$

x	y

2. $y = \frac{1}{3}(x - 5)^2$

x	y

3. $y = {}^{-}2(x - 7)^2$

x	y

4. $y = \frac{1}{2}(x + 3)^2 - 1$

x	y

5. $y = -(x + 8)^2 + 1$

x	y

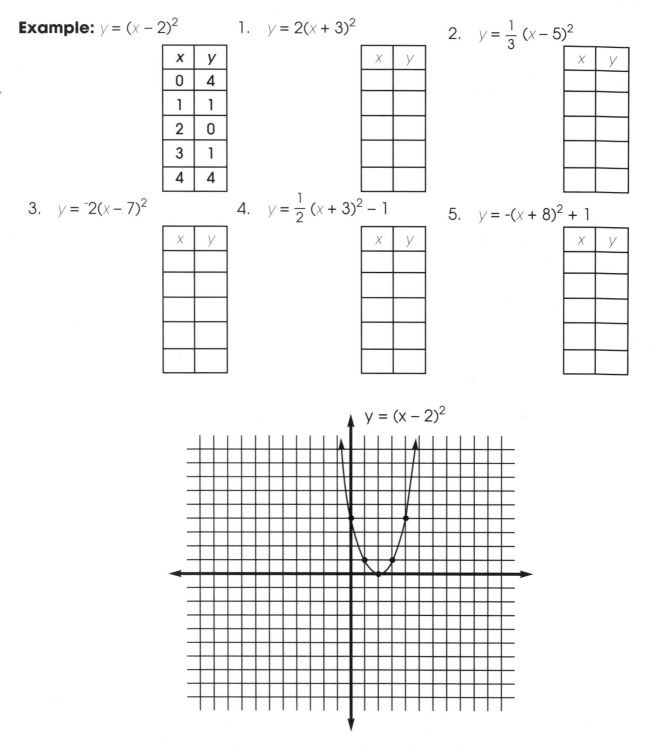

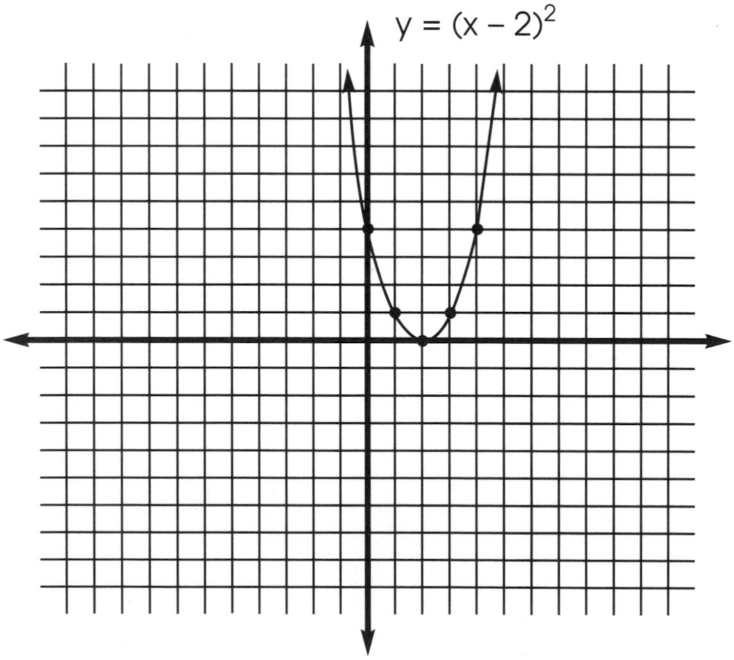

How do the constants *b* and *-b* alter the graph?

Name ____________________ Date ____________________

Factoring Binomials

Factor each binomial equation.

Example: $9x^2 - 4 = (3x + 2)(3x - 2)$

1. $4x^2 - 1 =$
2. $x^2 - 9 =$
3. $36x^2 - 9 =$
4. $100x^2 - 81 =$
5. $25x^2 - 4 =$
6. $81x^2 - 121 =$
7. $x^2 - 16 =$
8. $144x^2 - 16 =$
9. $x^2 - 25 =$
10. $625 - 16x^2 =$
11. $100 - x^2 =$
12. $x^2 - 36 =$
13. $121x^2 - 49 =$
14. $49x^2 - 16 =$

Cross out the correct answers below. Use the remaining letters to complete the statement.

$(x + 13)(x - 13)$ THE	$16(3x - 1)(3x - 1)$ SUM	$(x - 4)(x + 4)$ OFA	$(6x + 5)(6x - 5)$ PRO	$(25 - 4x)(25 + 4x)$ QUO	$(x + 1)(x - 1)$ DUC
$(9 + x)(9 - x)$ TOF	$9(2x - 1)(2x + 1)$ TIE	$(x + 7)(x - 7)$ THE	$(2x + 1)(2x - 1)$ NTA	$(9x + 1)(9x - 1)$ SUM	$(x + 2)(x - 2)$ AND
$(10 - x)(10 + x)$ WAS	$(5x + 3)(5x - 3)$ DIF	$(x - 5)(x + 5)$ HAS	$(8x + 1)(8x - 1)$ FER	$(11x - 7)(11x + 7)$ MAN	$(x - 6)(x + 6)$ NER
$(x + 18)(x - 18)$ ENC	$(10x - 9)(10x + 9)$ THA	$(x - 3)(x + 3)$ TIS	$(5x - 2)(5x + 2)$ MYP	$(7x + 11)(7x - 11)$ EOF	$(x + 8)(x - 8)$ THE
$(x + 15)(x - 15)$ SQU	$(9x - 11)(9x + 11)$ ROB	$(x + 9)(x - 9)$ ARE	$(3x + 2)(3x - 2)$ ROO	$(7x - 4)(7x + 4)$ LEM	$(x + 9)(x - 9)$ TS.

15. The factored form of the difference of the two squares is

_ _

_ _

_ _ _ _ _ _

Name ______________________ Date ______________________

Factoring Trinomials

Factor each trinomial equation. Example: $x^2 - 8x + 12 = (x - 6)(x - 2)$

1. $x^2 - 12x + 36 =$

2. $x^2 + 24x + 144 =$

3. $x^2 - 16x - 36 =$

4. $x^2 - 9x - 22 =$

5. $x^2 + 18x + 32 =$

6. $x^2 - x - 56 =$

7. $6x^2 + 7x + 2 =$

8. $3x^2 + 2x - 16 =$

9. $6x^2 - 5x - 4 =$

10. $15x^2 - x - 2 =$

11. $18x^2 + 9x + 1 =$

12. $20x^2 + 13x + 2 =$

13. $5x^2 - 26x + 5 =$

14. $x^2 - 9x - 10 =$

Name ______________________ Date ______________________

Finding the Vertex of Quadratic Equations

Find the vertex of each quadratic using the following equation:

If $y = ax^2 + bx + c$, then vertex $= \left(\frac{^-b}{2a}, \frac{^-b^2}{4a} + c\right)$

Example: $y = x^2 + 2x + 1$

$a = 1$

$b = 2$

$c = 1$

$\left(\frac{^-2}{2(1)}, \frac{^-(2)^2}{4(1)} + (1)\right) = (-1,0)$

1. $y = x^2 - 2x + 1$

2. $y = 8x^2 - 16x + 1$

3. $y = {}^-3x^2 + 6x - 1$

4. $y = x^2 - 9$

5. $y = 2x^2 + 1$

6. $y = x^2$

7. $y = {}^-10x^2$

8. $y = 2x^2 + 6x + 0$

9. $y = {}^-4x^2 - 7$

10. Once you have found the x-coordinate by using $\frac{^-b}{2a}$, how can you find the y-coordinate if you don't remember $(\frac{^-b^2}{4a}) + c$?

____

0-7424-1789-1 *Algebra II*

Name ______________________ Date ______________________

Finding *X*-Intercepts

Find the x-intercepts using the following quadratic formula:

If $y = ax^2 + bx + c$, then $x = \dfrac{^-b \pm \sqrt{b^2 - 4ac}}{2a}$

Example: $y = x^2 + 2x - 1$

$a = 1 \quad b = 2 \quad c = {^-1}$

$$x = \frac{^-2 \pm \sqrt{2^2 - 4(1)(^-1)}}{2(1)} = \frac{^-2 \pm \sqrt{8}}{2}$$

$$= \frac{^-2 \pm 2\sqrt{2}}{2} = {^-1} \pm \sqrt{2}$$

1. $y = 3x^2 - 14x + 1$

2. $y = 2x^2 - x - 1$

3. $y = {^-3}x^2 - 6x + 1$

4. $y = 3x^2 + x$

5. $y = {^-7}x^2 - 14x$

6. $y = 4x^2 - 9$

7. $y = x^2 - 2$

8. $y = (x - 3)(x + 2)$

9. $y = (x)(2x - {^-6})$

0-7424-1789-1 Algeb

Name ______________________ Date ______________________

Quick Graphs of Quadratic Equations

Create a quick graph using the x-intercept and the vertex.

Example: $y = x^2 - 5x - 14$

x-intercept:

$(x - 7)\ (x + 2)$

$x - 7 = 0 \quad x = 7$

$x + 2 = 0 \quad x = {}^{-}2$

vertex:

$\left(\frac{{}^{-}b}{2a}, \frac{{}^{-}b^2}{4a} + c\right)$

$\left(\frac{-({}^{-}5)}{(2)\ (1)}, \frac{-({}^{-}5)^2}{(4)\ (1)} + {}^{-}14\right)$

$\left(\frac{5}{2}, \frac{81}{4}\right)$

$a = 1$

$b = {}^{-}5$

$c = {}^{-}14$

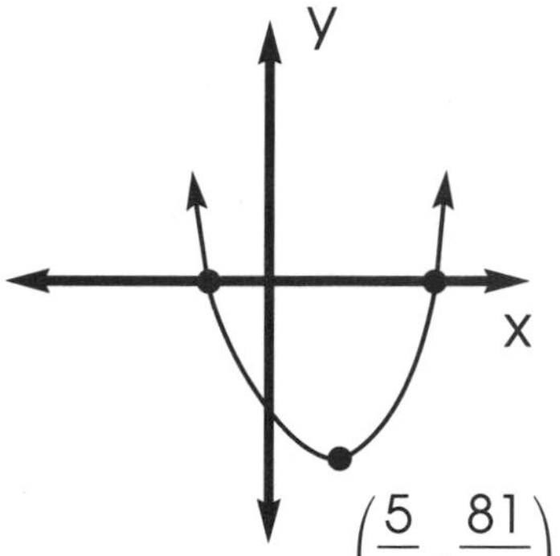

$\left(\frac{5}{2}, \frac{81}{4}\right)$

1. $y = x^2 - 8x + 12$

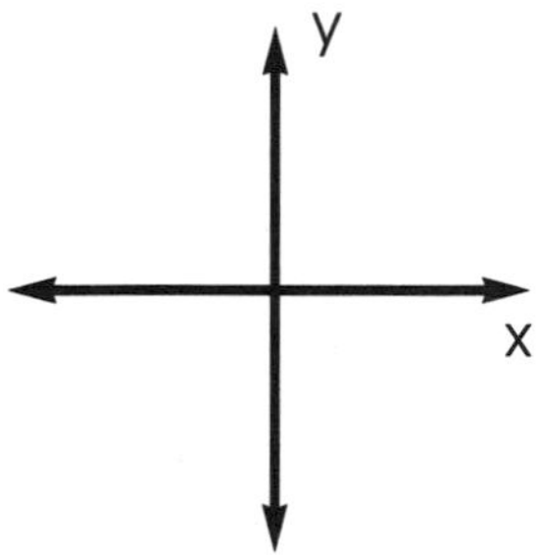

2. $y = 6x^2 - 10x - 4$

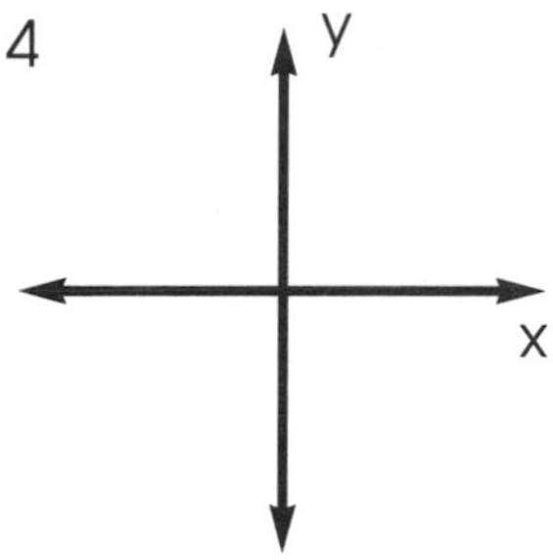

3. $y = {}^{-}15x^2 + x + 2$

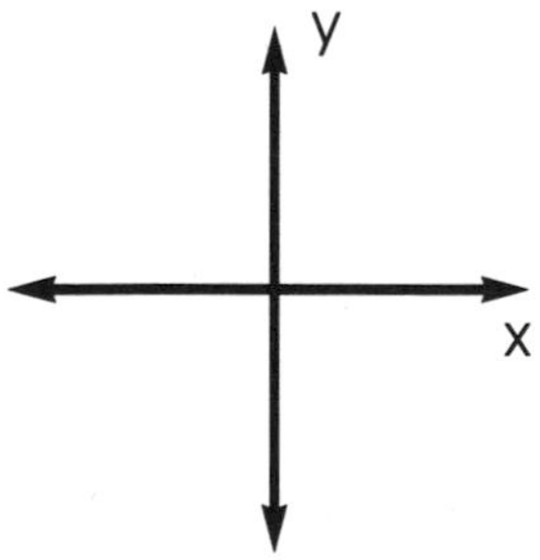

4. $y = x^2 - 16$

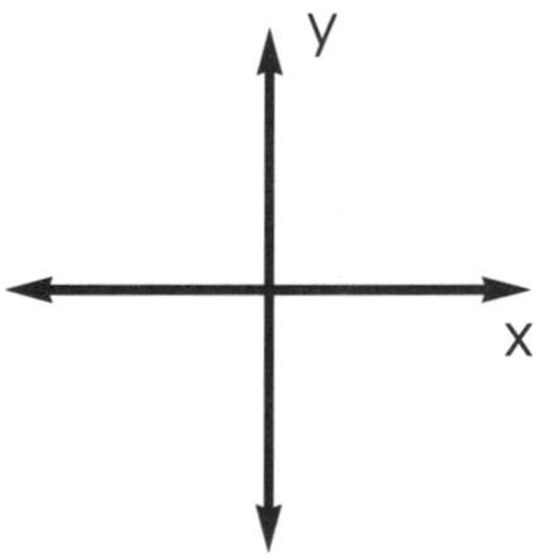

5. $y = (x - 2)\ (x + 3)$

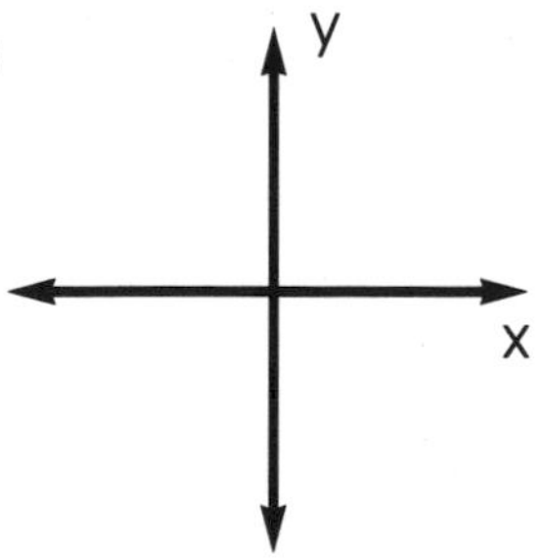

6. $y = (x - 5)\ (x + 5)$

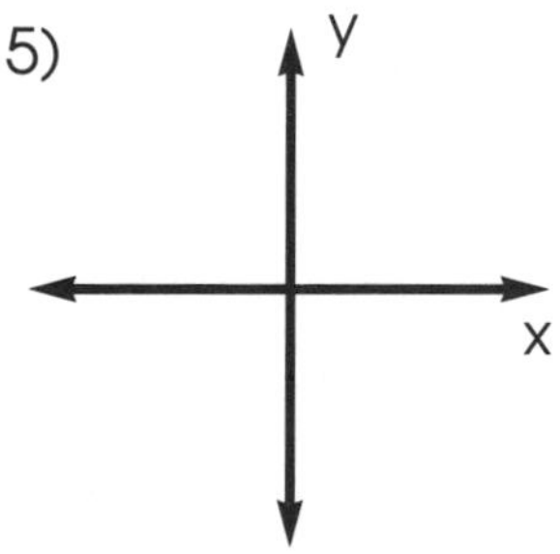

7. $y = -x^2 - 5x - 6$

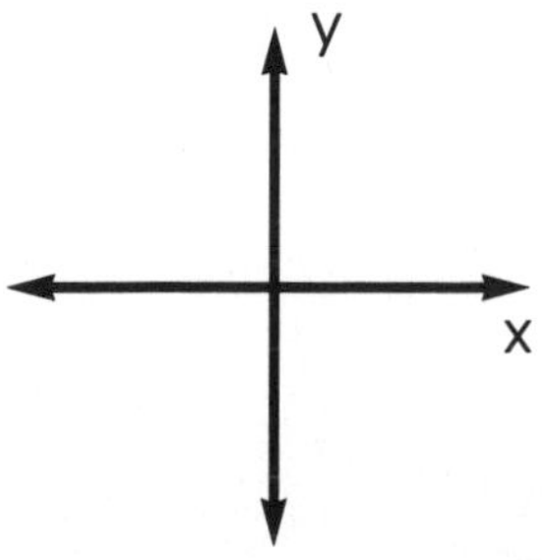

8. $y = 3x^2$

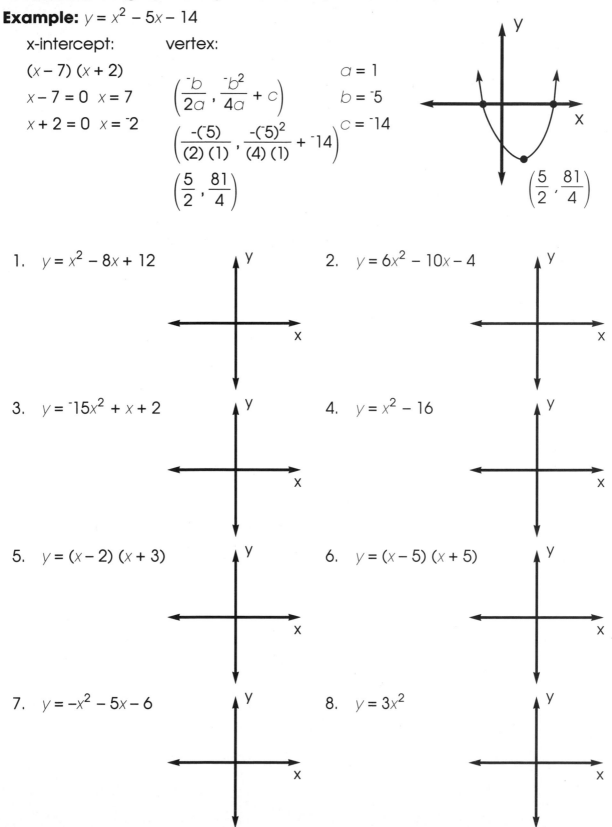

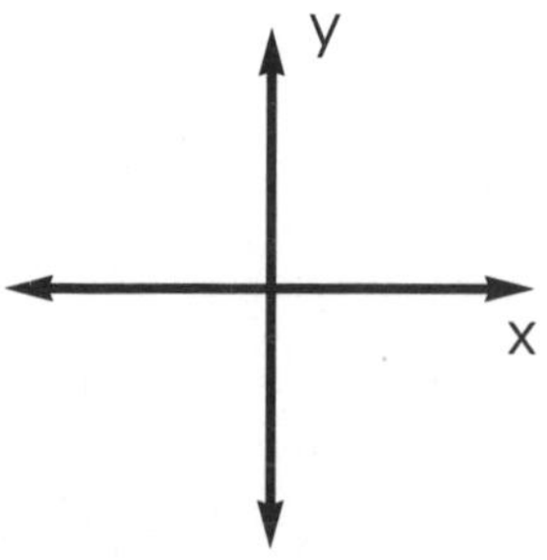

Name ______________________ Date ______________________

Graphing Quadratic Equations

Graph each quadratic equation on a piece of graph paper.

1. $y = {}^{-}5x^2 + 1$

2. $y = (x - 1)(x + 5)$

3. $y = {}^{-}4x^2$

4. $y = 3x^2 - x$

5. $y = x^2 + 6x + 8$

6. $y = {}^{-}3x^2 - 6x + 1$

7. $y = {}^{-}4x^2 - 7$

8. $y = x^2 + 2x - 3$

9. $y = 2x^2 + 1$

10. $y = -x^2 - x - 1$

Name ______________________ Date ______________________

Using the Vertical Line Test

Determine whether or not each graph is a function by applying the vertical line test. Remember: A graph represents a function if every x is associated with a unique y.

Example: YES

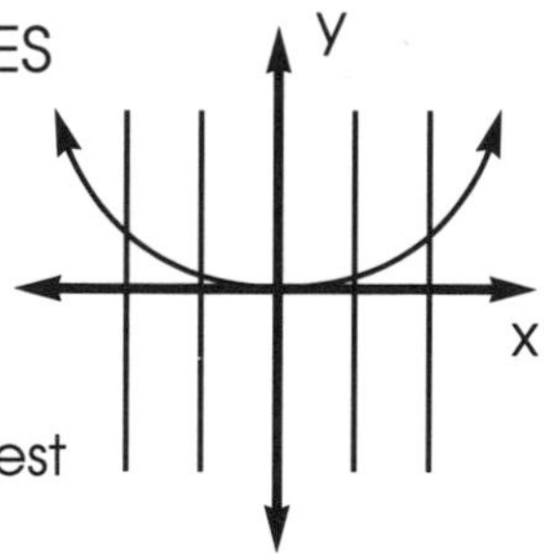

vertical line test

Example: NO

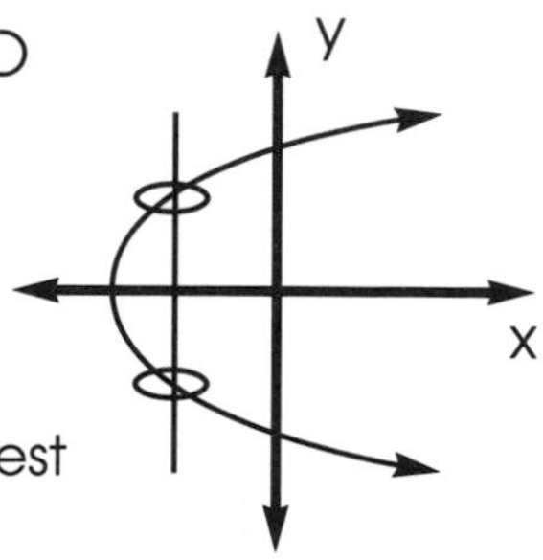

vertical line test

1.

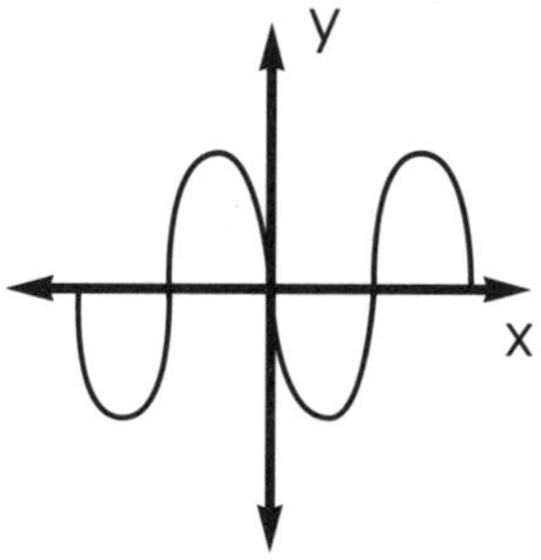

2.

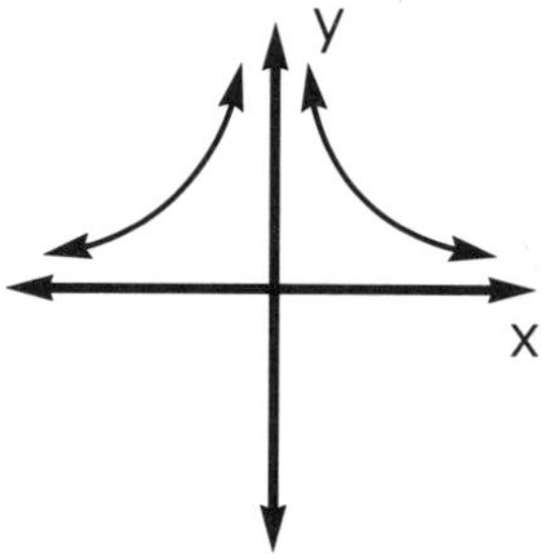

3.

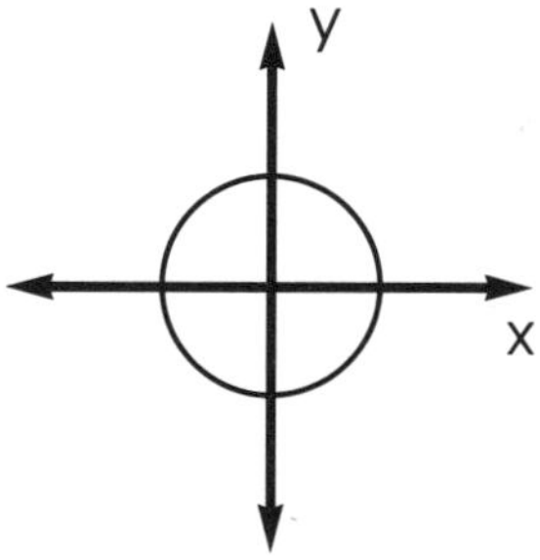

4.

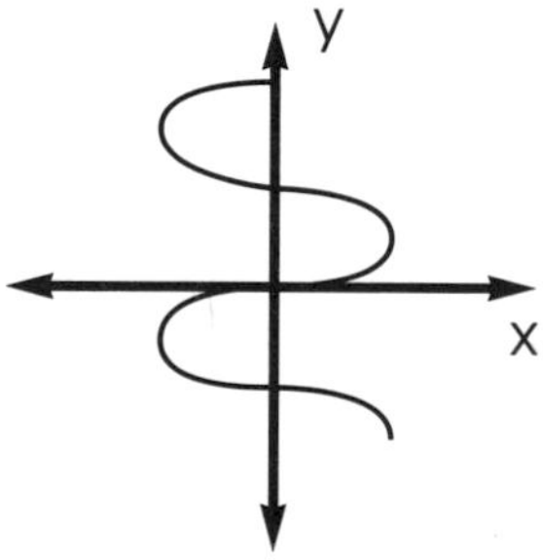

5.

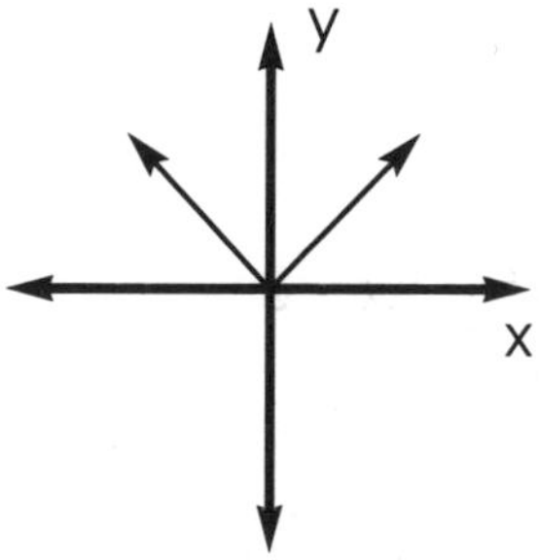

6.

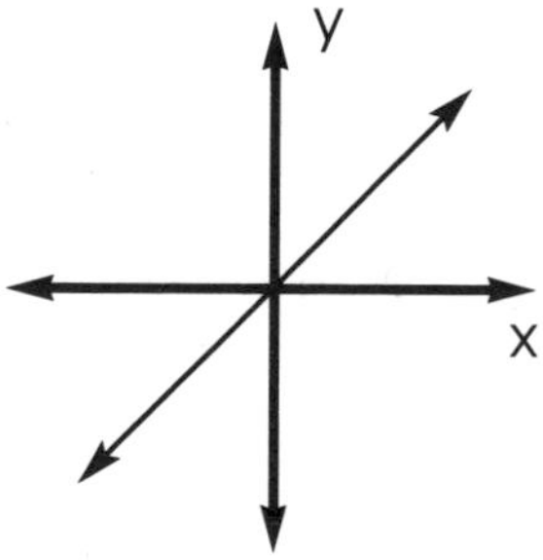

7.

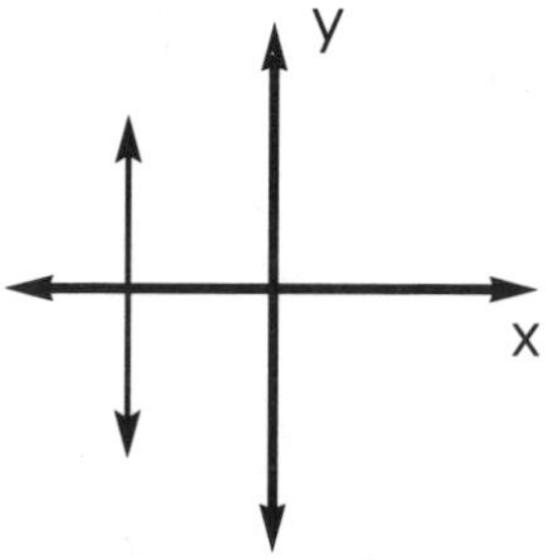

8.

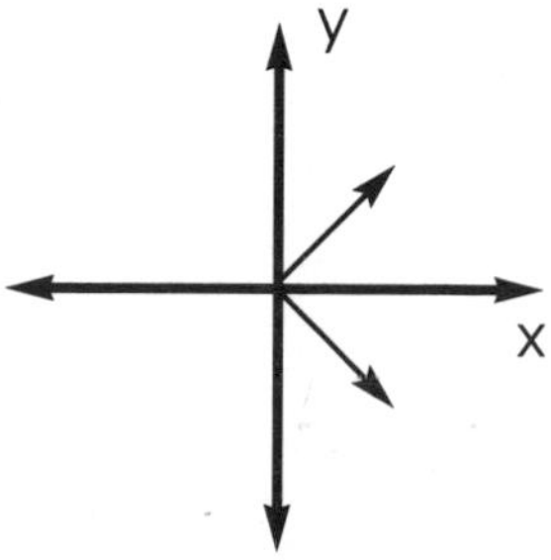

0-7424-1789-1 *Algebra II*

Name ______________________ Date ______________________

Composition of Functions

Write the composition of the functions given.

Given: $f(x) = {}^{-}2x + 7$ $g(x) = x^2$ $h(x) = x - 1$

Example: $g(h(x))$

$g(h(x)) = (x - 1)^2$

$= x^2 - x - x + 1$

$g(h(x)) = x^2 - 2x + 1$

1. $f(g(x))$

$x^2(-2x+7)$

$-2x^3+7x^2$

2. $g(f(x))$

$-2x+7(x^2)$

$-4x^3+7x^2$

3. $h(g(x))$

x^2-1

4. $f(h(x))$

$-2(x-1)+7$

$-2x+2+7$

$-2x+9$

5. $h(f(x))$

$(-2x+7)-1$

$-2x+6$

6. $f(g(h(x)))$

$-2(x^2-2x+1)+7$

$-2x^2+4x-2+7$

$-2x^2+4x+5$

7. $h(g(f(x)))$

$x(x^2-2+7)-1$

8. $f(f(x))$

$-2(-2x+7)+7$

$4x-14+7$

$4x-7$

0-7424-1789-1 Algeb

Name ______________________________ Date ______________________________

Using a Table of Values

Complete each table of values and graph the function.

$y = 2x - 1$ Euler notation: $f(x) = y$ so $f(x) = 2x - 1$

Example: $f(x) = {}^{-}3x + 2$

x	$f(x)$
-1	5
0	2
1	-1

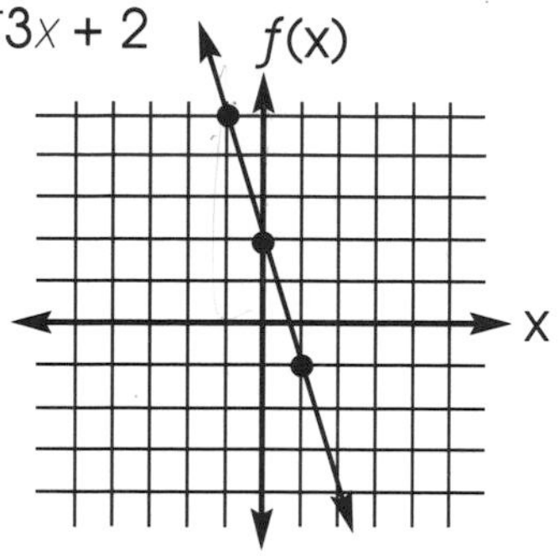

1. $f(x) = -x^2 + 3$

x	$f(x)$
-1	5
0	3
1	2

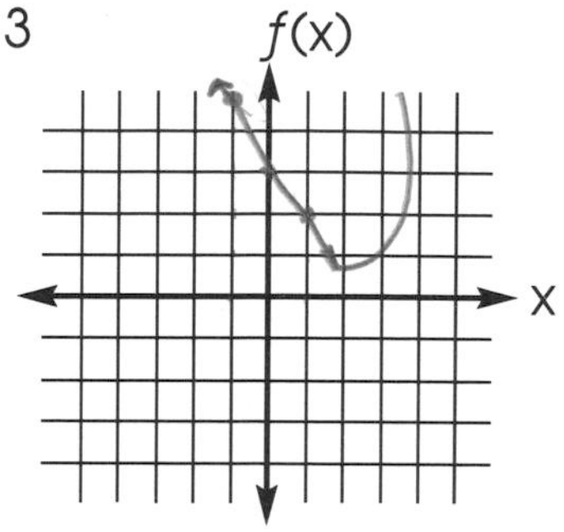

2. $f(x) = \frac{-1}{2}x + 1$

x	$f(x)$
-2	2
0	1
2	-1

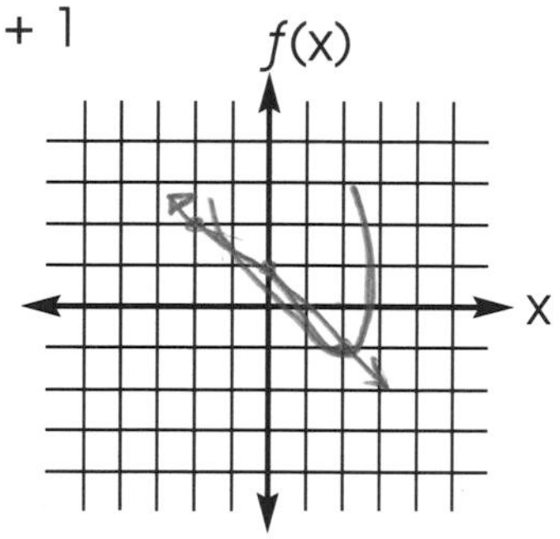

3. $f(x) = x^2 - 2x + 1$

x	$f(x)$
-1	4
0	1
1	0

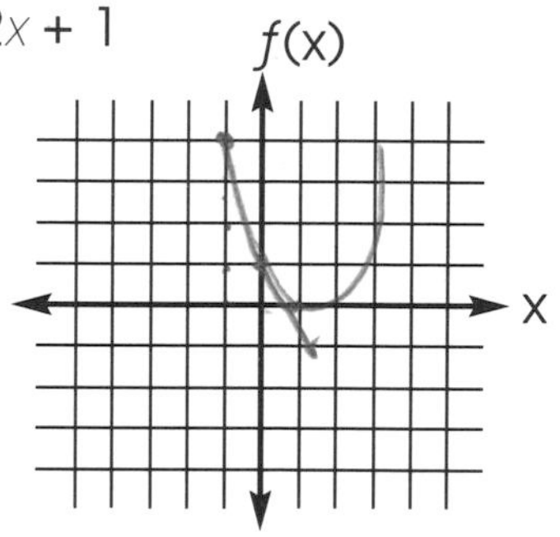

4. $f(x) = 2x^2 - 4$

x	$f(x)$
0	-4
1	-2
2	4

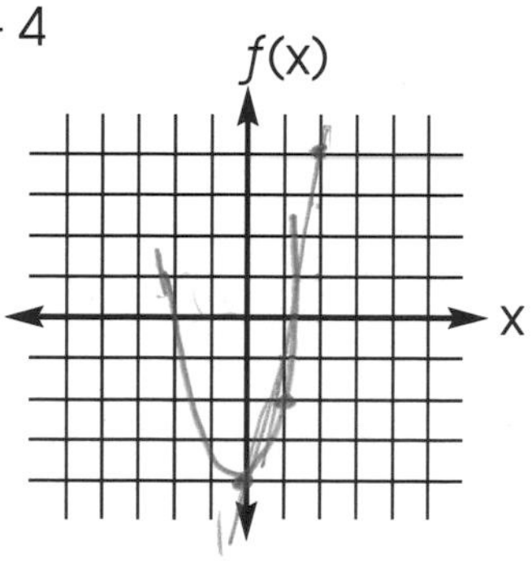

5. $f(x) = 2x - 5$

x	$f(x)$
-1	-7
0	-5
1	-3

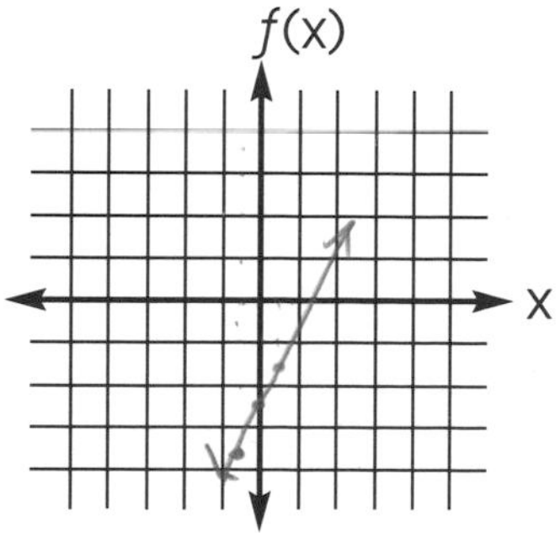

6. $f(x) = |x|$

x	$f(x)$
-1	
0	
1	

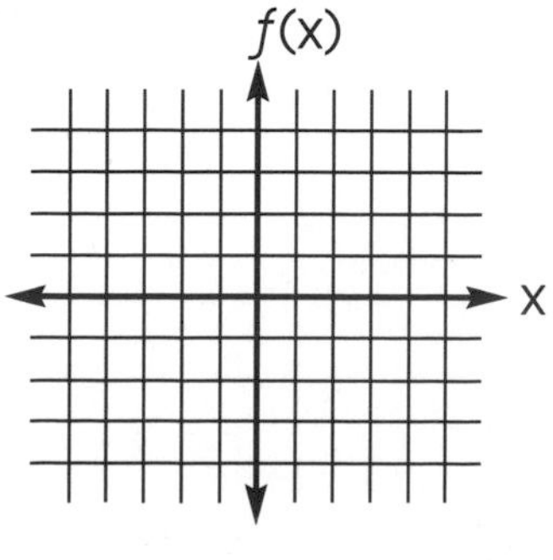

7. $f(x) = x^3$

x	$f(x)$

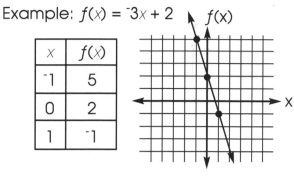

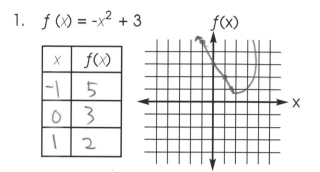

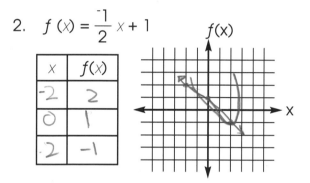

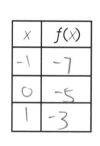

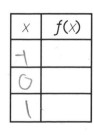

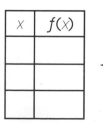

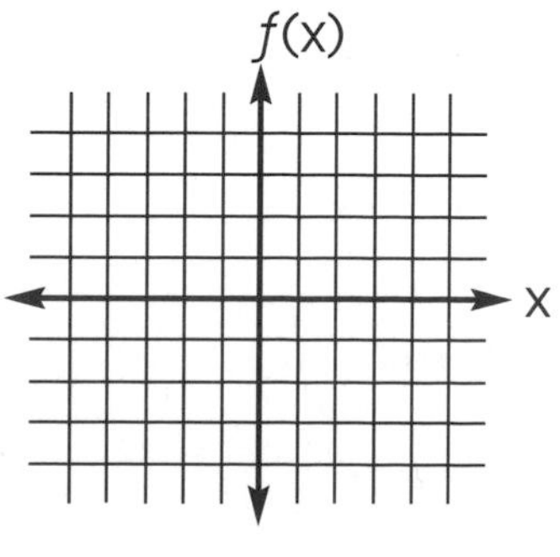

0-7424-1789-1 *Algebra II*

Name ______________________________ Date ______________________________

Graphing the Inverse of a Function

Fill in each table of values, then graph the inverse of each function.

Example:

function x	function $f(x)$	inverse x	inverse $f(x)$
-2	4	4	-2
-1	1	1	-1
-1/2	1/4	1/4	-1/2
0	0	0	0
1/2	1/4	1/4	1/2
1	1	1	1
2	4	4	2

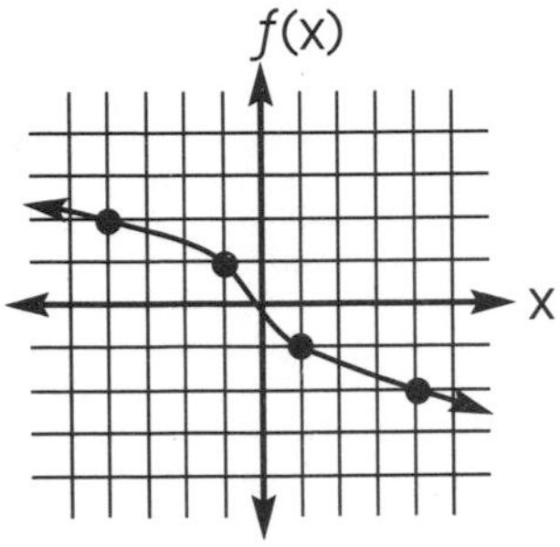

1.

function x	function $f(x)$	inverse x	inverse $f(x)$
-2	2		
-1	1		
-1/2	1/2		
0	0		

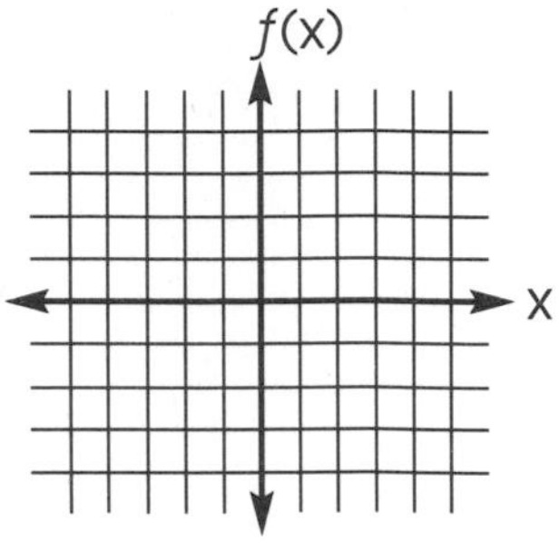

2.

function x	function $f(x)$	inverse x	inverse $f(x)$
-2	-8		
-1	-1		
-1/2	-1/8		
0	0		
1/2	1/8		
1	1		
2	8		

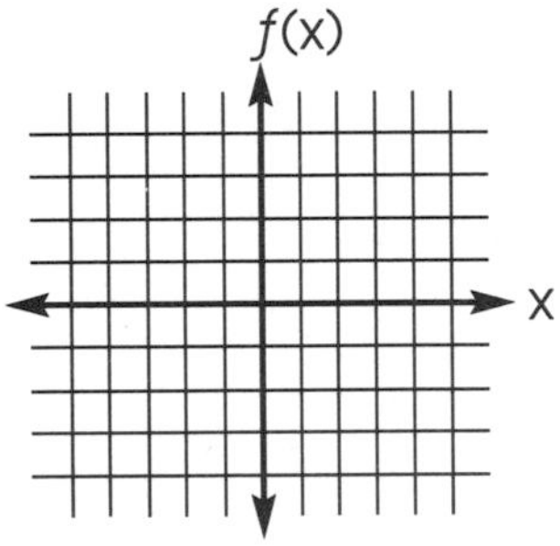

3.

function x	function $f(x)$	inverse x	inverse $f(x)$
-3	-11		
-2	-9		
-1	-7		
0	-5		
1	-3		
2	-1		
3	1		

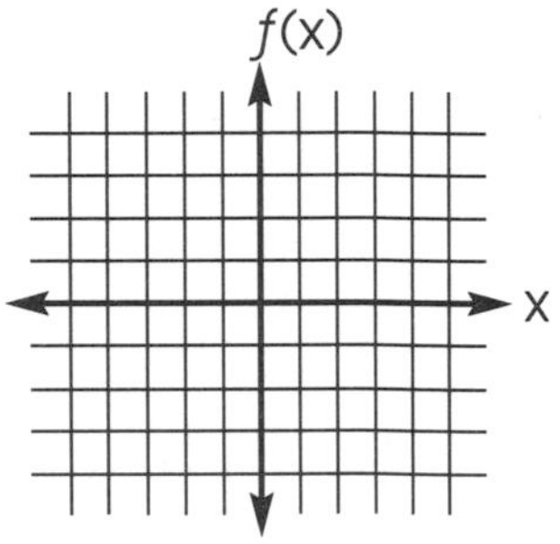

4.

function x	function $f(x)$	inverse x	inverse $f(x)$
-2	-8		
-1	-2		
-1/2	-1/2		
0	0		

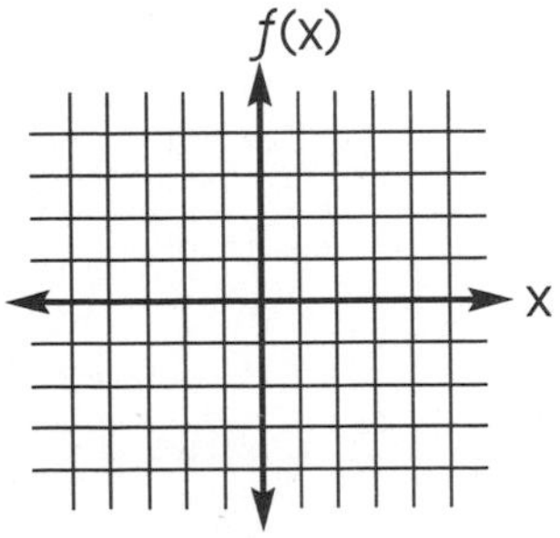

5.

function x	function $f(x)$	inverse x	inverse $f(x)$
-2	8		
-1	1		
-1/2	1/8		
0	0		
1/2	-1/8		
1	-1		
2	-8		

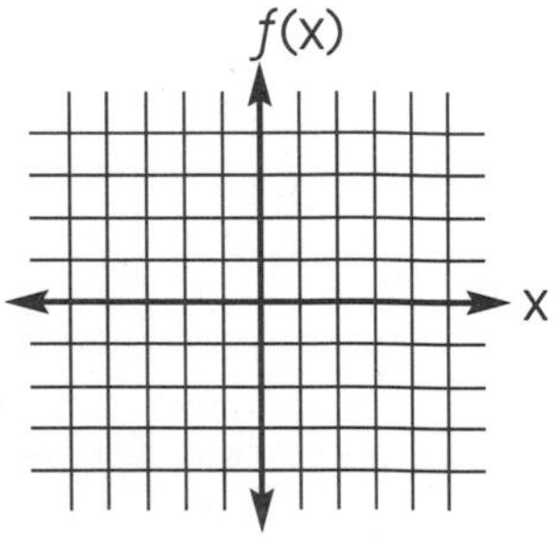

0-7424-1789-1 Algeb

Name ______________________ Date ______________________

Graphing the Inverse of a Function

Find and graph the inverse of each function.

Example: $f(x) = 4x - 5$

$y = 4x - 5$

$x = 4y - 5$

$4y = x + 5$

$y = \frac{1}{4}x + \frac{5}{4}$

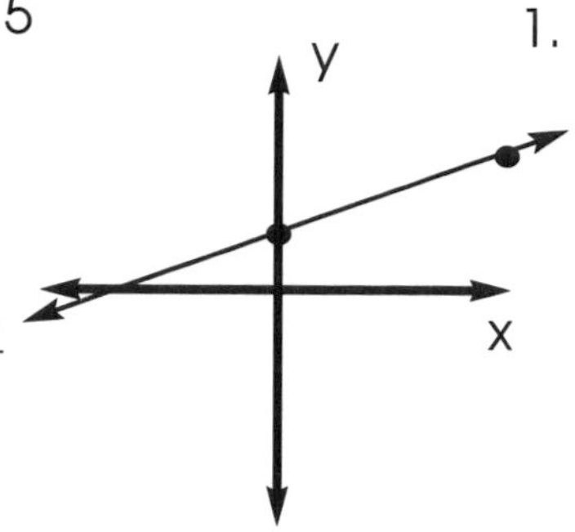

1. $f(x) = 2x^2$
(where $x \geq 0$)

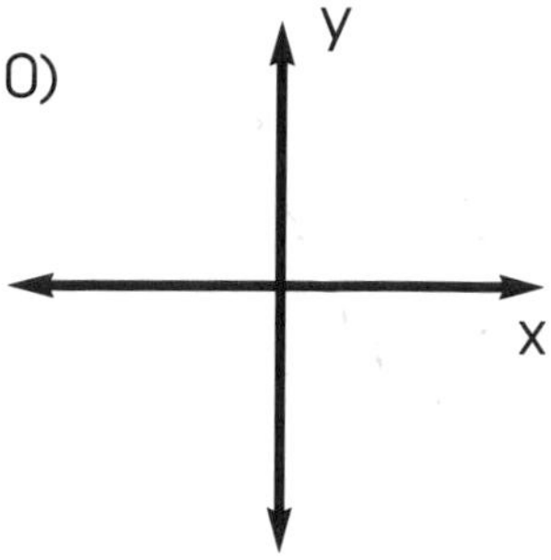

2. $f(x) = |x| + 2$
(where $x \geq 0$)

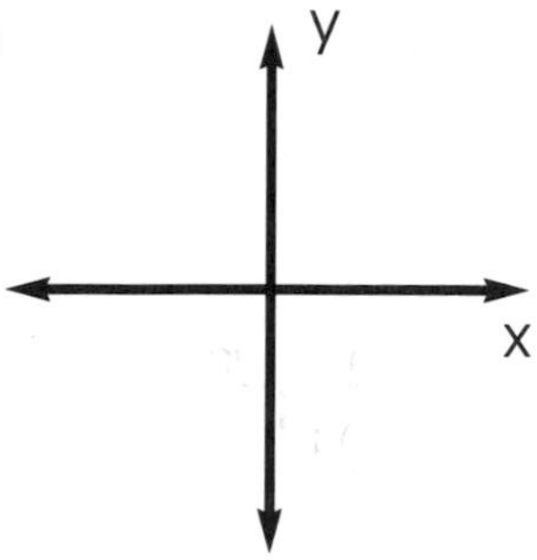

3. $f(x) = -x^2 + 1$
(where $x \geq 0$)

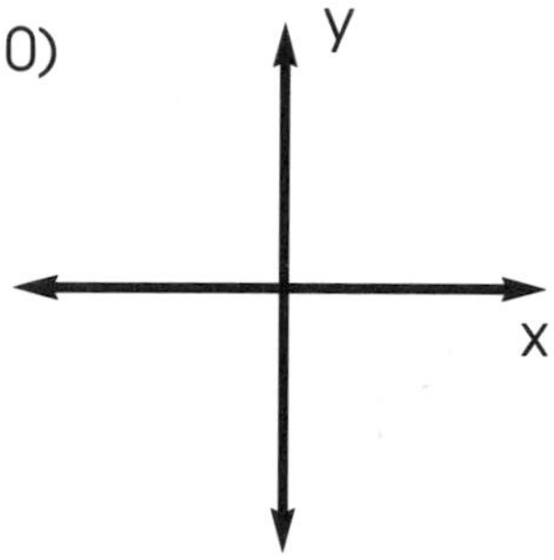

4. $f(x) = \frac{-1}{2}x^3$

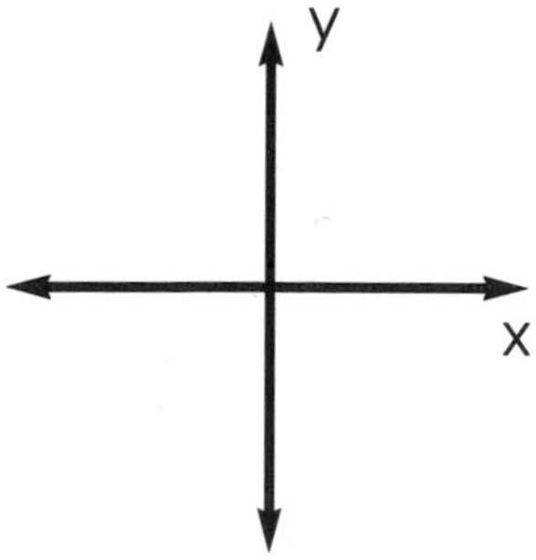

5. $f(x) = |x - 1|$
(where $x \geq 0$)

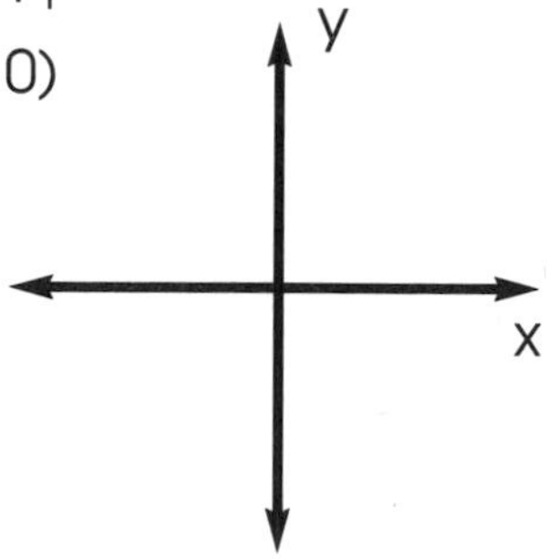

6. $f(x) = -4x + 7$

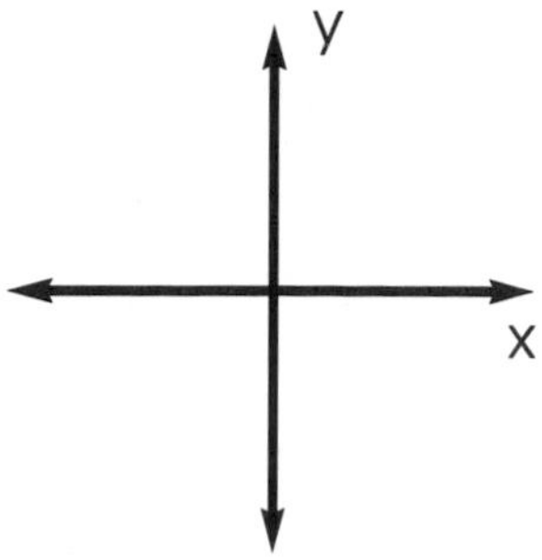

7. $f(x) = -x^2 + 5$
(where $x \geq 0$)

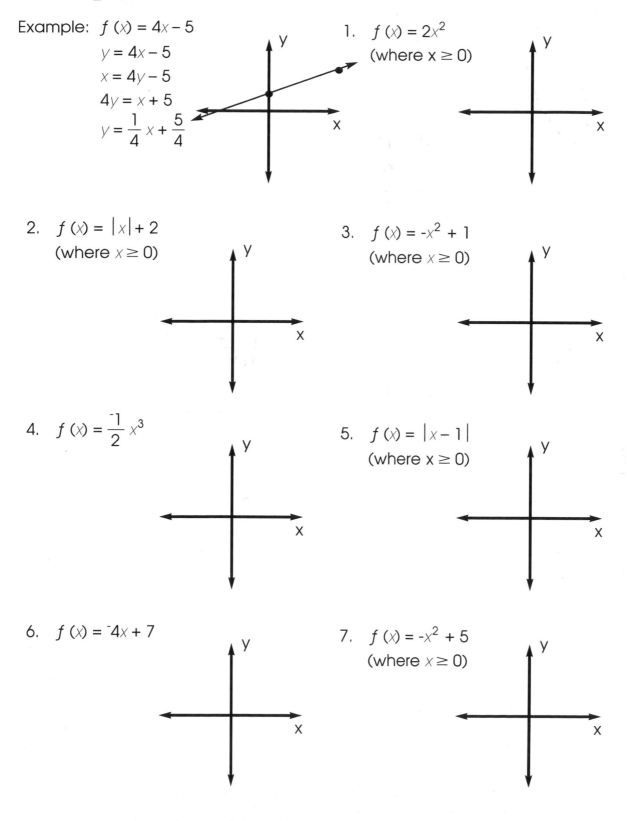

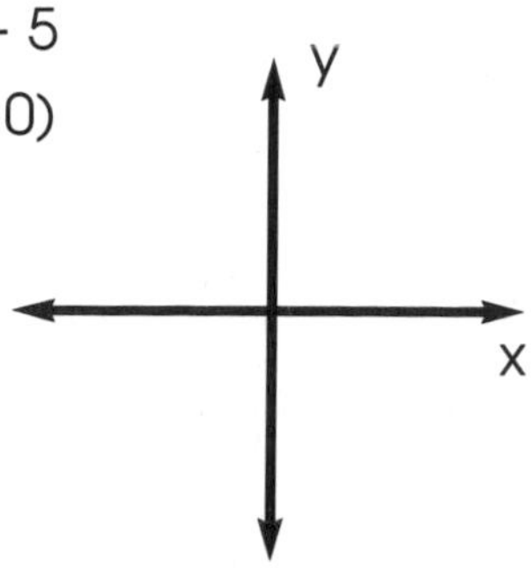

0-7424-1789-1 *Algebra II*

Name ______________________ Date ______________________

Domain and Range I

Find the domain and range of each function.
Domain: Allowable values of *x* Range: y values

Example:

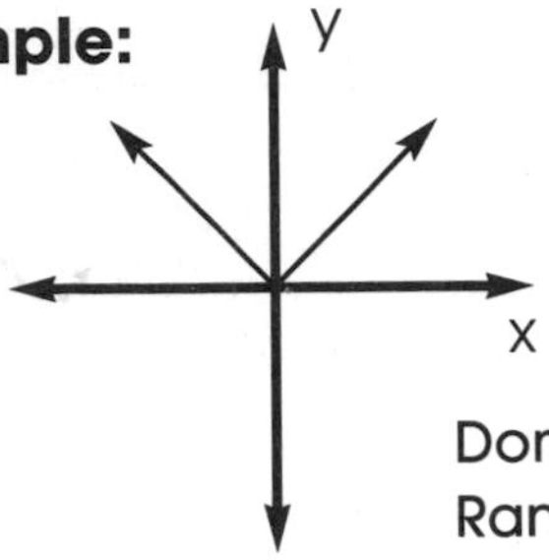

Domain: all Reals $\{\mathbb{R}\}$
Range: positive Reals (including 0) $\{\mathbb{R} : y \geq 0\}$

1.

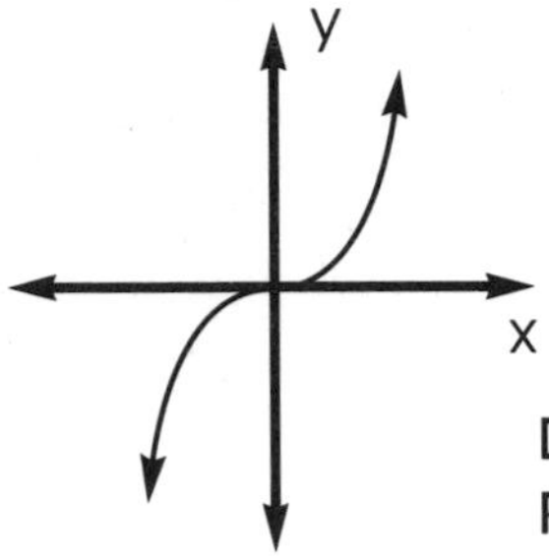

Domain:
Range:

2.

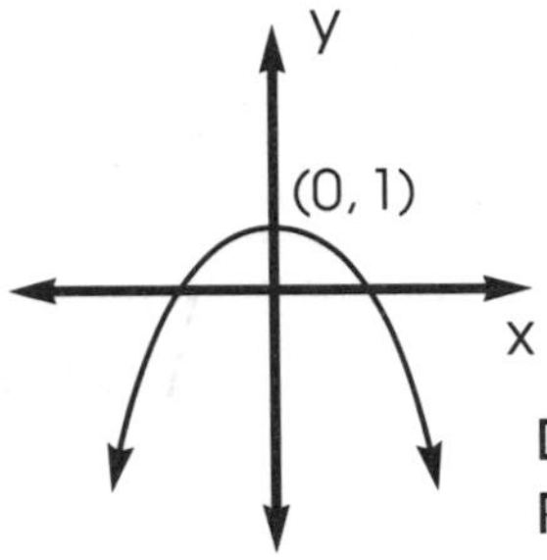

Domain:
Range:

3.

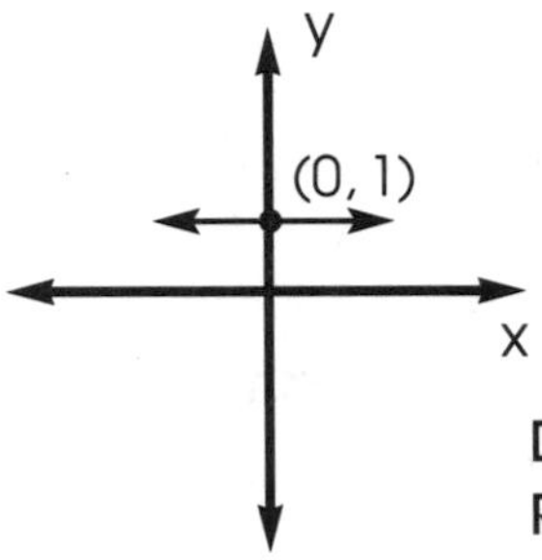

Domain:
Range:

4.

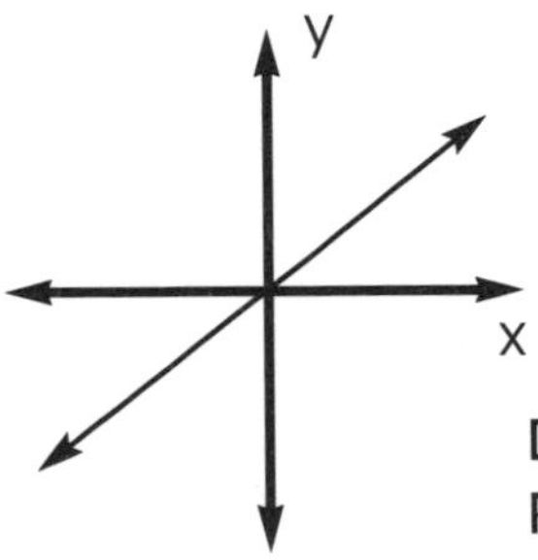

Domain:
Range:

5.

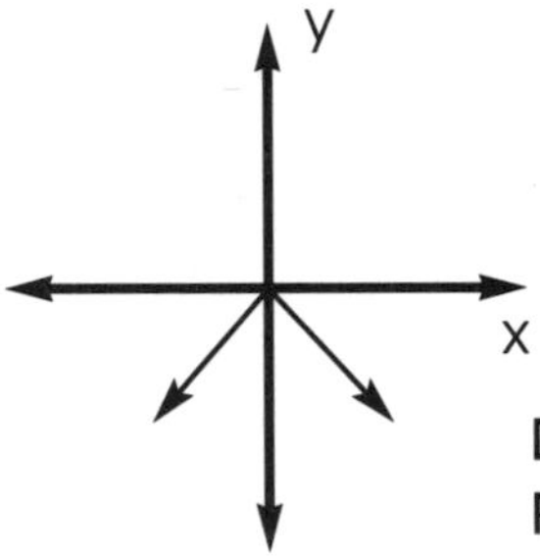

Domain:
Range:

6.

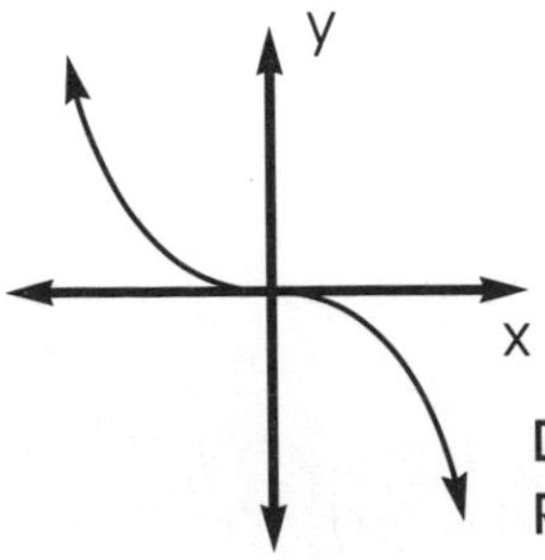

Domain:
Range:

7.

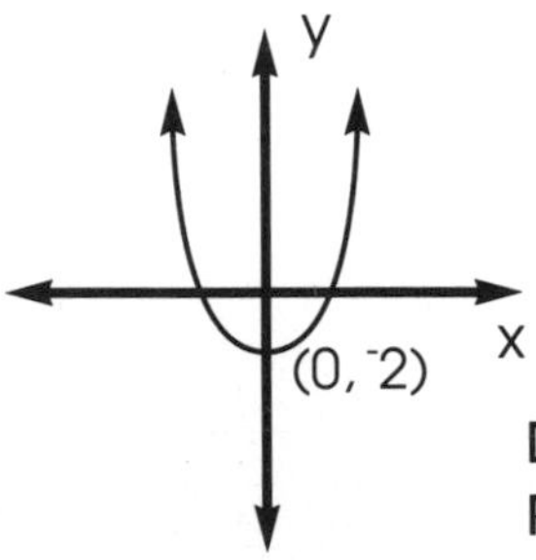

Domain:
Range:

8.

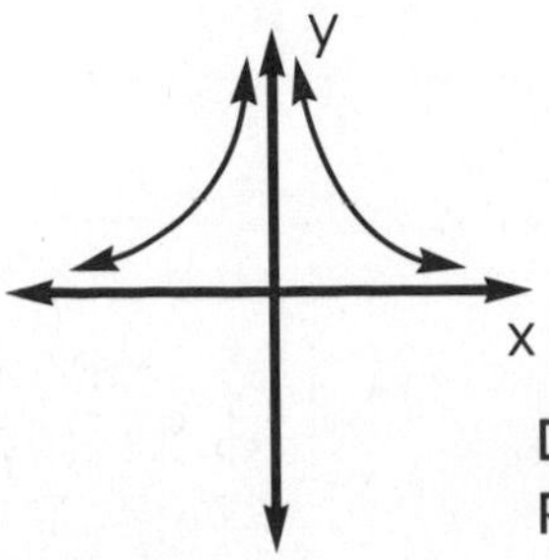

Domain:
Range:

9.

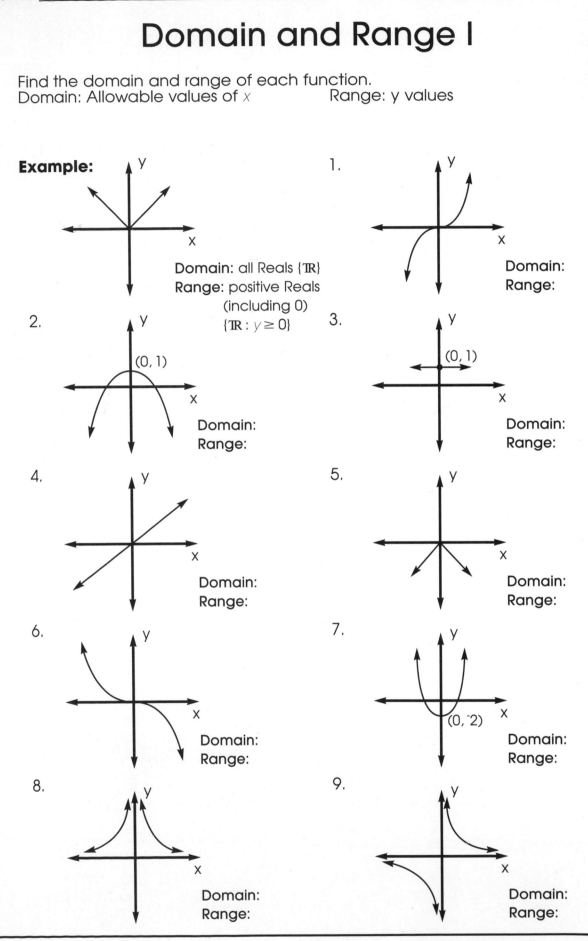

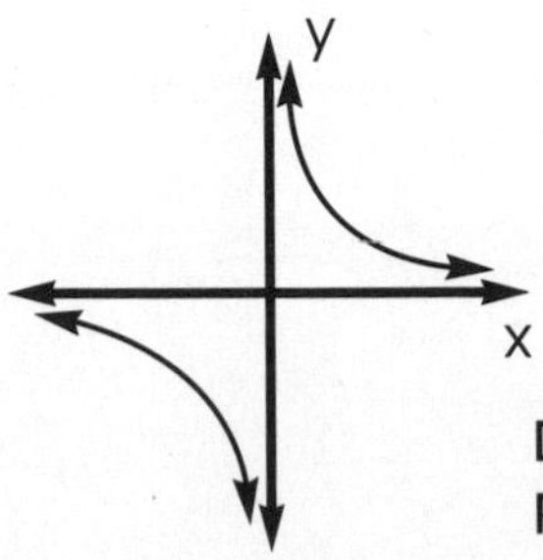

Domain:
Range:

Name ______________________ Date ______________________

Domain and Range II

Find the domain and range from the graph.
Each box on the graph equals 1 unit.

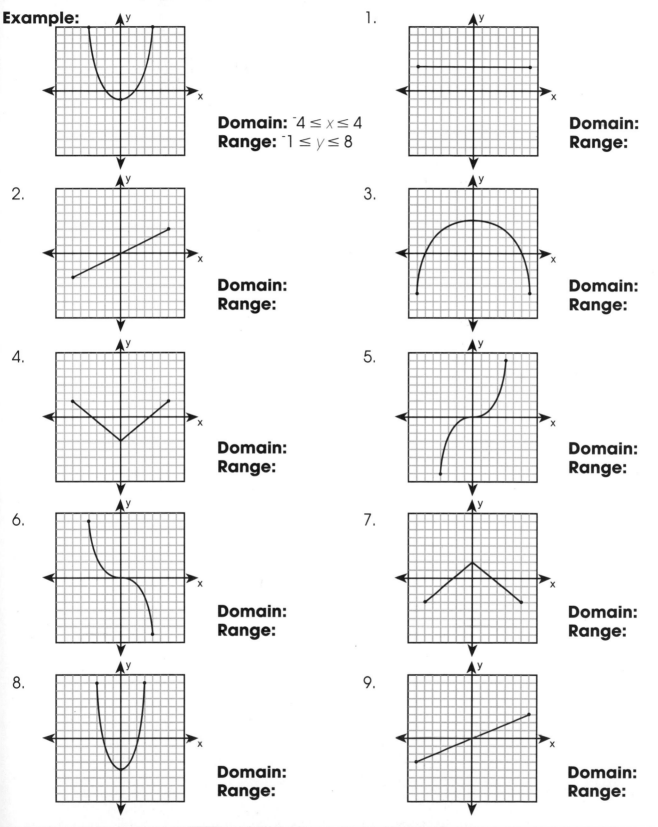

Example:

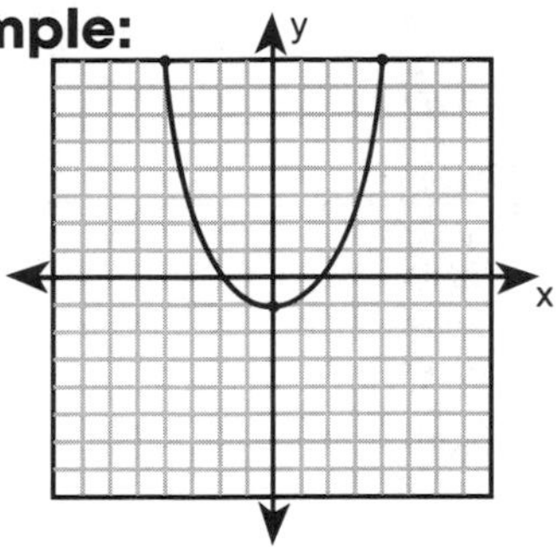

Domain: $^{-}4 \le x \le 4$
Range: $^{-}1 \le y \le 8$

1.

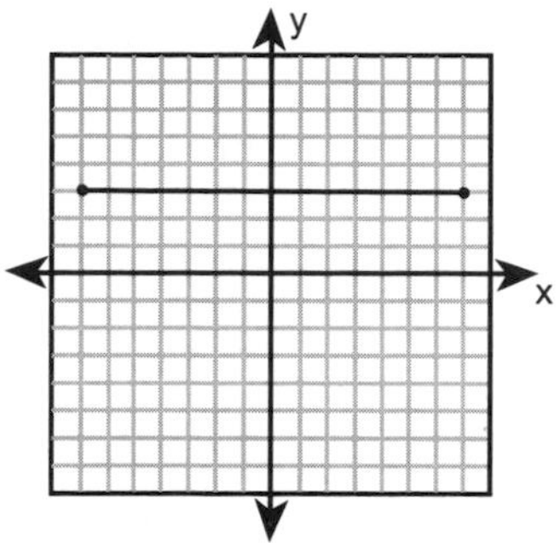

Domain:
Range:

2.

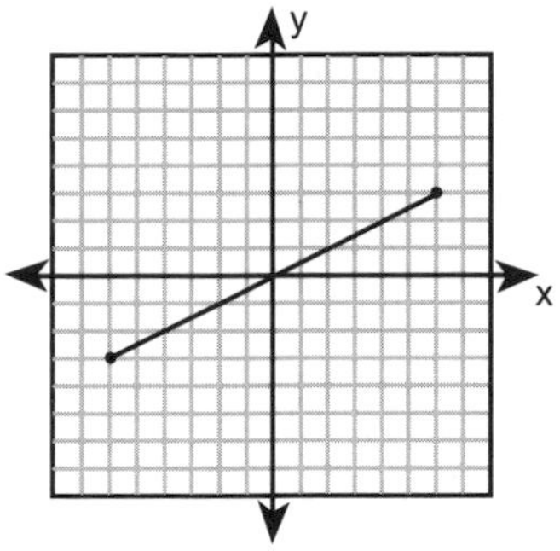

Domain:
Range:

3.

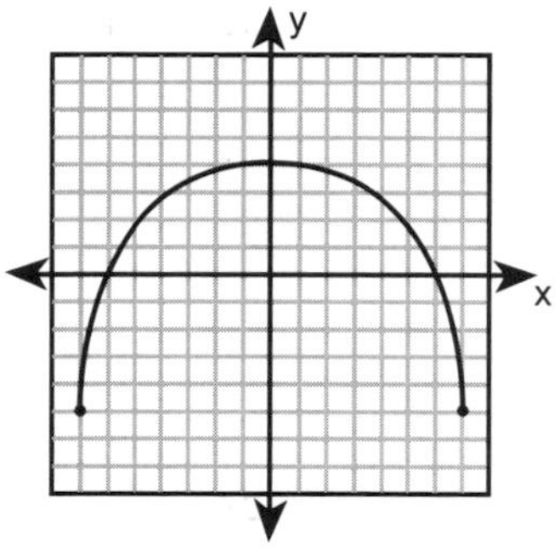

Domain:
Range:

4.

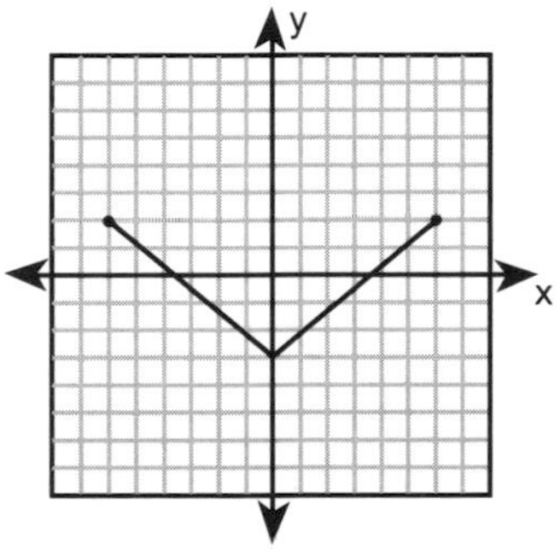

Domain:
Range:

5.

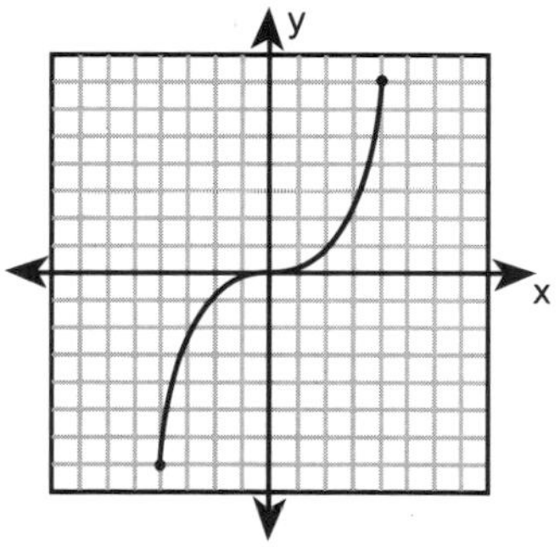

Domain:
Range:

6.

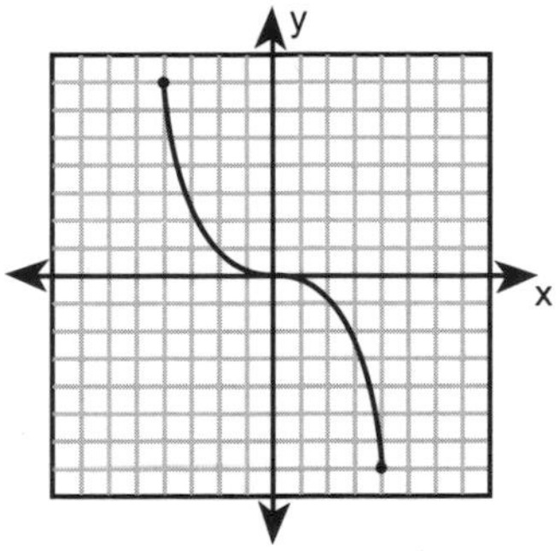

Domain:
Range:

7.

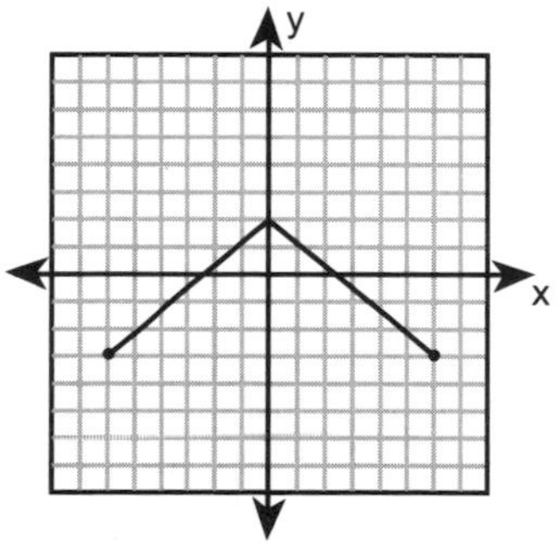

Domain:
Range:

8.

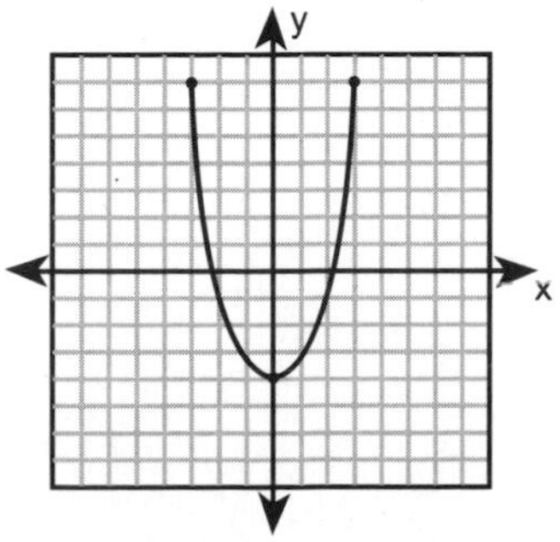

Domain:
Range:

9.

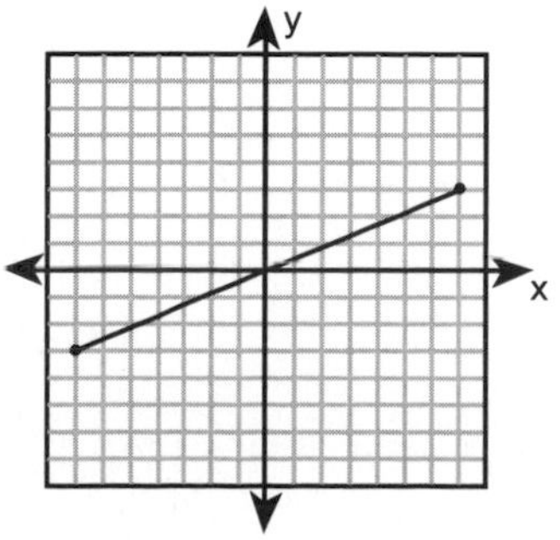

Domain:
Range:

0-7424-1789-1 *Algebra II*

Name ____________________ Date ____________________

Manipulating Powers

1) $(a^x)^y = a^{xy}$	4) $(ab)^x = a^x b^x$	7) $\frac{1}{a^{-x}} = a^x$
2) $a^x \cdot a^y = a^{x+y}$	5) $\left(\frac{a}{b}\right)^x = \frac{a^x}{b^x}$	
3) $\frac{a^x}{a^y} = a^{x-y}$	6) $a^{-x} = \frac{1}{a^x}$	

Simplify each expression.

Example: $(x^2)^4 = x^{2 \cdot 4} = x^8$

1. $x^4 \cdot x^2$

2. $\frac{x^8}{}$

3. $(x^2y)^3$

4. $\left(\frac{x}{}\right)^5$

5. y^{-15}

6. $\frac{1}{}$

7. $\frac{a^6}{}$

8. $(2c^2)^3$

9. $\frac{n^4 \cdot n^6}{n^8 \cdot n^2}$

10. $4a^5 \cdot 3a^3$

11. $\left(\frac{v}{3}\right)^4 \cdot \left(\frac{5}{v}\right)^2$

12. $(x^{-2})^2$

13. $\left(\frac{2}{x}\right)^{-1}$

0-7424-1789-1 *Algebra*

Name ______________________________ Date ______________________________

Manipulating Powers

14. $(x^{-2} \cdot y)^{-3}$

15. $\dfrac{12x^5}{3x^7}$

16. $\dfrac{8d}{}$

17. $^{-}2x^{-2}$

18. $x^{1/3} \cdot x^{2/3}$

19. $\left(\dfrac{8x}{125}\right)^{-2}$

20. $\dfrac{a^4 \cdot b^6 \cdot a^9}{}$

21. $\dfrac{x^{-4}y^{-6}}{}$

22. $\left(\dfrac{x^2}{(xz)^2}\right)^{-2}$

23. $\left(\dfrac{x^2y^1z}{a^4b^{-7}}\right)^{-3}$

24. $(x^2y^2)^{-2} \cdot x^4y^{19}$

25. $\left(\dfrac{x^{-4}}{}\right)^3 \cdot \left(\dfrac{x}{}\right)^{-4}$

26. $(a^2b^1c^8)^6 \cdot a^{-9} \cdot b^4 \cdot x$

27. $\left(\dfrac{x^{-4}b^{-1}}{4}\right)^{-3} \cdot 2x^5$

28. $(a^9b^{-2}c^1)^{-4} \cdot \left(\dfrac{ab}{x}\right)^3$

29. $\left(\dfrac{x^{-4}y^{-6}z^{10}}{}\right)^{-2} \cdot \left(\dfrac{a^1bc^{-4}}{x^6yz^9}\right)^5$

0-7424-1789-1 *Algebra II*

Name ______________________ Date ______________________

Evaluating Rational Exponents

Simplify the expressions.

Example 1: $\left(\frac{64}{343}\right)^{\frac{1}{3}} = \frac{64^{\frac{1}{3}}}{343^{\frac{1}{3}}} = \frac{4}{7}$

Example 2: $\left(\frac{1000}{64}\right)^{-\frac{2}{3}} = \left(\frac{64}{1000}\right)^{\frac{2}{3}} = \left(\frac{(64)^{\frac{1}{3}}}{(1000)^{\frac{1}{3}}}\right)^2 = \left(\frac{4}{10}\right)^2 = \frac{16}{100} = \frac{4}{25}$

1. $\left(\frac{216}{729}\right)^{\frac{2}{3}}$

12. $\left(\frac{81}{16}\right)^{\frac{3}{2}}$

3. $\left(\frac{1}{32}\right)^{\frac{3}{5}}$

4. $\left(\frac{1}{25}\right)^{\frac{1}{2}}$

5. $\left(\frac{256}{625}\right)^{\frac{3}{4}}$

6. $\left(\frac{81}{256}\right)^{\frac{-3}{4}}$

7. $\left(\frac{121}{36}\right)^{\frac{-1}{2}}$

8. $\left(\frac{32}{243}\right)^{\frac{2}{5}}$

9. $\left(\frac{729}{343}\right)^{\frac{-2}{3}}$

10. $\left(\frac{4}{81}\right)^{\frac{-3}{2}}$

11. $\left(\frac{343}{64}\right)^{\frac{2}{3}}$

Calculator Challenge:

12. $\left(\frac{225}{289}\right)^{\frac{-5}{2}}$

As a check, for each problem number substitute the answer.

$1 \cdot 2 \cdot 3 \div 4 \cdot 5 \cdot 6 \div 7 \div 8 \div 9 \div 10 \cdot 11 = \frac{22}{25}$

$\_\_ \cdot \_\_ \cdot \_\_ \div \_\_ \cdot \_\_ \cdot \_\_ \div \_\_ \div \_\_ \div \_\_ \div \_\_ \cdot \_\_ = \frac{22}{25}$

Name ______________________ Date ______________________

Simplifying Radicals

Simplify each radical.

Example: $\sqrt[3]{24m^3x^5}$

2 12 — $2 \cdot m \cdot x\sqrt[3]{3x^2}$

2 6 — $2mx\sqrt[3]{3x^2}$

2 3

1. $\sqrt{49m^2t^3}$

2. $\sqrt[4]{81x^4}$

3. $\sqrt{64a^2b^4}$

4. $\sqrt[4]{16x^5y^3}$

5. $\sqrt[3]{27x^6y^9}$

6. $\sqrt[10]{1000x^{12}y^{100}}$

7. $\sqrt[3]{343d^6}$

8. $-\sqrt{(2x+1)^2}$

9. $\sqrt[3]{(x+1)^6}$

10. $\sqrt{x^2+2x+1}$ **Hint:** factor

11. $\sqrt{4x^2-12x+9}$

Name ________________________ Date ________________________

Finding Real Roots I

Find all real roots for each equation.

Example: $\frac{12x^4}{12} = \frac{15552}{12}$

$x^4 = 1296$

$x = 6$ or $^-6$

Note: An even root gives two values.

1. $\sqrt[3]{x} + 2 = 9$

2. $2x^2 = 200$

3. $^-6x^7 = {}^-768$

4. $x^4 = 625$

5. $-4\sqrt[3]{x} = -20$

6. $2\sqrt{x} = 10$

7. $^-10\sqrt{x} = {}^-1000$

8. $13x^5 = 3159$

9. $^-14\sqrt[3]{x} = 378$

10. $^-11x^3 = 704$

Calculator Challenge

11. $\sqrt[4]{x} = 81$

Above each problem number place the letter associated with its answer from the Answer Bank.

Non-real roots of an equation are the

__ __ __ __ __ __ __ __ __   __ __ __ __ __ .
2 3 4 7 2 1 4 5 8   5 6 6 9 10

Answer Bank

A. ± 5	C. ± 36	D. ± 9	E. 100	G. 10,000	H. 1,000	I. ± 10	K. $^-81$	L. 16	M. 2
N. 343	O. 25	P. 8	R. 125	S. $^-4$	T. $^-19{,}683$	U. 64	V. ± 12	W. $^-27$	Y. 3

Name ______________________ Date ______________________

Finding Real Roots II

Find all real roots of each equation.

Example: $\sqrt{3x + 1} = \frac{60}{3}$

$$\sqrt{3x + 1}^2 = (20)^2$$
$$3x + 1 = 400$$
$$3x + 1 - 1 = 400 - 1$$
$$\frac{3x}{3} = \frac{399}{3}$$
$$x = 133$$

1. $^-9(2x + 6)^5 = 288$

2. $^-5\sqrt[3]{2x + 1} = 35$

3. $3(x - 1)^2 = 432$

4. $\frac{1}{2}(x - 2)^2 = 8$

5. $3(2x - 5)^4 = 19683$

6. $(5x - 1)^4 = 2401$

7. $^-6\sqrt{10x - 18} = {}^-294$

8. $11(12x - 1)^3 = 2376$

9. $8(4x + 3)^{\frac{1}{2}} = 648$

10. $7(x - 15)^{\frac{3}{5}} = 2401$

11. $^-4(13x - 23)^{\frac{3}{4}} = {}^-32$

Name ______________________ Date ______________________

Graphing Exponential Functions

Graph each equation using a table of values. Include x values which are both negative and positive. Graph the equations on a separate piece of graph paper.

Example: $y = 2^x$

x	y
-1	1/2
0	1
1	2
2	4

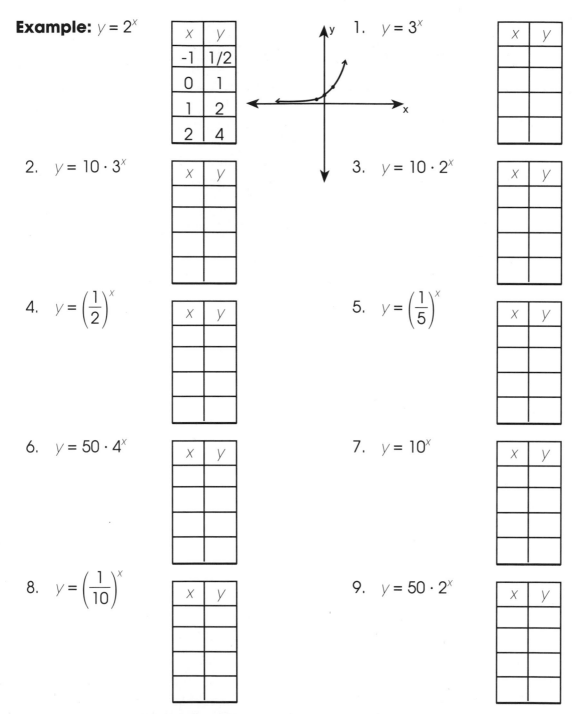

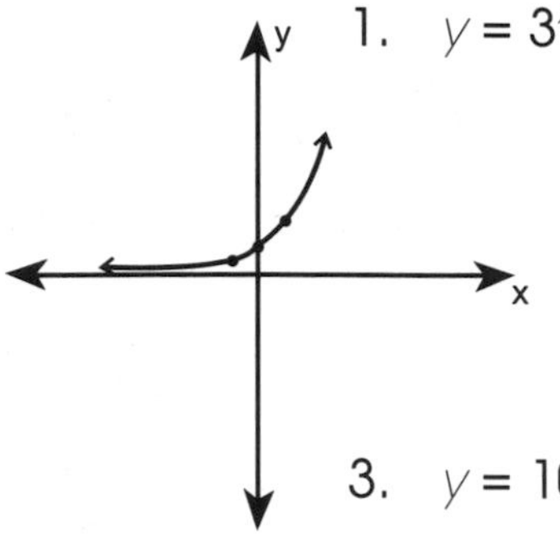

1. $y = 3^x$

x	y

2. $y = 10 \cdot 3^x$

x	y

3. $y = 10 \cdot 2^x$

x	y

4. $y = \left(\frac{1}{2}\right)^x$

x	y

5. $y = \left(\frac{1}{5}\right)^x$

x	y

6. $y = 50 \cdot 4^x$

x	y

7. $y = 10^x$

x	y

8. $y = \left(\frac{1}{10}\right)^x$

x	y

9. $y = 50 \cdot 2^x$

x	y

What do each of these sets of functions have in common?

Problems 1, 4, 5, 7, and 8:

Problems 4, 7, and 8:

0-7424-1789-1 *Algebra*

Name ______________________ Date ______________________

Calculating Compound Interest

Compound Interest

$$A = P\left(1 + \frac{r}{n}\right)^{nt}$$

where A = amount, P = principal, r = rate, t = time in years, and n = number of times compounded per year.

Solve the story problems assuming no deposits or withdrawals.

1. Heather received $100 for her 13th birthday. If she saves it in a bank with 3% interest compounded quarterly, how much money will she have in the bank by her 16th birthday?

2. Roland earned $1,500 last summer. If he deposited the money in a certificate of deposit that earns 4% interest compounded monthly, how much money will he have next summer?

3. The C.R.E.A.M. Company has an employee savings plan. If an employee makes an initial contribution of $2,500 and the company pays 5% interest compounded quarterly, how much money will the employee have after 10 years?

4. Juan invests $7,500 at 6% interest for one year. How much money would he have if the interest were compounded
   a. Yearly?
   b. Daily?
   c. Why are the amounts in answers *a* and *b* different?

5. Carmen is saving for a new car that costs $15,000. If she puts $5,000 in an account that earns 6% interest compounded monthly, how long will it take for her to save enough money to buy the car?

Name ______________________ Date ______________________

Exponential Decay (Half-life)

$$y = a\left(\frac{1}{2}\right)^x$$

where a = initial amount

x = number of half-lives = $\dfrac{\text{time}}{\text{half-life}}$

y = remaining

Solve each problem.

1. There are 10 grams of Curium-245 which has a half-life of 9,300 years. How many grams will remain after 37,200 years?

2. There are 80 grams of Cobalt-58 which have a half-life of 71 days. How many grams will remain after 213 days?

3. The half-life of Rhodium-105 is 1.5 days. If there are initially 7500 grams of this isotope, how many grams would remain after 30 days?

4. Two hundred ten years ago there were 132,000 grams of Cesium-137. How much is there today? The half-life of Cesium is 30 years.

5. In a nuclear reaction, 150 grams of Plutonium-239 are produced. How many grams would remain after one million years? The half-life of Plutonium-239 is 24,400 years.

6. Using carbon dating, scientists can determine how old a fossil is by how much Carbon-14 is present. If an average animal carcass contains 1 gram of Carbon-14, how old is a fossil with 0.0625 grams of Carbon-14? The half-life of Carbon-14 is 5730 years.

0-7424-1789-1 *Algebra*

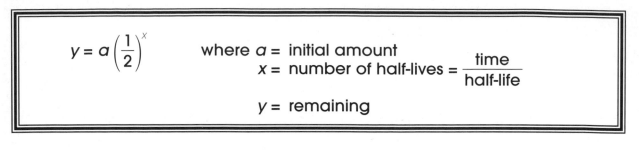

Name ______________________ Date ______________________

Manipulating Common Logs (Base 10)

$y = \log_b x$ where b = base
Common logarithm $b = 10$.
When no base is given, assume base 10.
$y = \log_{10} x$ is equivalent to $10^y = x$

Solve without using a calculator.

Example: $\log_{10} 100 = y$
$10^y = 100$
$y = 2$

1. $\log 1000$

2. $\log \sqrt[5]{10}$

3. $\log \sqrt[3]{10^2}$

4. $\log 0.1$

5. $\log 0.0001$

6. $\log \sqrt[4]{10}$

7. $\log \sqrt{10}$

8. $\log 10^6$

9. $\log 1$

10. $\log 10{,}000$

0-7424-1789-1 *Algebra II*

Name ______________________ Date ______________________

Converting from Logarithmic to Exponential Form

Convert each equation from logarithmic form to exponential form or from exponential to logarithmic. $y = \log_b x \leftrightarrow b^y = x$

Example: $\log_{11} 121 = 2$
$11^2 = 121$

1. $5^3 = 125$

2. $10^6 = 1{,}000{,}000$

3. $\log_{10} 1 = 0$

4. $\log_3 \frac{1}{243} = {}^-5$

5. $7^5 = 16{,}807$

6. $y = \log x$

7. $12^x = 87$

8. $y = \log_{15} 30$

9. $y = \log_Q x$

10. $y = \log_{180} B$

11. $10^y = x$

12. $\log_b 64 = 3$

13. $\log_x 5 = 10$

14. $7^x = 343$

Name ______________________ Date ______________________

Graphing Logarithms

Complete the table of values and graph each function on graph paper.

Example:
$y = \log_{10} x$
Convert to exponential form.
$10^y = x$
Choose y values that are both positive and negative.

x	y
$\frac{1}{100}$	$^-2$
$\frac{1}{10}$	$^-1$
1	0
10	1
100	2
1000	3

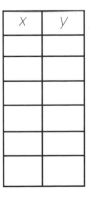

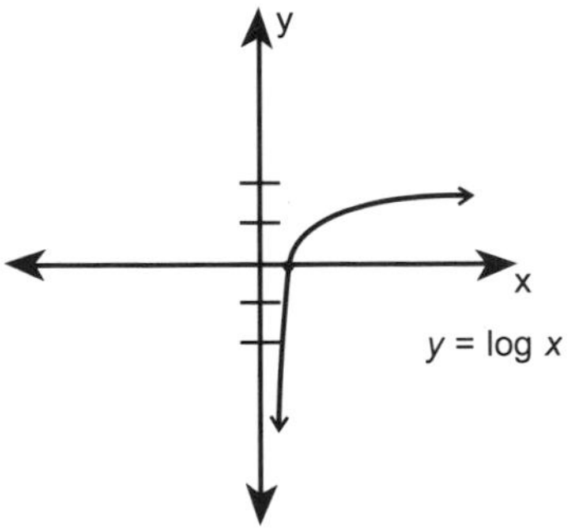

1. $y = \log_3 x$

x	y

2. $y = \log_5 x$

x	y

3. $y = \log_7 x$

x	y

4. $y = \log_2 x$

x	y

5. $y = \log_4 x$

x	y

6. $y = \log_{11} x$

x	y

7. $y = \log_{15} x$

x	y

0-7424-1789-1 *Algebra II*

Name ____________________ Date ____________________

Simplifying Logarithms

product property: $\log_b (m \cdot n) = \log_b m + \log_b n$

quotient property: $\log_b (\frac{m}{n}) = \log_b m - \log_b n$

power property: $\log_b (m^n) = n \cdot \log_b m$

Simplify.

Example 1: $\log_5 6 + \log_5 8 = \log_5 (6 \cdot 8) = \log_5 48$

Example 2: $\log_7 9 - \log_7 3 = \log_7 \frac{9}{3} = \log_7 3$

Example 3: $\log_{12} 6^3 = 3 \log_{12} 6$

1. $\log_9 4 + \log_9 6$

2. $\log_{12} 12 + \log_{12} 11$

3. $\log_{16} 36 - \log_{16} 12$

4. $\log 3 - \log 2$

5. $\log 14^6$

6. $\log_{20} 10^{16}$

7. $\log_3 16 + \log_2 4$

8. $\log 10 + \log 10$

9. $\log 125$

10. $\log_2 2^4$

Name ______________________ Date ______________________

Simplifying and Solving Logarithms

Simplify each expression, then solve. Place the letter of the correct answer above the problem number below.

Example 1: $\log_3 x - \log_3 4 = \log_3 12$

$\log_3 \left(\frac{x}{4}\right) = \log_3 (12)$

therefore $\frac{x}{4} = 12$

$x = 48$

Example 2: $\log_5 7 + \frac{1}{2} \log_5 4 = \log_5 x$

$\log_5 7 + \log_5 4^{\frac{1}{2}} = \log_5 x$

$\log_5 7 + \log_5 2 = \log_5 X$

$\log_5 14 = \log_5 x$

$X = 14$

1. $\log_3 x - 2 \log_3 2 = 3 \log_3 3$
   M. 23
   N. 108
   O. $6\frac{3}{4}$

2. $\log_2 x = 9$
   A. 18
   E. 512
   I. 81

3. $\log_2 128 = x$
   C. 16
   D. 64
   E. 7

4. $\log_x 144 = {}^-2$
   N. 12
   O. 72
   P. $\frac{1}{12}$

5. $\log_2 x = \frac{1}{3} \log_2 27$
   N. 3
   O. 9
   P. 27

6. $\log_{16} 32 - \log_{16} 2 = x$
   W. 2
   X. 1
   Y. 16

7. $5 \log 2 = \log x$
   E. 10
   I. 16
   O. 32

8. $\log_2 x - \log_2 5 = \log_2 10$
   R. 25
   S. 15
   T. 50

A logarithm is an __ __ __ __ __ __ __ __ .
2 6 4 7 5 3 1 8

Name ______________________ Date ______________________

Using Logarithms to Solve $B^x = A$

Solve for x, rounding to the nearest tenth.

Example: $5^x = 30$

$\log 5^x = \log 30$

$x \cdot \log 5 = \log 30$

$x = \dfrac{\log 30}{\log 5} = 2.1113 = 2.1$

1. $9^x = 27$

2. $7^x = 343$

3. $10^x = 0$

4. $6^x = 127$

5. $12^x = 303$

6. $13^x = 2839$

7. $2^x = 90$

8. $4^x = 512$

9. $3^x = 5.2$

10. $11^x = 153$

Name ______________________ Date ______________________

Classifying Polynomials

General expression of a polynomial

$a_n x^n + a_{n-1} x^{n-1} + a_{n-2} x^{n-2} + \ldots a_1 x^1 + a_0 x^0$

Note: $x^0 = 1$

$a_0 \cdot 1 = a_0$

<u>Types of Polynomial</u>

monomial = 1 term
binomial = 2 terms
trinomial = 3 terms

1st degree = linear polynomial
2nd degree = quadratic polynomial
3rd degree = cubic polynomial
(Degree is the highest power on the variable.)

Classify each polynomial.

Example 1: $4x + 7$ — linear binomial

Example 2: $7x^4 + 12x^2 + 79$ — 4th degree trinomial

1. $x^3 + 1$

2. $10x^5 + x$

3. x^{10}

4. $15x^6 + x^4 + 1$

5. $10 + x^6$

6. $10x^{15}$

7. $x^2 + 10x^1 + x^3$

8. $x^2 + 70\,x^4$

9. $1500x$

10. $17x^7 + 1$

11. $5x^6 + 4$

12. $21x^3 + 4x + 10$

Name ______________________ Date ______________________

Ordering Polynomials

Write each polynomial in descending order including missing degrees of x.

Example 1: $5x^3 + x + 4$

$5x^3 + 0x^2 + x + 4$

Example 2: $9x + 6x^5 + 2x$

$6x^5 + 0x^4 + 0x^3 + 0x^2 + 11x + 0$

1. $7x^4 + x^3 + x$

2. $23 + 6x^3 + x^2$

3. $19x^6 + 1$

4. $4x + 14x^2$

5. x^3

6. $10x^1 + 3x^2$

7. $1 + 2x + x^2$

8. $8x^3 + 4x$

9. $1 + x$

10. $x + 3x^3 + 2x^2$

11. $18 + 20x + x^4$

12. $25x^2 + 5x$

13. $18x^3 + x$

0-7424-1789-1 Algebra

Name ______________________ Date ______________________

Evaluating Polynomials

Given: $P(x) = 4x^2 + 1$
$Q(x) = {}^{-}2x^3 + x^2 - 6$
$R(x) = {}^{-}9x^2 - x + 16$

Evaluate each polynomial expression.

Example: $P(2)$
$P(2) = 4(2)^2 + 1$
$= 4(4) + 1 = 17$

1. $Q(5)$

2. $R(6)$

3. $Q({}^{-}2)$

4. $P(4)$

5. $R({}^{-}3)$

6. $R({}^{-}1)$

7. $P(10)$

8. $Q({}^{-}8)$

9. $P({}^{-}14)$

10. $Q(2)$

Cross out the correct answers below. Use the remaining letters to complete a statement, then rewrite the statement as a common adage.

101 SIM	⁻231 THE	⁻118 ILA	5 RAV	65 LAS	17 IAR	401 TMA	41 YSP	⁻18 NIS	37 ECI
⁻314 STA	⁻14 ESC	⁻62 NDI	341 ONG	⁻894 REG	1082 NG	⁻17 ATE	14 IST	8 HEO	785 NE.

_ _

_ _ _ _ _ _ _ _ _ _ .

Common adage: ______________________________ .

Name ______________________________ Date ______________________________

Multiplying Polynomials

Multiply each polynomial expression.

Example: $(x + 2)(3x^2 + x - 5)$

$$\begin{array}{r} 3x^3 + x^2 - 5x \\ \underline{+ \quad 6x^2 + 2x - 10} \\ 3x^3 + 7x^2 \; 3x - 10 \end{array}$$

1. $(x - 1)(2x^3 - 3x^2)$

2. $(x + 1)^3$

3. $(x + 1)(x^2 + 6x + 10)$

4. $(2x + 1)(x^3 - 6)$

5. $(x^2 - 1)(x^2 + 1)$

6. $(9x - 4)(6x^2 - x + 1)$

7. $(5x^2 + x - 8)(x - 1)$

8. $(6x^2 + 2x + 1)(x - 4)$

9. $(2x - 3)^3$

10. $(3x^2 + 1)^3$

11. $(14x + 1)(x^3 + x^2 - 7)$

12. $(^-2x + 1)(3x^3 + 2x + 1)$

13. $(11x^2 - 1)^3$

14. $(^-2x^2 + x)^3$

Name ______________________ Date ______________________

Factoring Polynomials

Patterns: Sum of cubes $(a^3 + b^3) = (a + b)(a^2 - ab + b^2)$
Difference of cubes $(a^3 - b^3) = (a - b)(a^2 + ab + b^2)$

Process:

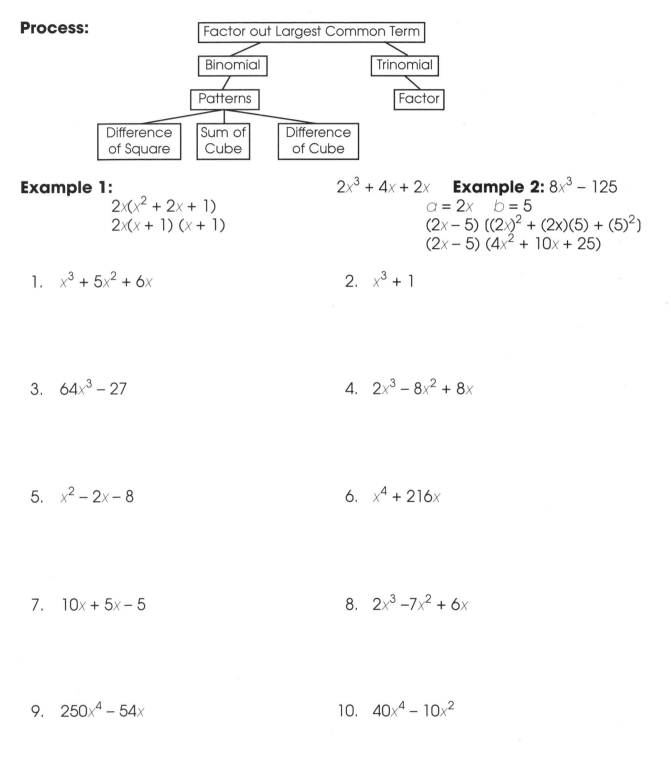

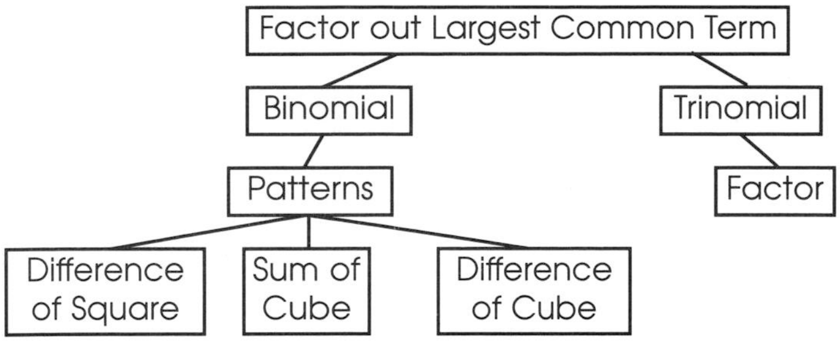

Example 1: $2x^3 + 4x + 2x$

$2x(x^2 + 2x + 1)$
$2x(x + 1)(x + 1)$

Example 2: $8x^3 - 125$

$a = 2x \quad b = 5$
$(2x - 5)((2x)^2 + (2x)(5) + (5)^2)$
$(2x - 5)(4x^2 + 10x + 25)$

1. $x^3 + 5x^2 + 6x$

2. $x^3 + 1$

3. $64x^3 - 27$

4. $2x^3 - 8x^2 + 8x$

5. $x^2 - 2x - 8$

6. $x^4 + 216x$

7. $10x + 5x - 5$

8. $2x^3 - 7x^2 + 6x$

9. $250x^4 - 54x$

10. $40x^4 - 10x^2$

Name ______________________ Date ______________________

Dividing Polynomials

Divide each polynomial expression. Check your answer.

Example: $\dfrac{(4x^2 - 2x + 6)}{}$

$$\begin{array}{r} 2x + 2 \\ 2x - 3\,\overline{)\,4x^2 - 2x + 6} \\ -\underline{4x^2 + 6x} \\ 4x + 6 \\ \underline{-4x + 6} \\ 12 \text{ remainder} \end{array}$$

$(2x + 2) + \dfrac{12}{2x - 3}$

Check: $(2x + 2)(2x - 3) + 12$

$4x^2 - 2x - 6 + 12 = 4x^2 - 2x + 6$

1. $(x^3 - 1) \div (x^2 - 1)$

2. $\dfrac{(2x^2 - 5x - 3)}{}$

3. $\dfrac{(x^2 - 3x - 7)}{}$

4. $(x^3 - 6) \div (x - 1)$

5. $(x^3 - 6x^2 + 1) \div (x + 2)$

6. $(5x^2 - 34x - 7) \div (x - 7)$

7. $\dfrac{(x^4 - 3x^3 - 5x - 6)}{(x + 2)}$

8. $\dfrac{(6x^2 - x - 7)}{(3x + 1)}$

Name ______________________ Date ______________________

Synthetic Division

Synthetic division is a short-hand method of dividing polynomials when the divisor is a binomial expression with a one as the coefficient of the variable. It serves as a useful tool in factoring and graphing polynomials. At first glance, the process seems involved. However, with practice, synthetic division is the fastest way to divide two polynomials.

The Process	**Example**
1. Write the polynomial in descending order.	$(-4x^2 + 3x^3 - 2 - 3x) \div (x - 3)$ $(3x^3 - 4x^2 - 3x - 2)$
2. Write the coefficients in a row.	$3 \quad -4 \quad -3 \quad -2$
3. Write the opposite of the constant of the divisor in front of the row of coefficients.	$\begin{array}{r\|rrrr} 3 & 3 & -4 & -3 & -2 \end{array}$
4. Bring the first coefficient straight down.	$\begin{array}{r\|rrr\|r} 3 & 3 & -4 & -3 & -2 \\ & & & & \\ \hline & 3 & & & \end{array}$
5. Multiply the first coefficient by the divisor and place the product under the second coefficient.	$\begin{array}{r\|rrr\|r} 3 & 3 & -4 & -3 & -2 \\ & & 9 & & \\ \hline & 3 & & & \end{array}$
6. Add the second coefficient to the product from step #5.	$\begin{array}{r\|rrr\|r} 3 & 3 & -4 & -3 & -2 \\ & & 9 & & \\ \hline & 3 & 5 & & \end{array}$
7. Multiply the sum from step #6 by the divisor and place under the third coefficient.	$\begin{array}{r\|rrr\|r} 3 & 3 & -4 & -3 & -2 \\ & & 9 & 15 & \\ \hline & 3 & 5 & & \end{array}$
8. Add the third coefficient to the product from step #7.	$\begin{array}{r\|rrr\|r} 3 & 3 & -4 & -3 & -2 \\ & & 9 & 15 & \\ \hline & 3 & 5 & 12 & \end{array}$
9. Multiply the sum from step #8 by the divisor and place it under the fourth coefficient.	$\begin{array}{r\|rrr\|r} 3 & 3 & -4 & -3 & -2 \\ & & 9 & 15 & 36 \\ \hline & 3 & 5 & 12 & \end{array}$
10. Add the fourth coefficient to the product from step #9.	$\begin{array}{r\|rrr\|r} 3 & 3 & -4 & -3 & -2 \\ & & 9 & 15 & 36 \\ \hline & 3 & 5 & 12 & 34 \end{array}$
11. Each coefficient in the last row corresponds to a new polynomial with the degree of the polynomial being decreased by one.	$3x^2 + 5x + 12$
12. If the sum from step #10 is any expression other than zero, write it over the original divisor.	$\dfrac{3x^2 + 5x + 12 + 34}{x - 3}$

Name ______________________ Date ______________________

Synthetic Division

Use synthetic division to divide the polynomials.

1. $(16 - 8x - 7x^2 + 2x^3) \div (x - 4)$

2. $(2x^2 + 3 + 5x) \div (x + 1)$

3. $(3x + x^2 - 18) \div (x + 3)$

4. $(2x^2 - 4x + 3) \div (x - 3)$

5. $(x - x^2 + 8 + x^3) \div (x - 1)$

6. $(-x^2 + 2x - 4 + 3x^3) \div (x - 2)$

0-7424-1789-1 *Algeb*

Name ______________________________ Date ______________________________

Factoring Using Synthetic Division

Sometimes when factoring polynomials, nothing seems to work. For example, there may not be a recognizable pattern or trinomial. In such cases, we can use synthetic division to reduce the polynomial to a trinomial or binomial, then look for patterns which are familiar.

In the following example, there are no familiar patterns or trinomials. The goal is to reduce the polynomial using synthetic division by trial and error and end up with a remainder of zero. If the remainer is not zero, choose a different factor and try again. **Hint:** Try factors of the constant term for your trial and error.

Example: Factor $x^3 - 2x^2 - 7x - 4$ using synthetic division.

Start by assuming that $(x - 2)$ is a factor of this polynomial.

$$\begin{array}{r|rrr|r} 2 & 1 & -2 & -7 & -4 \\ & & 2 & 0 & -14 \\ \hline & 1 & 0 & -7 & -18 \end{array}$$

Since the remainder is not zero, $(x - 2)$ is not a factor of this polynomial.

This time, try $(x - 4)$ as a factor.

$$\begin{array}{r|rrr|r} 4 & 1 & -2 & -7 & -4 \\ & & 4 & 8 & 4 \\ \hline & 1 & 2 & 1 & 0 \end{array}$$

Since the remainder is zero, $(x - 4)$ is a factor of the polynomial $x^3 - 2x^2 - 7x - 4$.

Now, rewrite the bottom line as a trinomial. $x^2 + 2x + 1$

Multiply the new trinomial by the factor $(x - 4)$. The problem at this point is $(x - 4)(x^2 + 2x + 1)$.

Factor the familiar trinomial. The final factors can be written in simplest terms. $(x - 4)(x + 1)(x + 1)$

0-7424-1789-1 *Algebra II*

Name ________________________ Date ________________________

Factoring Using Synthetic Division

Use synthetic division to factor the polynomials. **Hint:** Try factors of the constant term for your trial and error.

1. $2x^3 - 3x^2 - 3x + 2$

2. $x^3 - x^2 - x + 1$

3. $x^3 + 7x^2 + 7x - 15$

4. $x^3 - x^2 - 10x - 8$

5. $2x^3 - 3x^2 - 2x + 3$

6. $3x^3 - 13x^2 - 11x + 5$

0-7424-1789-1 *Algeb*

Name ______________________ Date ______________________

Graphing Polynomials

Graph the polynomials using x-intercepts.

Process: 1. Factor the polynomial.
2. Solve for the x-intercept.
3. Graph the x-intercept.
4. Determine the general shape.
5. Graph

Example: $y = 2x^3 + 4x^2 + 2x$

step 1: $= 2x(x^2 + 2x + 1)$

$= 2x(x + 1)(x + 1)$

step 3:

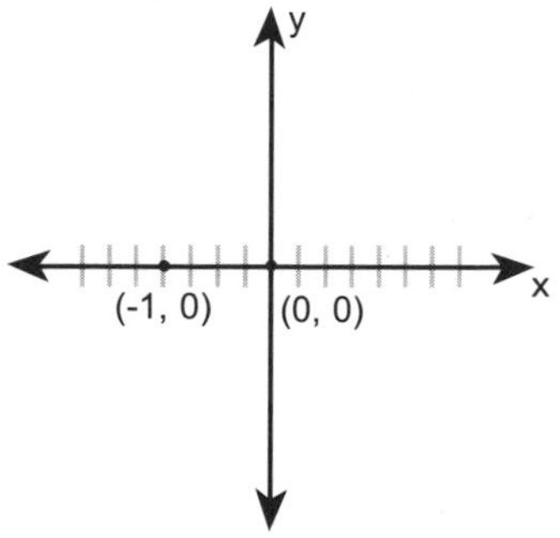

step 2: $2x = 0 \rightarrow x = 0$

$x + 1 = 0 \rightarrow x = {}^-1$

$x + 1 = 0 \rightarrow x = {}^-1$

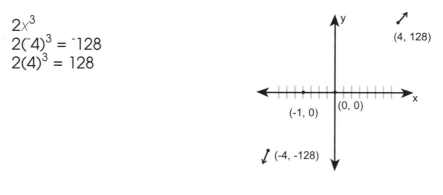

step 4: The shape of the graph is determined by the term with the highest power of x.
Plug in two x values; one positive and one negative.

$2x^3$

$2({}^-4)^3 = {}^-128$

$2(4)^3 = 128$

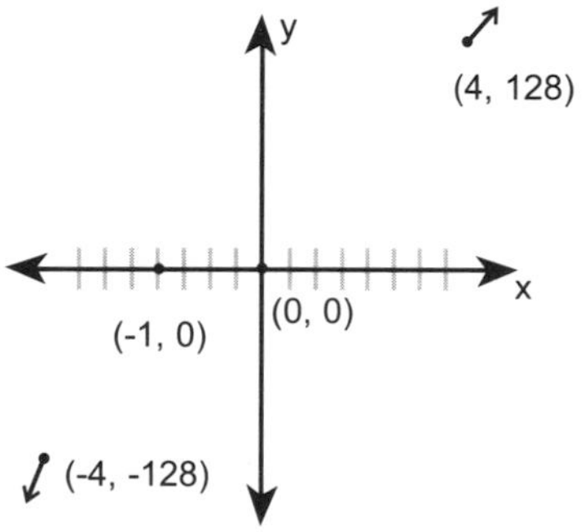

step 5: Since the same solution for the x-intercept appears twice (in this example $x = {}^-1$), the graph hits the x-axis at this point and moves away, not through the x-axis.

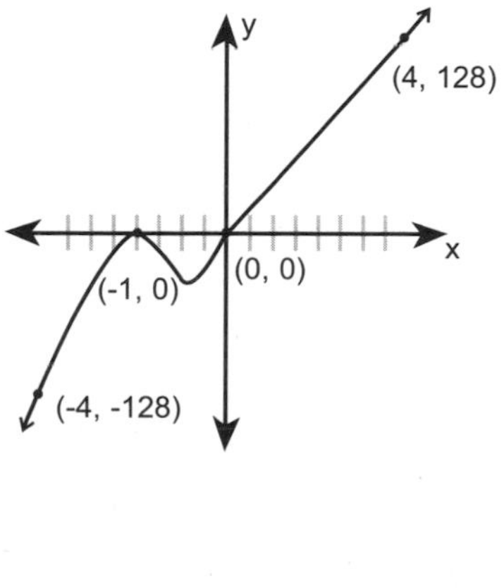

Note: If the coefficient on the x^3 term were negative, the shape of the graph would also change.

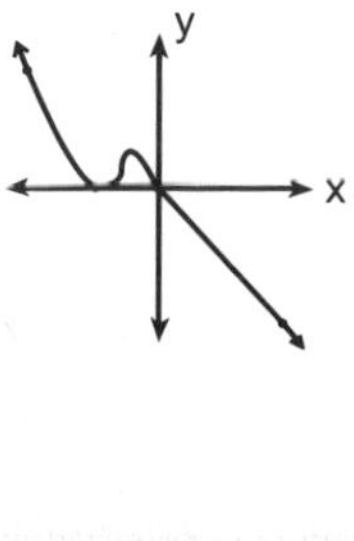

Name ______________________ Date ______________________

Graphing Polynomials

Graph the polynomials using the x-intercept.

1. $2x^3 - 7x^2 + 6x = y$

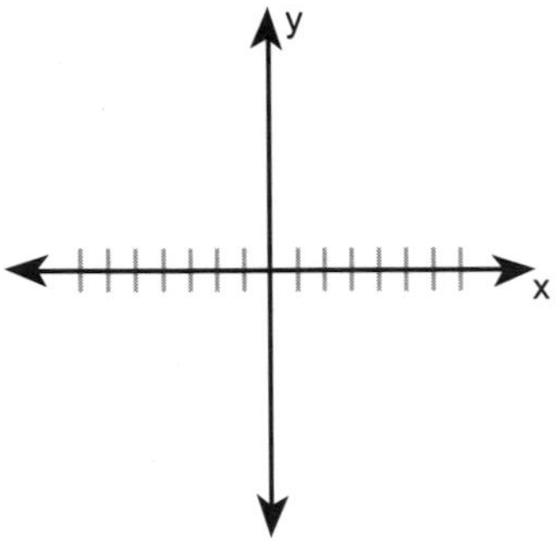

2. $-x^3 + 5x^2 - 6x = y$

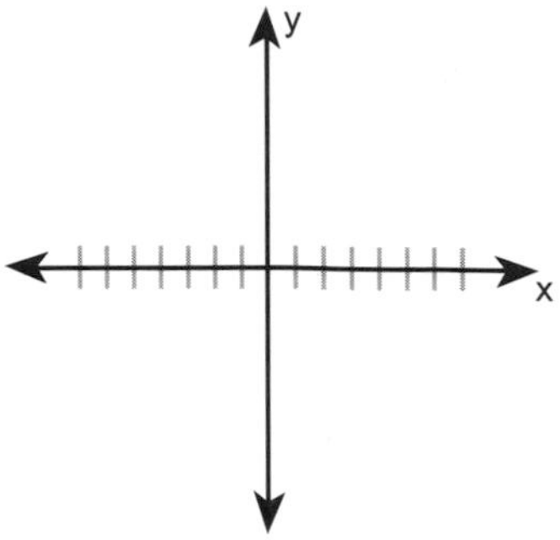

3. $^{-}4x^3 - 12x^2 + x + 3 = y$

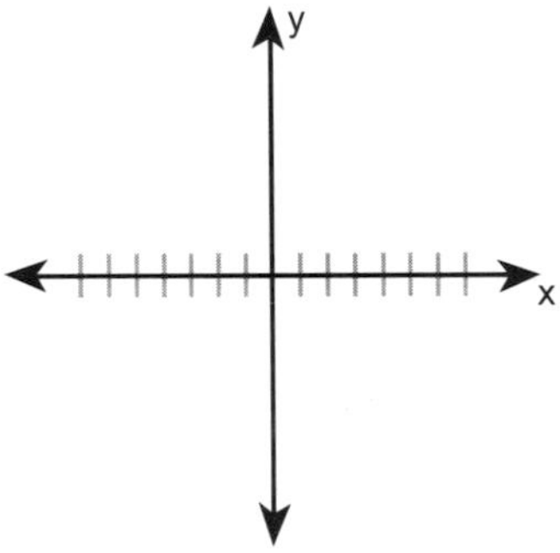

4. $x^3 + x^2 - x - 1 = y$

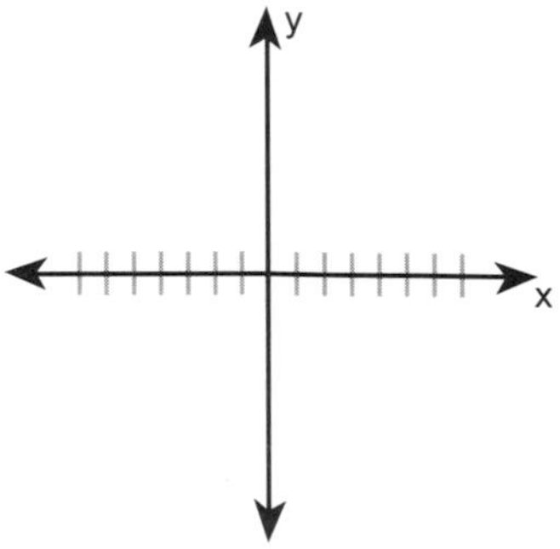

5. $40x^4 - 10x^2 = y$

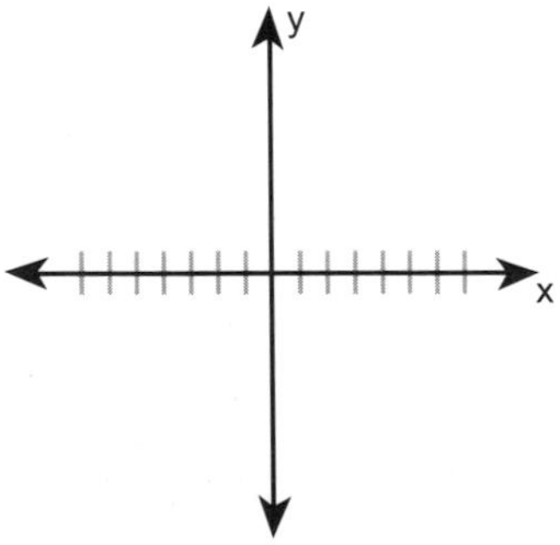

6. $x^4 - 9x^3 + 20x^2 = y$

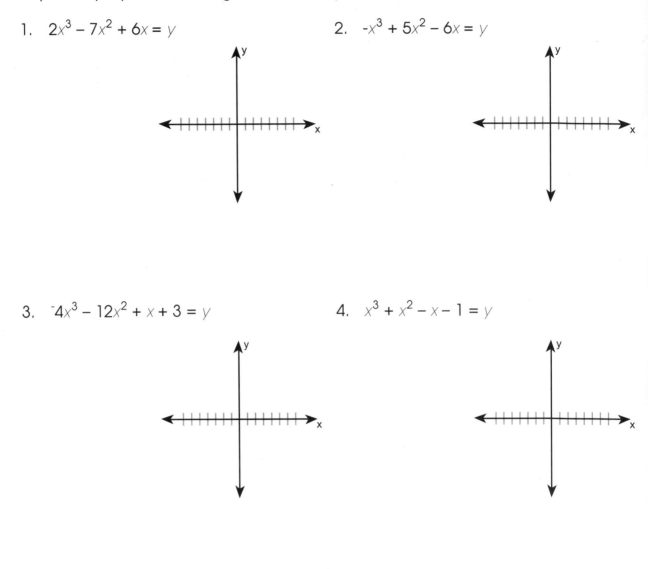

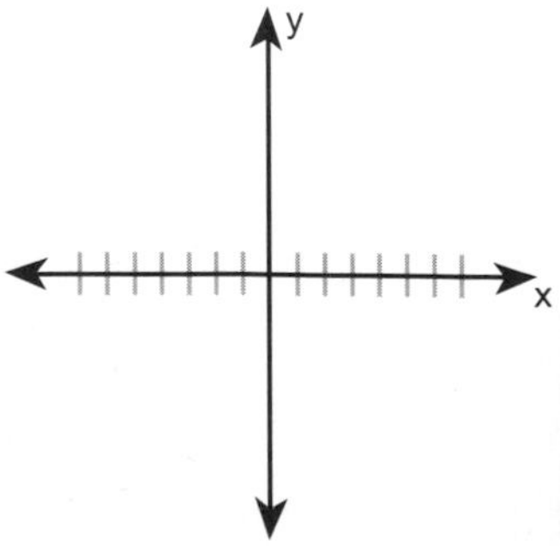

0-7424-1789-1 *Algeb*

Name ______________________________ Date ______________________________

Graphing Parabolas

General Equation: $y = a(x - h)^2 + k$ or $x = a(y - k)^2 + h$

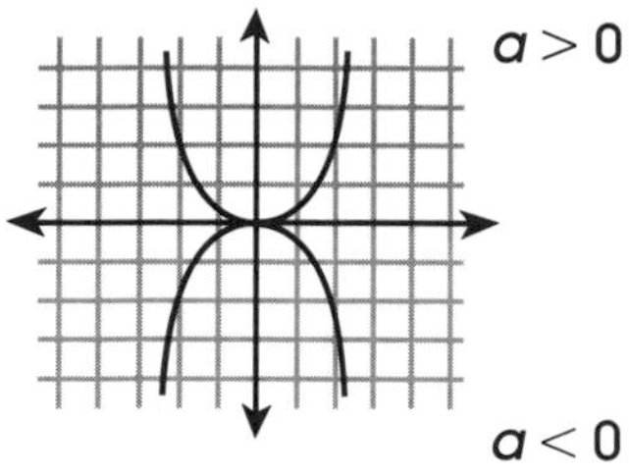

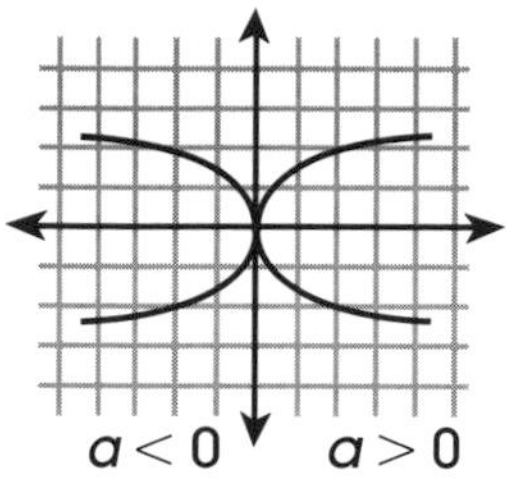

The vertex of the parabola is (h, k).

Graph each parabola and label its vertex.

Example: $y = 3(x - 3)^2 + 2$

x	y
2	5
4	5

Choose one x value on either side of vertex.
vertex (3, 2)

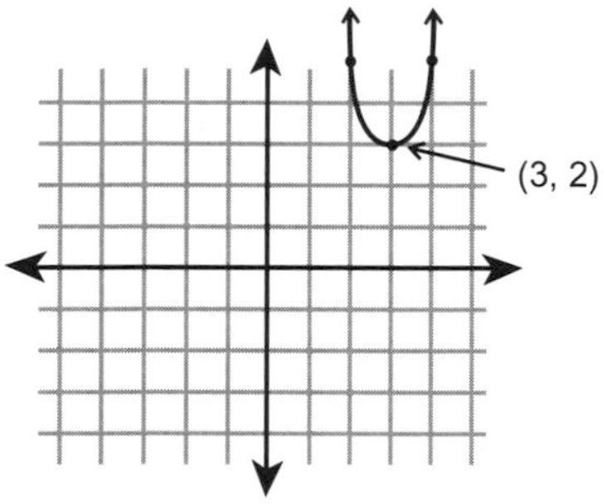

1. $x = (y + 2)^2 + 4$

x	y

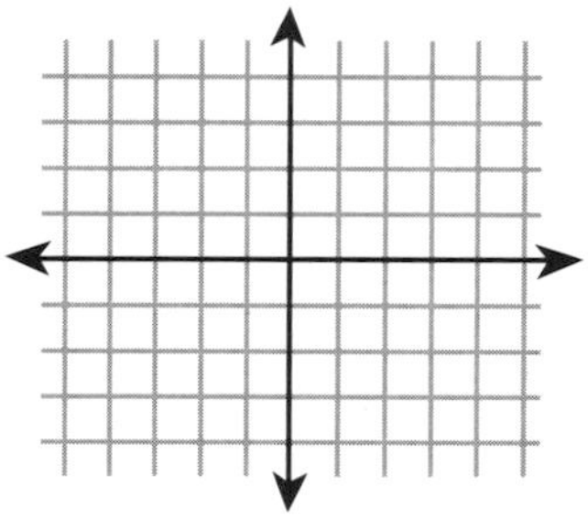

2. $x = {}^{-}2(y - 2)^2 + 3$

x	y

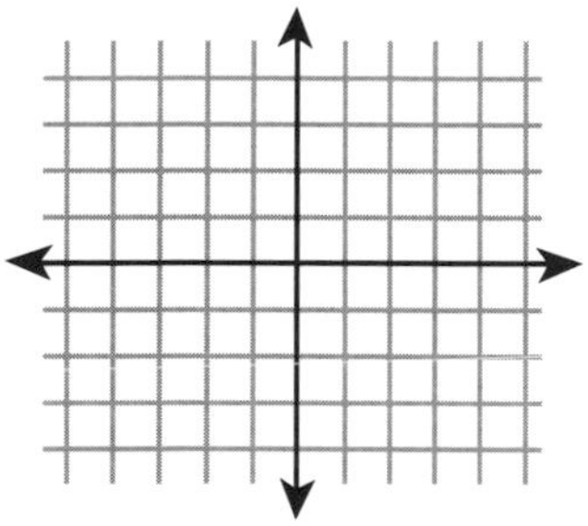

3. $y = -(x + 3)^2 - 1$

x	y

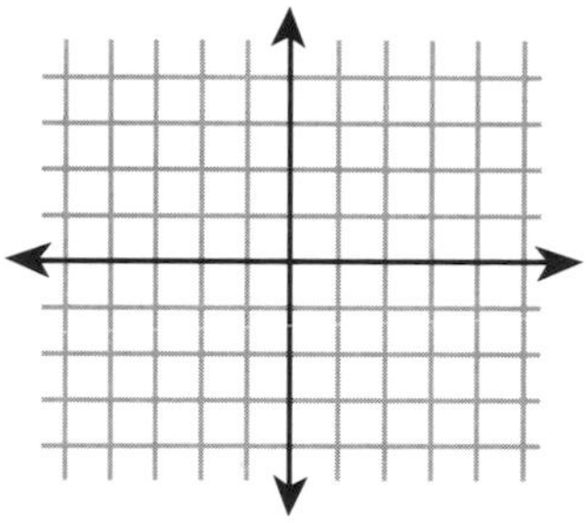

4. $y = \frac{1}{3}(x + 5)^2$

x	y

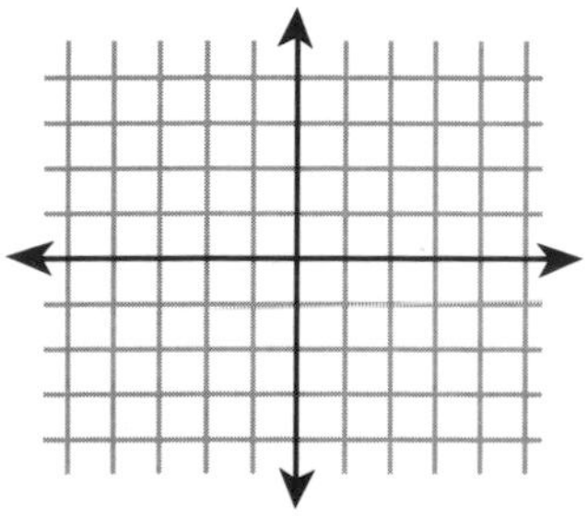

5. $x = \frac{1}{10}(y + 2)^2 + 2$

x	y

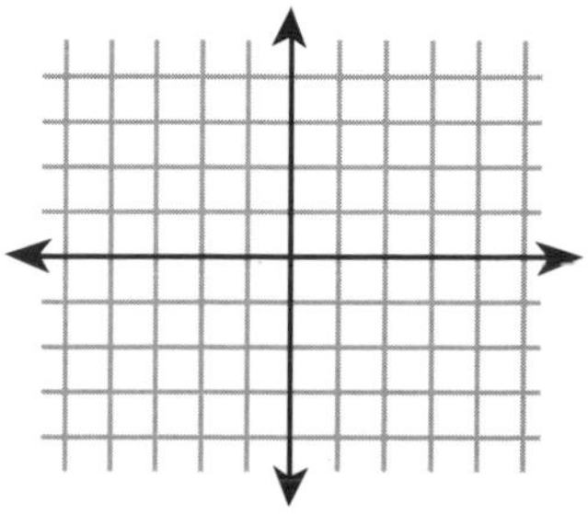

0-7424-1789-1 *Algebra II*

Name ______________________ Date ______________________

Completing the Square

Parabolas as well as other conic sections are not always given in their general form. To put a conic section in its general form it is sometimes necessary to "complete the square."

Example: $y = 3x^2 - 18x - 10$

To complete the square. . .

1. Isolate the x terms. $y + 10 = 3x^2 - 18x$
2. Divide by the x^2 coefficient. $\frac{(y + 10)}{3} = 1x^2 - 6x$
3. Divide the coefficient of the x term by two, then square it and add the product to both sides of the equation. $\frac{(y + 10)}{3} + 9 = 1x^2 - 6x + 9$
4. Factor the right side of the equation. $\frac{(y + 10)}{3} + 9 = (x - 3)(x - 3)$
   $3\left[\frac{(y + 10)}{3} + 9\right] = 3(x - 3)^2$
5. Solve for y. $y + 10 + 27 = 3(x - 3)^2$
   $y + 37 = 3(x - 3)^2$
   $y = 3(x - 3)^2 - 37$

vertex of parabola (3, ⁻37)

Complete the square and name the vertex for each parabola.

1. $y = 2x^2 - 4x + 8$
2. $y = {}^-3x^2 - 12x - 13$
3. $y = \frac{1}{3}x^2 - 2x + 3$
4. $y = \frac{1}{5}x^2 - \frac{2}{5}x + \frac{11}{5}$
5. $x = y^2 + 10y - 6$
6. $x = y^2 - 10y + 35$
7. $x = 5y^2 + 40y + 77$
8. $x = \frac{1}{2}y^2 - \frac{3}{2}y - \frac{1}{4}$

Name ______________________ Date ______________________

Equations for Circles

General equation: $(x-h)^2 + (y-k)^2 = r^2$

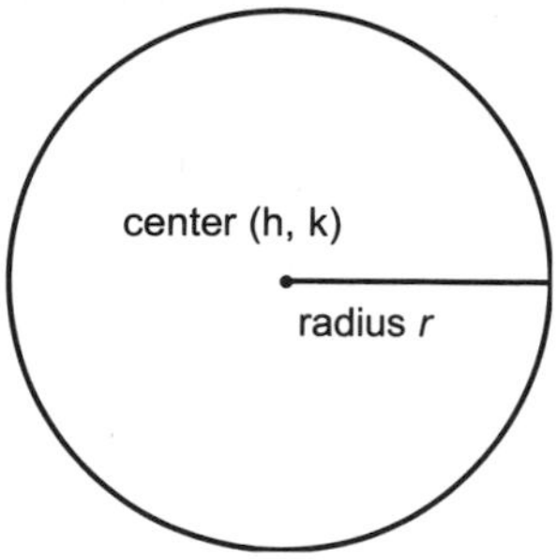

Given the equation for a circle, identify its center and its radius.

Example: $(x-2)^2 + (y-3)^2 = 25$

center (2, 3)

radius = 5

1. $(x-4)^2 + (y+10)^2 = 144$

2. $x^2 + (y-7)^2 = 49$

3. $x^2 + y^2 = 1$

4. $(x+3)^2 + (y+11)^2 = 15$

5. $(x-15)^2 + y^2 = 10$

Given the center and the radius of a circle, write the equation describing the circle.

Example: $(0, 4), r = 9$

$(x-0)^2 + (y-4)^2 = 81$

$x^2 + (y-4)^2 = 81$

1. $(0, 0), r = 8$

2. $(^-2, 3), r = 2$

3. $(^-7, ^-18), r = 14$

4. $(12, 9), r = 1$

5. $(10, 0), r = 22$

0-7424-1789-1 *Algebra II*

Name ____________________ Date ____________________

Graphing Circles

Graph each circle and label its center and radius.

Example:
$x^2 + (y - 3)^2 = 16$

center (2, ⁻5)
radius = 2

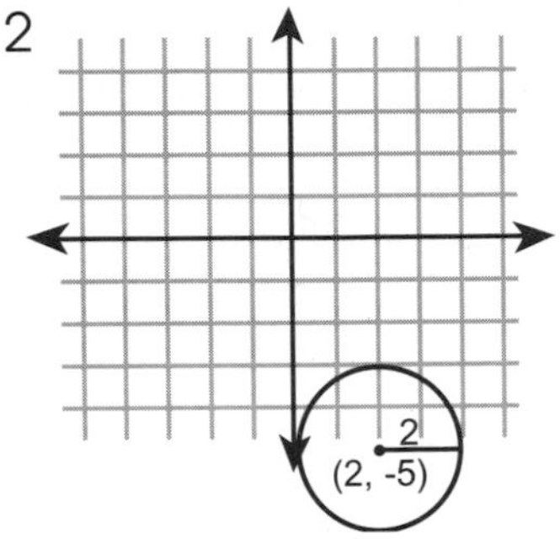

1. $(x - 2)^2 + (y + 5)^2 = 4$

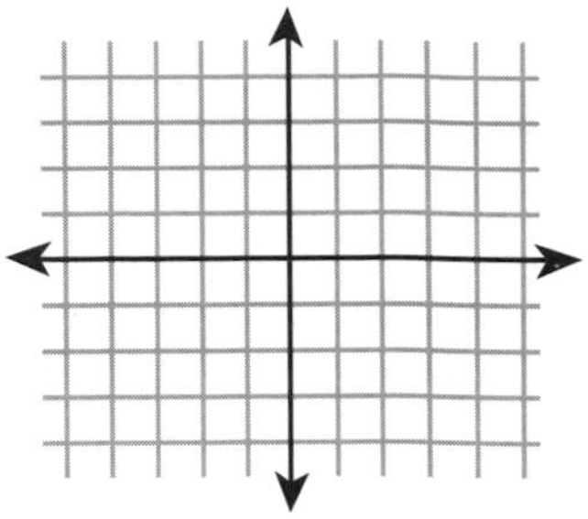

2. $x^2 + y^2 = 64$

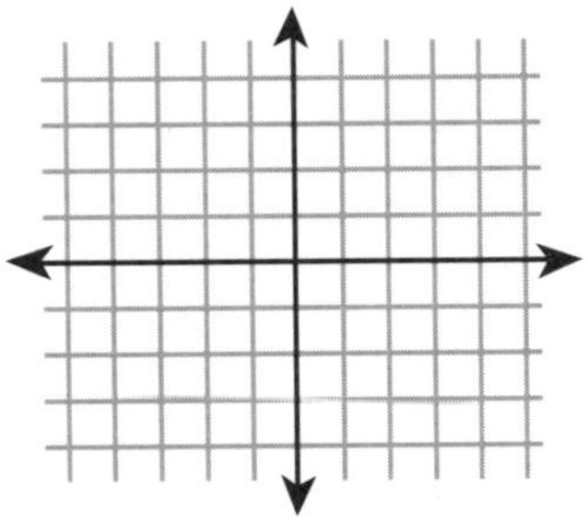

3. $(x - 1)^2 + (y + 1)^2 = 1$

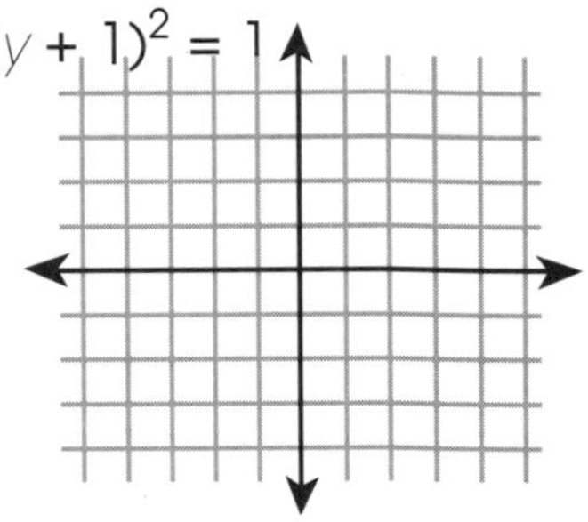

4. $(x - 7)^2 + (y - 2)^2 = 25$

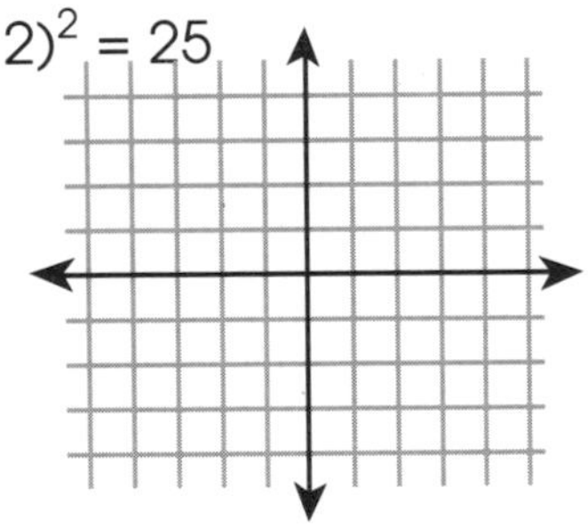

5. $(x + 4)^2 + y^2 = 9$

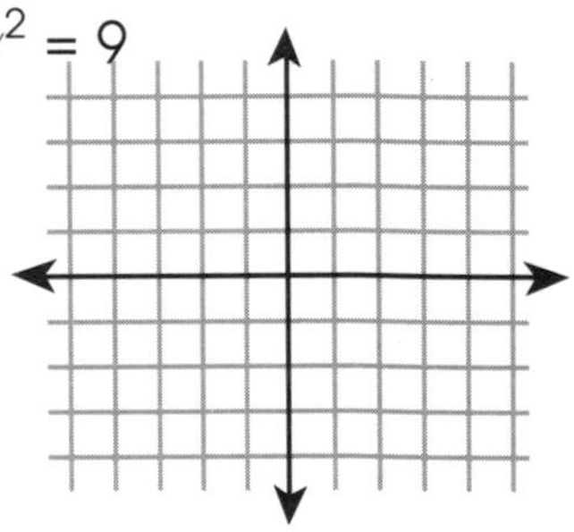

6. $x^2 + (y - 12)^2 = 20$

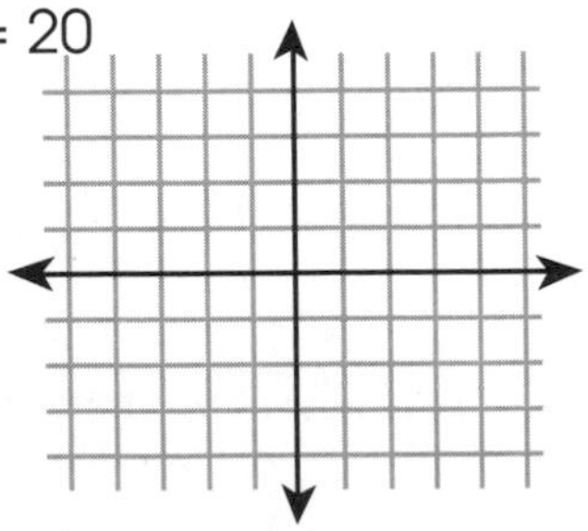

7. $(x + 6)^2 + (y + 9)^2 = 15$

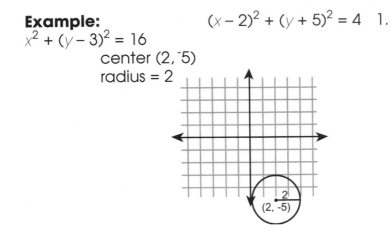

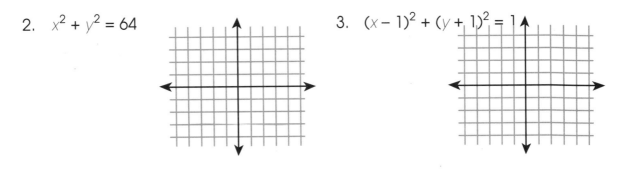

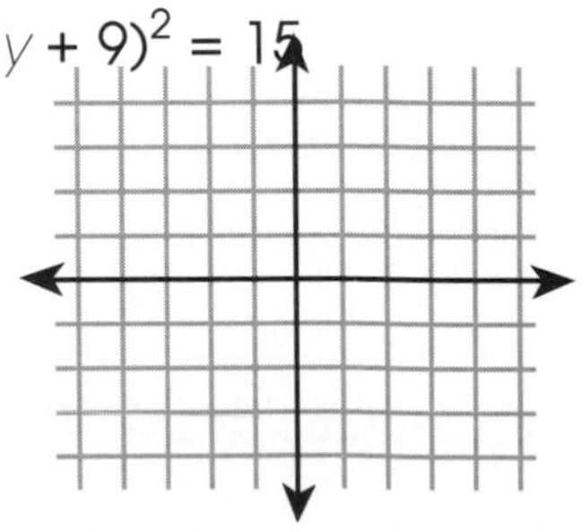

0-7424-1789-1 Alge

Name ______________________ Date ______________________

Graphing an Ellipse with Center (0, 0)

Two different types of ellipses may have the center (0, 0). The first type has its two foci on the x-axis, and the second type has its two foci on the y-axis. The axis which contains the foci is called the major axis. The other axis is called the minor axis.

Type one: x-axis as the major axis

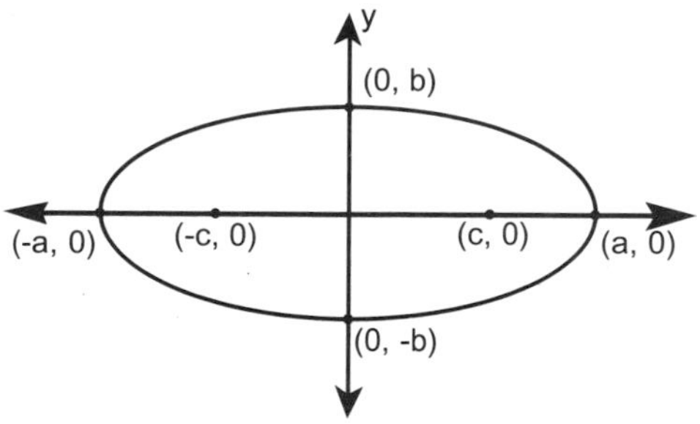

General equation: $\frac{x^2}{\quad} + \frac{y^2}{\quad} = 1$

The vertices of the ellipse are $(-a, 0)$, $(a, 0)$, $(0, b)$, $(0, -b)$.

The foci of the ellipse are $(c, 0)$, $(-c, 0)$.

The equation relating a, b, and c is $c^2 = a^2 - b^2$.

Note: $c^2 = a^2 - b^2$ looks like the Pythagorean theorem and it is derived from it, but a is the hypotenuse rather than c.

Type two: y-axis as the major axis

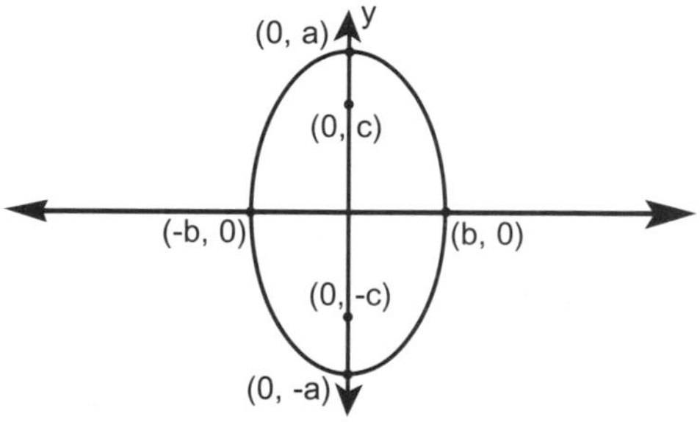

General equation: $\frac{x^2}{\quad} + \frac{y^2}{\quad} = 1$

The vertices of the ellipse are $(0, -a)$, $(0, a)$, $(b, 0)$, $(-b, 0)$.

The foci of the ellipse are $(0, -c)$, $(0, c)$.

The equation relating a, b, and c is $c^2 = a^2 - b^2$.

Note: In the general equation, the variable a^2 is always the larger of the two denominators and is under the variable of the major axis.

Name ____________________ Date ____________________

Graphing an Ellipse with Center (0, 0) (cont.)

Graph each ellipse and label the four vertices and the foci.

Example: $\frac{x^2}{9} + \frac{y^2}{25} = 1$

$b^2 = 9$ so $b = 3$ and $a^2 = 25$ so $a = 5$
and $c^2 = a^2 - b^2$ therefore $c = \sqrt{a^2 - b^2}$
finally, $c = \sqrt{25 - 9}$ so $c = 4$

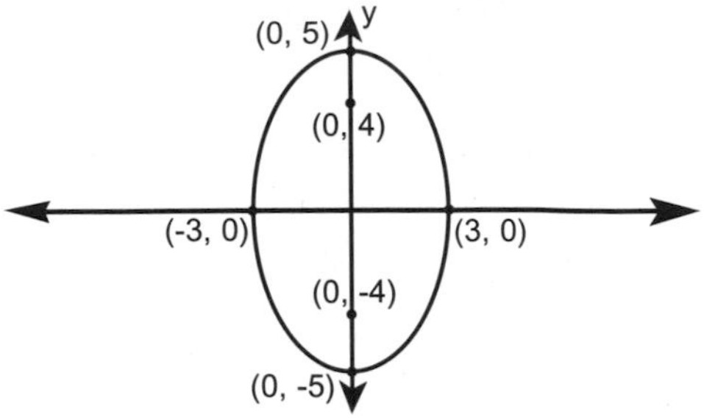

1. $\frac{x^2}{4} + \frac{y^2}{25} = 1$

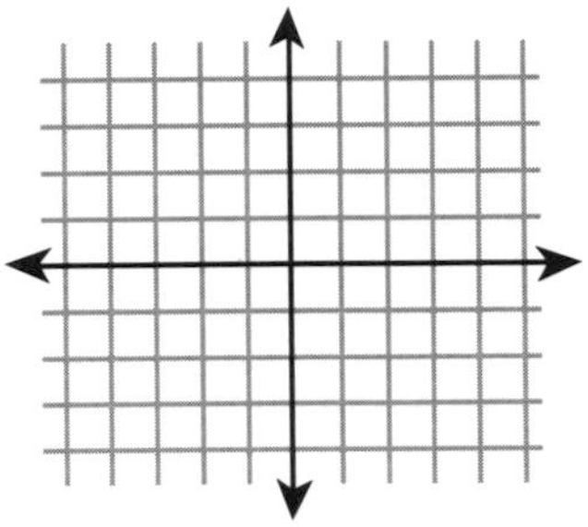

2. $\frac{x^2}{64} + y^2 = 1$

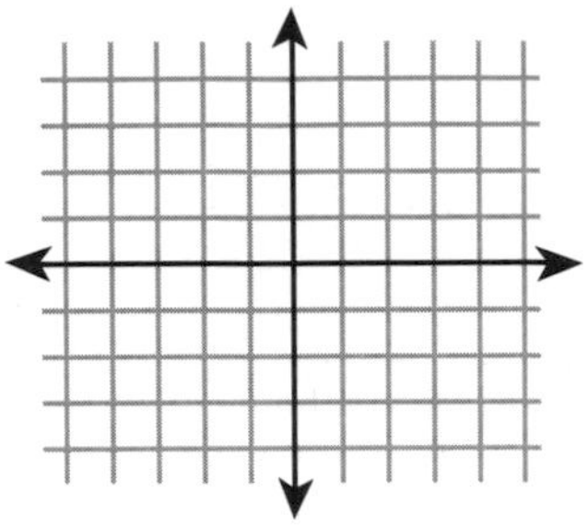

3. $\frac{x^2}{100} + \frac{y^2}{36} = 1$

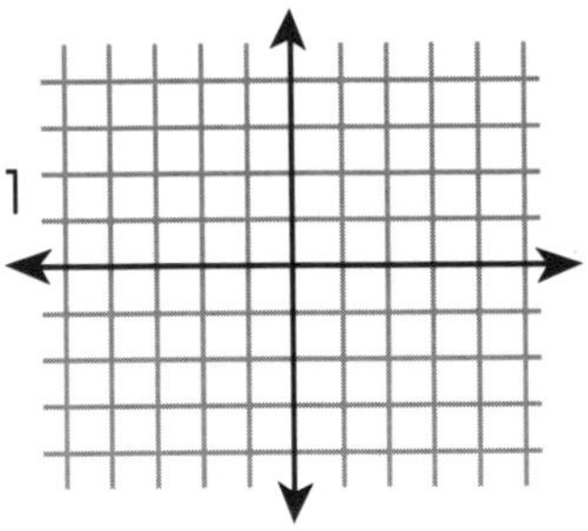

4. $\frac{x^2}{49} + \frac{y^2}{144} = 1$

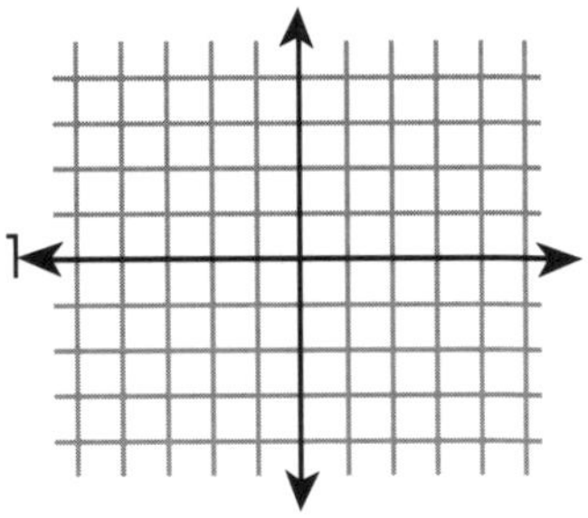

5. $x^2 + \frac{y^2}{25} = 1$

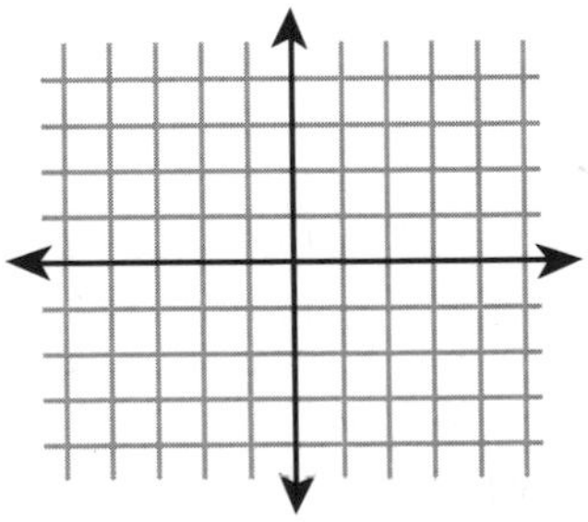

6. $\frac{x^2}{16} + \frac{y^2}{121} = 1$

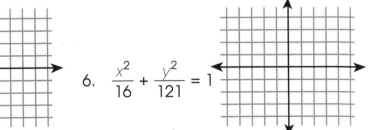

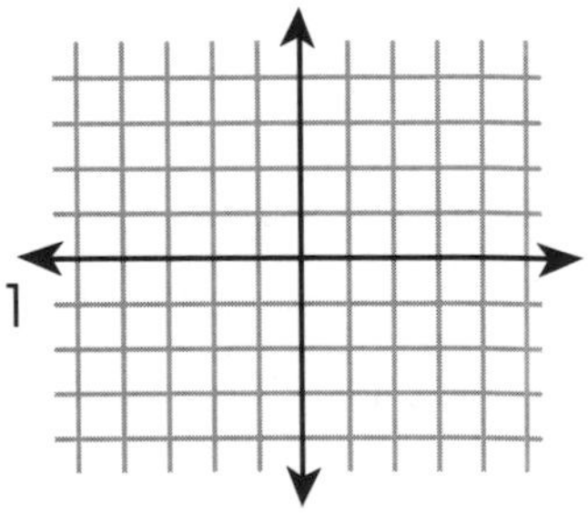

Name ______________________________ Date ______________________________

Graphing Ellipses with Center (h, k)

There are two types of ellipses with center (h, k). The first type has its two foci on a horizontal major axis, and the second type has its two foci on a vertical major axis.

Type one: horizontal major axis

General equation:

$$\frac{(x-h)^2}{} + \frac{(y-k)^2}{} = 1$$

Type two: vertical major axis

General equation:

$$\frac{(x-h)^2}{} + \frac{(y-k)^2}{} = 1$$

Graph each ellipse, labeling the four vertices and the center. Mark units on both axes.

Example: $\frac{(x+1)}{36} + \frac{(y-2)}{9} = 1$

center = $(^{-}1, 2)$, $a = 6$, $b = 3$

Note: a^2 is under the variable x. The x-axis is a horizontal line, therefore, this equations has a horizontal major axis.

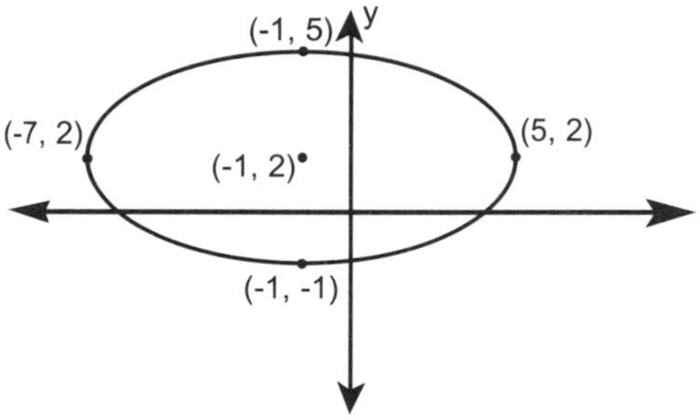

1. $\frac{(x-3)^2}{81} + \frac{(y+5)^2}{25} = 1$

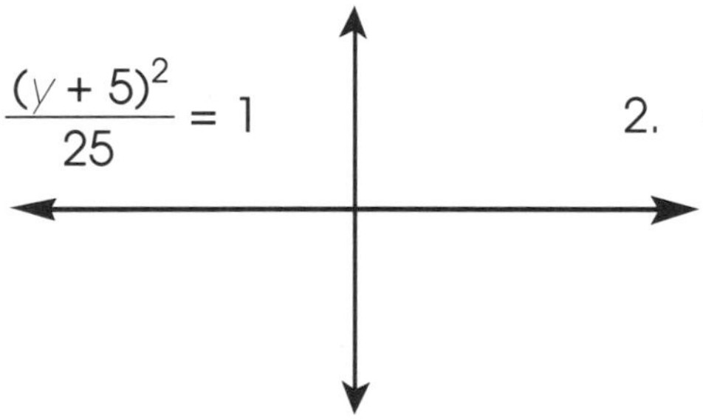

2. $\frac{(x+8)^2}{64} + (y-6)^2 = 1$

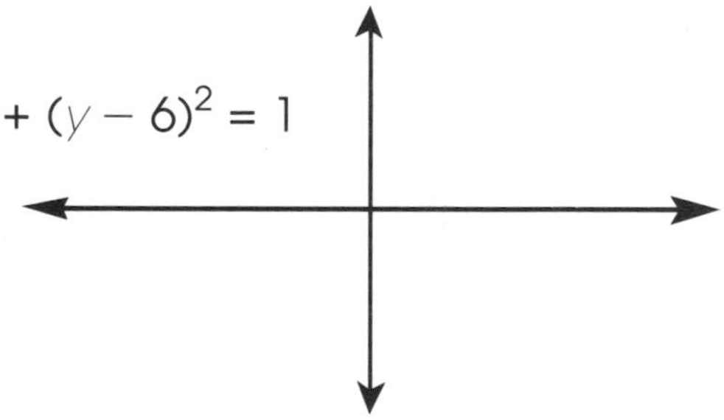

3. $\frac{x^2}{9} + \frac{y^2}{64} = 1$

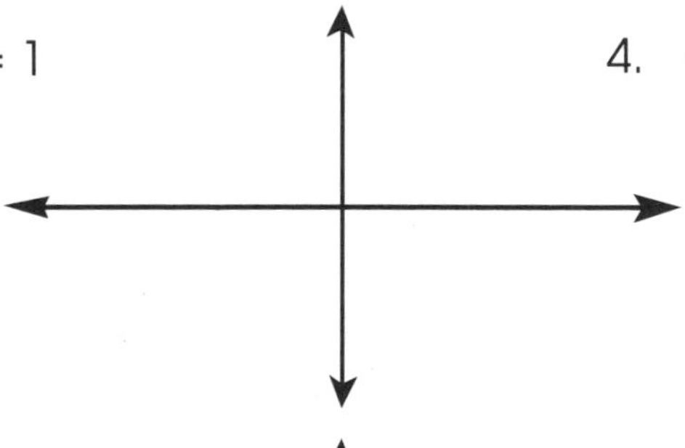

4. $\frac{(x+2)^2}{49} + \frac{(y+3)^2}{225} = 1$

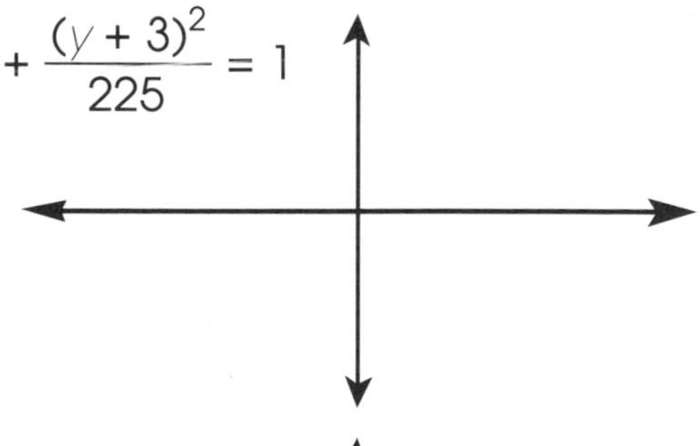

5. $\frac{(x+4)^2}{25} + \frac{(y-16)^2}{30} = 1$

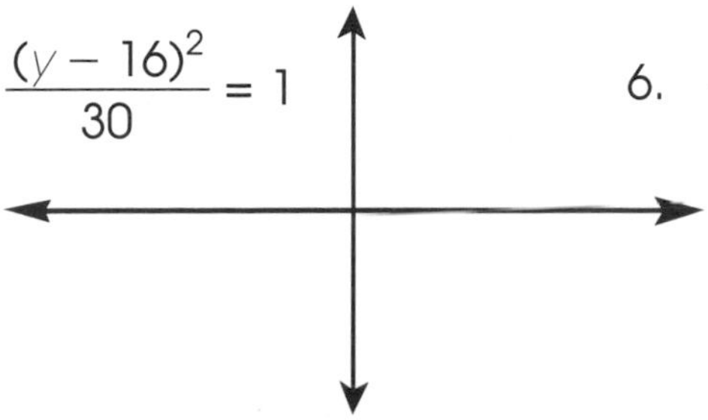

6. $\frac{(x-5)^2}{20} + \frac{(y-11)^2}{16} = 1$

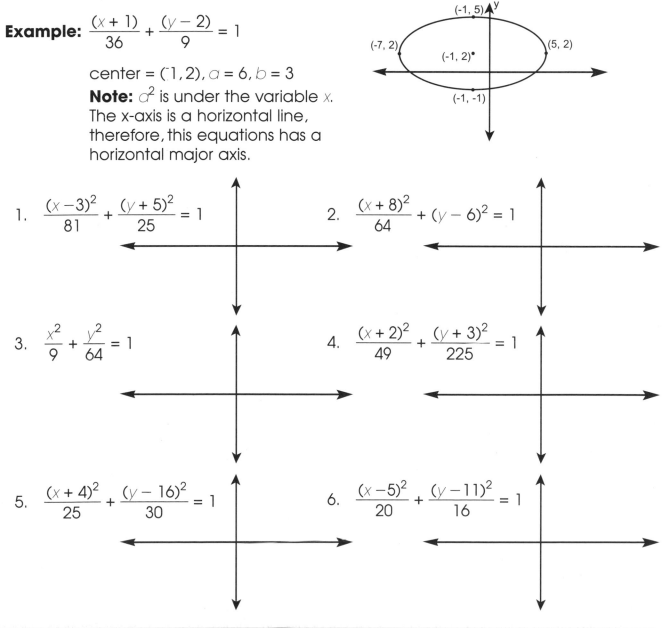

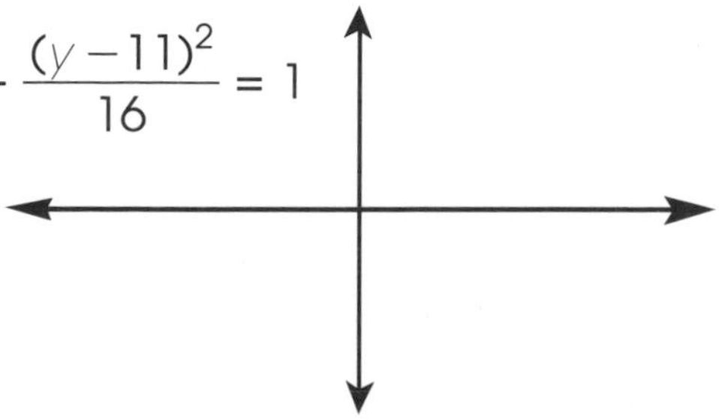

0-7424-1789-1 *Algebra II*

Name ______________________ Date ______________________

Graphing Hyperbolas with Center (0, 0)

There are two types of hyperbola with center (0, 0). The first type has its vertex and foci on the x-axis, and the second type has its vertex and foci on the y-axis.

Type one: vertex and foci on the x-axis

General equation: $\frac{x^2}{\quad} - \frac{y^2}{\quad} = 1$

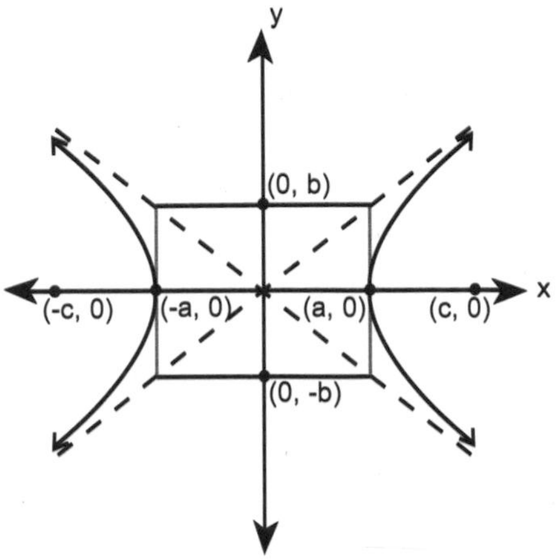

The vertices of the hyperbola are $(-a, 0)$, $(a, 0)$.

The foci of the hyperbola are $(c, 0)$, $(-c, 0)$.

The equation relating a, b, and c is $c^2 = a^2 + b^2$.

The two dashed lines are the asymptotes. The hyperbola gets very close to but does not touch either of these two dashed lines.

Note: The asymptotes are the diagonals of the quadrilateral with dimensions 2a by 2b.

Type two: vertex and foci on y-axis

General equation: $\frac{y^2}{\quad} - \frac{x^2}{\quad} = 1$

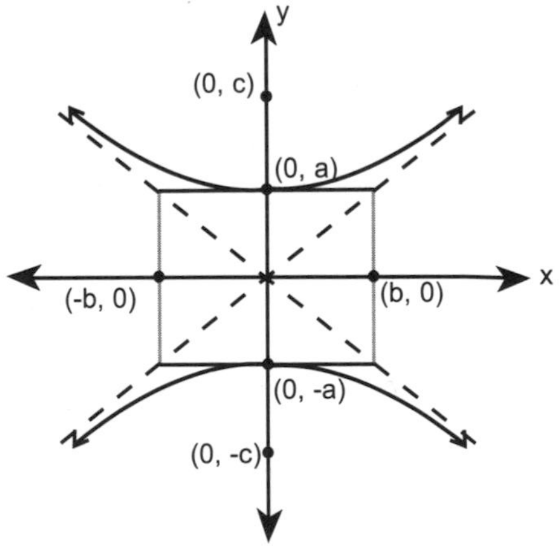

The vertices of the hyperbola are $(0, -a)$, $(0, a)$.

The foci of the hyperbola are $(0, -c)$, $(0, c)$.

The equation relating a, b, and c is $c^2 = a^2 + b^2$.

Note: The equations for hyperbolas and ellipses are identical except for a minus sign. In graphing either, the positive axis variable, x or y, is the axis which contains the vertex and the foci.

0-7424-1789-1 *Algeb*

Name ______________________ Date ______________________

Graphing Hyperbolas with Center (0, 0) (cont.)

Graph each hyperbola labeling the vertices and foci.

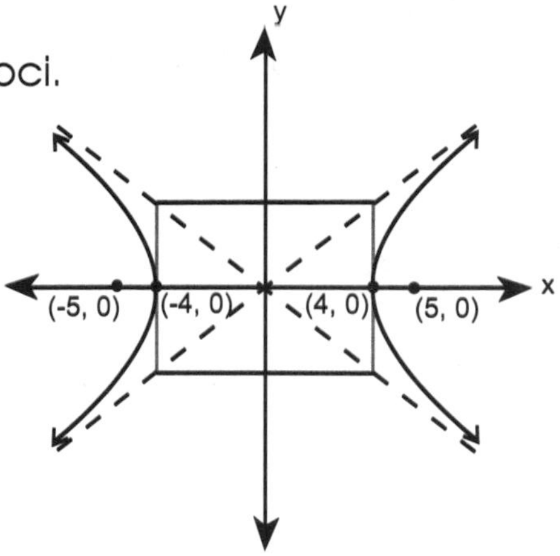

Example: $\frac{x^2}{16} - \frac{y^2}{9} = 1$

$a^2 = 16$ so $a = 4$ $\quad$ $b^2 = 9$ so $b = 3$

$c^2 = a^2 + b^2$ therefore $c = \sqrt{a^2 + b^2}$

finally, $c = \sqrt{16 + 9}$ so $c = 5$

1. $\frac{x^2}{25} - \frac{y^2}{49} = 1$

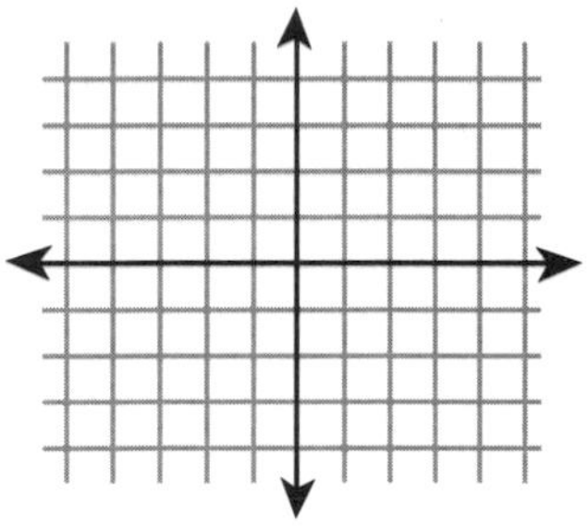

2. $\frac{y^2}{16} - \frac{x^2}{81} = 1$

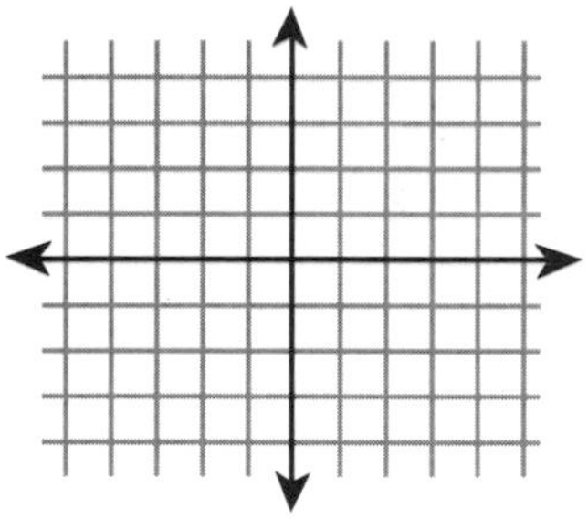

3. $\frac{y^2}{36} - \frac{x^2}{100} = 1$

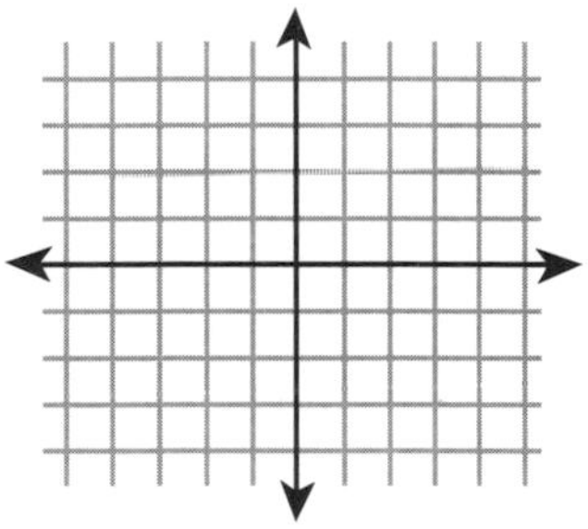

4. $\frac{x^2}{49} - \frac{y^2}{144} = 1$

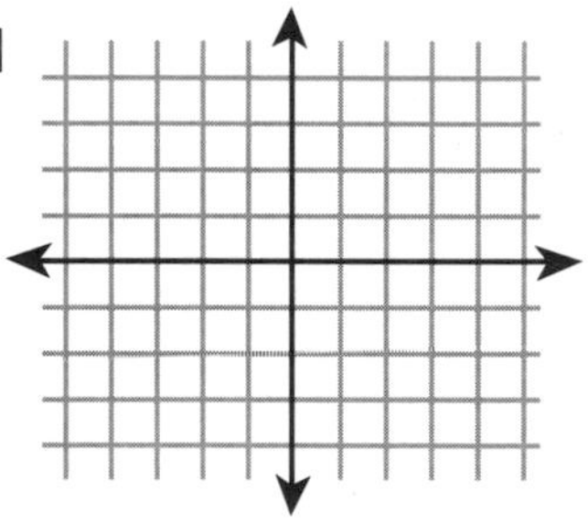

5. $x^2 - \frac{y^2}{25} = 1$

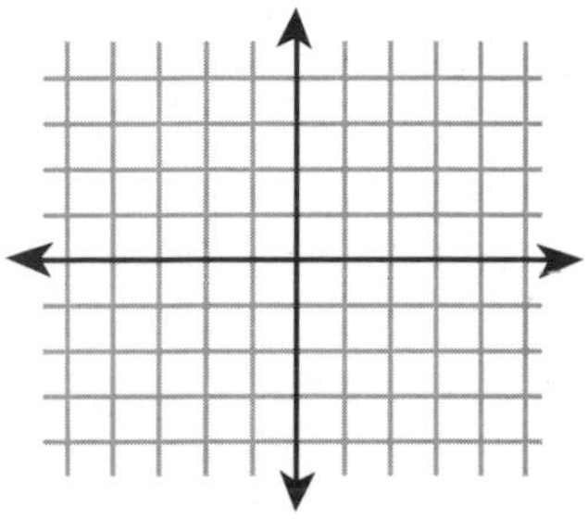

6. $\frac{y^2}{121} - \frac{x^2}{16} = 1$

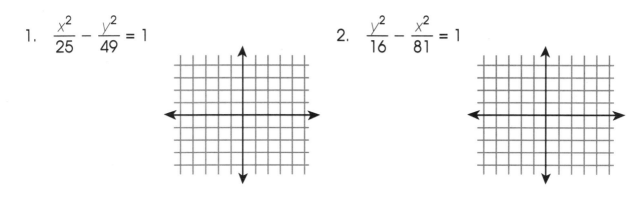

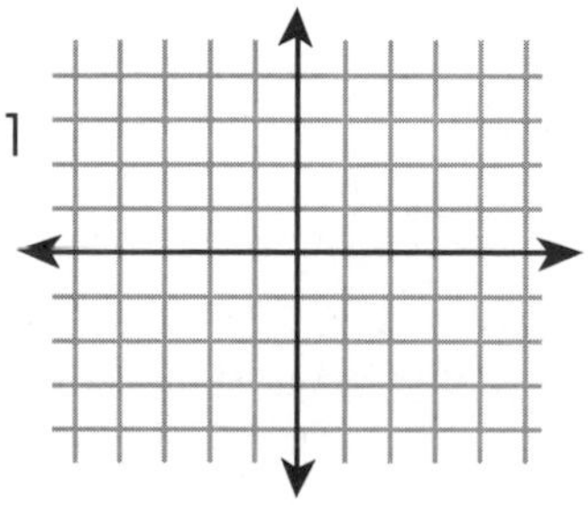

Name ______________________________ Date ______________________________

Graphing Hyperbolas with Center (h, k)

There are two types of hyperbola with center (h, k). In the first type, the vertex and foci are on the horizontal line $y = k$. In the second type, the vertex and foci are on the vertical line $x = h$.

Type one: horizontal line $y = k$.

General equation: $\frac{(x-h)^2}{} - \frac{(y-k)^2}{} = 1$

Type two: vertical line $x = h$.

General equation: $\frac{(y-k)^2}{} - \frac{(x-h)^2}{} = 1$

Graph each hyperbola, labeling the vertices and the center.

Example: $\frac{(x+1)}{36} - \frac{(y-2)}{9} = 1$

center = $(^-1, 2)$, $a = 6$, $b = 3$

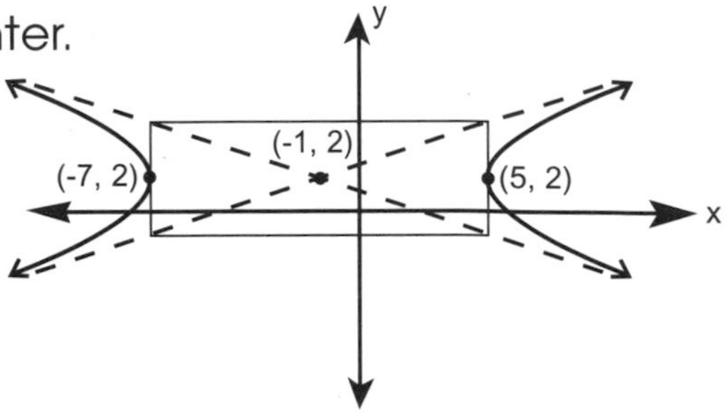

Note: The variable x is positive since the x-axis is a horizontal line. The vertex and foci are on the horizontal line $y = k$.

1. $\frac{(x-3)^2}{4} - \frac{(y+5)^2}{121} = 1$

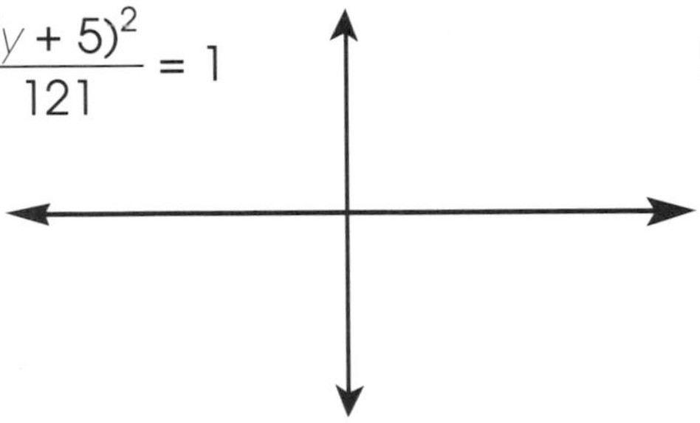

2. $(y+6)^2 - \frac{(x+8)^2}{16} = 1$

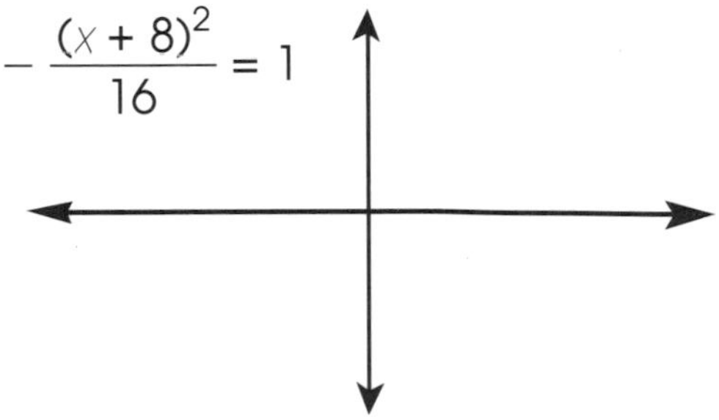

3. $\frac{x^2}{100} - \frac{y^2}{36} = 1$

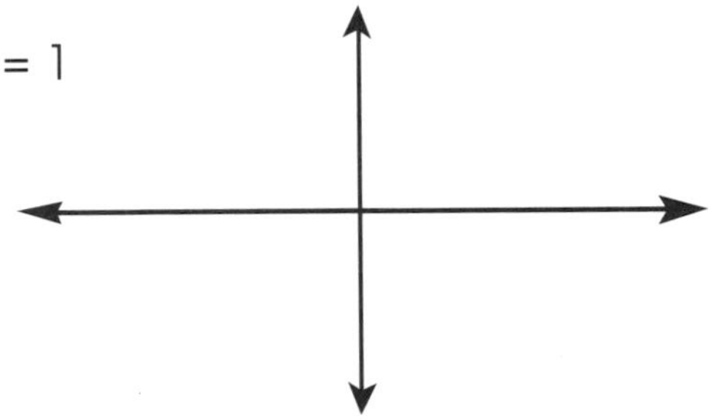

4. $\frac{(y+3)^2}{225} - \frac{(x+2)^2}{1} = 1$

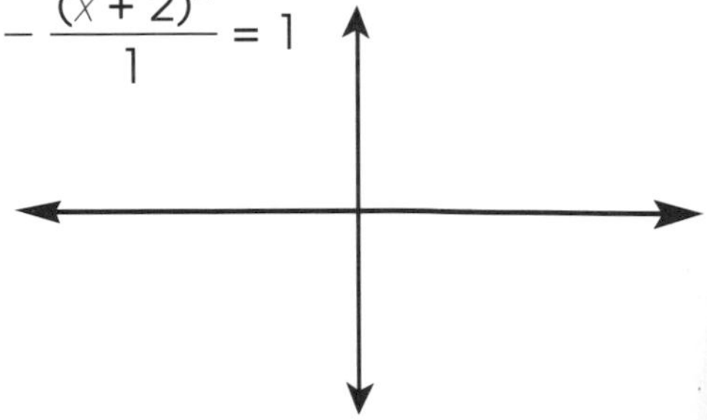

5. $\frac{(y-16)^2}{36} - \frac{(x+4)^2}{25} = 1$

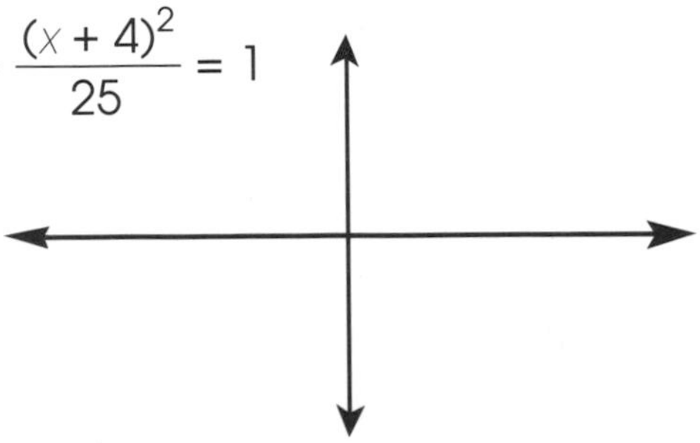

6. $\frac{(x-5)^2}{16} - \frac{(y-11)^2}{121} = 1$

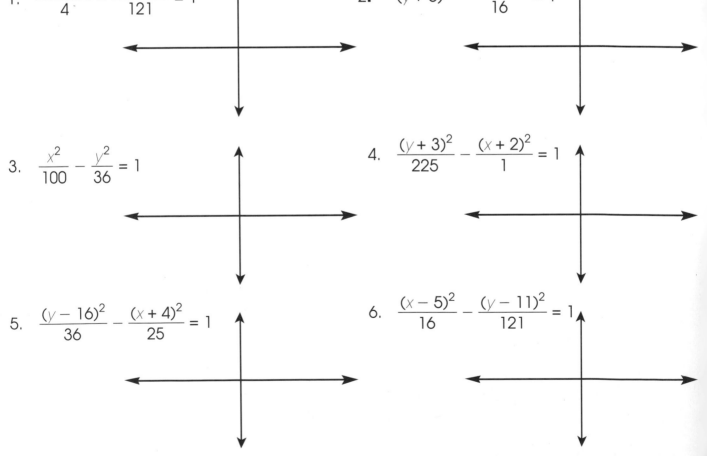

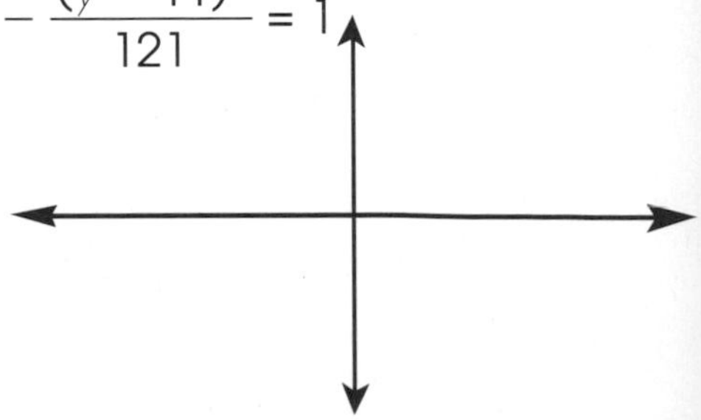

Name ______________________ Date ______________________

Identifying Different Types of Conic Sections

Complete the square, then identify the type of conic section and its center.

Example: $y = 16x^2 - 9y^2 - 32x + 72y - 272 = 0$

1. Isolate the x and y terms.

   $16x^2 - 32x - 9y^2 - 72y = 272$

2. Factor by the coefficients of the squared terms.

   $16(x^2 - 2x) - 9(y^2 - 8y) = 272 + 16(\quad) + {}^-9(\quad)$

3. Divide the coefficient of the x and y term by two, then square them, and add them to both sides of the equation.

   $16(x^2 - 2x + 1) - 9(y^2 - 8y + 16) = 272 + 16(1) + {}^-9(16)$

4. Factor the left side of the equation.

   $16(x - 1)^2 - 9(y - 4)^2 = 272 + 16(1) + {}^-9(16)$

5. Simplify.

   $16(x - 1)^2 - 9(y - 4)^2 = 272 + 16 + {}^-144$

   $16(x - 1)^2 - 9(y - 4)^2 = 144$

6. Divide by the product of the leading coefficients.

   $$\frac{16(x-1)^2}{144} - \frac{9(y-4)^2}{144} = \frac{144}{144}$$

   This is the equation of a hyperbola with center at (1, 4).

   $$\frac{(x-1)^2}{9} - \frac{(y-4)^2}{16} = 1$$

Write your answers in complete sentences.

1. $x^2 + y^2 - 4x + 6y + 4 = 0$

2. $9x^2 + 4y^2 + 54x + 8y + 49 = 0$

3. $25x^2 + y^2 - 300x + 8y + 891 = 0$

4. $16x^2 - y^2 + 96x + 8y + 112 = 0$

5. $x^2 + y^2 + 8x + 20y + 112 = 0$

Name ______________________ Date ______________________

Graphing Conic Sections

Graph each conic section, name it, then label its vertices and center.

1. $x^2 + (y - 2)^2 = 25$

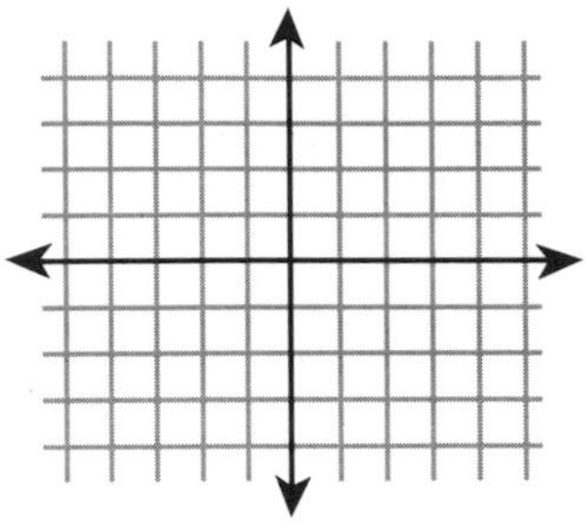

2. $\frac{x^2}{4} + \frac{(y-3)^2}{16} = 1$

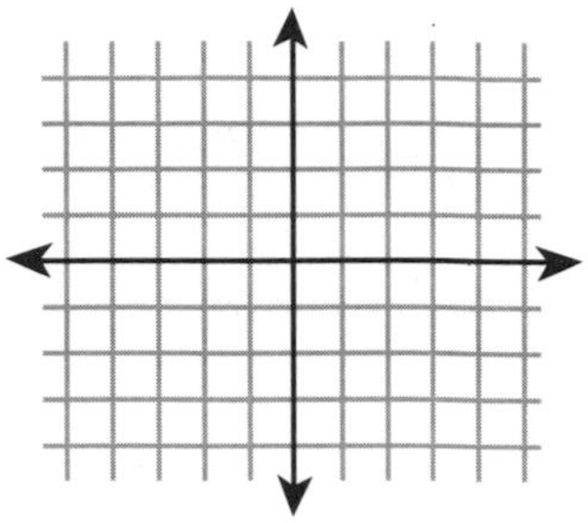

3. $\frac{(x-1)^2}{16} - \frac{(y+5)^2}{25} = 1$

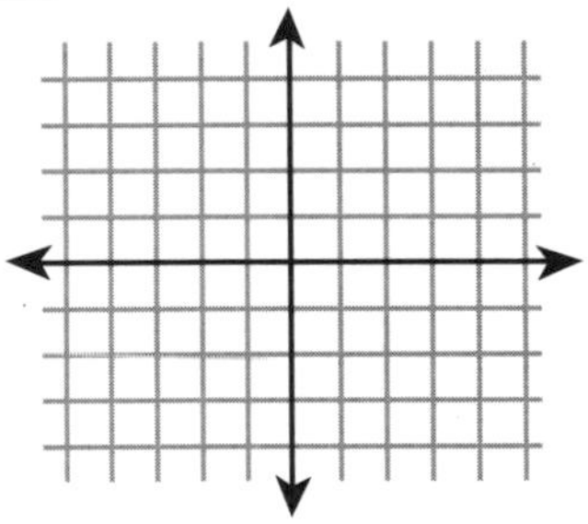

4. $y = (x + 2)^2 - 3$

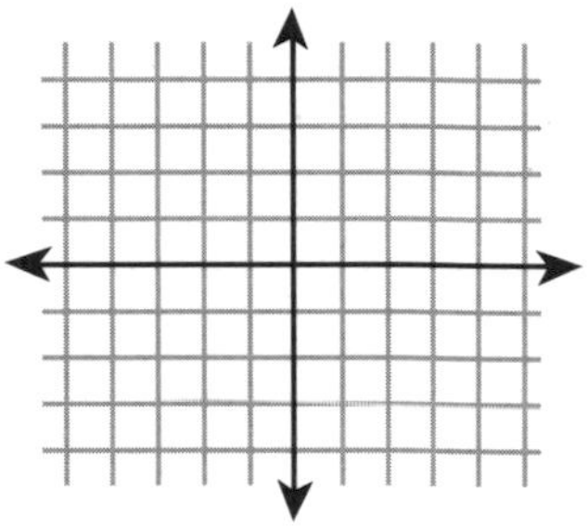

5. $x^2 + y^2 + 6x - 2y - 15 = 0$

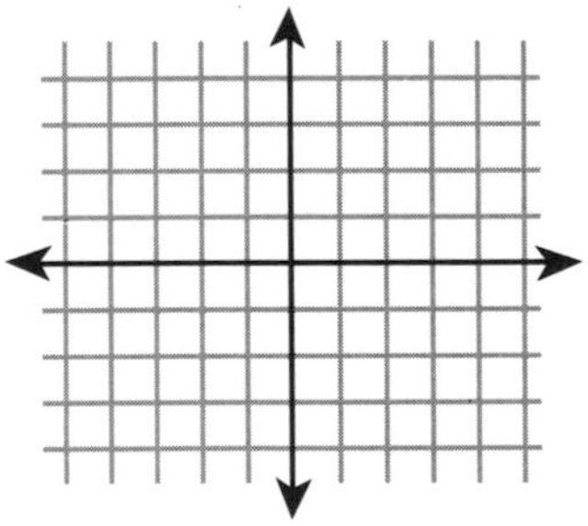

6. $x^2 + 4y^2 + 2x - 24y + 33 = 0$

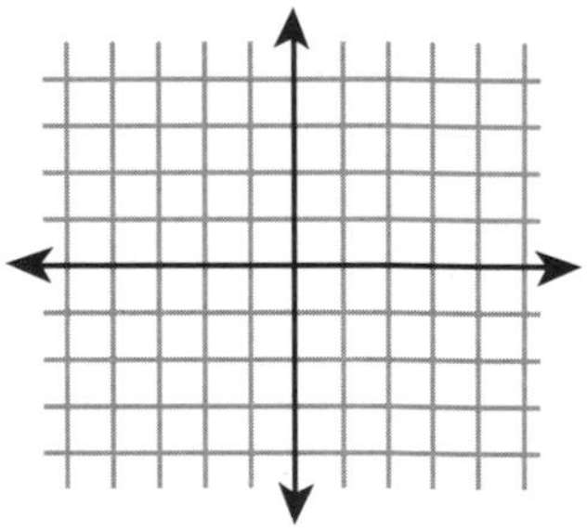

7. $y^2 - 4x^2 - 2y - 16x - 19 = 0$

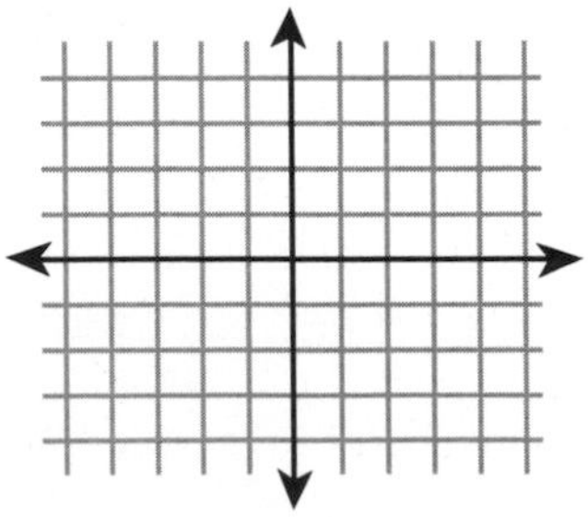

8. $y = x^2 + 8x + 20$

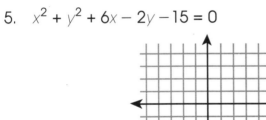

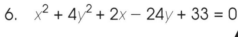

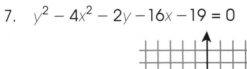

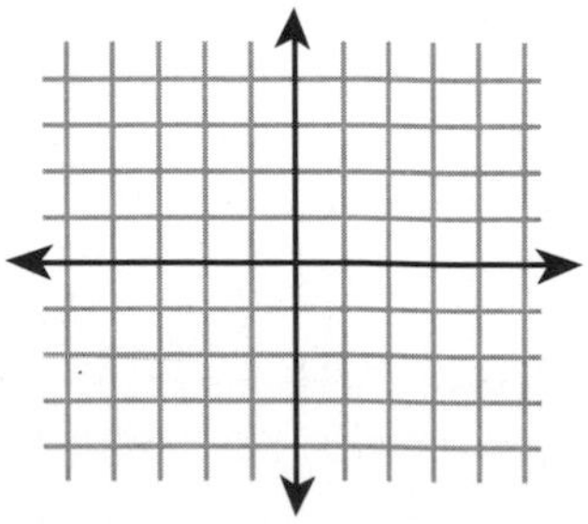

0-7424-1789-1 *Algebr*

Name ______________________________ Date ______________________________

Manipulating Special Right Triangles

30° 60° 90° Right Triangle   45° 45° 90° Right Triangle

Example: Find the missing sides of each triangle. Leave in radical form.
Note: Since these are right triangles, you can check your answer using the Pythagorean theorem.

1.

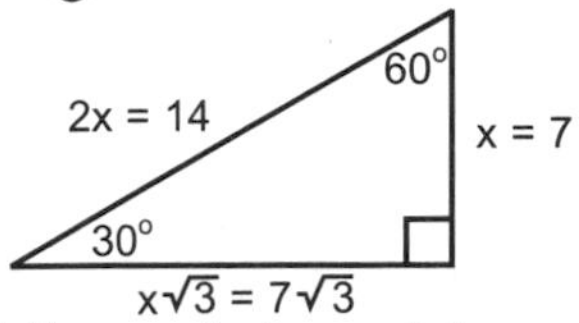

2.

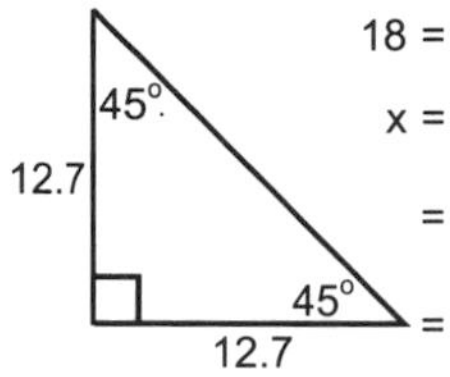

$18 = x\sqrt{2}$

$x = \frac{18}{\sqrt{2}}$

$= \frac{18\sqrt{2}}{2}$

$= 12.7$

Find the missing sides of each triangle. Check your answers using the Pythagorean theorem.

1.

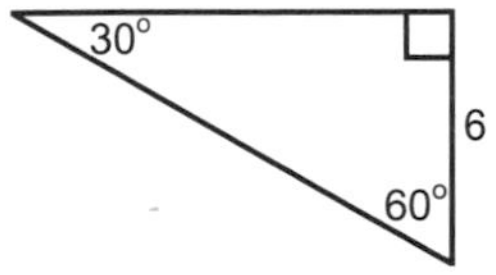

2.

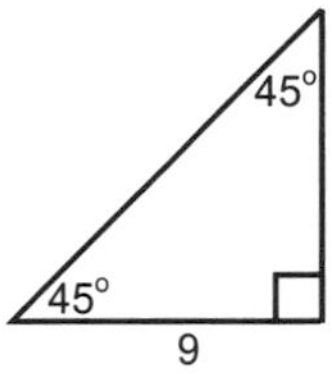

3.

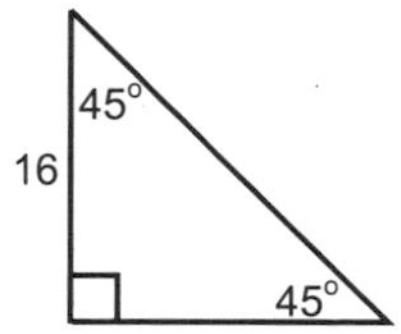

4.

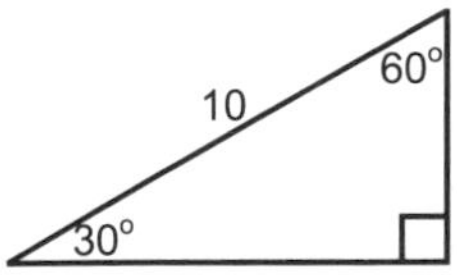

5.

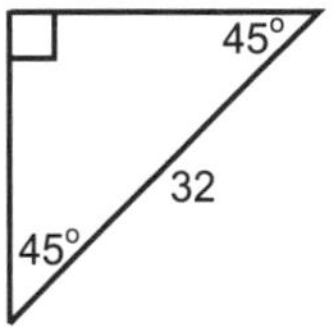

6.

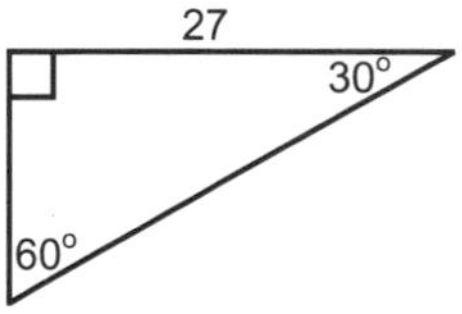

7.

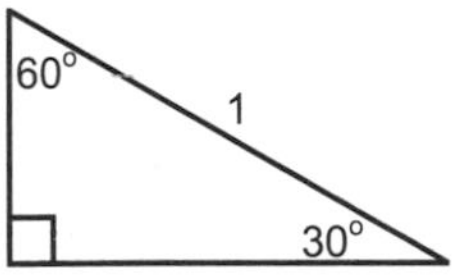

8.

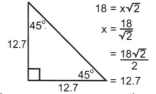

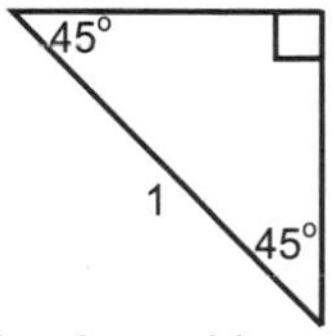

Cross out the correct answers below. Use the remaining letters to complete the statement.

9 O	9/2 I	$16\sqrt{2}$ N	1/4 S	24 H	$9\sqrt{2}$ F	25 A	$\sqrt{2}$ L	$16\sqrt{2}$ O	$\sqrt{3}$ F	3 T	12 U
10 H	5 R	81 E	1/2 T	$6\sqrt{3}$ H	$9\sqrt{3}$ O	5/2 H	1/8 Y	7 P	$16\sqrt{2}$ F	$7\sqrt{2}$ O	$\sqrt{2}/2$ T
$5\sqrt{3}$ H	$\sqrt{2}/2$ E	$11\sqrt{2}$ T	11/2 E	15 N	25/2 U	16 L	$\sqrt{3}/2$ E	3/2 S	$16\sqrt{3}$ E	$18\sqrt{3}$ G	15/2 .

In a 30–60 degrees right triangle, the side opposite the 30-degree angle

_ _   _ _ _ _ _   _ _ _   _ _ _ _ _ _ _ _ _ _ _

Name ______________________________ Date ______________________________

Trigonometric Ratios

Use this helpful mnemonic to remember the following ratios:
Oscar **H**as **A** **H**eap **O**f **A**pples.

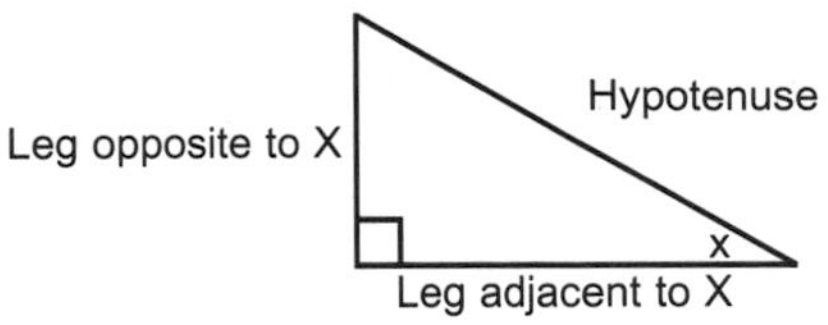

$$\text{Sine } x = \frac{\textbf{O}\text{pposite leg}}{\textbf{H}\text{ypotenuse}}$$

$$\text{Cosine } x = \frac{\textbf{A}\text{djacent leg}}{\textbf{H}\text{ypotenuse}}$$

$$\text{Tangent } x = \frac{\textbf{O}\text{pposite leg}}{\textbf{A}\text{djacent leg}}$$

Note: The trigonometric ratios hold only for right triangles.

Given a right triangle, find each trigonometric ratio. Leave your answer as a fraction. The first one has been started for you.

1.
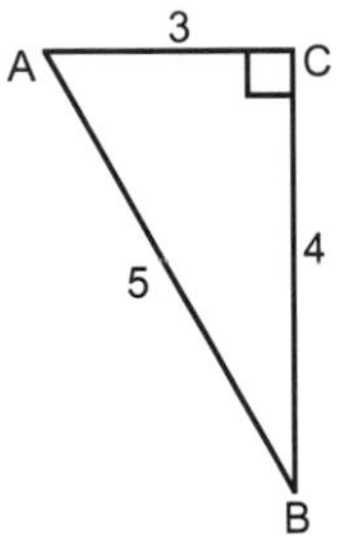

$\sin A = \frac{4}{5}$ $\sin B =$

$\cos A = \frac{3}{5}$ $\cos B =$

$\tan A = \frac{4}{3}$ $\tan B =$

2.
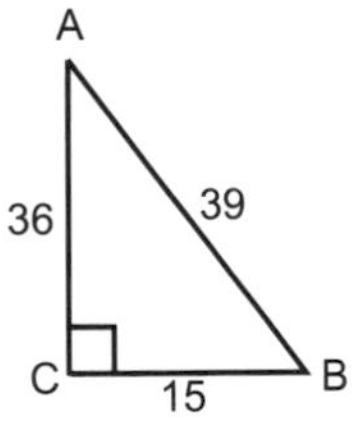

$\sin A =$ $\sin B =$

$\cos A =$ $\cos B =$

$\tan A =$ $\tan B =$

3.
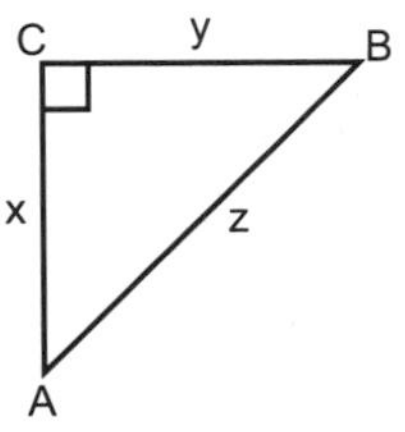

$\sin A =$ $\sin B =$

$\cos A =$ $\cos B =$

$\tan A =$ $\tan B =$

4.
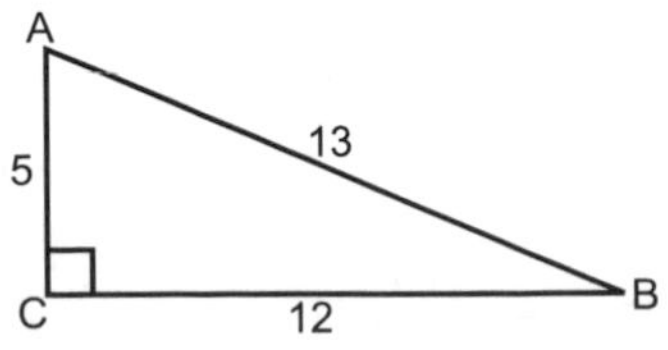

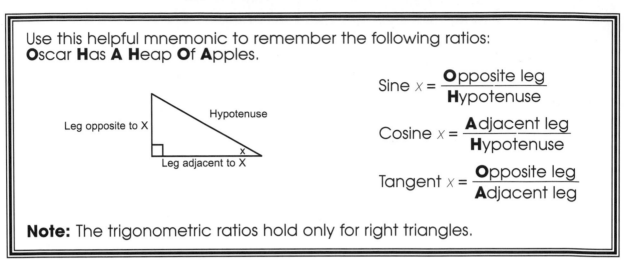

$\sin A =$ $\sin B =$

$\cos A =$ $\cos B =$

$\tan A =$ $\tan B =$

Name ______________________ Date ______________________

Evaluating Trigonometric Functions

Evaluate each trigonometric function. Round to the nearest hundredth. You will need a scientific calculator.

Example: sin 60°

The calculator key sequence is [sin] [60] [=] 0.8660254° = 0.87°

Note: If you do not get the above answer, check the mode on your calculator. The mode should be in degrees. If you still do not get the correct answer, try [60] [sin] [=].

1. tan 45°
2. cos 10°
3. cos 220°
4. sin 80°
5. sin 23°
6. tan 135°

Find the angle with the given trigonometric ratio. Round your answer to the nearest degree.

Example: $\cos x = \left(\frac{6}{11}\right)$

calculator key sequence: [2nd] [cos] [6] [÷] [11] [=] 56.94426885° = 57°

Note: The mode on your calculator should still be in degrees. If you are not getting the correct answer, try [6] [÷] [11] [2nd] [cos] [=].

1. $\cos x = \left(\frac{7}{19}\right)$
2. $\tan x = \left(\frac{101}{90}\right)$
3. $\sin x = \left(\frac{20}{21}\right)$
4. $\cos x = \left(\frac{45}{76}\right)$
5. $\tan x = \left(\frac{15}{4}\right)$
6. $\sin x = \left(\frac{8}{99}\right)$

0-7424-1789-1 *Algebra II*

Name ______________________ Date ______________________

Applying Trigonometric Ratios

Using the trigonometric ratios, solve for the missing sides *x* and *y* of each right triangle. Round your answers to the nearest tenth.

Example:

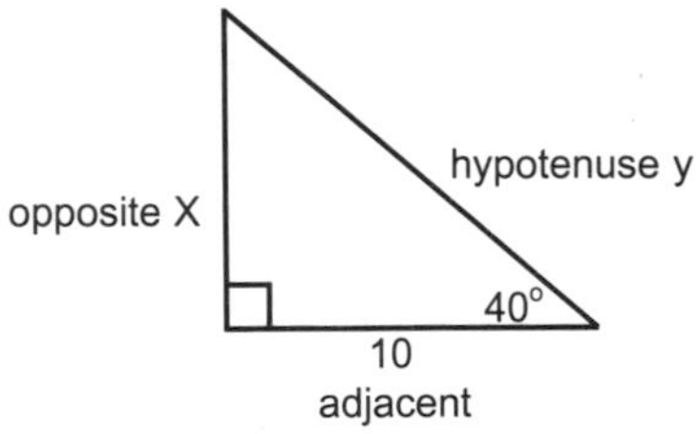

Ratios: $\sin 40 = \left(\frac{x}{y}\right)$ ← **Note:** having two variables in one ratio means it can not be solved.

$\cos 40 = \left(\frac{10}{y}\right)$

$\tan 40 = \left(\frac{x}{10}\right)$

Use the tan and the cos to solve for *x* and *y*.

$\cos 40^\circ = \frac{10}{y}$

$y \cos 40^\circ = 10$

$y = \frac{10}{\cos 40^\circ} = 13.05407$

$y = 13.1$

$\tan 40^\circ = \frac{x}{10}$

$x = 10 \tan 40^\circ = 8.39099$

$x = 8.4$

Note: Since these are right triangles, you can check your answer using the Pythagorean theorem. The answers will not be exact due to rounding.

1. 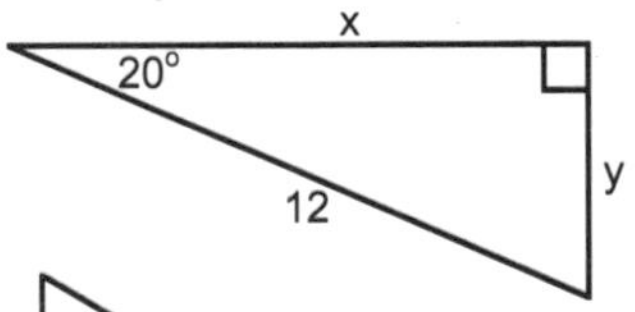

2. 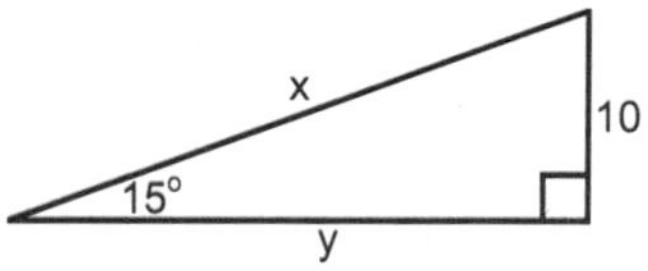

3. 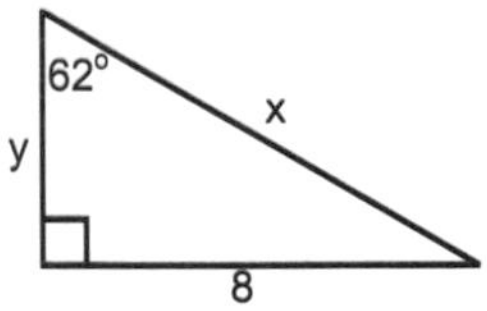

4. 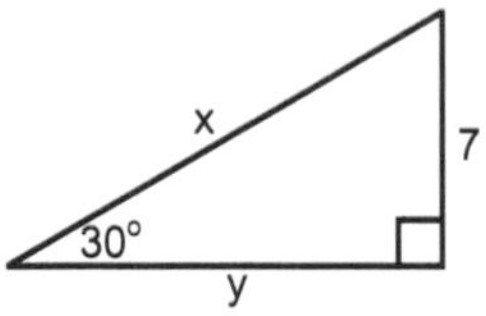

5. 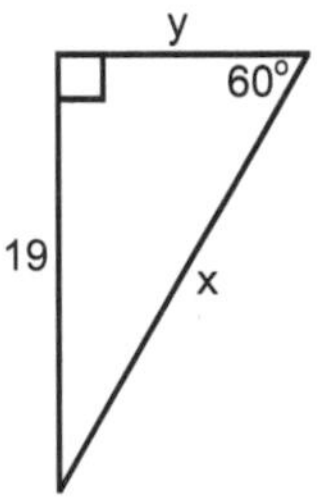

6. 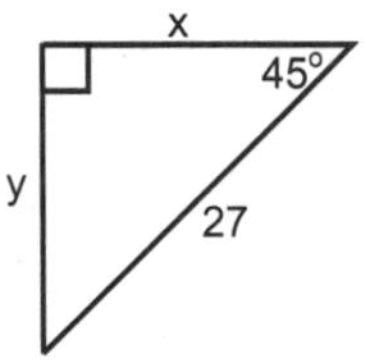

7. 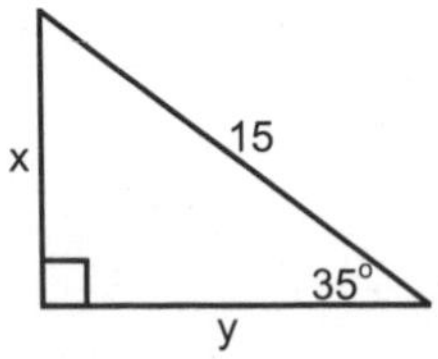

8. 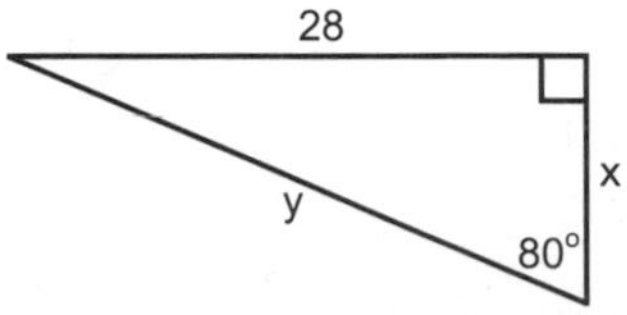

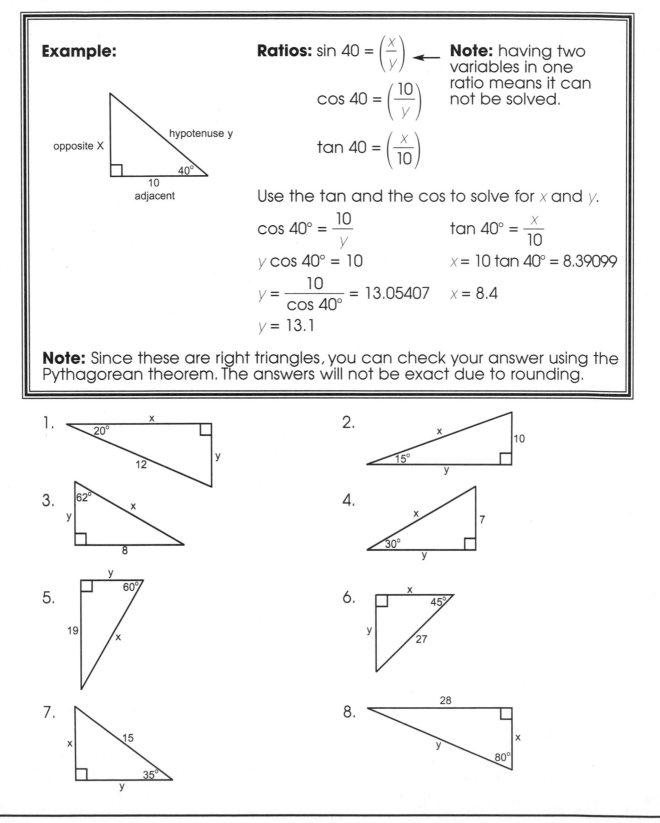

Name ______________________ Date ______________________

Using Trigonometric Ratios to Find Angles

Using the trigonometric ratios, solve for the missing angles x and y of each right triangle. Round your answers to the nearest tenth.

Example:

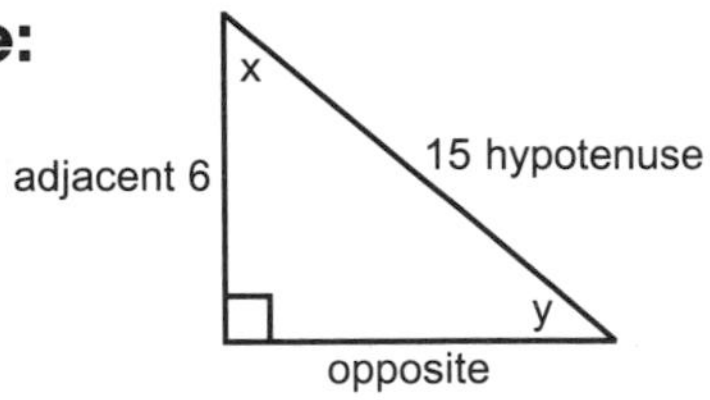

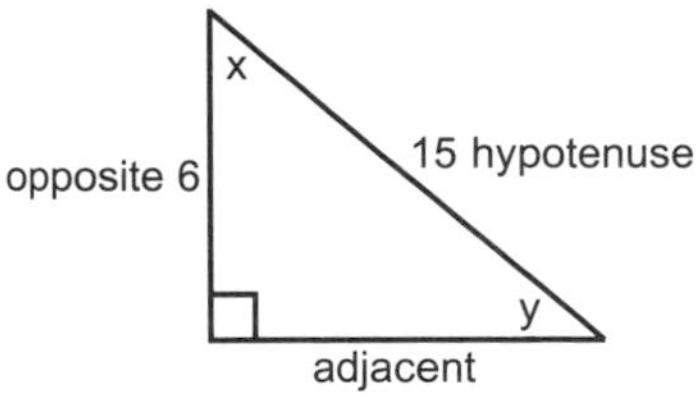

Solving for angle x:

$\cos x = \left(\frac{6}{15}\right)$

$x = \cos^{-1}\left(\frac{6}{15}\right)$

$x = 66.421 = 66°$

Solving for angle y:

$\sin y = \left(\frac{6}{15}\right)$

$y = \sin^{-1}\left(\frac{6}{15}\right)$

$y = 23.578 = 24°$

Check: $66° + 24° = 90°$

Check: The three angles of a triangle always add up to 180 degrees. Since these are right triangles, one angle must equal 90 degrees. Therefore the other two must add up to 90 degrees. Remember, rounding may cause the answers to be slightly off.

1.
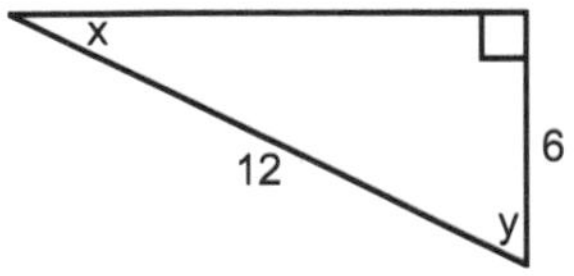

2.
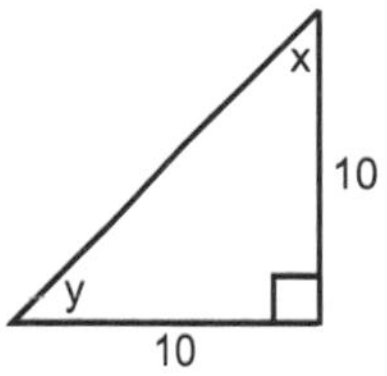

3.
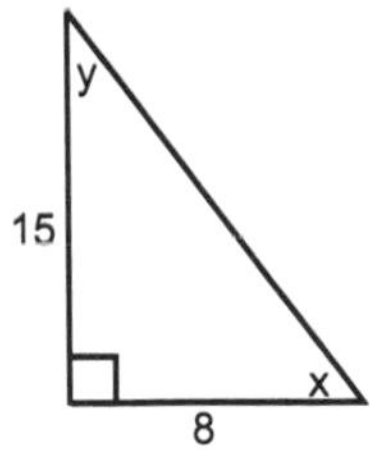

4.
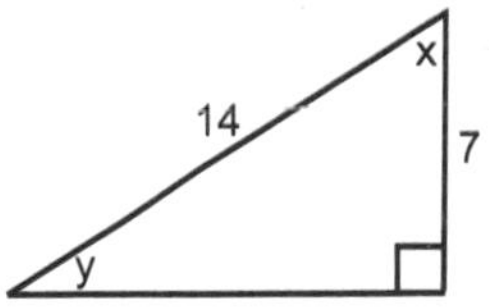

5.
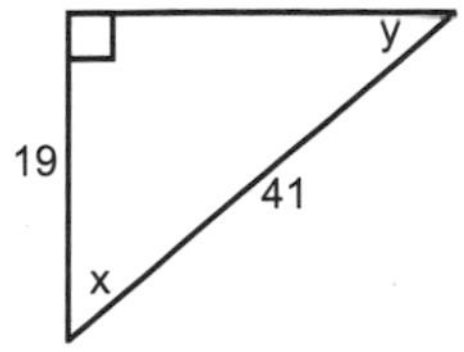

6.
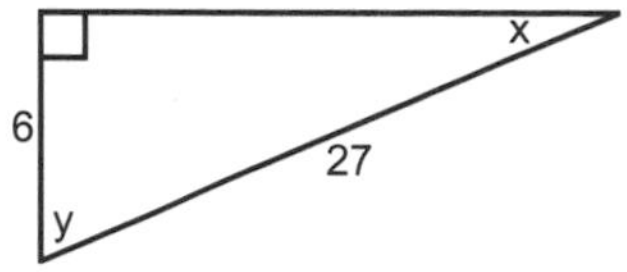

7.
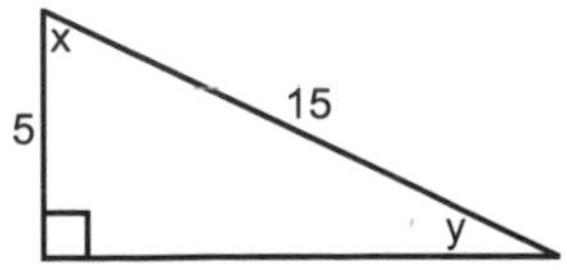

8.
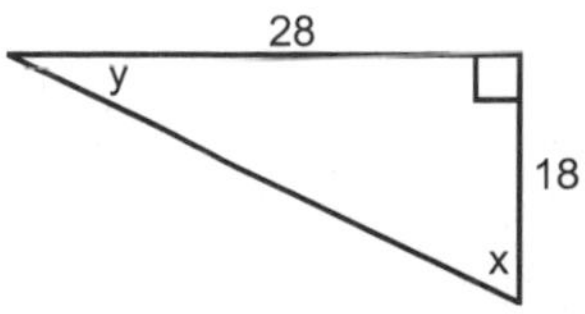

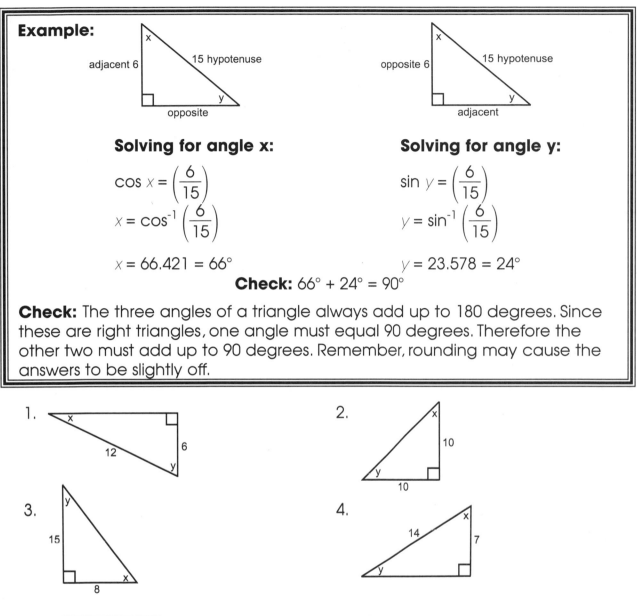

0-7424-1789-1 *Algebra II*

Name ______________________ Date ______________________

Problem Solving with Trigonometric Ratios

Draw a picture and solve the story problem using trigonometric ratios.

Example: An eagle spotted a mouse 20 feet below at an angle of 42 degrees with the horizon. If the eagle flies along its line of sight, how far will it have to fly to reach its prey?

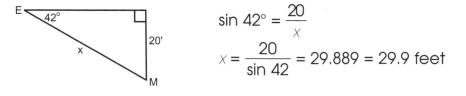

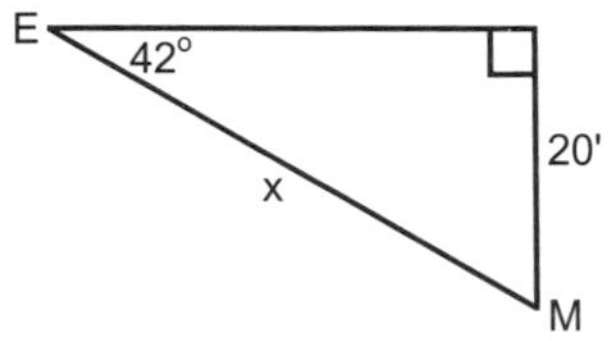

$$\sin 42° = \frac{20}{x}$$

$$x = \frac{20}{\sin 42} = 29.889 = 29.9 \text{ feet}$$

1. A 20-foot ladder is leaning against a wall. The base of the ladder is 3 feet from the wall. What angle does the ladder make with the ground?

2. How tall is a bridge if a 6-foot-tall person standing 100 feet away can see the top of the bridge at an angle of 30 degrees to the horizon?

3. An air force pilot must descend 1500 feet over a distance of 9000 feet to land smoothly on an aircraft carrier. What is the plane's angle of descent?

4. In a movie theater 150 feet long, the floor is sloped so there is a difference of 30 feet between the front and back of the theater. What is the angle of depression?

5. A bow hunter is perched in a tree 15 feet off the ground. If he sees his prey on the ground at an angle of 30 degrees, how far will the arrow have to travel to hit his target?

0-7424-1789-1 *Algebra*

Name ____________________ Date ____________________

Creating the Unit Circle

One of the most useful tools in trigonometry is the unit circle. The unit circle is a circle with a radius of one unit placed on an x-y plane. The angles are measured from the positive x-axis counterclockwise. The x-axis corresponds to the cosine function and the y-axis corresponds to the sine function. To create the unit circle, one uses the special right triangles: 30° 60° 90° and 45° 45° 90°. Study the following diagrams to learn how to create the unit circle instead of merely memorizing it!

a.

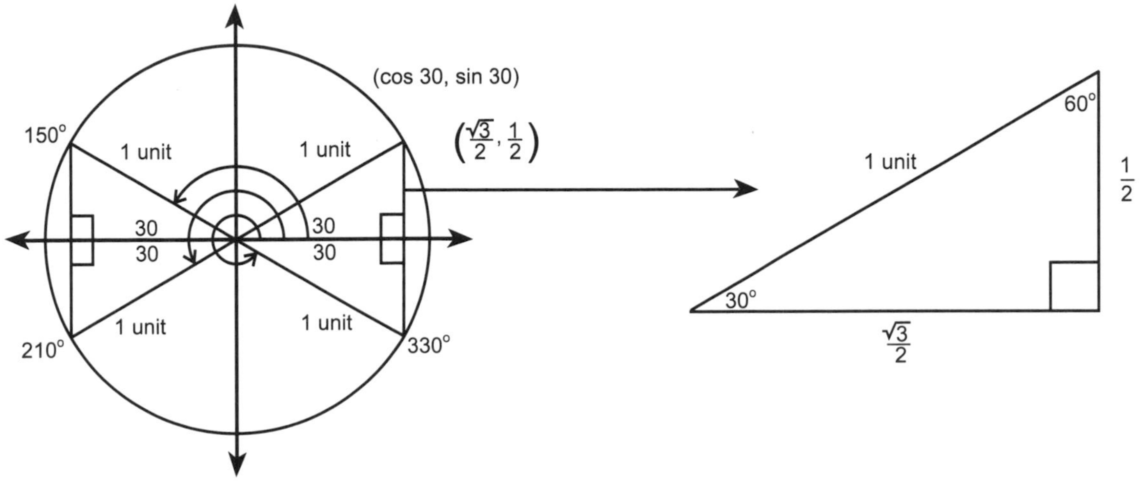

b.

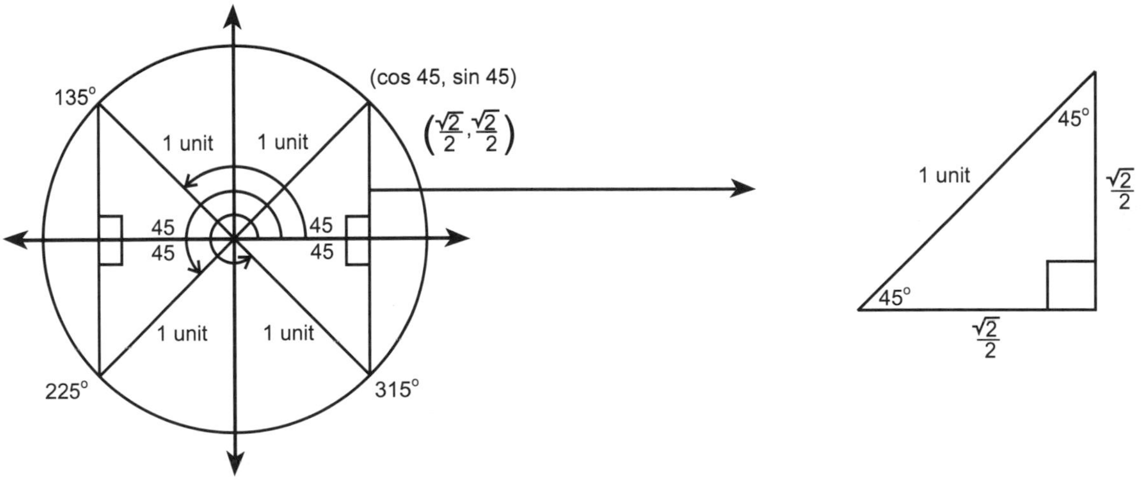

c.

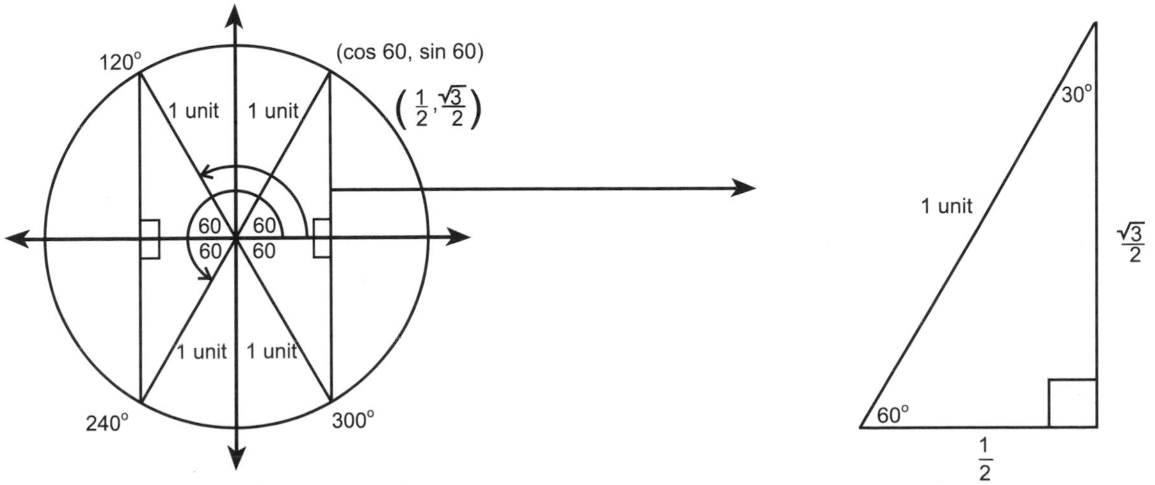

0-7424-1789-1 *Algebra II*

Name ______________________ Date ______________________

Creating the Unit Circle (cont.)

Note: Three congruent right triangles are created in each different quadrant. Therefore, the length of the sides will be the same in each triangle. The only difference will be the sign (positive or negative) of the numbers.

Complete the unit circle below, being watchful of the signs of the numbers in each quadrant.

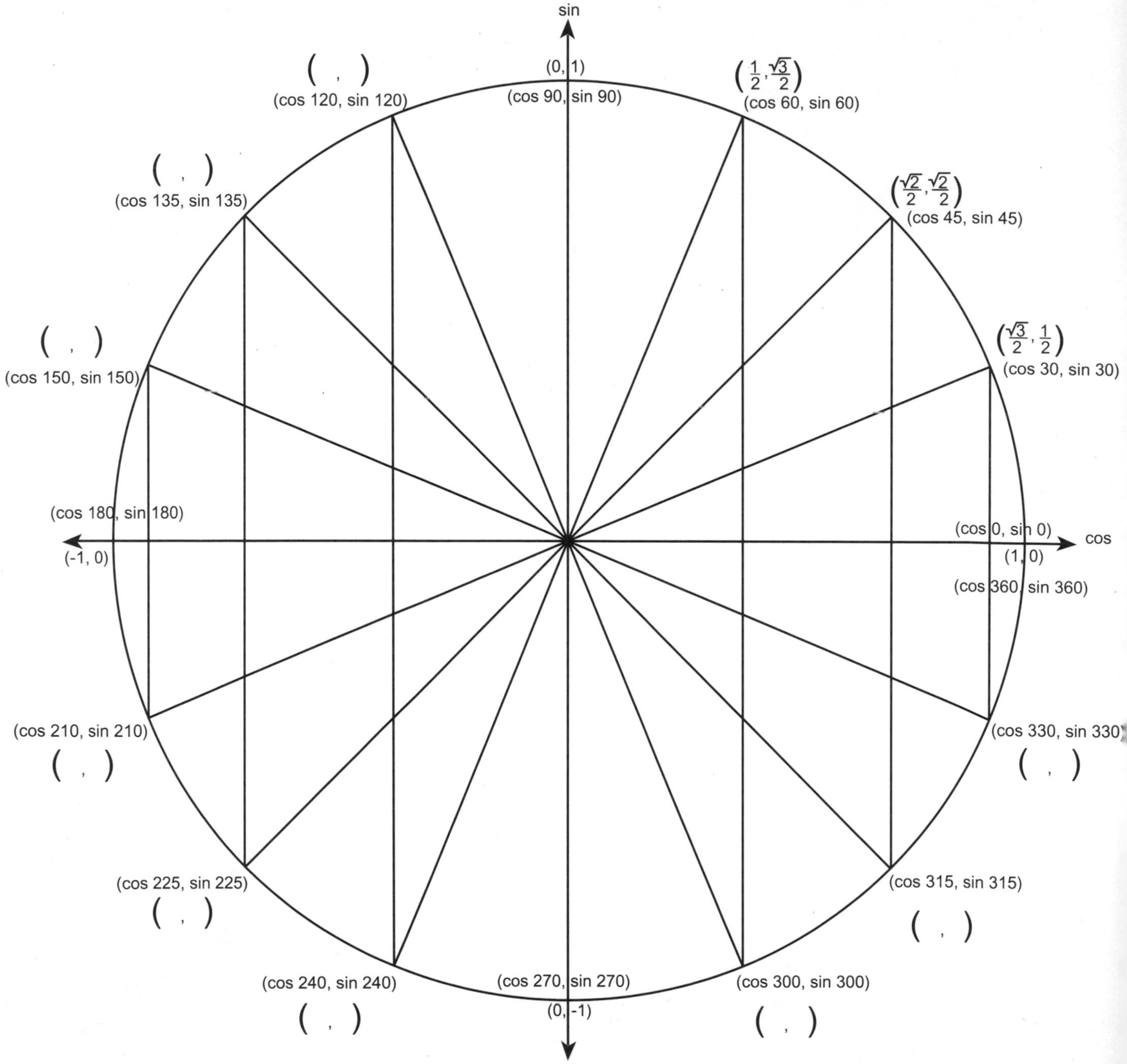

Name ______________________ Date ______________________

Unit Circle with Negative Angle Measures

Recall that the angles of the unit circle are measured from the positive x-axis counter-clockwise. The angles can be measured from the positive x-axis going in the clockwise direction, but in such a case the sign of the angle measured are negative.

Complete the unit circle using negative angle measures.

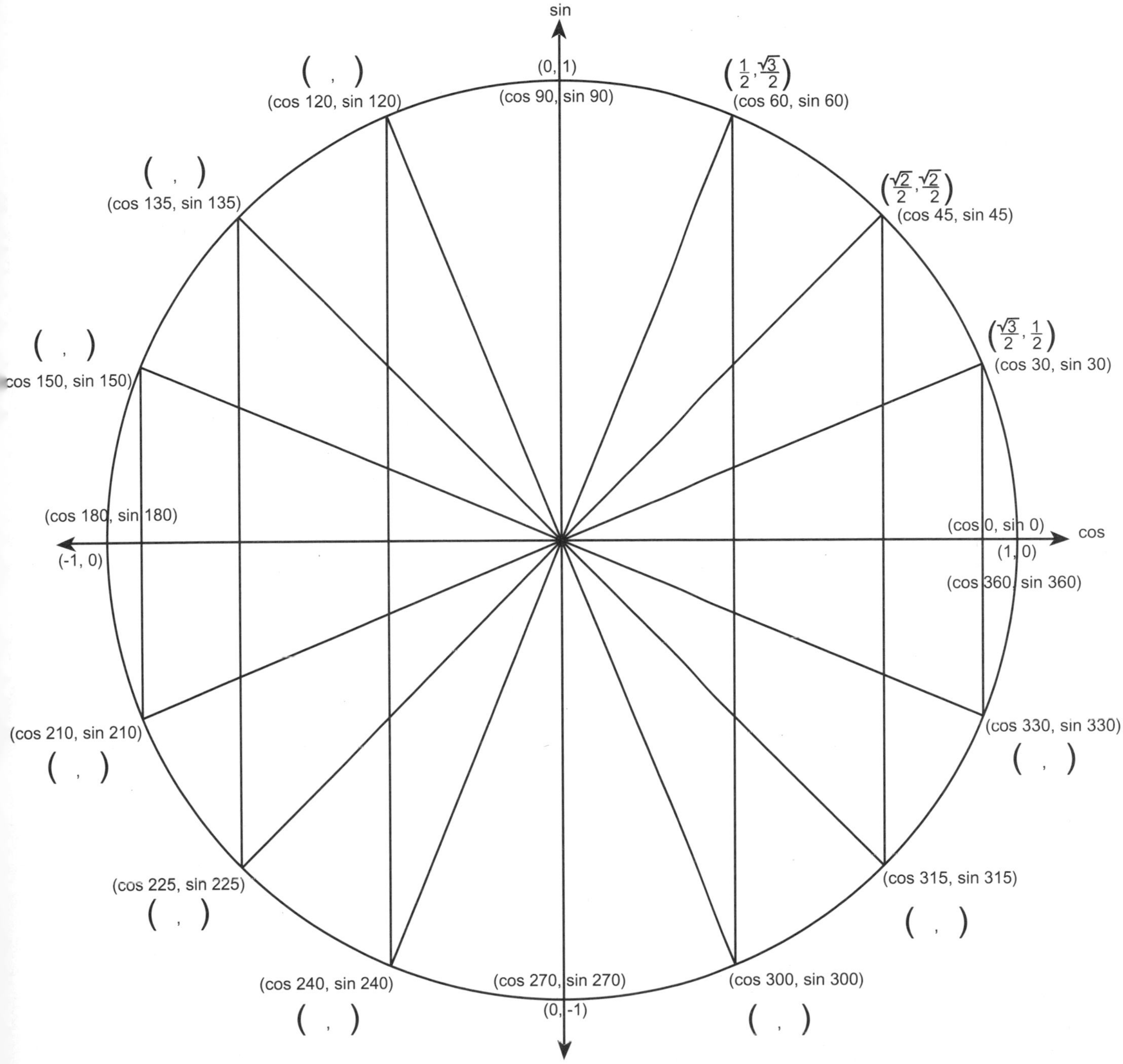

What did you notice about the positive and negative angles measured at each point?

____

Name ______________________ Date ______________________

Angles Greater Than 360 Degrees

Without a calculator, evaluate the following trigonometric functions.
Hint: Rewrite each statement using an angle $\leq 360^\circ$.

Example: $\sin 450^\circ$

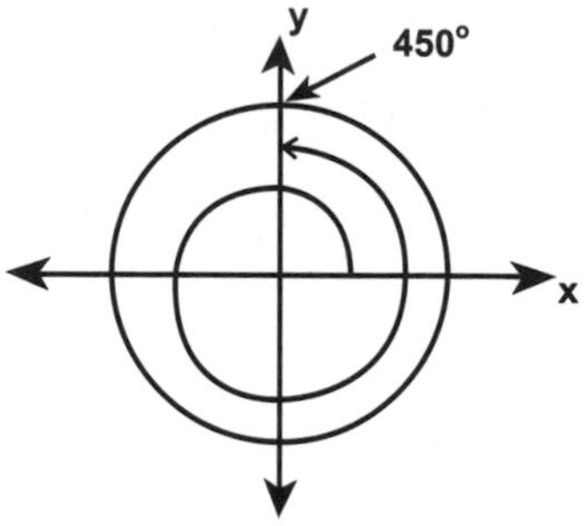

360 degrees represents one complete revolution about the unit circle.
So 450 degrees is one complete revolution plus 90 degrees more in the counter clockwise direction.

$450 - 360 = 90$
The problem reduces to $\sin 90 = 1$.

Note: Refer to the unit circle diagram while you complete this assignment.

1. $\sin 630^\circ$
2. $\sin {}^{-}750^\circ$
3. $\cos {}^{-}480^\circ$
4. $\sin {}^{-}420^\circ$
5. $\sin 510^\circ$
6. $\cos 1020^\circ$
7. $\cos {}^{-}540^\circ$
8. $\cos {}^{-}675^\circ$
9. $\sin {}^{-}540^\circ$
10. $\cos {}^{-}930^\circ$
11. $\sin 405^\circ$
12. $\sin {}^{-}600^\circ$
13. $\sin 3600^\circ$
14. $\cos {}^{-}1830^\circ$

Each sine problem has the same value as one of the cosine problems. List the pairs.

1 & ____; 2 & ____; 4 & ____; 5 & ____; 9 & ____; 11 & ____; 12 & ____

In each pair, what is the relationship of the reference angles? ______________

____

0-7424-1789-1 *Algebra*

Name ______________________ Date ______________________

Converting Angle Measurements

On the unit circle, the angles are given in degrees. Another way to measure an angle is with radians. π Radians = 180°. The two unit conversions are as follows:

radians to degrees	degrees to radians
$\frac{180°}{\pi}$	$\frac{\pi}{180°}$

Convert the angle from degrees to radians, leaving your answer as a fraction.

Example: 90° Simply multiply. $\frac{90°}{1} \times \frac{\pi}{180°} = \frac{90°\pi}{180°} = \frac{1}{2}\pi$

1. 310°
2. 150°
3. 30°
4. 420°
5. 120°
6. 350°

Convert from radians to degrees.

Example: $\frac{3}{2}\pi$ Simply multiply. $\frac{3}{2}\pi \times \frac{180°}{\pi} = \frac{540°}{2} = 270°$

1. $\frac{5}{4}\pi$
2. 4π
3. $\frac{7}{6}\pi$
4. $\frac{1}{6}\pi$
5. $\frac{7}{4}\pi$
6. $\frac{9}{2}\pi$

Name ______________________ Date ______________________

Unit Circle with Radian Angle Measures

Complete the unit circle using radian angle measures. Use as a reference when completed.

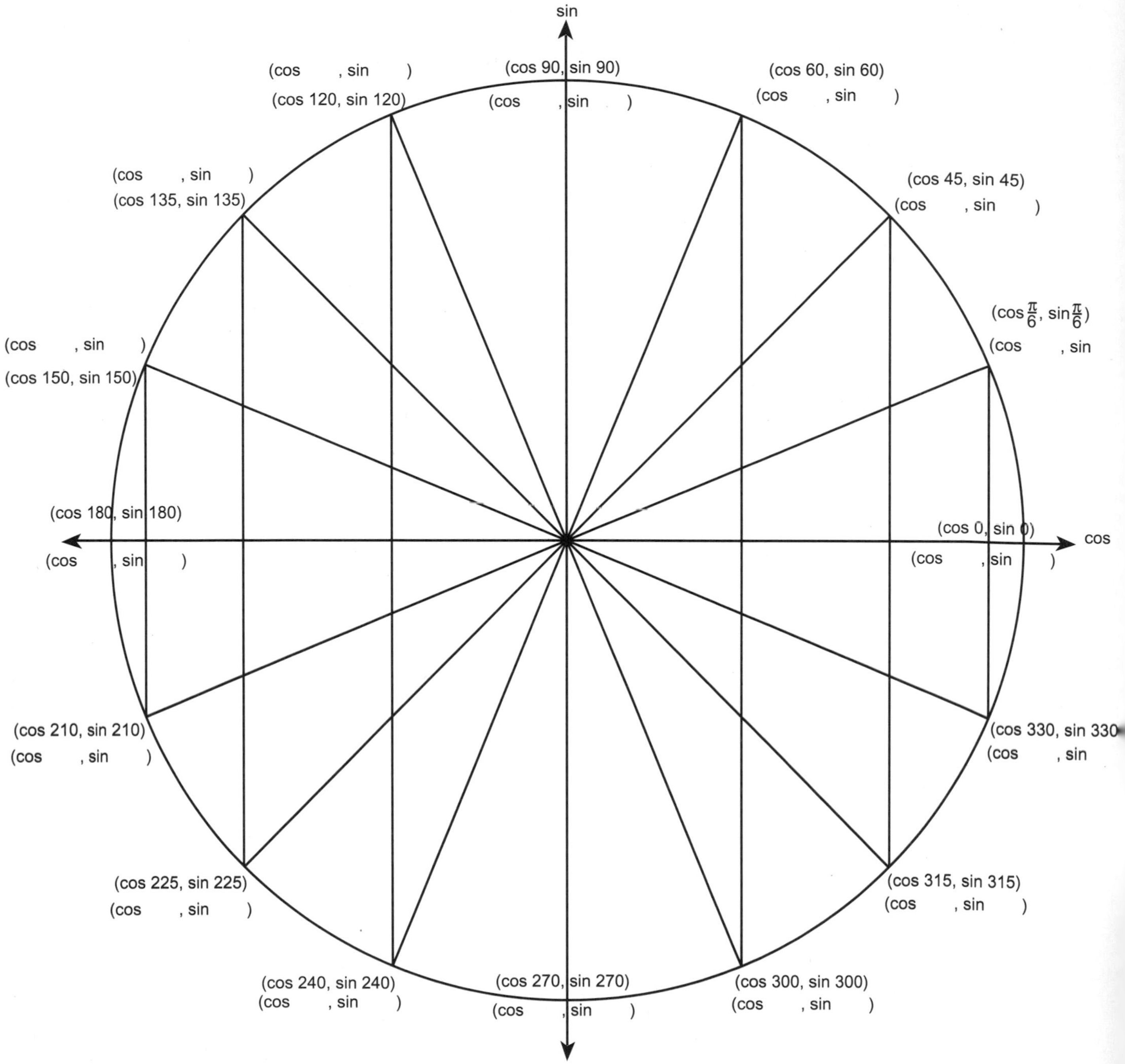

0-7424-1789-1 *Algebra*

Name ______________________ Date ______________________

Manipulating Properties of Sine and Cosine

General Properties		**Examples:**
$\sin x = \cos(90° - x)$	$\longrightarrow$	$\sin 30° = \cos(90° - 30°) = \cos 60°$
$\cos x = \sin(90° - x)$	$\longrightarrow$	$\cos 75° = \sin(90° - 75°) = \sin 15°$
$\sin x = \sin(180° - x)$	$\longrightarrow$	$\sin 45° = \sin(180° - 45°) = \sin 135°$
$\cos x = \cos(360° - x)$	$\longrightarrow$	$\cos 120° = \cos(360° - 120°) = \cos 240°$

Given the sin x, name two angles such that $\sin x = \cos y$.

1. $\sin 60°$

2. $\sin 15°$

3. $\sin 180°$

4. $\sin {}^-45°$

5. $\sin {}^-120°$

Given cos x, name two angles such that $\cos x = \sin y$.

1. $\cos 30°$

2. $\cos {}^-60°$

3. $\cos 90°$

4. $\cos {}^-225°$

5. $\cos 50°$

Name ______________________________ Date ______________________________

Graphing the Sine and Cosine Functions

Graph each function using a table of values over the specified domain. Add units to both axes.

Example: $y = \sin x$,
where $0° \leq x \leq 360°$

$x°$	y
0	0
30	0.5
45	0.7
60	0.9
90	1
135	0.7
180	0
270	$^{-}1$
360	0

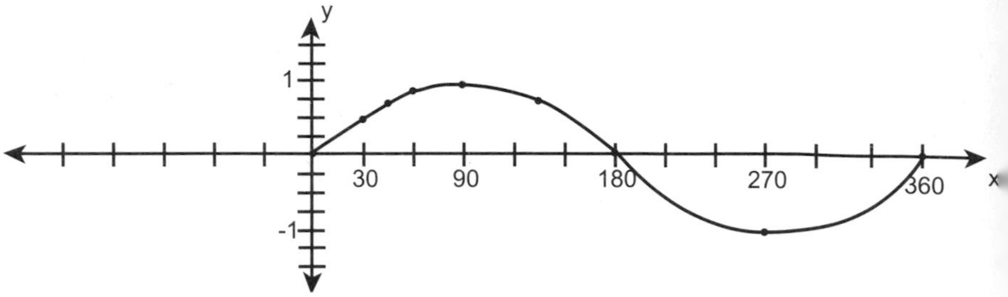

1. $y = \cos x$
where $0° \leq x \leq 360°$

$x°$	y
0	
30	
45	
60	
90	
135	
180	
270	
360	

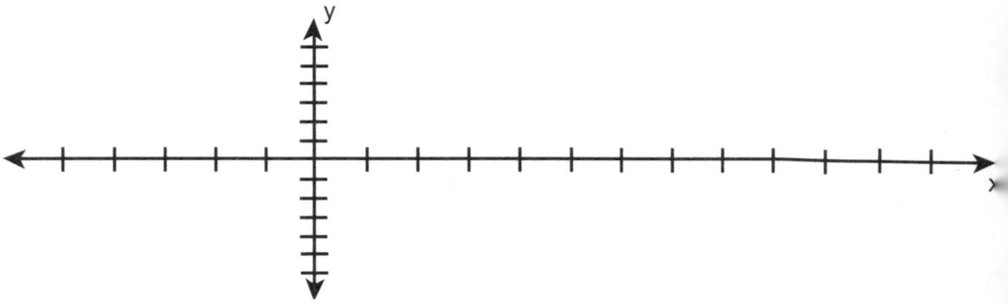

2. $y = \sin x$
where $90° \leq x \leq 450°$

$x°$	y

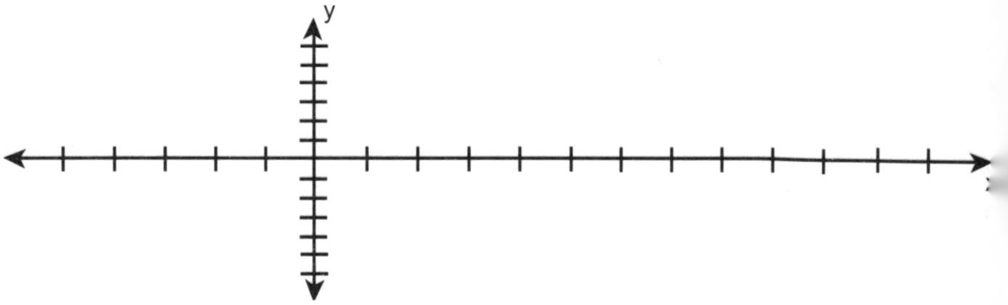

3. $y = \sin x$
where $^{-}90° \leq x \leq 270°$

$x°$	y

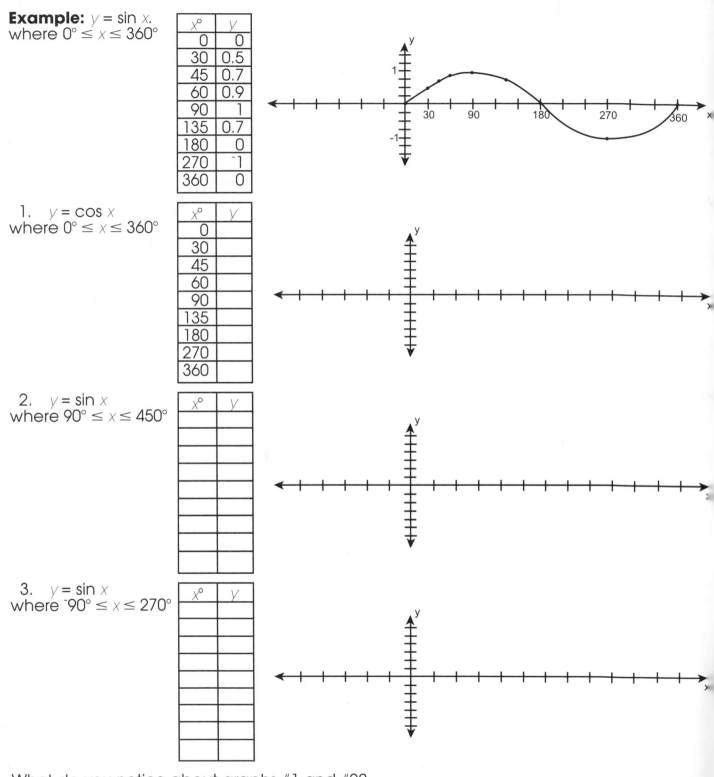

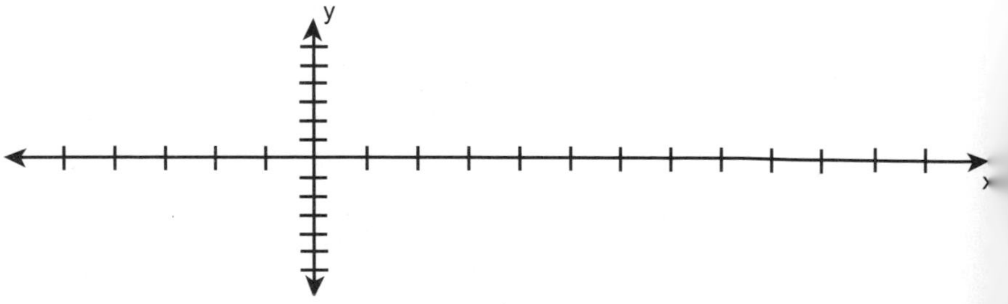

What do you notice about graphs #1 and #2?

____

0-7424-1789-1 *Algebr*

Name ______________________________ Date ______________________________

Graphing the Sine and Cosine Functions (cont.)

4. $y = \sin x$
where $^{-}360° \leq x \leq 360°$

$x°$	y

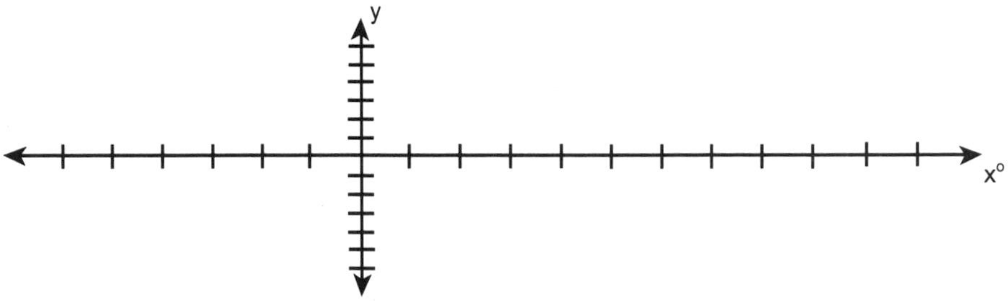

5. $y = \cos x$
where $^{-}360° \leq x \leq 360°$

$x°$	y

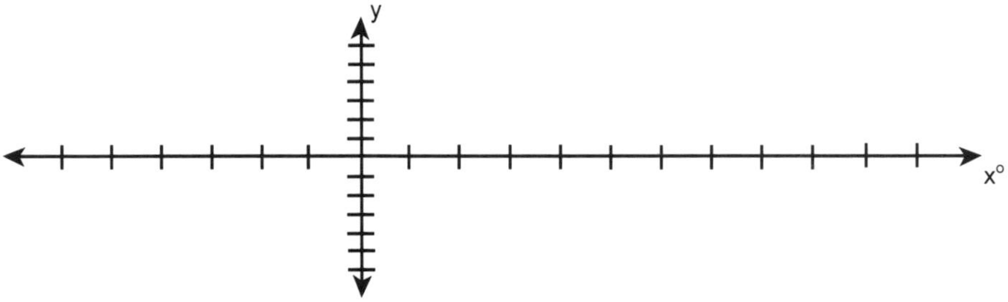

6. $y = \sin x$
where $0° \leq x \leq 720°$

$x°$	y

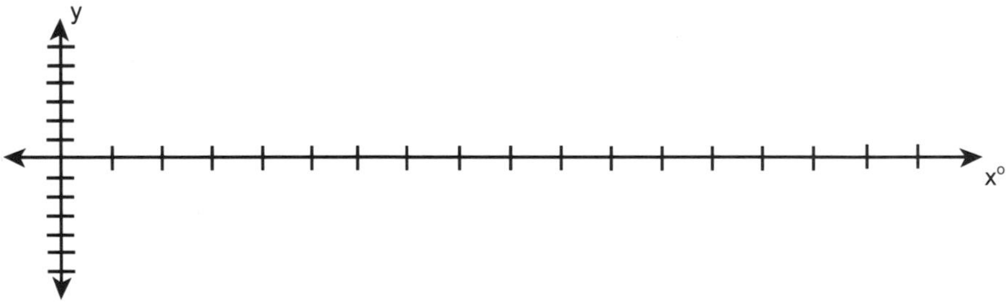

7. $y = \cos x$
where $0° \leq x \leq 720°$

$x°$	y

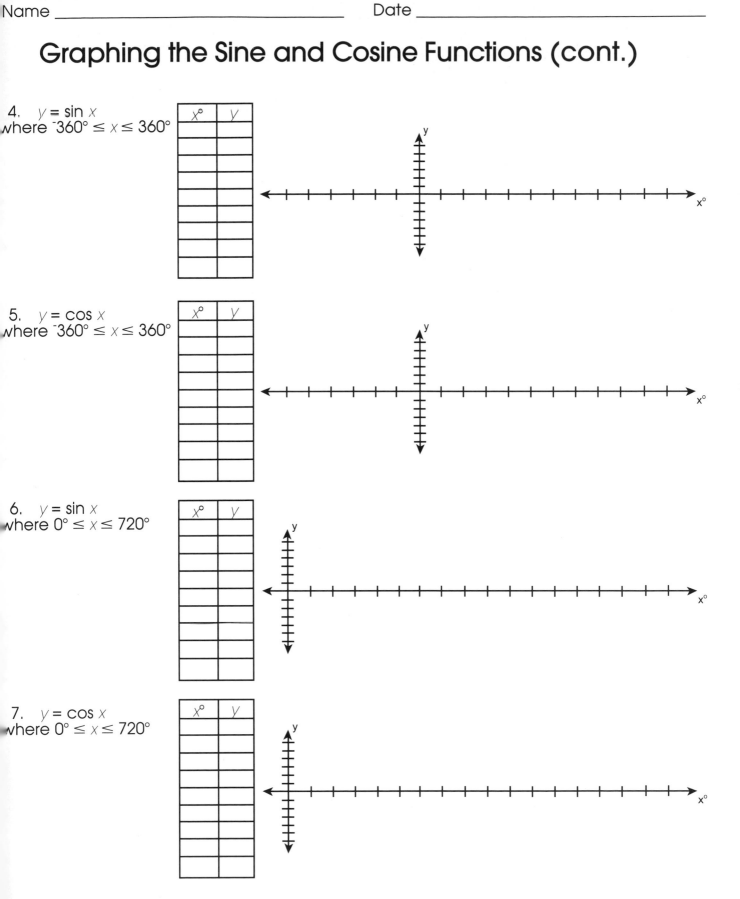

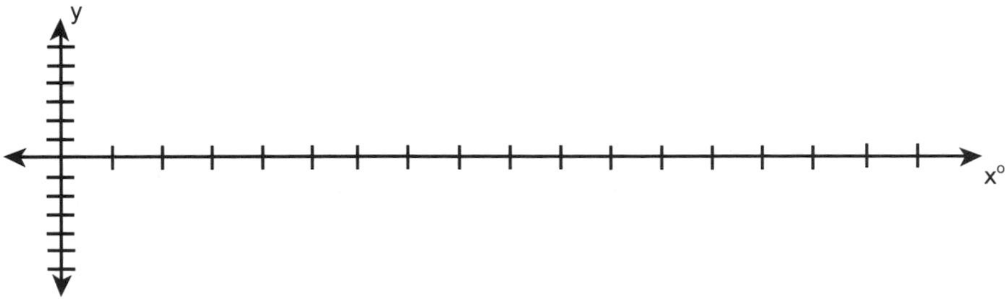

Name ______________________________ Date ______________________________

Graphing $y = a \sin x$ or $y = a \cos x$

Graph each function. Add units to both axes.

Example: $y = {}^{-}2 \cos x$

x°	y
0	$^{-}2$
90	0
180	2
270	0
360	$^{-}2$

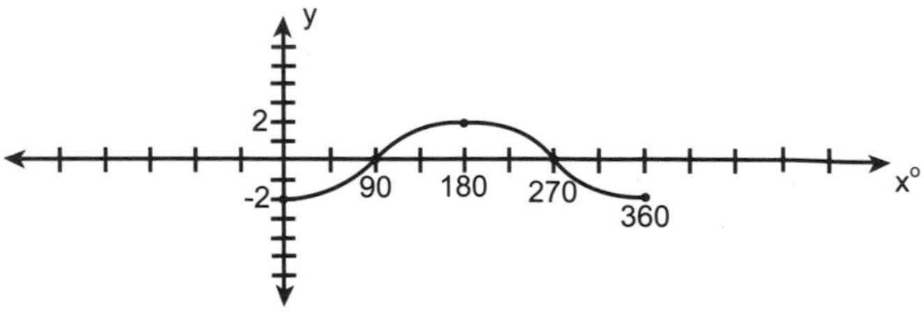

1. $y = 4 \cos x$

x°	y
0	
90	
180	
270	
360	

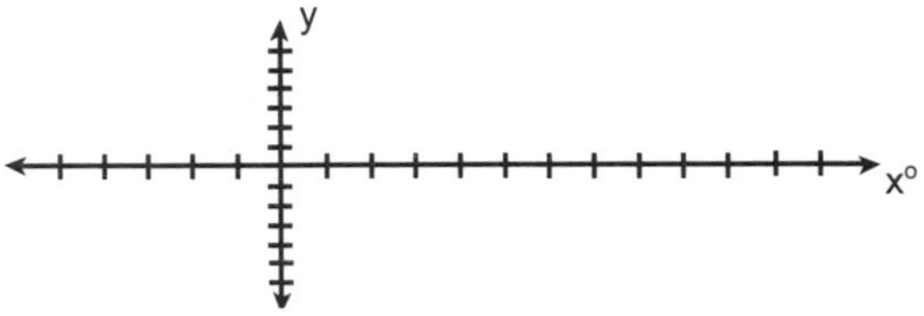

2. $y = \frac{3}{2} \sin x$

x°	y
0	
90	
180	
270	
360	

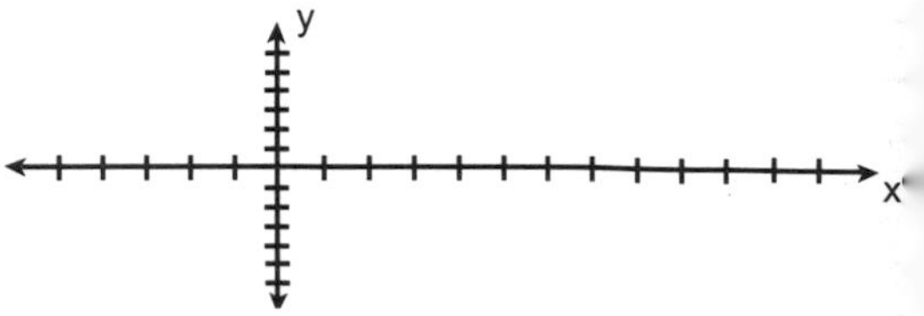

3. $y = \frac{1}{2} \cos x$

x°	y
0	
90	
180	
270	
360	

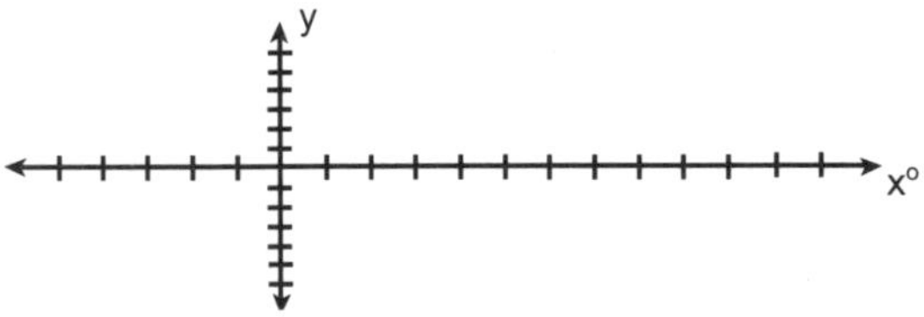

4. $y = {}^{-}3 \sin x$

x°	y
0	
90	
180	
270	
360	

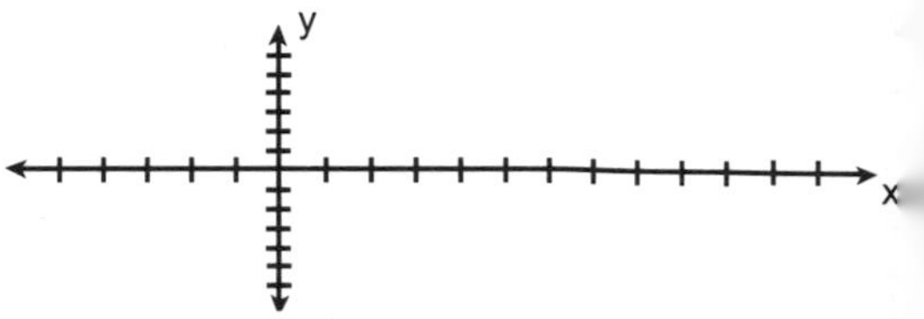

5. $y = 4 \sin x$

x°	y
0	
90	
180	
270	
360	

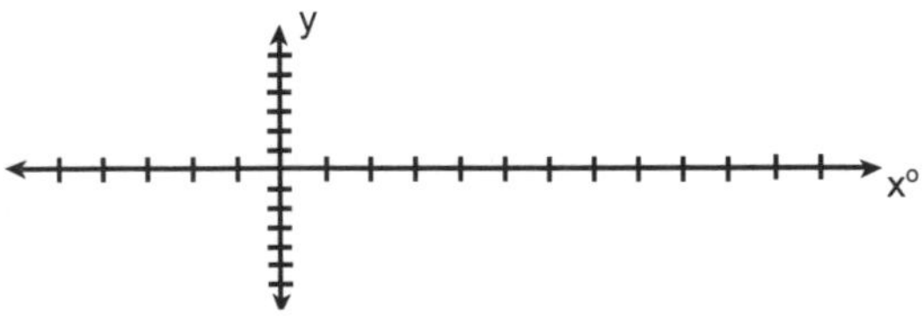

6. $y = -\frac{1}{3} \sin x$

x°	y
0	
90	
180	
270	
360	

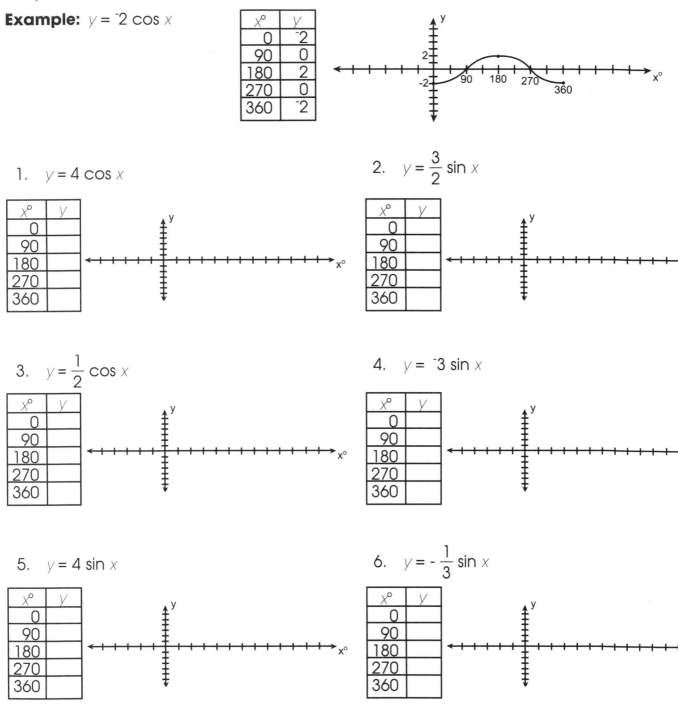

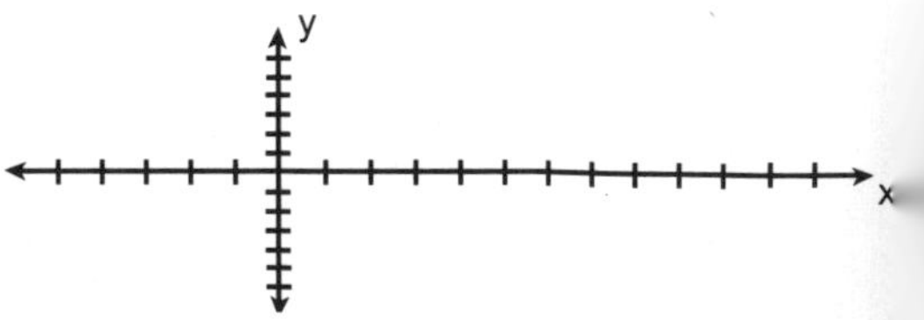

What does a do to the sin and cos function?
What does $-a$ do to the sin and cos function?

Name ______________________ Date ______________________

Graphing $y = c + a \sin x$ or $y = c + a \cos x$

Graph each function. Add units to both axes.

Example: $y = 1 + \sin x$

$x°$	y
0	$^{-}2$
90	0
180	2
270	0
360	$^{-}2$

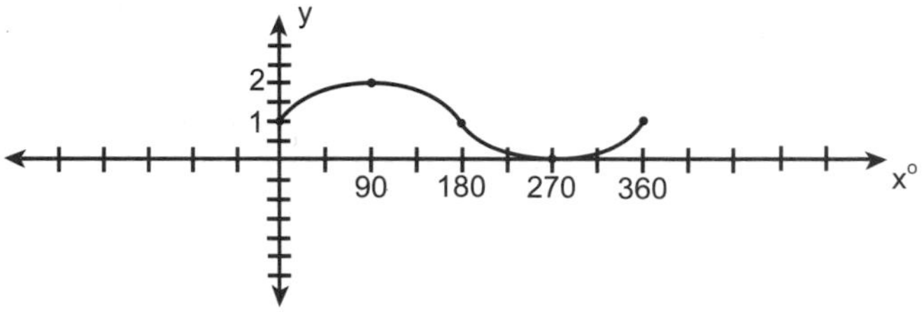

1. $y = 3 + \cos x$

$x°$	y
0	
90	
180	
270	
360	

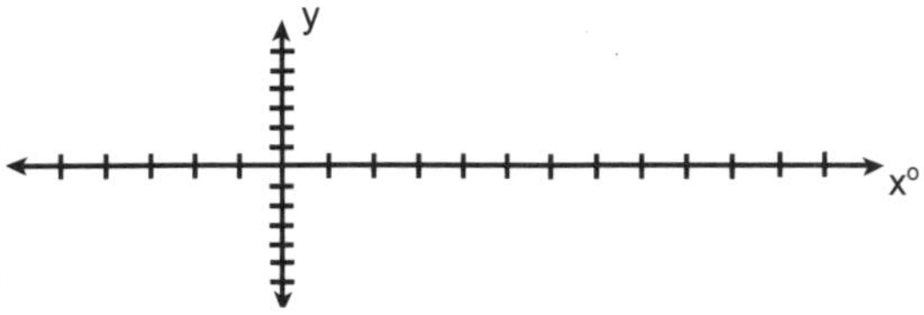

2. $y = 2 + \sin x$

$x°$	y
0	
90	
180	
270	
360	

3. $y = \frac{1}{2} + \cos x$

$x°$	y
0	
90	
180	
270	
360	

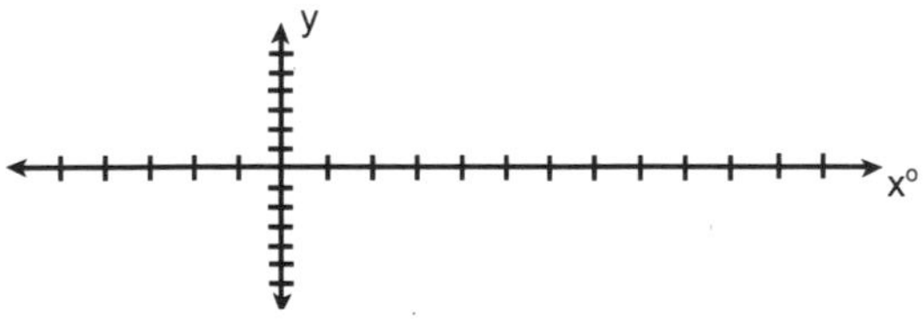

4. $y = {}^{-}3 + \sin x$

$x°$	y
0	
90	
180	
270	
360	

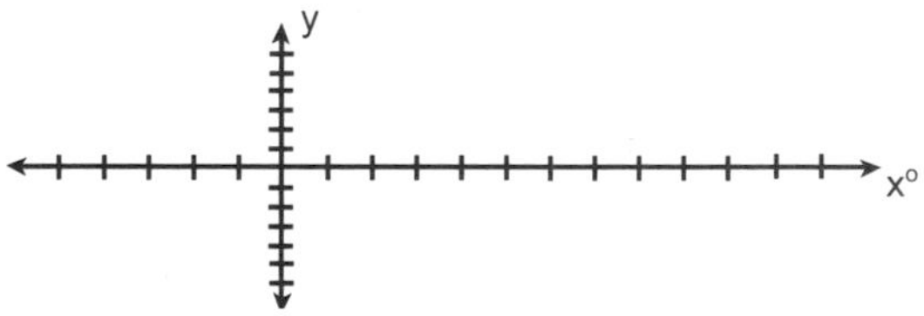

5. $y = {}^{-}1 + \cos x$

$x°$	y
0	
90	
180	
270	
360	

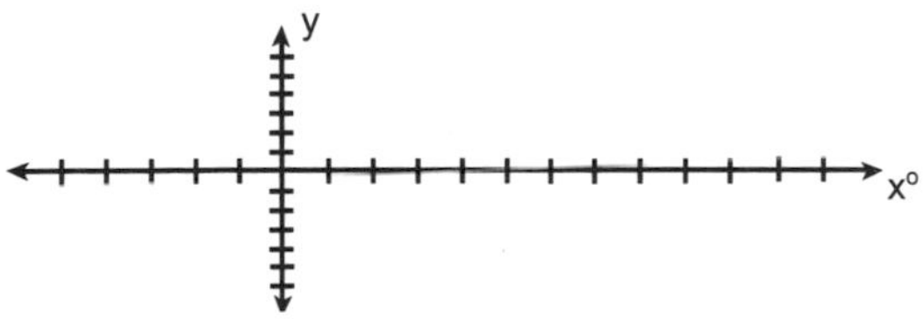

6. $y = -\frac{1}{3} + \sin x$

$x°$	y
0	
90	
180	
270	
360	

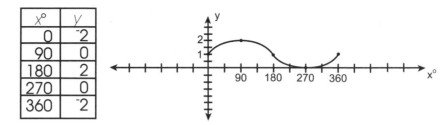

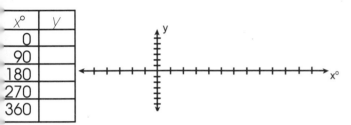

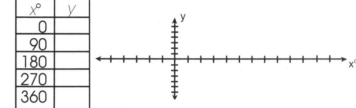

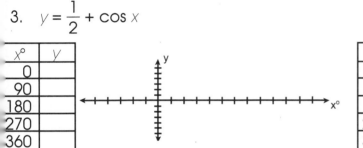

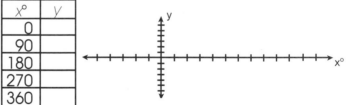

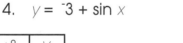

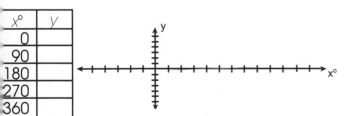

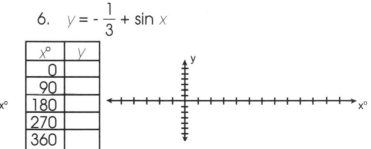

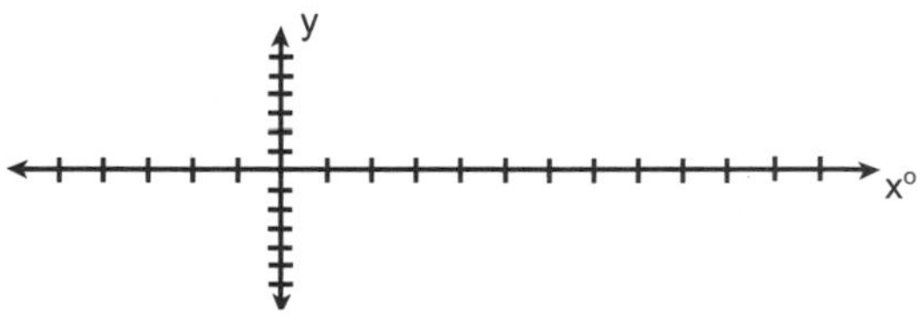

What does a positive c value do?
What does a negative c value do?

Name ______________________ Date ______________________

Graphing $y = \sin bx$ or $y = \cos bx$

The normal period, one complete wave, of a sine or cosine function is 360 degrees. However, the period will change due to the constant b in the general equation, $y = \sin bx$, $y = \cos bx$. In general, the period will be $\frac{360}{b}$. For example, the equation $y = \sin 2x$ has a period of $\frac{360}{2}$ or 180 degrees, that is, one complete sine wave in 180 degrees or two complete sine waves in 360 degrees. Refer to the table of values and the graph below. Notice that the table of values has three columns instead of the usual two. The middle column is always bx, and the usual values of 0, 90, 180, 270, and 360 are placed here. The first column contains the values in the middle column divided by b (or in this case two). The third column contains the value of the function y. **Note:** To graph the function, use only the first and last columns of the table of values.

Complete the table of values and graph the function. Write the units on both axes.

Example: $y = \sin 2x$

$x°$	$2x°$	y
0	0	0
45	90	1
90	180	0
135	270	$^-1$
180	360	0

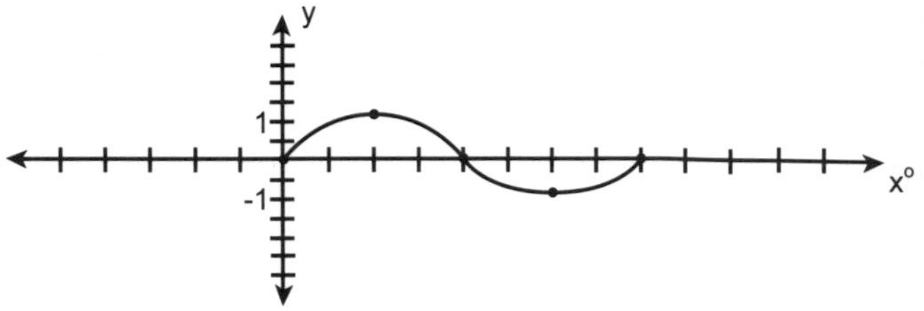

1. $y = \cos 4x$

$x°$		y
	0	
	90	
	180	
	270	
	360	

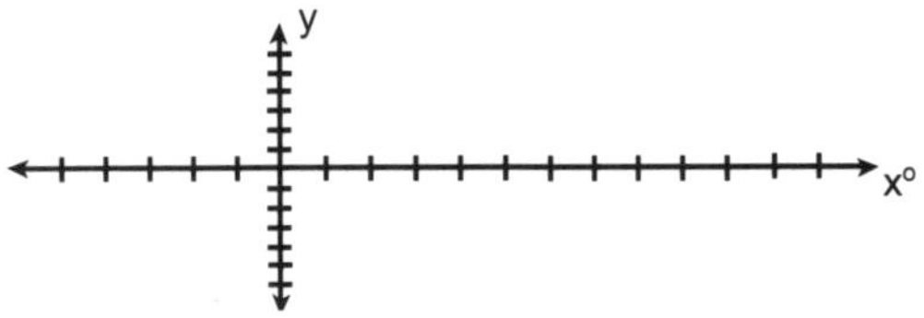

2. $y = \sin 3x$

$x°$		y
	0	
	90	
	180	
	270	
	360	

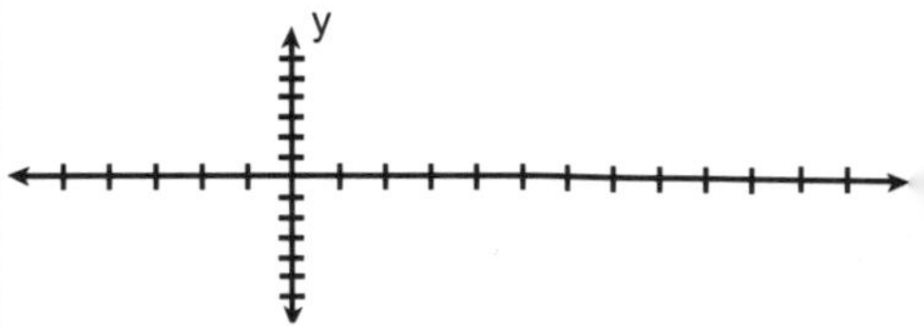

3. $y = \sin \frac{1}{2}x$

$x°$		y
	0	
	90	
	180	
	270	
	360	

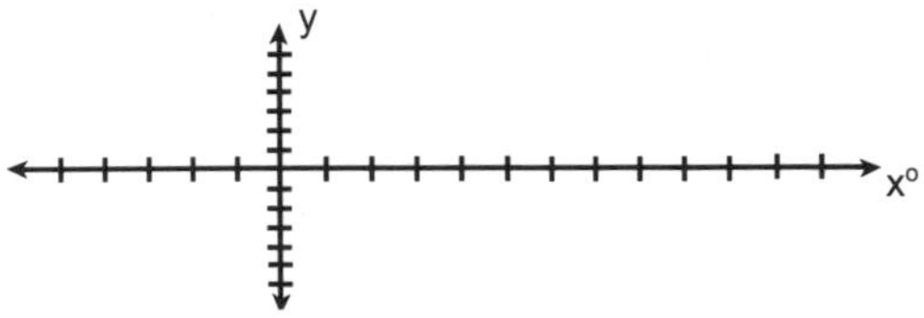

4. $y = \cos \frac{1}{3}x$

$x°$		y
	0	
	90	
	180	
	270	
	360	

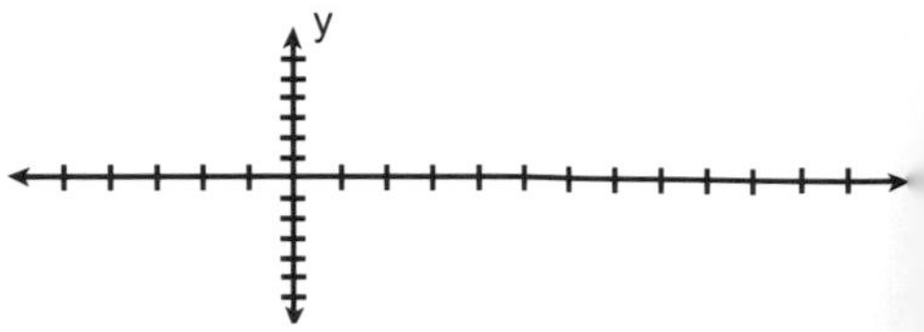

5. $y = \sin \frac{1}{4}x$

$x°$		y
	0	
	90	
	180	
	270	
	360	

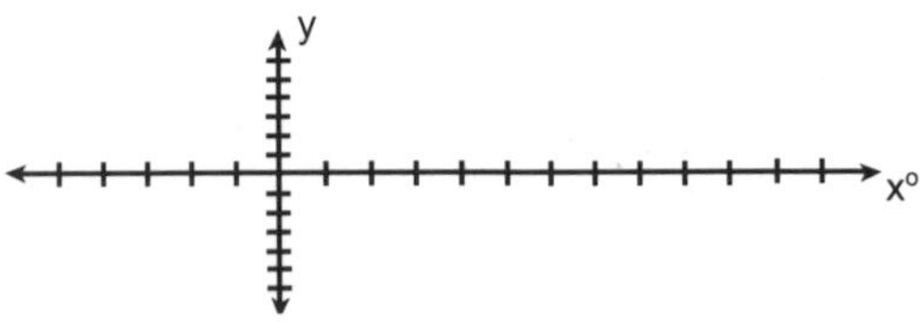

6. $y = \cos 2x$

$x°$		y
	0	
	90	
	180	
	270	
	360	

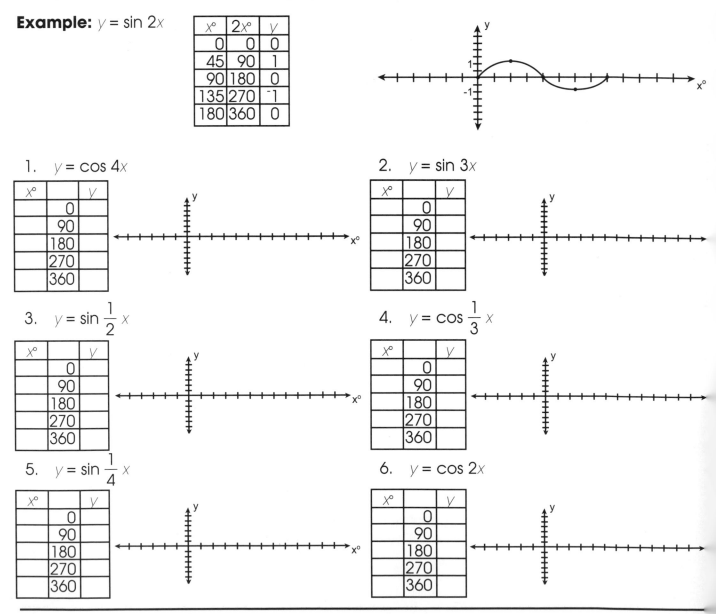

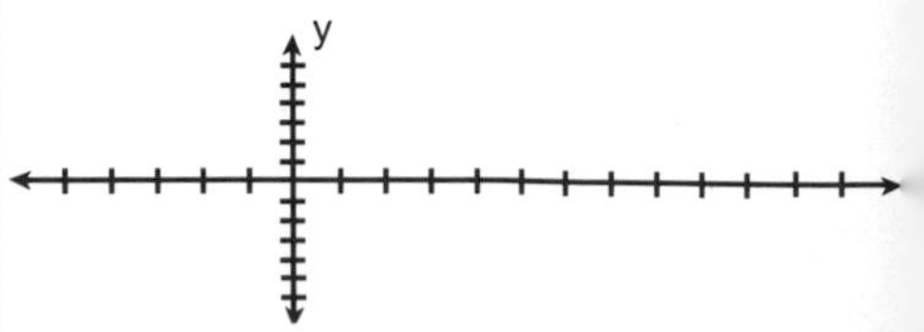

0-7424-1789-1 Algeb

Name ______________________ Date ______________________

Graphing $y = \sin(x - d)$ or $y = \cos(x - d)$

n the general equation $y = \sin(x - d)$ or $y = \cos(x - d)$, $(x - d)$ is known as the argument of the function. $(x - d)$ corresponds to a phase shift or horizontal shift of d degrees. To graph functions of this type, a table of values with three three columns is used. The first column is for the variable . The middle column is for the argument $(x - d)$, and the last column is for the value of the function y. **Note:** Use only the first and last columns to graph the function. The numbers in the middle column insure that the graph will have one complete sine or cosine wave.

Complete the table of values and graph the function. Write the units on both axes.

xample: $y = \sin(x - 90°)$

$x°$	$(x-90)$	y
0	0	0
45	90	1
90	180	0
135	270	$^{-}1$
180	36	0

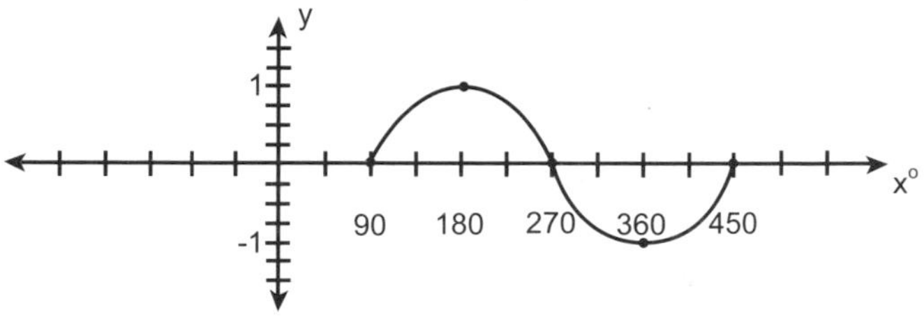

1. $y = \cos(x - 90°)$

$x°$		y
	0	
	90	
	180	
	270	
	360	

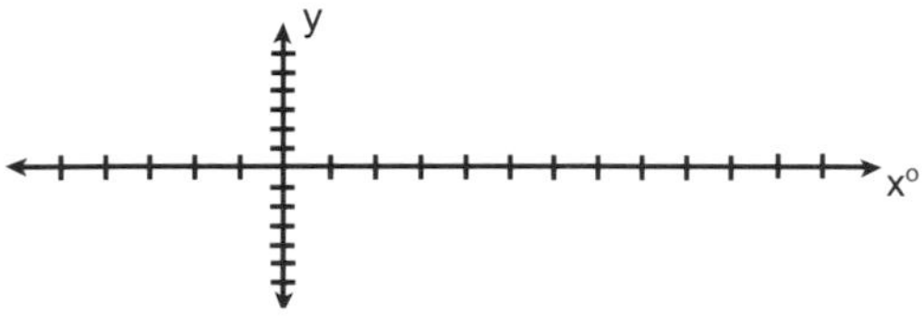

2. $y = \sin(x + 90°)$

$x°$		y
	0	
	90	
	180	
	270	
	360	

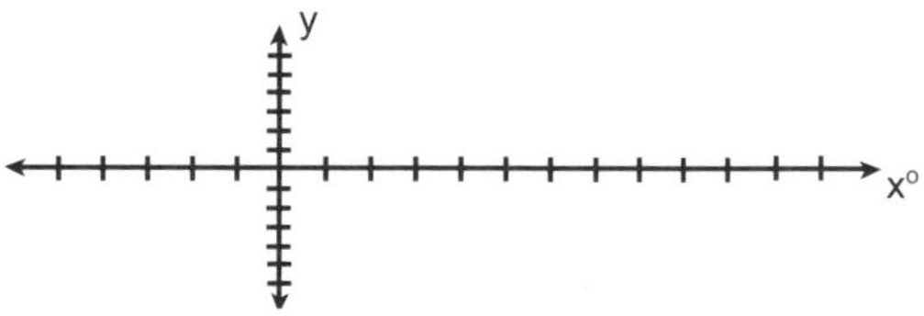

3. $y = \sin(x - 180°)$

$x°$		y
	0	
	90	
	180	
	270	
	360	

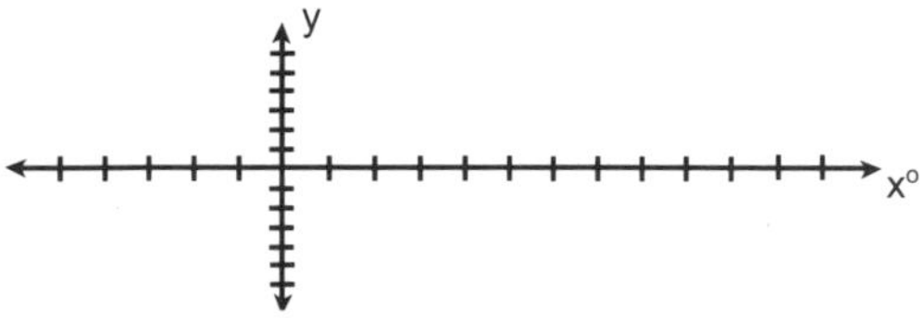

4. $y = \cos(x + 45°)$

$x°$		y
	0	
	90	
	180	
	270	
	360	

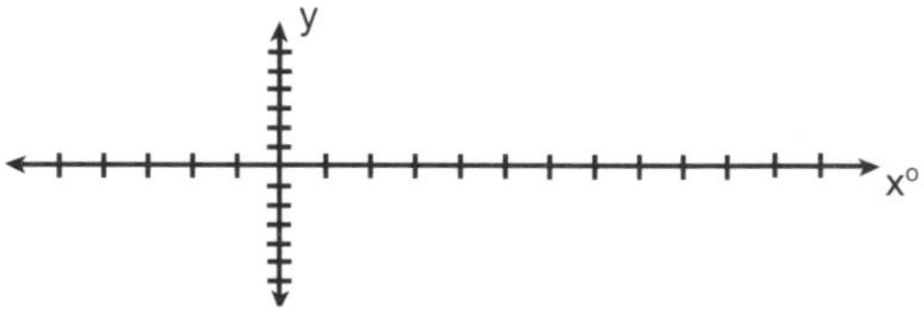

5. $y = \sin(x - 270°)$

$x°$		y
	0	
	90	
	180	
	270	
	360	

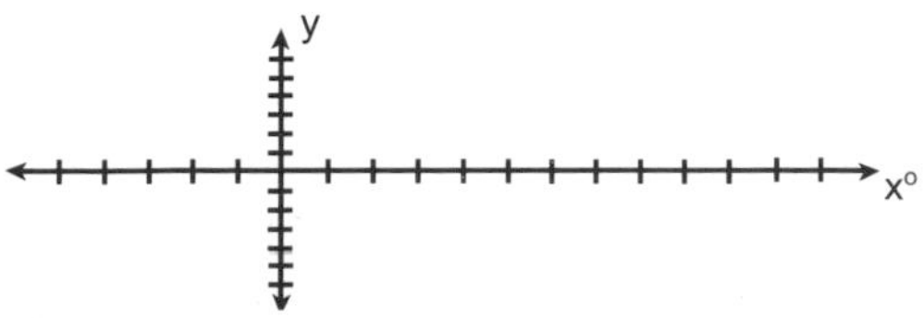

6. $y = \cos(x + 30°)$

$x°$		y
	0	
	90	
	180	
	270	
	360	

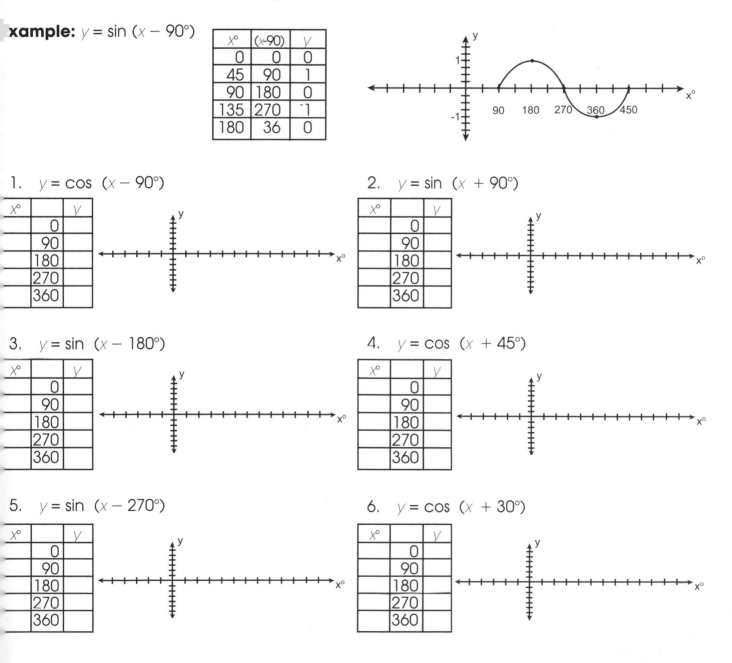

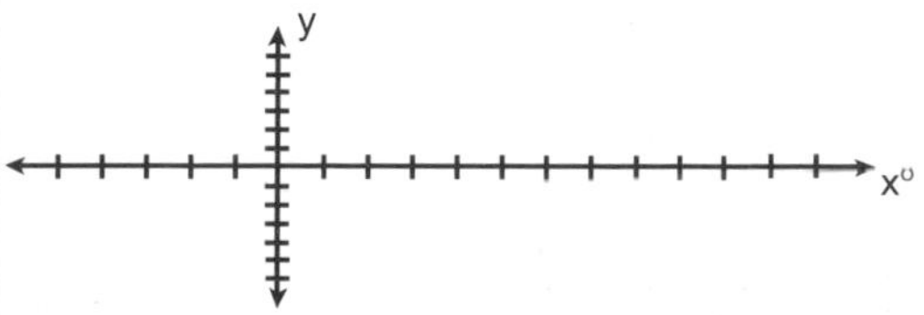

Name ______________________ Date ______________________

Graphing $y = c + \sin(x - d)$ or $y = c + \cos(x - d)$

In the general equation $y = c + \sin(x - d)$ or $y = c + \cos(x - d)$, the variable c is known as the vertical translation and the variable d is known as the horizontal translation. Now that we are familiar with the general shape of the sine and cosine functions, we will not use a table of values, but simply translate the origin graph from (0,0) to (d,c). Note that when both c and d are accounted for by translating the origin, the function simplifies to $y = \sin x$ or $y = \cos x$.

Graph each function.

Example: $y = 2 + \sin(x + 90)$

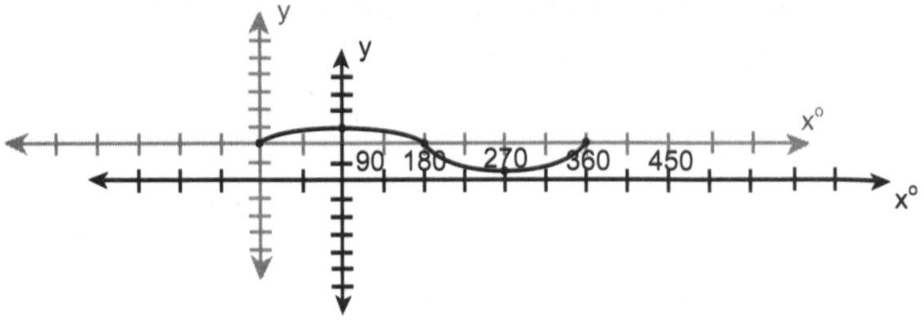

1. $y = 1 + \sin(x - 90)$

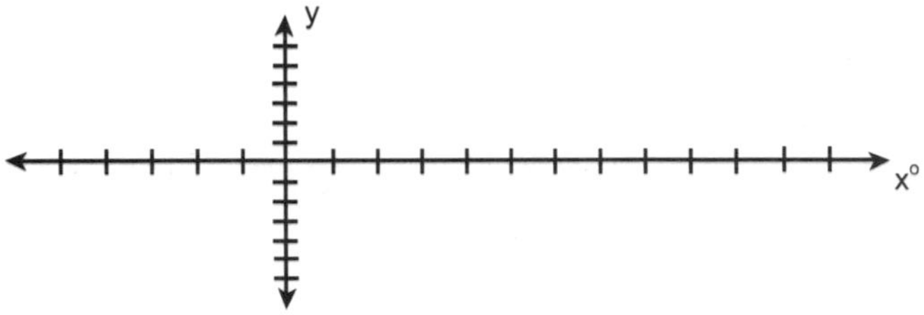

2. $y = 2 + \cos(x - 45)$

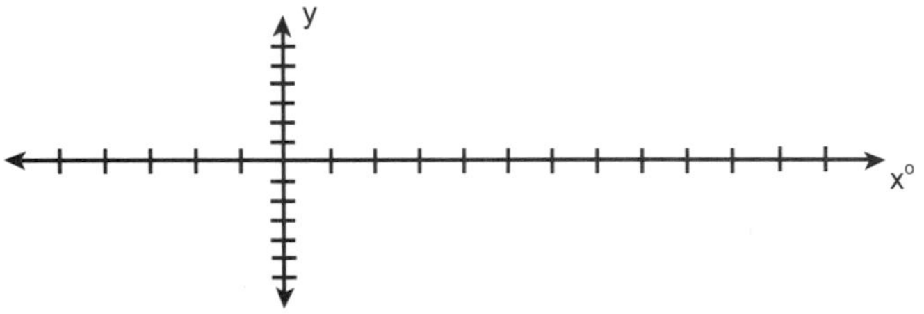

3. $y = {}^-1 + \cos(x + 90)$

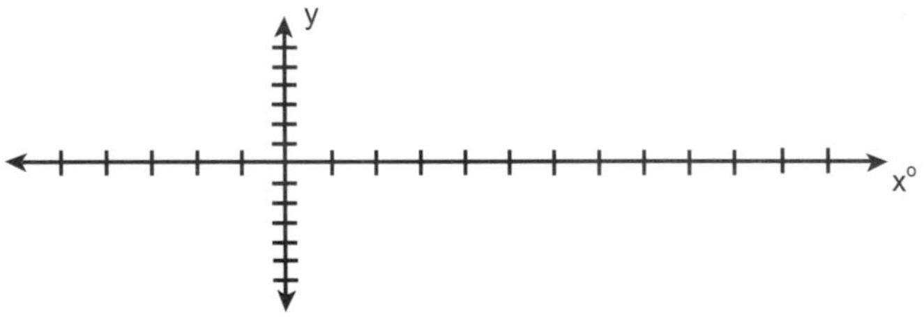

4. $y = {}^-2 + \sin(x + 180)$

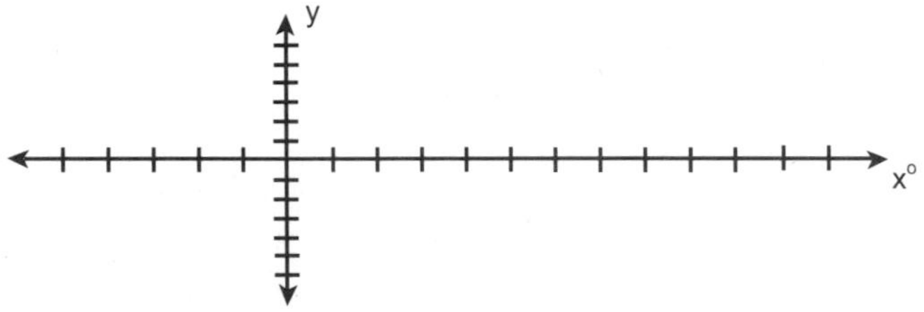

5. $y = {}^-3 + \cos(x - 180)$

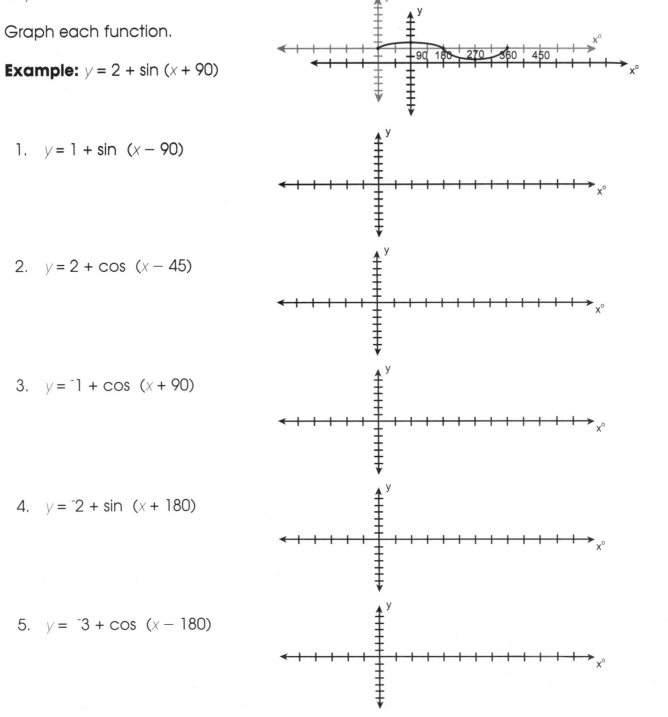

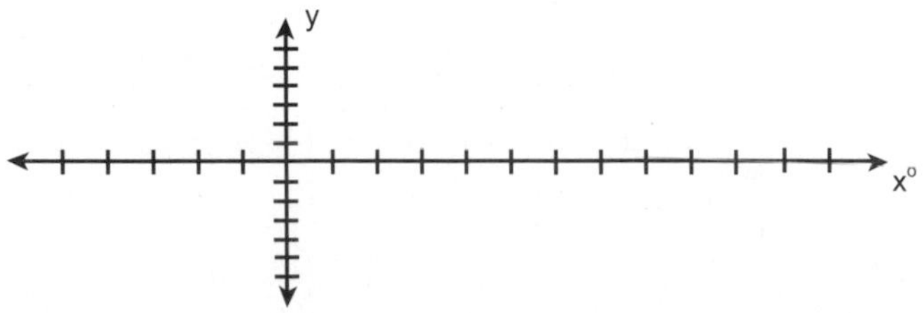

0-7424-1789-1 *Algeb*

Name ________________________ Date ________________________

Graphing $y = c + a \sin b(x - d)$ or $y = c + a \cos b(x - d)$

In the general equation $y = c + a \sin b(x - d)$ or $y = c + a \cos b(x - d)$...

$|a|$ is the amplitude.

$\frac{360}{b}$ is the period.

c is the vertical translation.
d is the horizontal translation.

To graph a complex equation of this type, first translate the origin of the graph from (0, 0) to (d, c) which will reduce the equation to $y = a \sin bx$ or $y = a \cos bx$. Then use a table of values with three columns (x, bx, and y) to graph the equation on the translated $x - y$ plane.

Example: $y = 1 + 3 \sin 2(x + 90)$

a. The first step is to translate the origin of the coordinate system from (0, 0) to ($^-90$, 1).

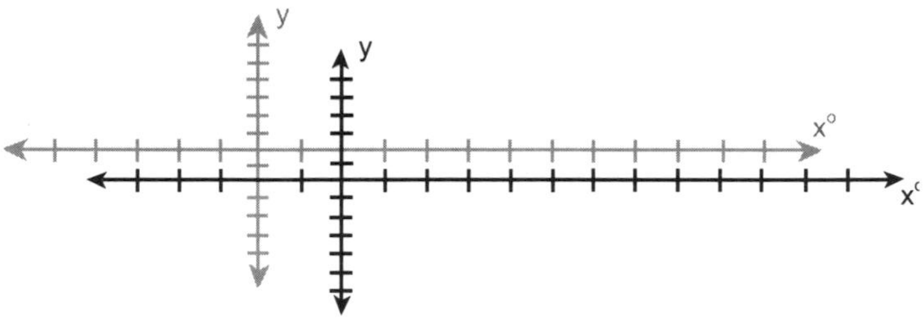

b. In translating the origin, the equation is reduced to $y = 3 \sin 2x$. The amplitude is 3, the period is 180 degrees.

c. After completing the table of values, graph the first and last columns only onto the translated coordinate system.

$x°$	$2x°$	y
0	0	0
45	90	3
90	180	0
135	270	$^-3$
180	360	0

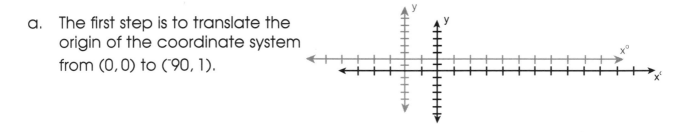

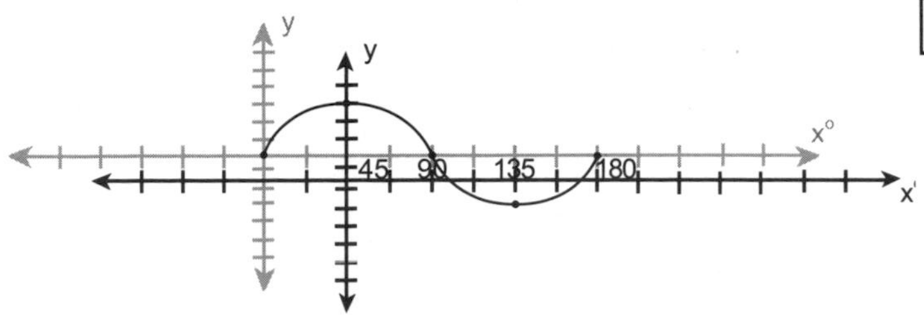

Name ______________________________ Date ______________________________

Graphing $y = c + a \sin b(x - d)$ or $y = c + a \cos b(x - d)$ (cont.)

Graph the following equations. Write the units on both axes.

1. $y = {}^{-}2 - 1 \cos 3(x - 90)$

$x°$		y

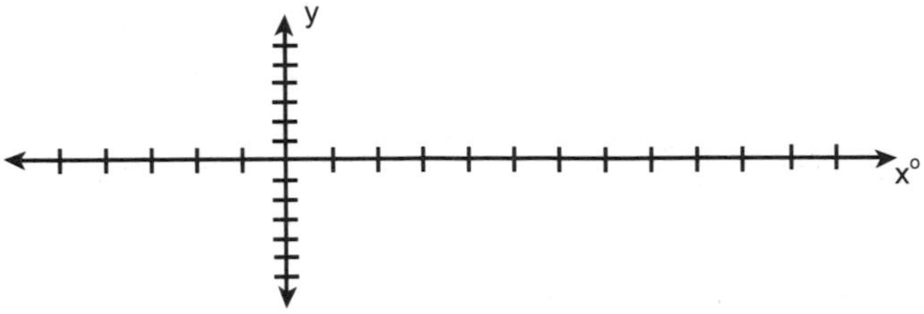

2. $y = {}^{-}1 + \frac{1}{2} \cos 2(x - 180)$

$x°$		y

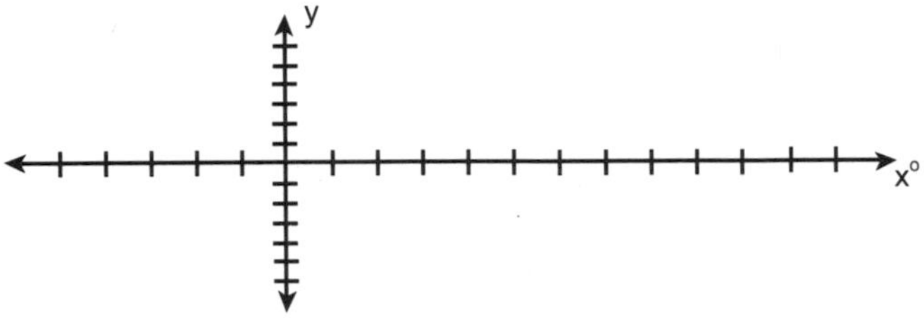

3. $y = 3 + 3 \sin (x + 90)$

$x°$		y

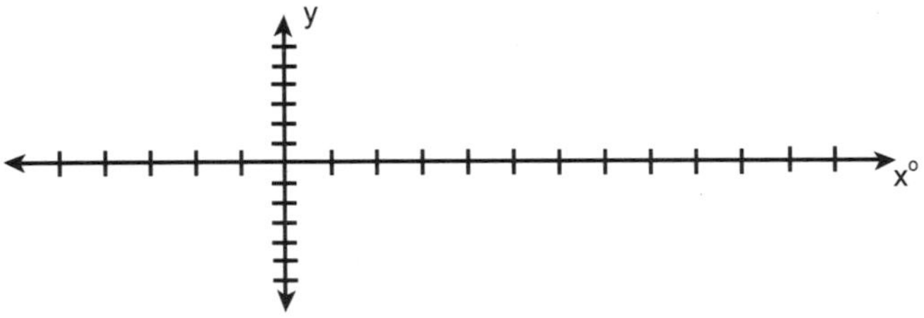

4. $y = {}^{-}6 - 2 \sin \frac{1}{2}(x + 45)$

$x°$		y

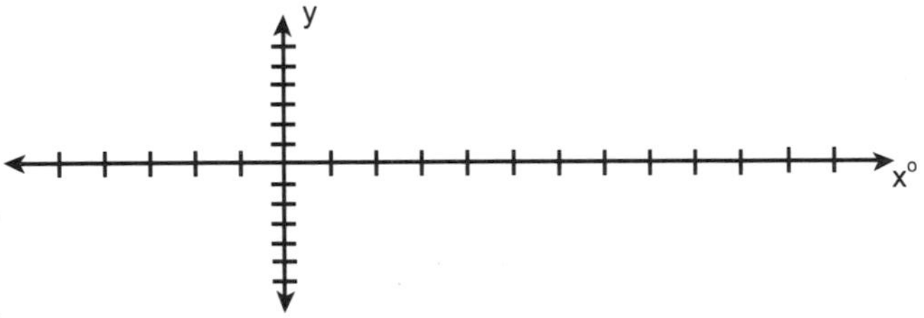

5. $y = 2 + 3 \cos 4(x - 45)$

$x°$		y

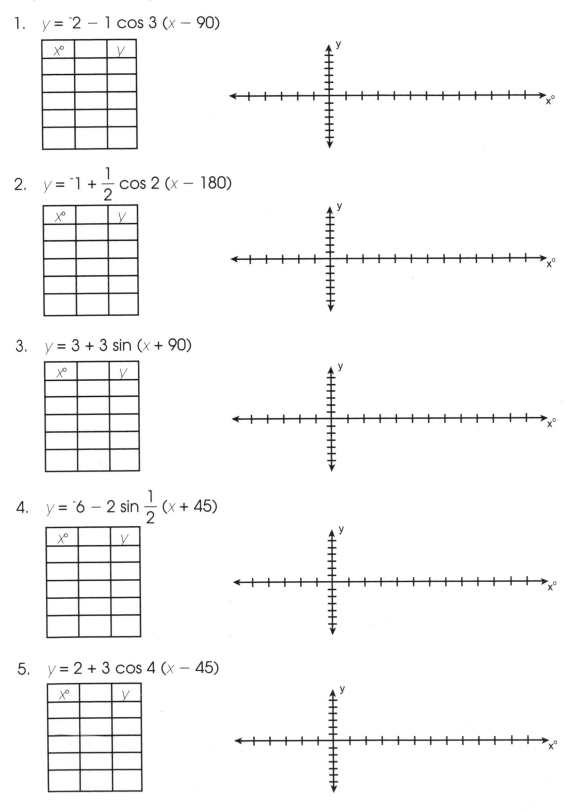

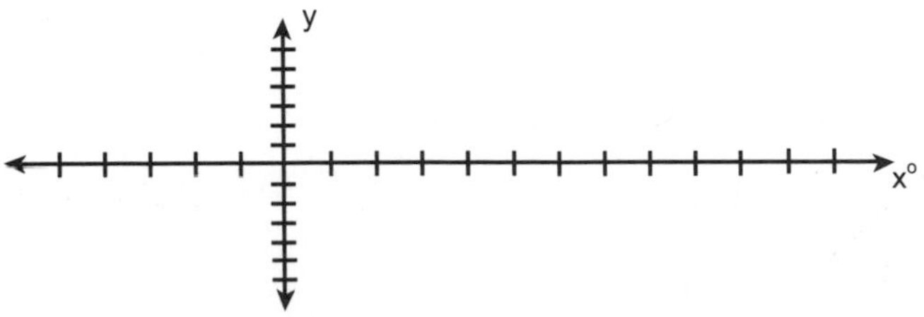

0-7424-1789-1 *Algeb*

Name ______________________ Date ______________________

Law of Sines

Given the triangle ABC with lengths a, b, c and angles A, B, and C then,

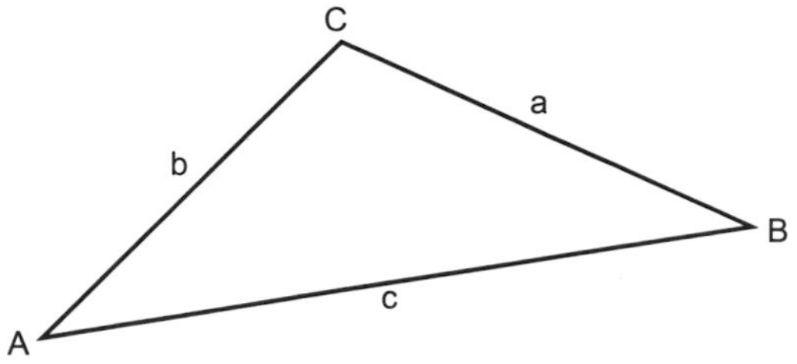

1. $\dfrac{\sin A}{a} = \dfrac{\sin B}{b}$
2. $\dfrac{\sin C}{c} = \dfrac{\sin B}{b}$
3. $\dfrac{\sin A}{a} = \dfrac{\sin C}{c}$

Note: a is the length of the side opposite angle A.

Solve for the all missing sides and angles in each triangle. Round sides to nearest tenth and angles to nearest degree.

Example:

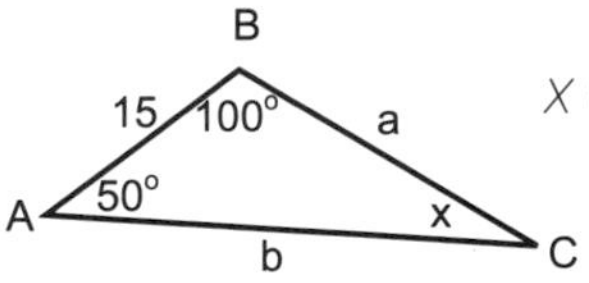

$100 + 50 + x = 180$

$x = 30$

$\dfrac{\sin 50}{a} = \dfrac{\sin 30}{15}$

$15 \sin 50 = a \sin 30$

$a = \dfrac{15 \sin 50}{\sin 30} = 22.981$

$a = 22.9$

$\dfrac{\sin 100}{b} = \dfrac{\sin 30}{15}$

$15 \sin 100 = b \sin 30$

$b = \dfrac{15 \sin 100}{\sin 30} = 29.50$

$b = 29.5$

Note: The law of sines works for all triangles.

1. 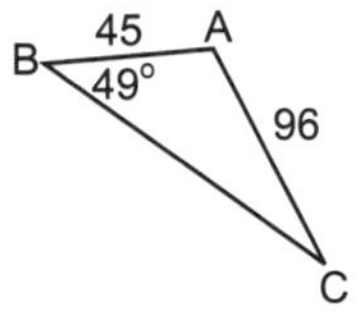

2. 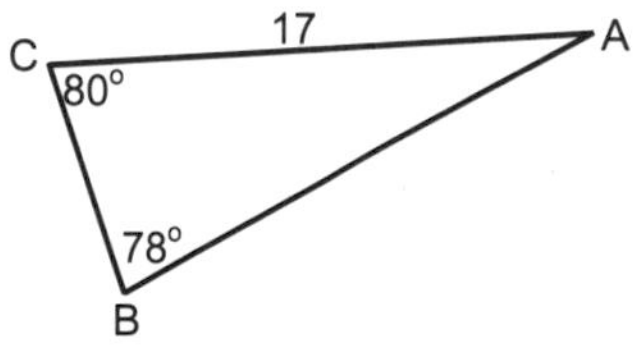

3. 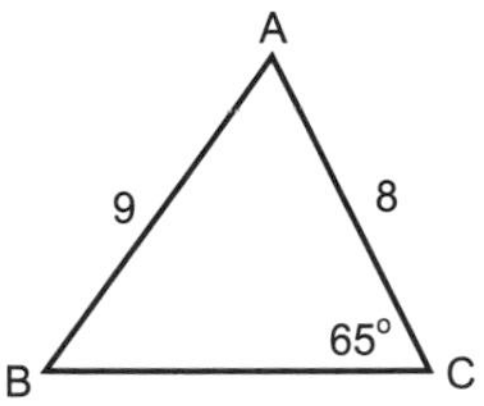

4. 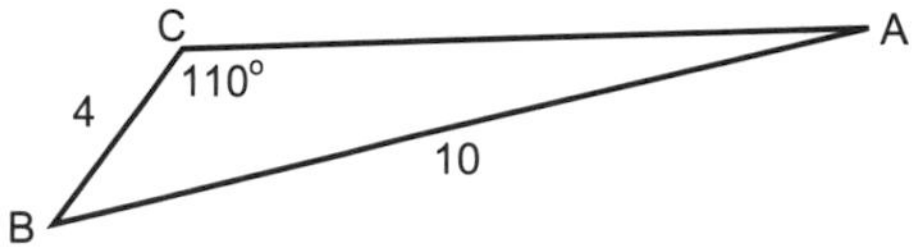

5. 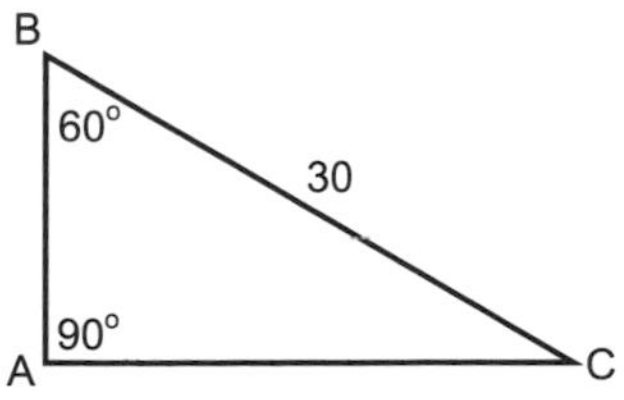

6. 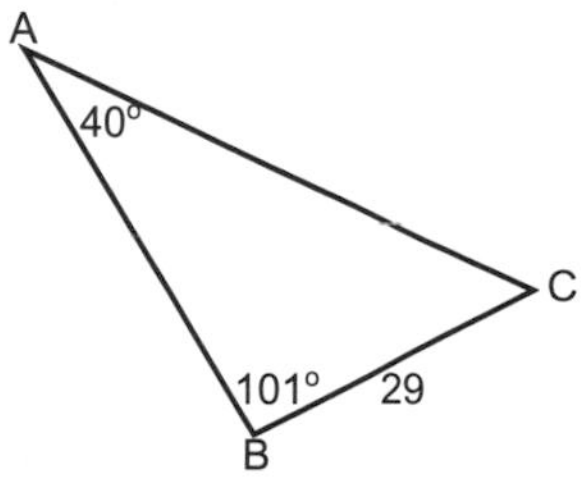

7. 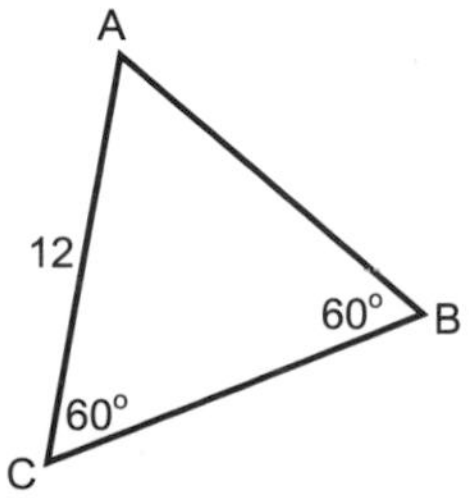

8. 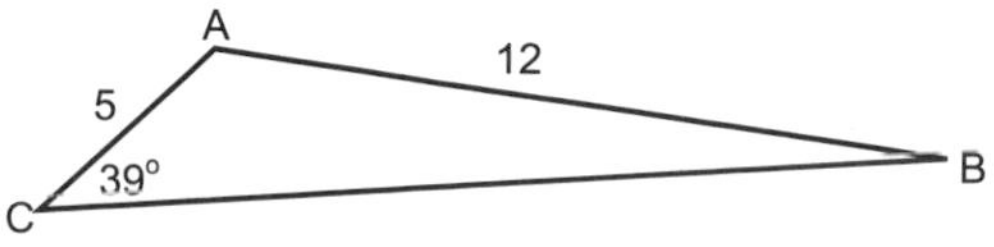

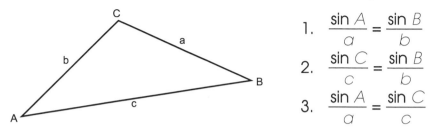

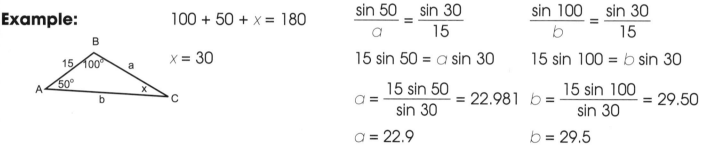

Name ______________________ Date ______________________

Law of Cosines

Given the triangle ABC with lengths a, b, c and angles A, B, and C then,

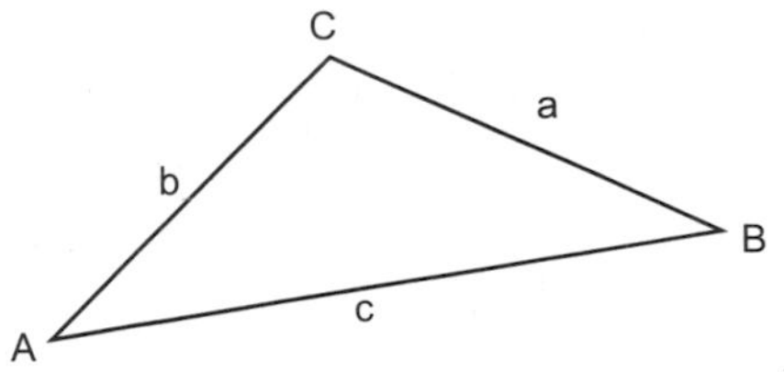

1. $a^2 = b^2 + c^2 - 2bc \cos A$
2. $b^2 = a^2 + c^2 - 2ac \cos B$
3. $c^2 = a^2 + b^2 - 2ab \cos C$

Note: a is the length of the side opposite angle A.

The law of cosines is significantly more difficult to use than that of the law of sines. Consider two cases: The first is solving for side a of a triangle, the second is solving for angle A.

1. $a^2 = \sqrt{b^2 + c^2 - 2bc \cos A}$ 2. $A = \cos^{-1}\left(\frac{a^2 - b^2 - c^2}{}\right)$

Solve for x on each triangle. Round length to nearest tenth and angle to the nearest degree.

Example:

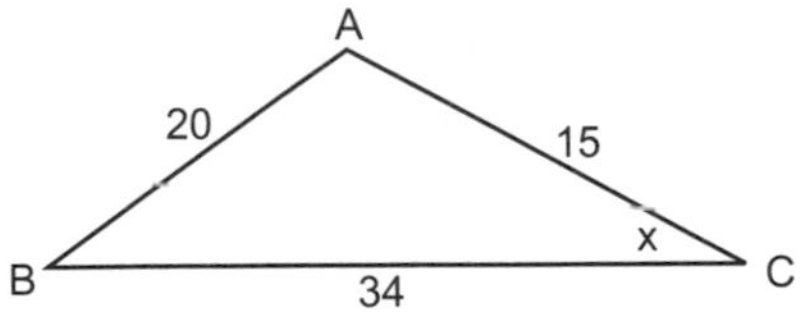

$$A = \cos^{-1}\left(\frac{34^2}{^-2} - \frac{15^2 - 20^2}{(15)(20)}\right) = \cos^{-1}\left(\frac{531}{^-600}\right) = \cos^{-1}(^-0.885) = 152.25$$

$$A = 152^\circ$$

Note: The law of cosines works for all triangles.

1. 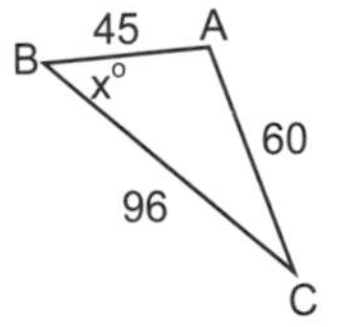

2. 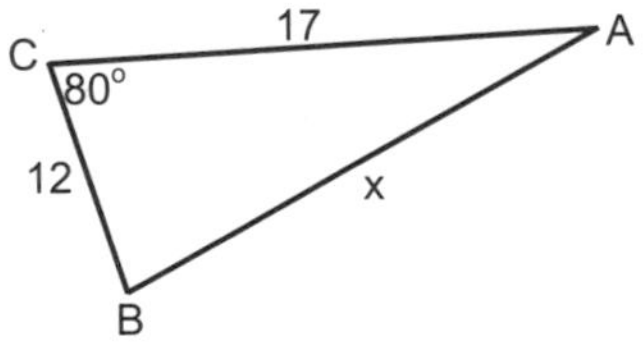

3. 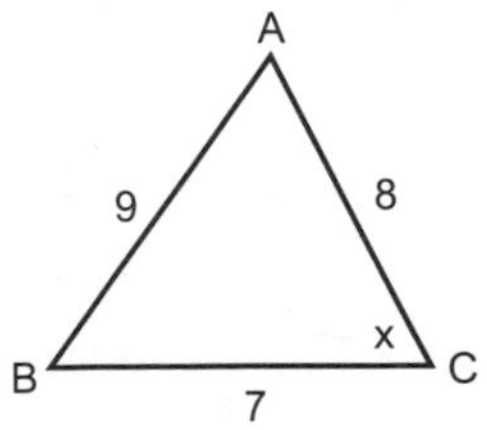

4. 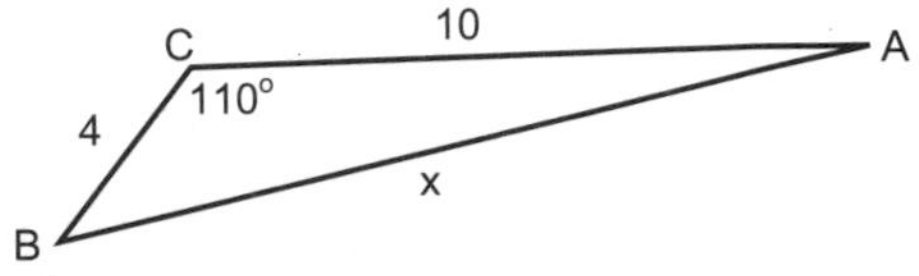

5. 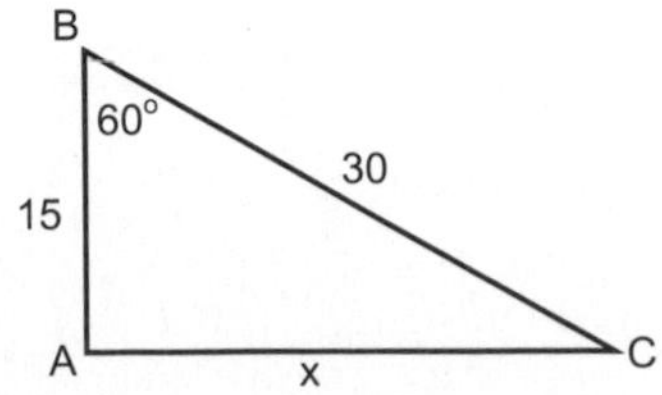

6. 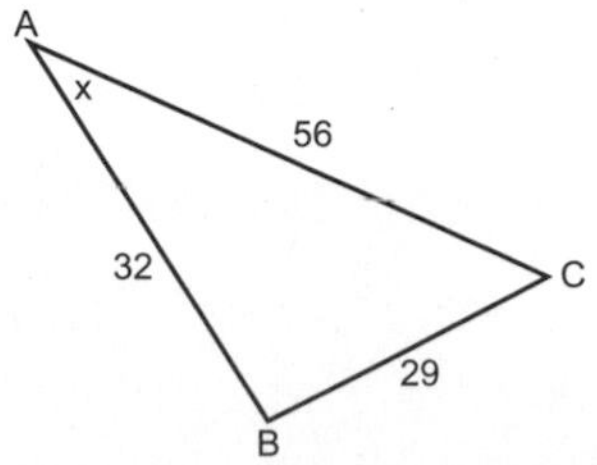

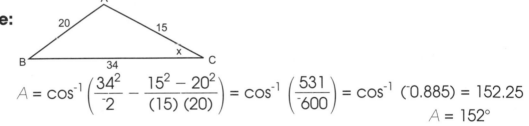

Name ______________________ Date ______________________

Problem Solving: The Law of Sines and the Law of Cosines

Draw a picture and solve.

1. Juan and Romelia are standing at the seashore 10 miles apart. The coastline is a straight line between them. Both can see the same ship in the water. The angle between the coastline and the line between the ship an Juan is 35 degrees. The angle between the coastline and the line between the ship and Romelia is 45 degrees. How far is the ship from Juan?

2. Jack is on one side of a 200-foot-wide canyon and Jill is on the other. Jack and Jill can both see the trail guide at an angle of depression of 60 degrees. How far are they from the trail guide?

3. Tom, Dick, and Harry are camping in their tents. If the distance between Tom and Dick is 153 feet, the distance between Tom and Harry is 201 feet, and the distance between Dick and Harry is 175 feet, what is the angle between Dick, Harry, and Tom?

4. Three boats are at sea: Jenny one (J1), Jenny two (J2), and Jenny three (J3). The crew of J1 can see both J2 and J3. The angle between the line of sight to J2 and the line of sight to J3 is 45 degrees. If the distance between J1 and J2 is 2 miles and the distance between J1 and J3 is 4 miles, what is the distance between J2 and J3?

5. Airplane A is flying directly toward the airport which is 20 miles away. The pilot notices airplane B 45 degrees to her right. Airplane B is also flying directly toward the airport. The pilot of airplane B calculates that airplane A is 50 degrees to his left. Based on that information, how far is airplane B from the airport?

Name ______________________ Date ______________________

Describing Vectors

A **vector** is a quantity specified by magnitude and direction, such as velocity. A **scalar** is a quantity specified by magnitude only, such as speed. For example, 65 mile per hour due North is a vector known as velocity. 65 miles per hour is scalar known as speed. When describing a vector, you must give both a magnitude and a direction.

Describe each vector.

Example:

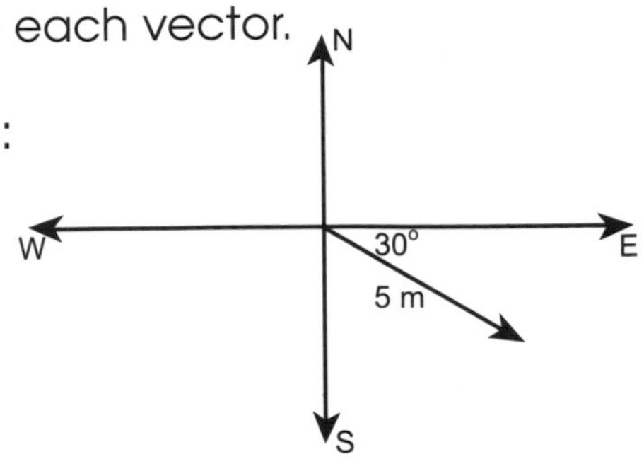

5 meters at 30 degrees south of east

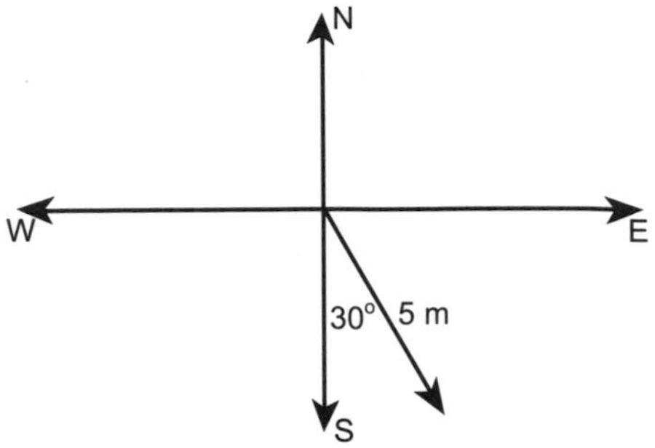

5 meters at 30 degrees east of south

1.

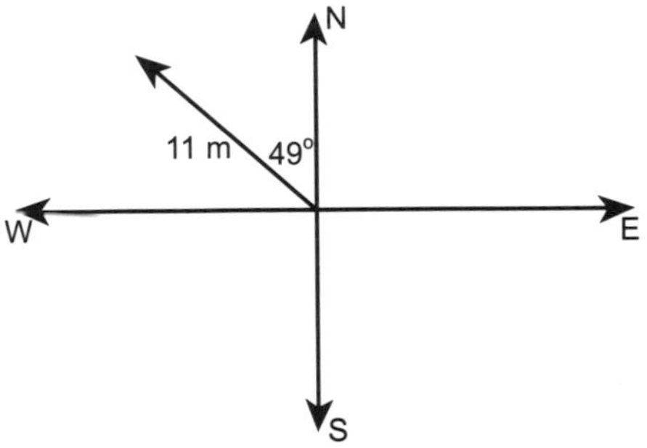

2.

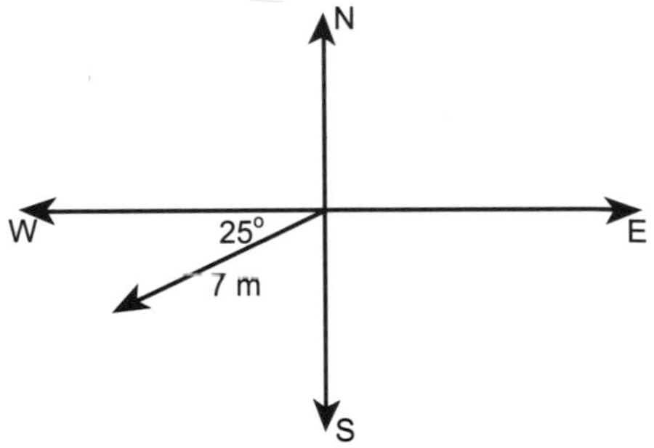

3.

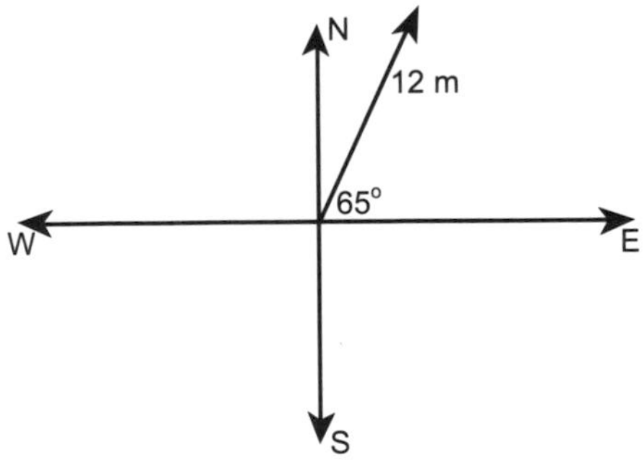

4.

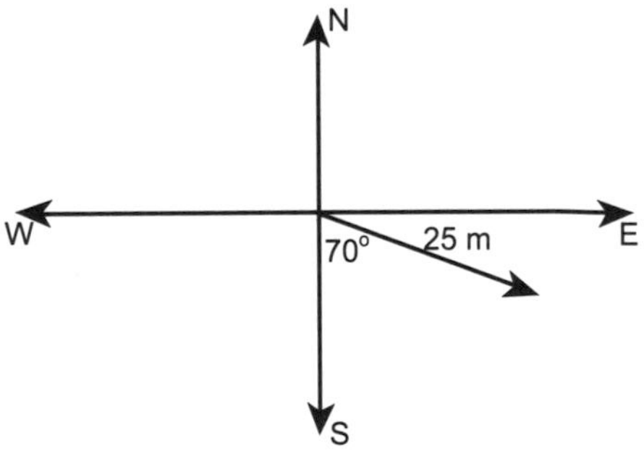

5.

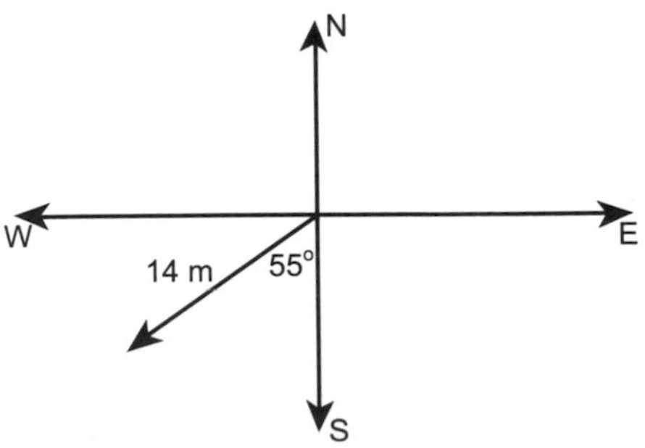

6.

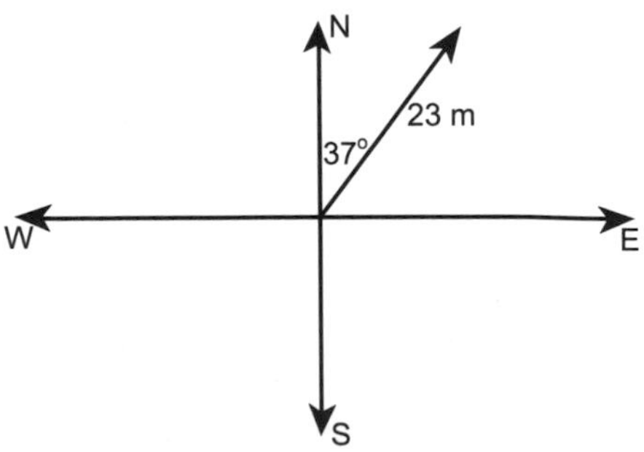

0-7424-1789-1 *Algeb*

Name ______________________________ Date ______________________________

Adding Vectors Graphically

Vectors are commonly denoted as an arrow where the tip indicates the direction of the vector and the tail depicts the origin (see vector *u*).

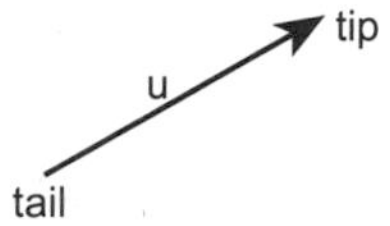

The length of the arrow is proportional to the magnitude of the vector. See examples *u* and *v* below.

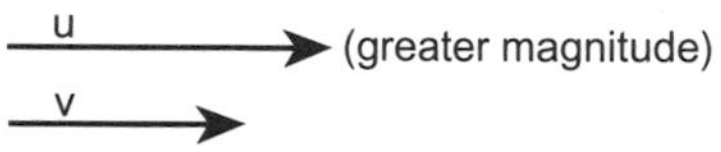

Using vectors *u*, *v*, *s*, and *t*, perform the following vector operations graphically.

Example: *u* + *s*

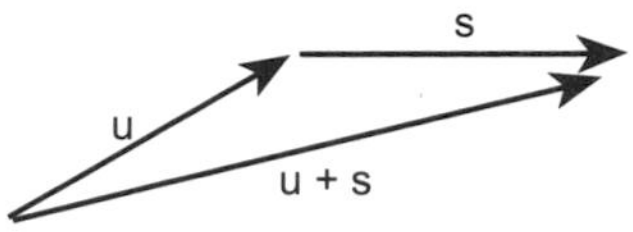

This method of addition is known as "tail to tip". Place vectors *u* and *s* together, then draw the resultant vector *u* + *s* from the tail of *u* to the tip of *s*.

1. *u* + *t*
2. *v* + *s*
3. *s* + *t*
4. *u* + *v*
5. *s* + *s*
6. *v* + *u*
7. *t* + *u*
8. *s* + *v*

Is vector addition commutative? Explain.

Name ______________________ Date ______________________

Vector Addition and Scalar Multiplication

Using the vectors, u, v, r, and t, perform the following vector operations.

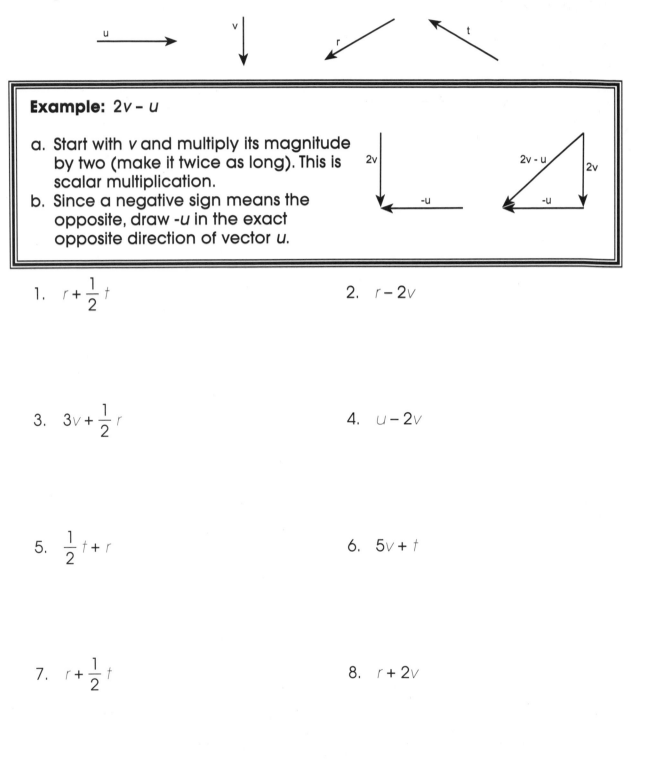

Example: $2v - u$

a. Start with v and multiply its magnitude by two (make it twice as long). This is scalar multiplication.
b. Since a negative sign means the opposite, draw $-u$ in the exact opposite direction of vector u.

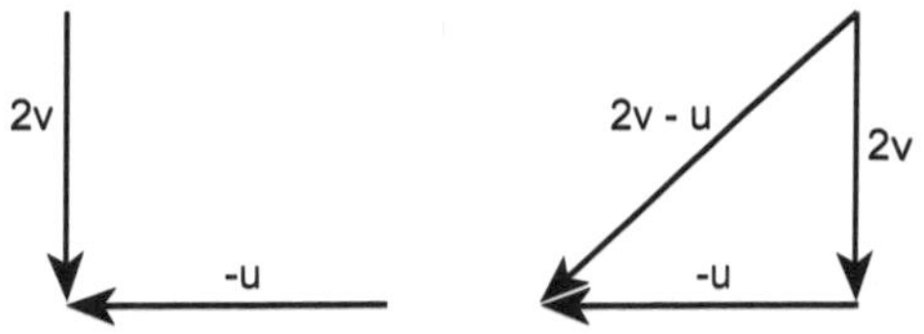

1. $r + \frac{1}{2}t$

2. $r - 2v$

3. $3v + \frac{1}{2}r$

4. $u - 2v$

5. $\frac{1}{2}t + r$

6. $5v + t$

7. $r + \frac{1}{2}t$

8. $r + 2v$

Is vector subtraction commutative? Explain.

0-7424-1789-1 *Algebr*

Name ______________________________ Date ______________________________

Resolving Vectors

Resolve each vector into its x and y components. Round to the nearest tenth of a meter.

Example:

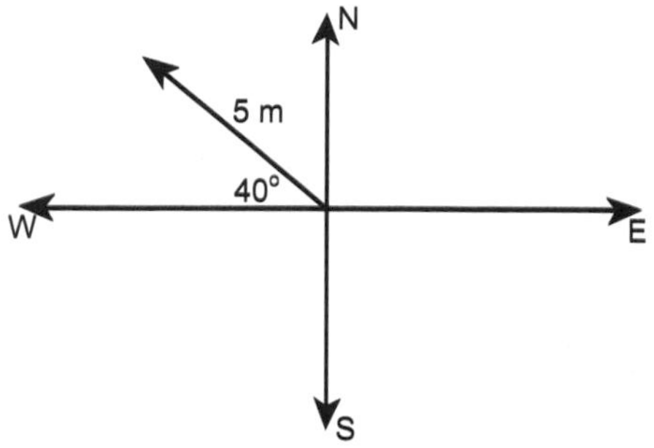

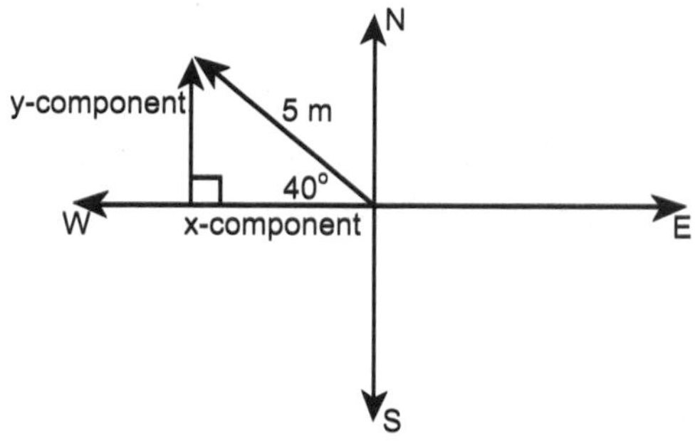

Note: The vector and its *x* and *y* components create a right triangle. Using the trigonometric ratios solve for the x-component (*x*) and the y-component (*y*).

$\sin 40 = \frac{y}{5}$

$y = 5 \sin 40 = 3.213938 = 3.2$ m

$\cos 40 = \frac{x}{5}$

$x = 5 \cos 40 = 3.830222 = 3.8 = {}^{-}3.8$ m

Note: the x-component is negative since it points west.

1.

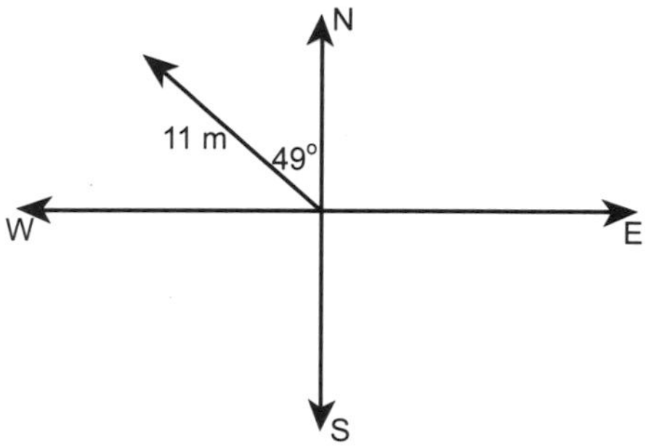

2.

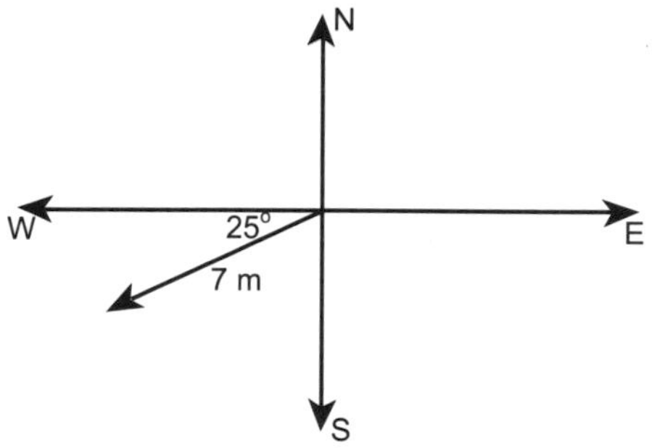

3.

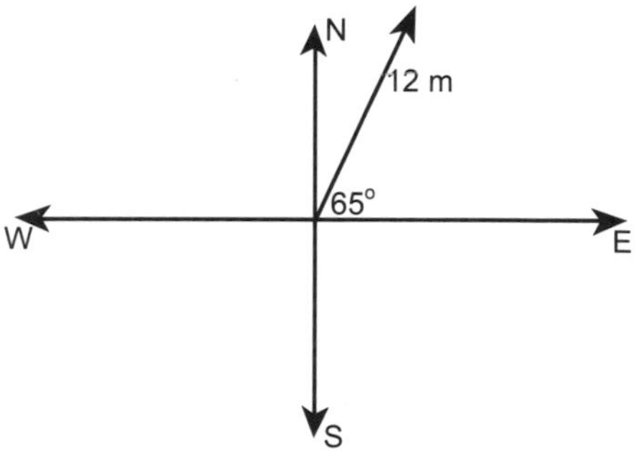

4.

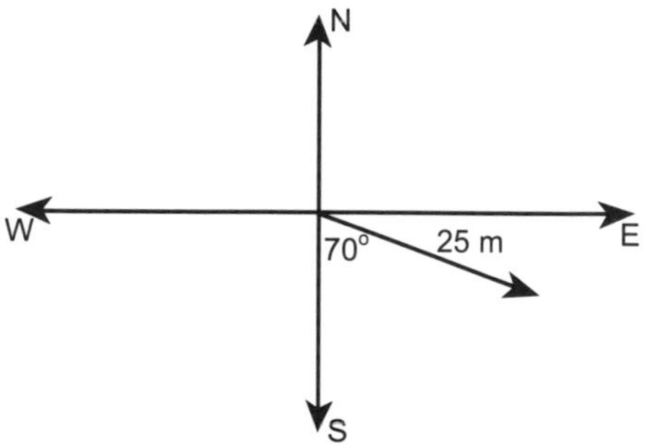

5.

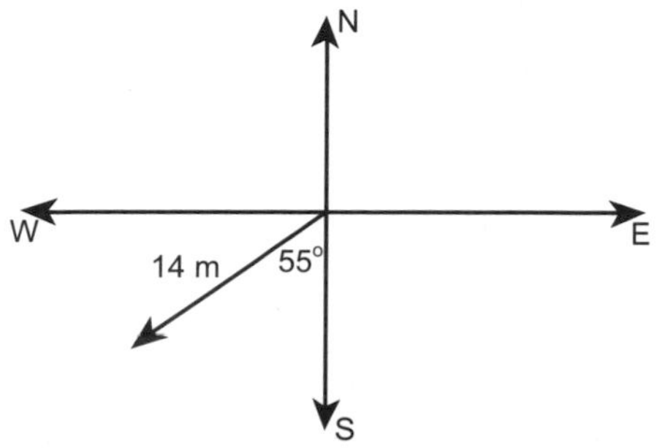

6.

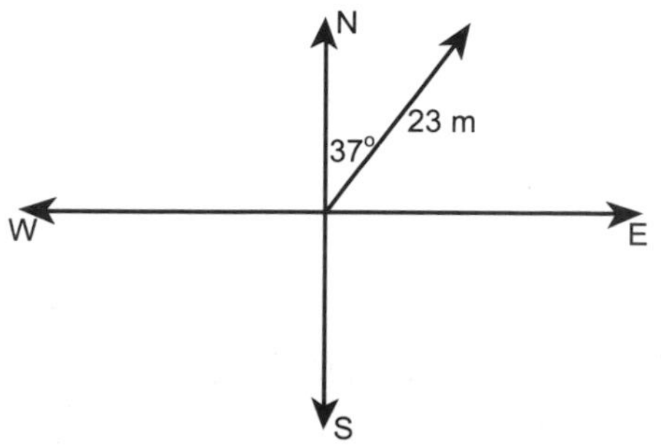

Name ______________________ Date ______________________

Describing Vectors from *x* and *y* Components

Given the x and y components, describe the resultant vector. Round magnitudes to the nearest tenth and directions to the nearest degree.

Example:

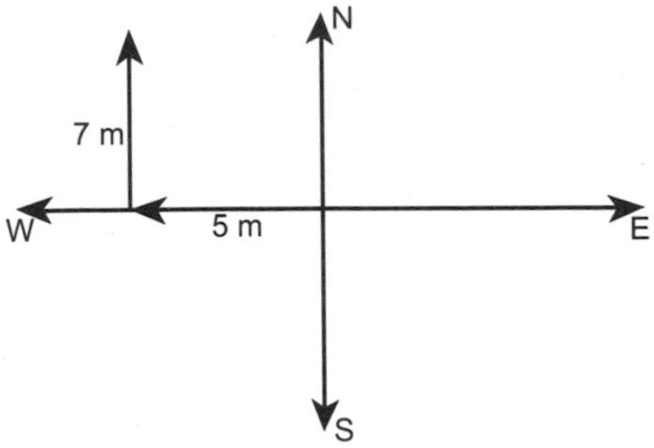

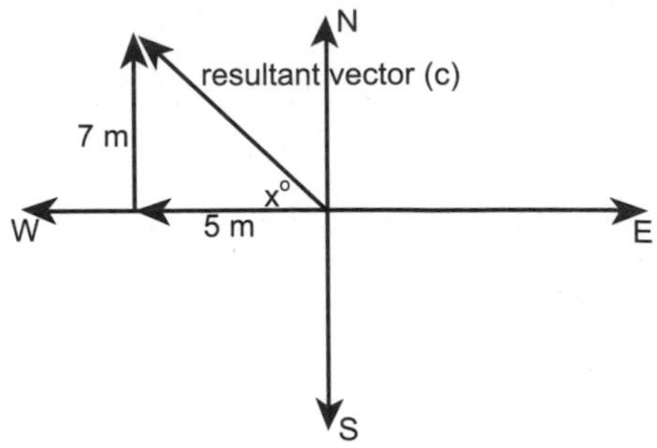

To find the magnitude, use the Pythagorean theorem

$c = \sqrt{a^2 + b^2} = \sqrt{7^2 + 5^2} = 8.602325 = 8.6$ m

To find the direction, use the trigonometric ratio.

$\tan x = \dfrac{\text{opposite}}{\text{adjacent}} = \dfrac{7}{5}$

$x = \tan^{-1}\left(\dfrac{7}{5}\right) = 54.4623222 = 54°$ North of West

1.

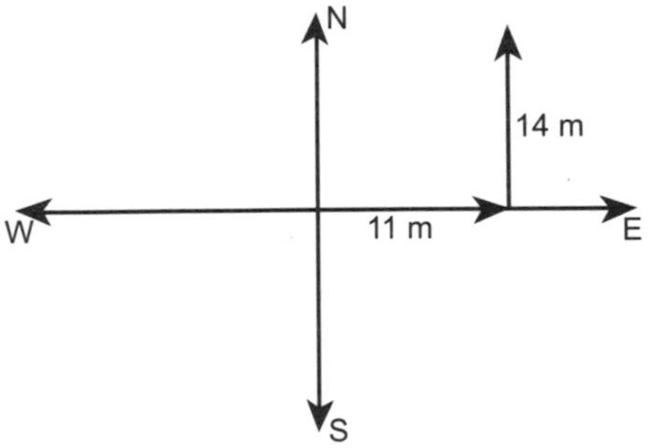

2.

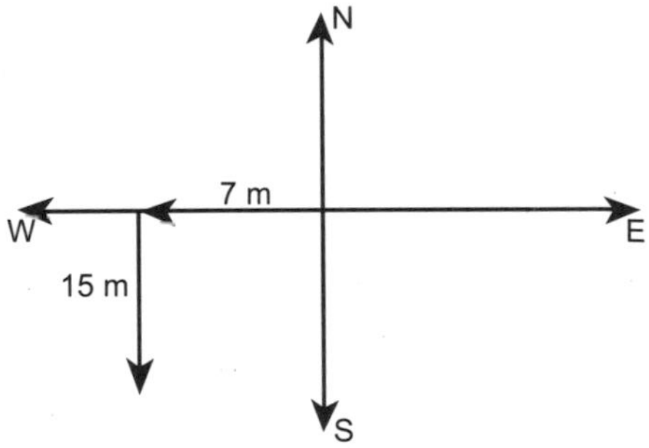

3.

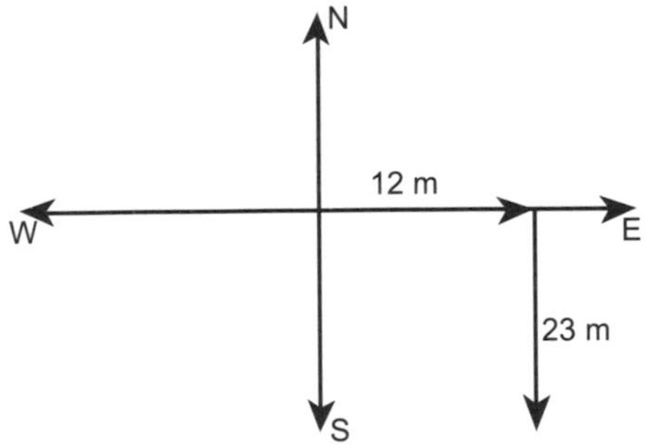

4.

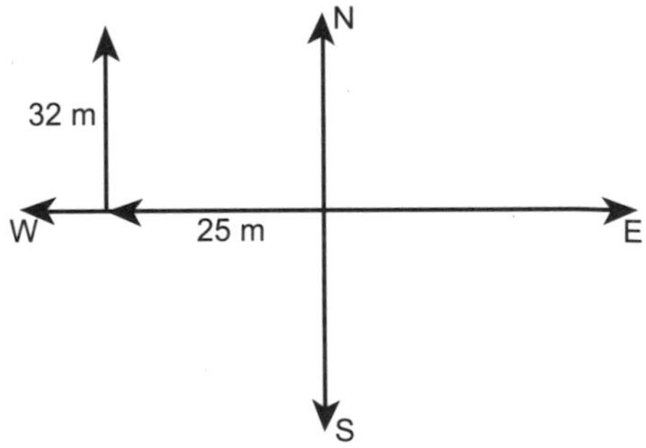

5.

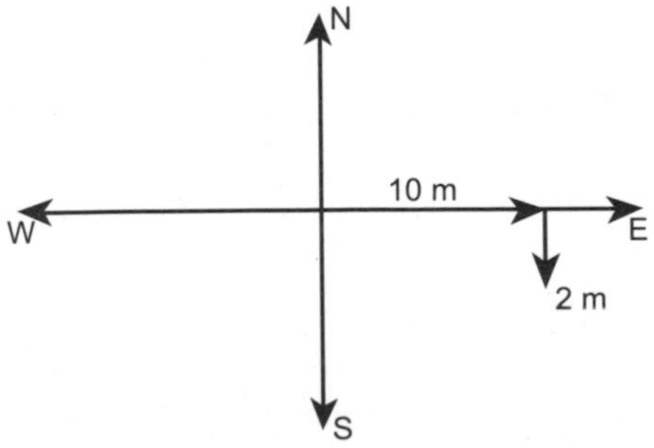

6.

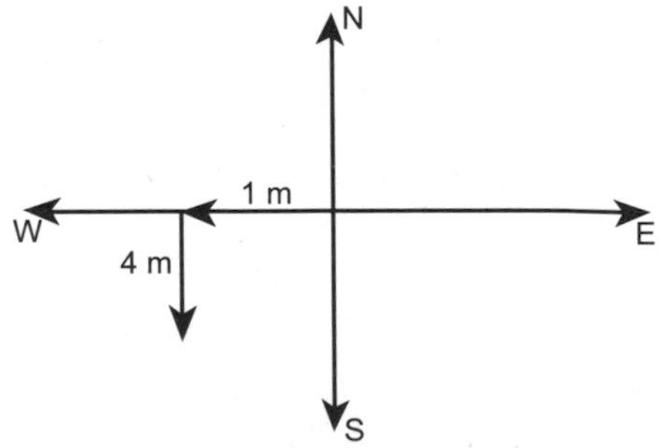

Name ____________________ Date ____________________

Problem Solving Involving Vectors

Draw a picture and solve each problem.

1. A boat is traveling directly across a river at 30 miles per hour. There is a current flowing down river at 5 miles per hour. What is the boat's resultant velocity vector?

2. An airplane pilot is traveling 500 miles per hour due south. He meets a wind current that is traveling 75 miles per hour due west. To continue flying due south, what adjustment in his navigation does he have to make?

3. A marathon runner runs 16 miles due north then 10 miles due west. What is his displacement?

4. In an explosion, a piece of debris is tossed 99 meters northwest. What is the displacement in the north and west directions?

5. A duck flies 402 miles at 30 degrees southwest for the winter. How far south does the duck actually travel?

Name ______________________ Date ______________________

Adding Vectors Algebraically

Given two vectors, describe their resultant algebraically. Round the magnitude to the nearest tenth and direction to the nearest degree.

1. 15 m 45 degrees north of east and 5 m 10 degrees south of east.

2. 25 m 35 degrees south of east and 8 m 60 degrees north of east.

3. 99 m 30 degrees south of west and 15 m 53 degrees north of west.

4. 4 m 75 degrees north of east and 12 m 20 degrees north of west.

5. 62 m 23 degrees south of east and 36 m 45 degrees north of east.

0-7424-1789-1 *Algebra*

Name ______________________ Date ______________________

Story Problems: Resolving Vectors

Draw a picture and solve each problem.

1. A glider is floating through the sky at 45 miles per hour with a heading of 50 degrees north of west when it meets a head wind of 10 miles per hour blowing 45 degrees south of east. What is its resultant velocity?

2. A river boat is crossing the Mississippi River at 12 miles per hour due north. The current in the mighty Mississippi is 5 miles per hour at 43 degrees south of west. What is the resulting velocity of the river boat?

3. A ship leaves port and sails 14 miles at 68 degrees south of west. Then the ship turns due east and sails 8 miles. How far is the ship from port and what heading would be the shortest way home?

4. A pilot wants to fly 430 miles per hour at 45 degrees north of east, but there is a westerly wind blowing 20 miles per hour. What course correction does the pilot have to make to fly on his desired heading?

5. A long-distance swimmer starts out swimming a steady 2 miles per hour at 30 degrees south of west. A 5 mile per hour current is flowing at 10 degrees north of east. What is the swimmer's resultant velocity?

0-7424-1789-1 *Algebra II*

Answer Key

Page 7

1.

x	y
$^{-}1$	9
0	6
1	3

2.

x	y
$^{-}1$	$^{-}3$
0	$^{-}2$
1	$^{-}1$

3.

x	y
$^{-}1$	0
0	$^{-}2$
1	$^{-}4$

4.

x	y
$^{-}1$	11/2
0	5/2
1	$^{-}1/2$

5.

x	y
$^{-}3$	1/2
0	3/2
3	5/2

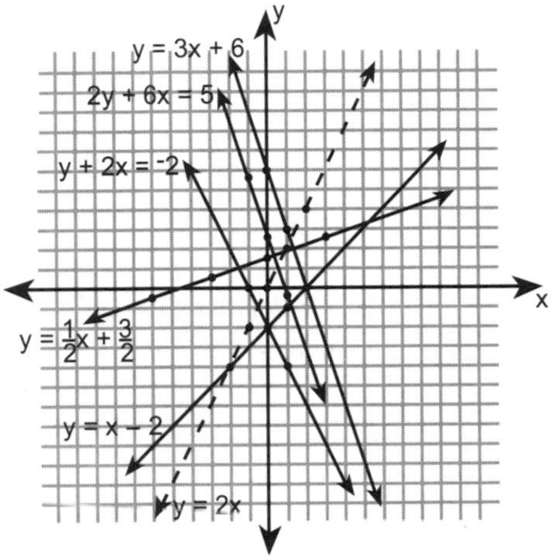

Page 8.

1. $\frac{^{-}2 + 12}{10 - 15} = \frac{10}{^{-}5} = {}^{-}2$
2. $\frac{^{-}12 - {}^{-}2}{5 - 15} = \frac{^{-}10}{^{-}10} = 1$
3. $\frac{14 - 28}{^{-}3 - {}^{-}1} = \frac{^{-}14}{^{-}2} = 7$
4. $\frac{6 - 6}{9 - 4} = 0$
5. $\frac{14 - {}^{-}9}{8 - 22} = \frac{23}{^{-}14}$
6. $\frac{59 - 0}{33 - 0} = \frac{59}{33}$
7. $\frac{21 - 6}{14 - 14} = \frac{^{-}15}{0}$ no slope
8. $\frac{17 - 9}{5 - {}^{-}18} = \frac{8}{23}$
9. $\frac{^{-}1 - 9}{16 - 8} = \frac{^{-}10}{8} = \frac{^{-}5}{4}$
10. $\frac{2 - 9}{^{-}4 - 6} = \frac{^{-}7}{^{-}10} = \frac{7}{10}$
11. $\frac{4 - {}^{-}3}{8 - 7} = \frac{7}{1} = 7$
12. $\frac{4 + 19}{^{-}15 + 1} = \frac{23}{^{-}14}$
13. $\frac{^{-}1 - 6}{^{-}8 - 6} = \frac{^{-}7}{^{-}14} = \frac{1}{2}$
14. #3 & #11; #5 & #12
15. #1 & #13; #4 & #7
16. Every vertical line is perpendicular to every horizontal line.

Page 9

1. slope: $^{-}1$, y-intercept: (0,0)
2. slope: 4, y-intercept: (0,0)
3. slope: $^{-}2$, y-intercept: (0,0)
4. slope: 0, y-intercept: (0,3)
5. slope: undefined, y-intercept: none
6. slope: 1, y-intercept: (0,1)
7. slope: $-\frac{1}{2}$, y-intercept: (0,$^{-}1$)

Page 10

1.

x	y
0	$^{-}6$
4	0

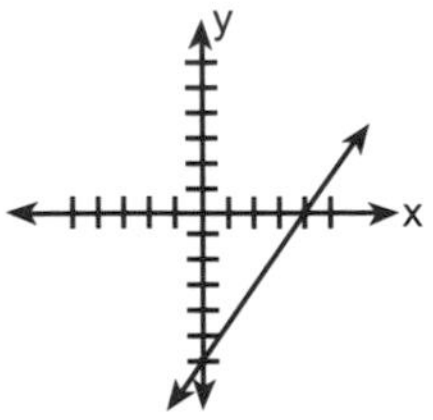

2.

x	y
0	5
$^{-}5$	0

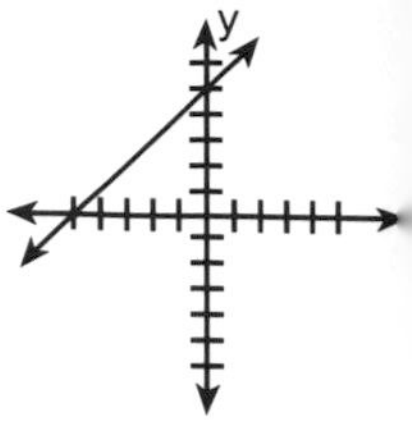

3.

x	y
0	$^{-}10$
2	0

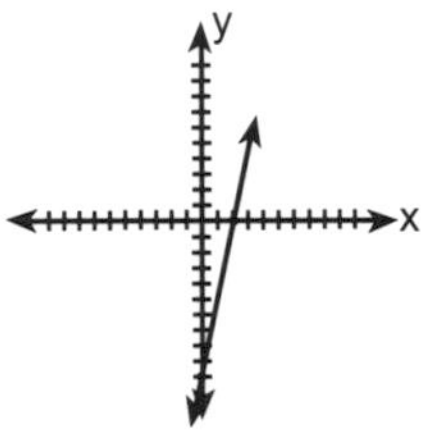

4.

x	y
0	5
10	0

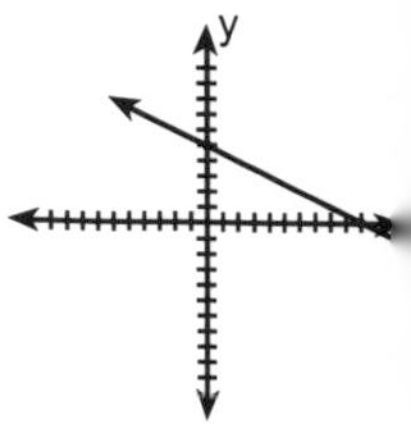

5.

x	y
0	5
$^{-}1$	0

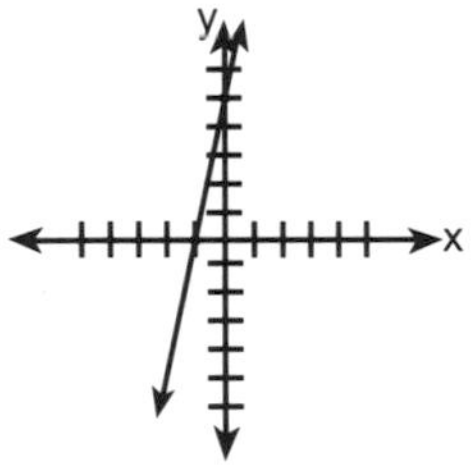

6.

x	y
0	$^{-}6$
2	0

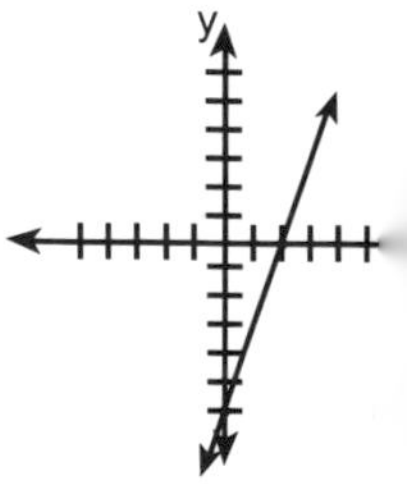

7.

x	y
0	$^{-}2$
$^{-}3$	0

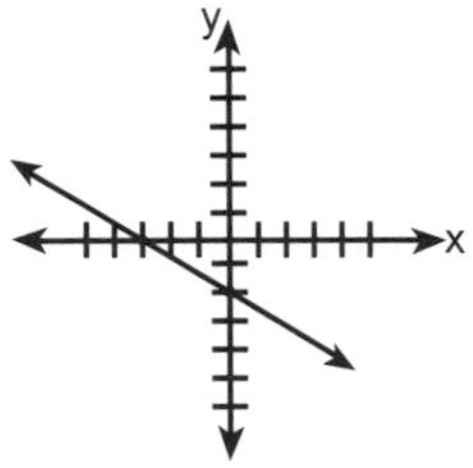

8.

x	y
0	$^{-}8$
1/2	0

9.

x	y
0	12
9	0

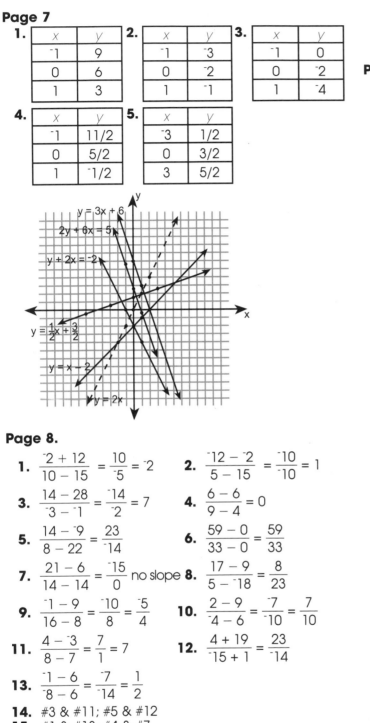

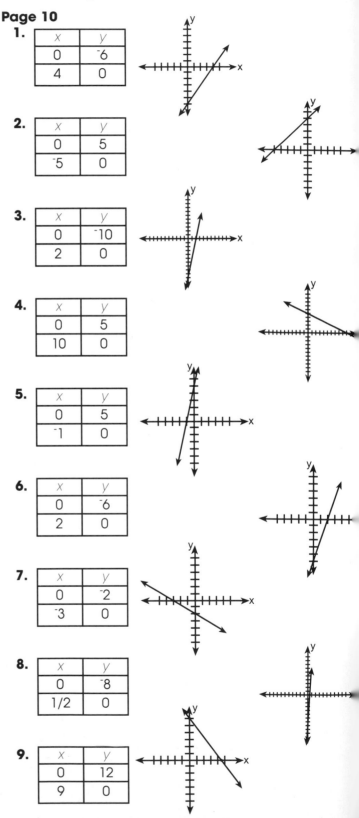

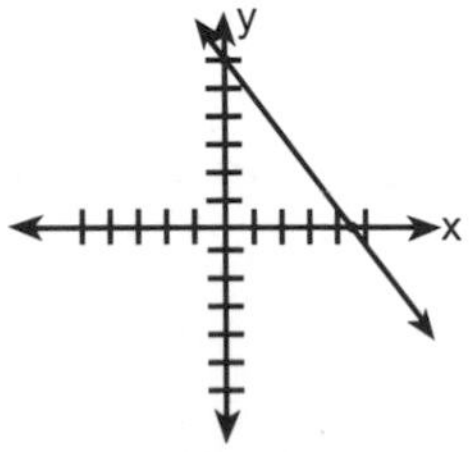

Answer Key

Page 11

1.

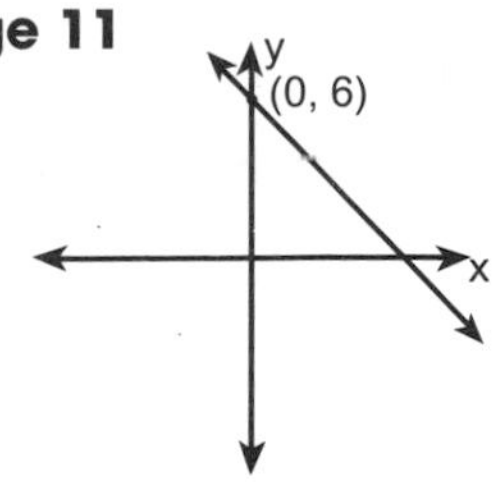

2.

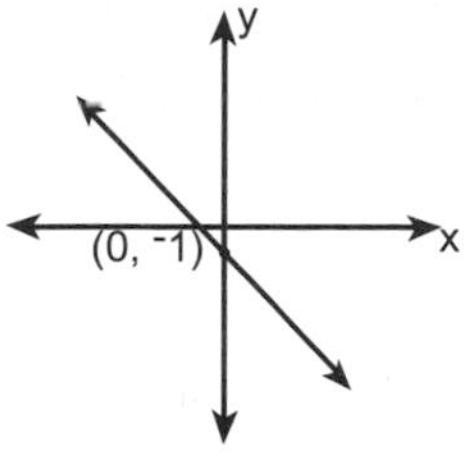

3.

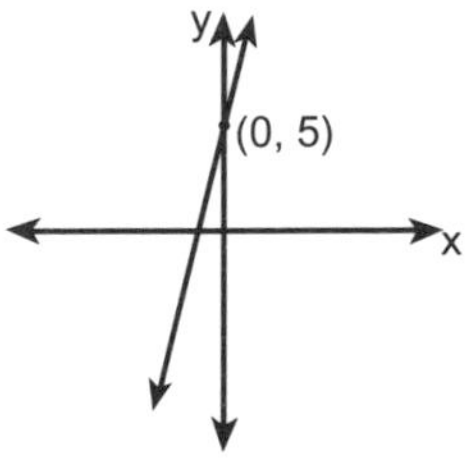

4.

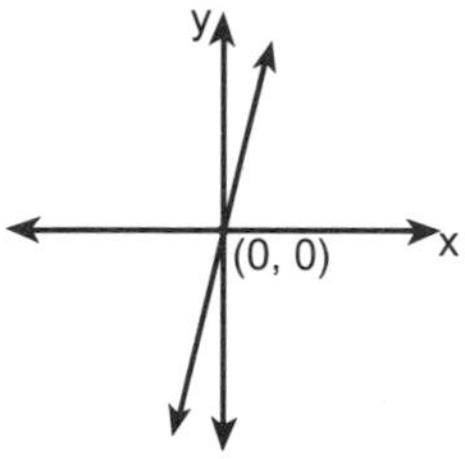

5.

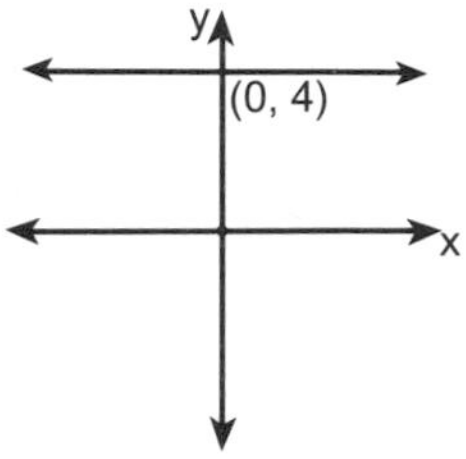

6.

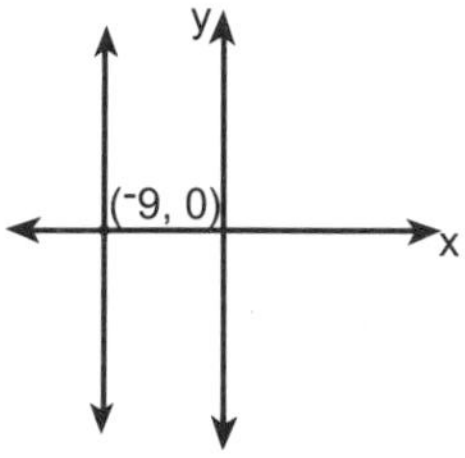

7.

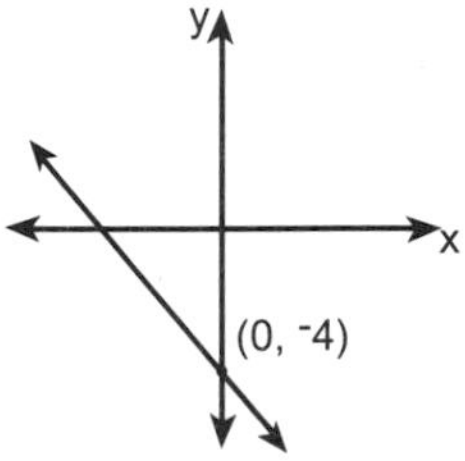

8.

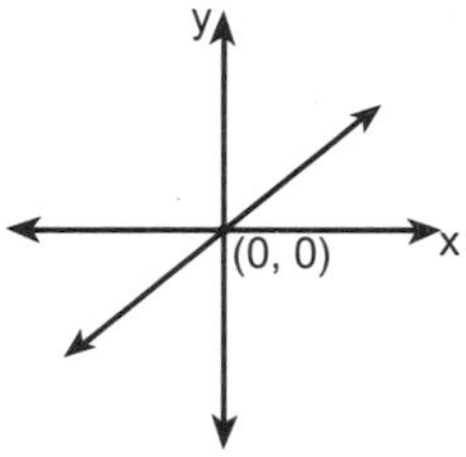

9.

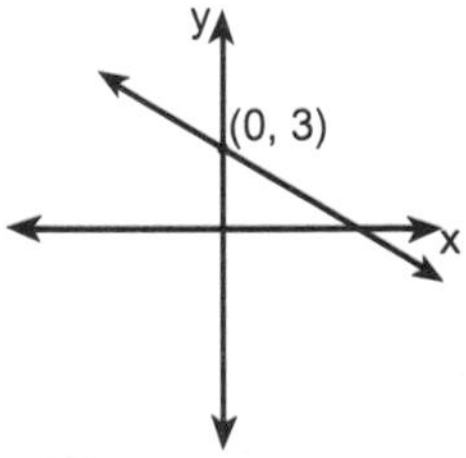

Page 12

1.

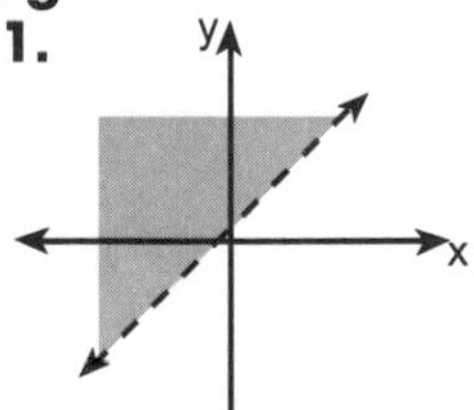

2.

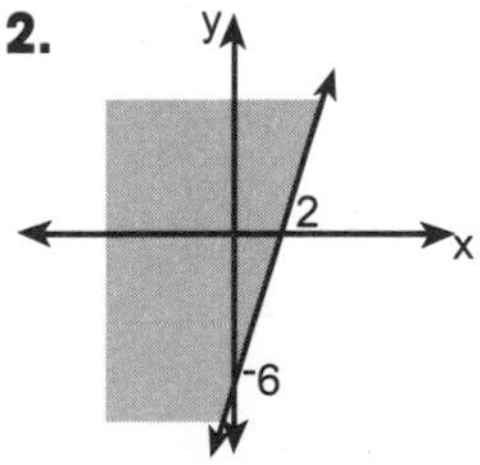

3.

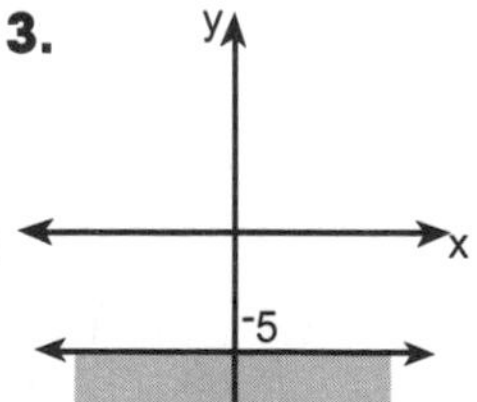

4.

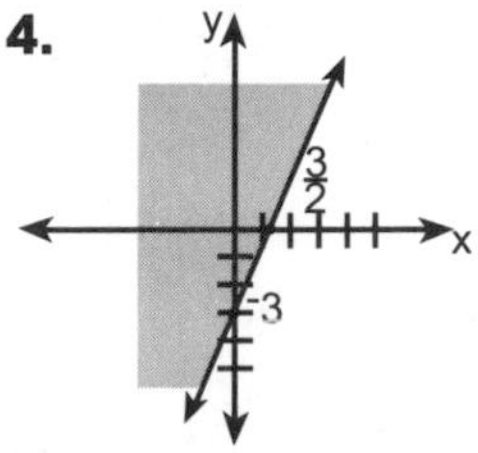

5.

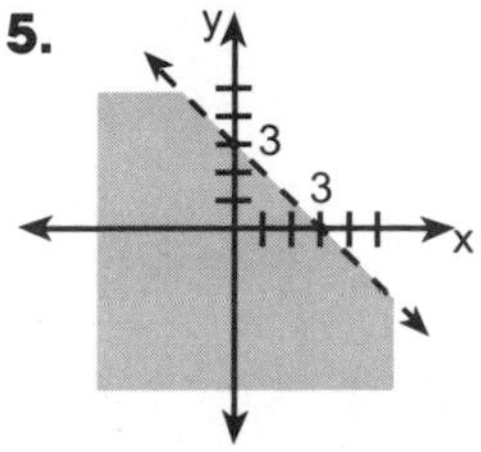

6.

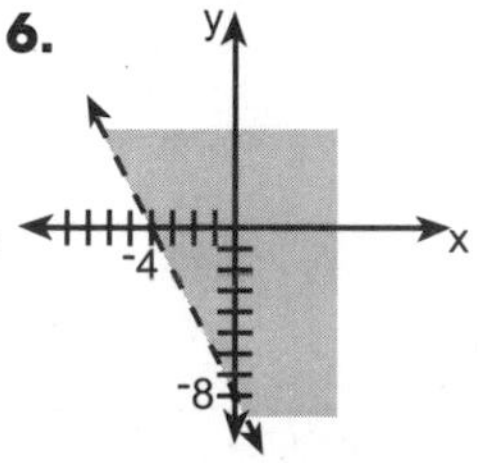

7.

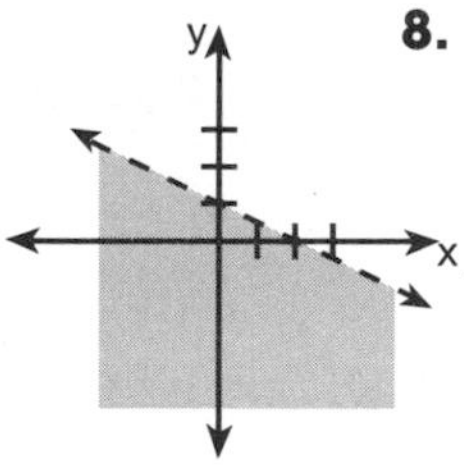

8.

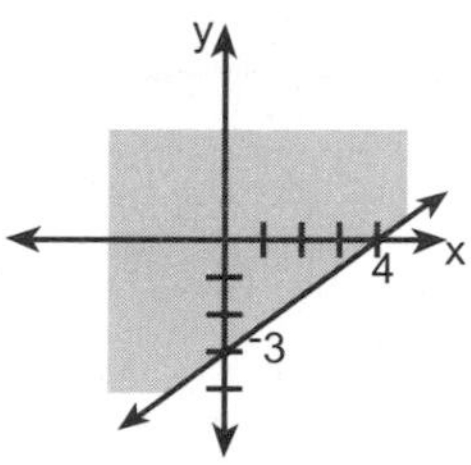

Page 13

1.

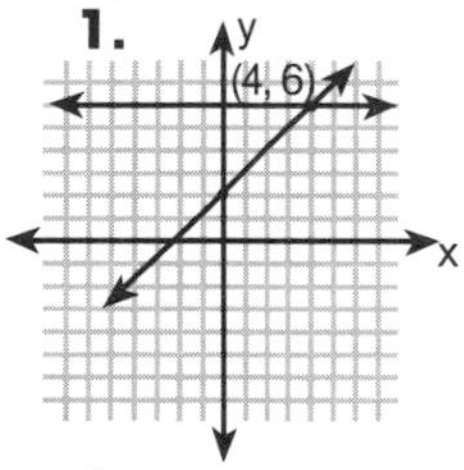

2.

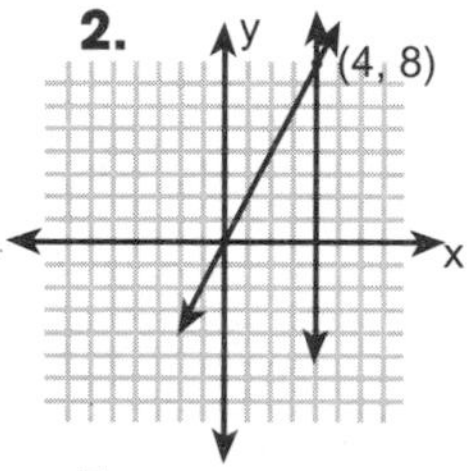

3.

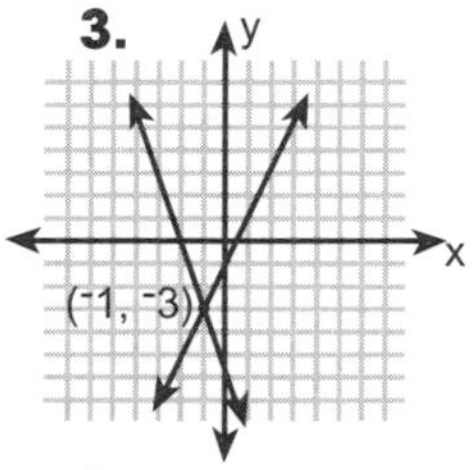

4.

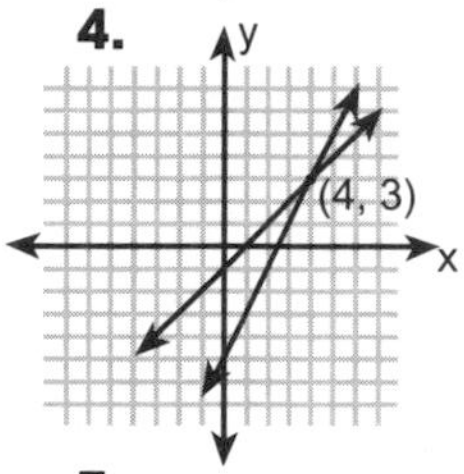

5.

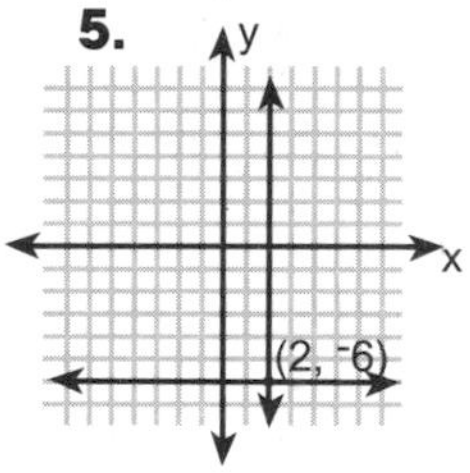

6.

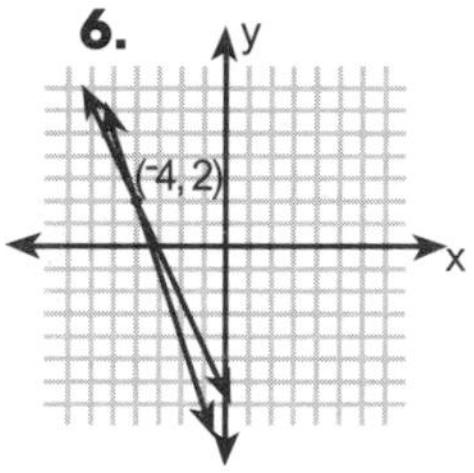

7.

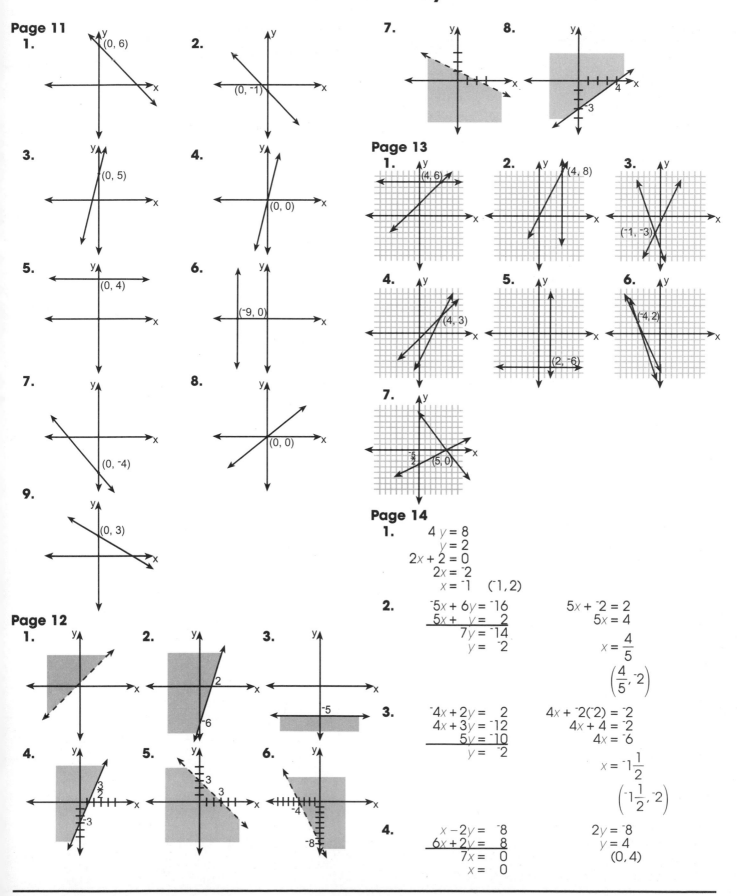

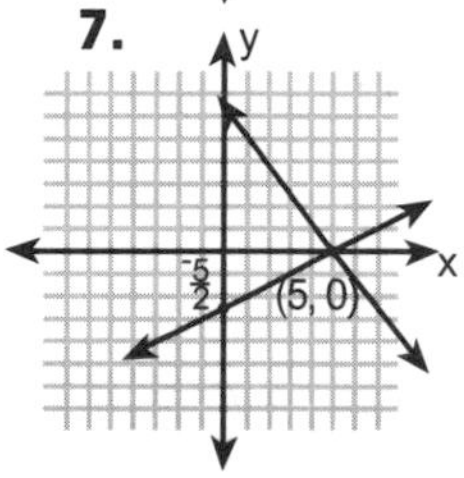

Page 14

1.

$4y = 8$
$y = 2$
$2x + 2 = 0$
$2x = {}^{-}2$
$x = {}^{-}1 \quad ({}^{-}1, 2)$

2.

$${}^{-}5x + 6y = {}^{-}16$$
$$\underline{5x + y = 2}$$
$$7y = {}^{-}14$$
$$y = {}^{-}2$$

$5x + {}^{-}2 = 2$
$5x = 4$
$x = \frac{4}{5}$
$\left(\frac{4}{5}, {}^{-}2\right)$

3.

$${}^{-}4x + 2y = 2$$
$$4x + 3y = {}^{-}12$$
$$\underline{5y = {}^{-}10}$$
$$y = {}^{-}2$$

$4x + {}^{-}2({}^{-}2) = {}^{-}2$
$4x + 4 = {}^{-}2$
$4x = {}^{-}6$
$x = {}^{-}1\frac{1}{2}$
$\left({}^{-}1\frac{1}{2}, {}^{-}2\right)$

4.

$$x - 2y = {}^{-}8$$
$$\underline{6x + 2y = 8}$$
$$7x = 0$$
$$x = 0$$

$2y = {}^{-}8$
$y = 4$
$(0, 4)$

Answer Key

Page 15

1. $x + 3x = 8$
$4x = 8$
$x = 2 \quad y = 3(2) = 6 \quad (2, 6)$

2. $2(3y - 3) = 3y$
$6y - 6 = 3y$
$3y = 6$
$y = 2 \quad x = 3(2) - 3 = 6 - 3 = 3 \quad (3, 2)$

3. $x + (x - 2) = 0$
$2x - 2 = 0$
$2x = 2$
$x = 1 \quad y = 1 - 2 = {}^-1 \quad (1, {}^-1)$

4. $3x - 2\left(\frac{{}^-5}{4}\right)x = 20$
$\frac{3}{2}x + \frac{5}{2}x = 20$
$\frac{8}{2}x = \frac{20}{1} \cdot \frac{2}{8} = \frac{40}{8}$
$x = 5$
$y = \frac{{}^-5}{4}(5) = \frac{{}^-25}{4} \quad \left(5, \frac{{}^-25}{4}\right)$

Page 16

1.
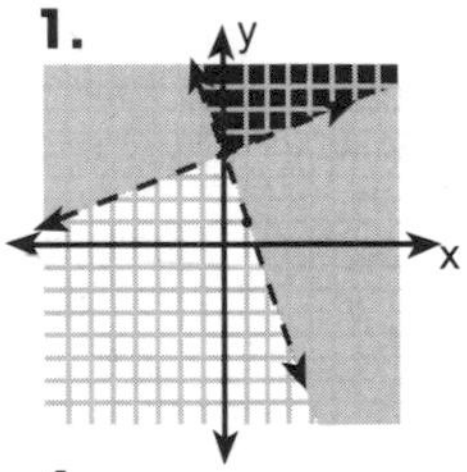

2.
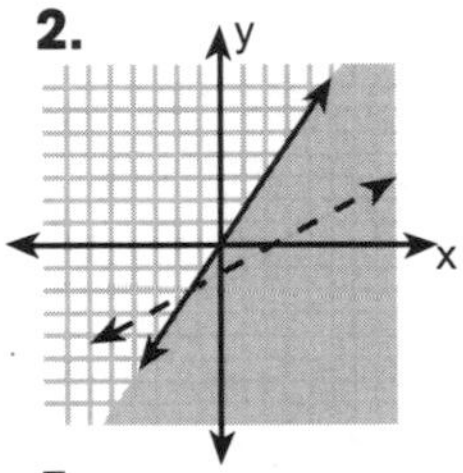

3.
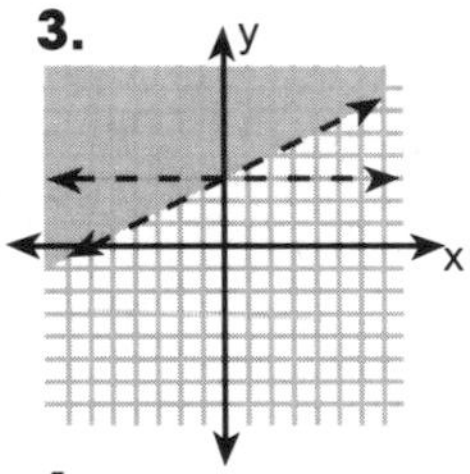

4.
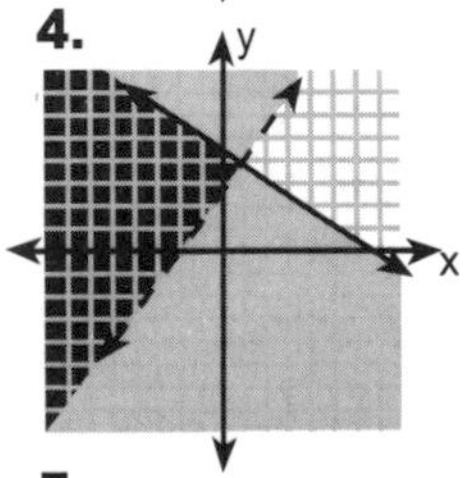

5.
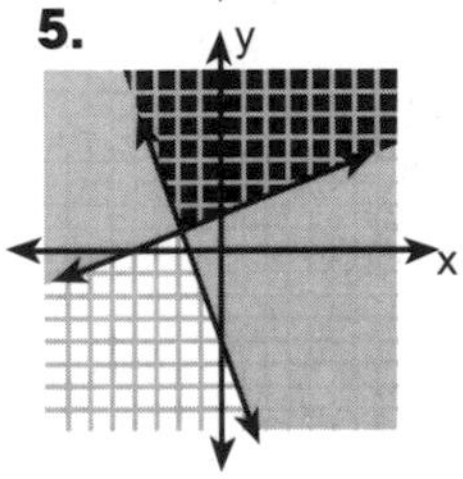

6.
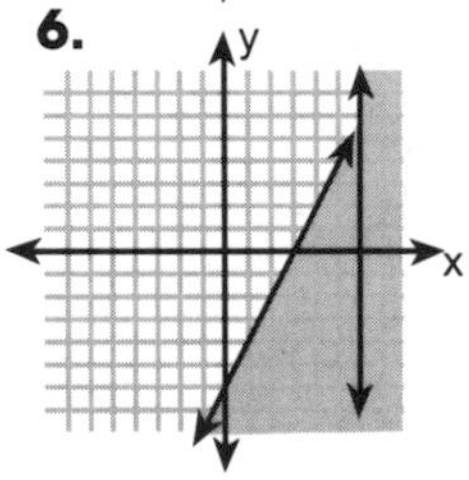

7.
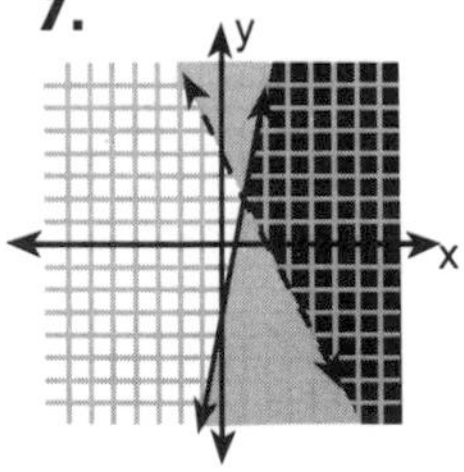

Page 17

1. $2x - 4y = 18$
${}^-12x + 4y = {}^-88$
${}^-10x = {}^-70$
$x = 7$
$2(7) - 4y = 18$
$14 - 4y = 18$
${}^-4y = 4$
$y = {}^-1$
$(7, {}^-1)$

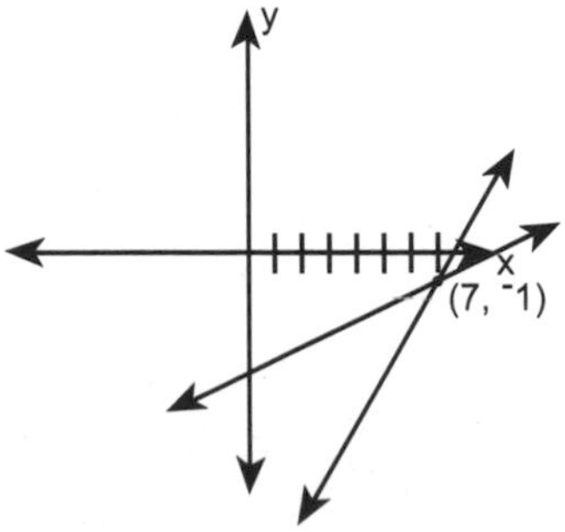

2. $3({}^-6y) + 10y = 16$
${}^-18y + 10y = 16$
${}^-8y = 16$
$y = {}^-2$
$x = {}^-6({}^-2) = 12$
$(12, {}^-2)$

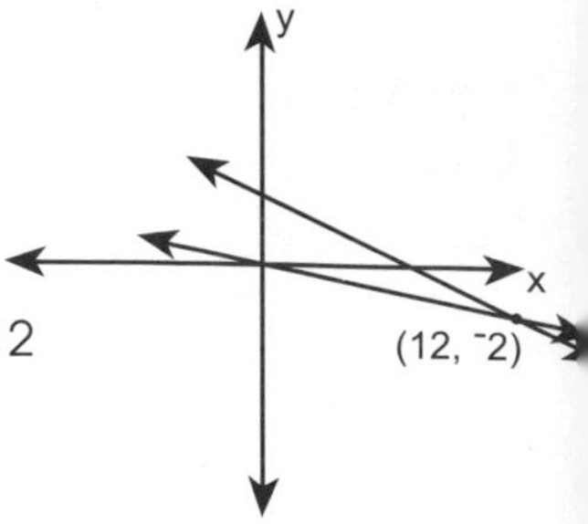

3. ${}^-3x + 2(5x) = {}^-28$
${}^-3x + 10x = {}^-28$
$7x = {}^-28$
$x = {}^-4$
$y = 5({}^-4) = {}^-20$
$({}^-4, {}^-20)$

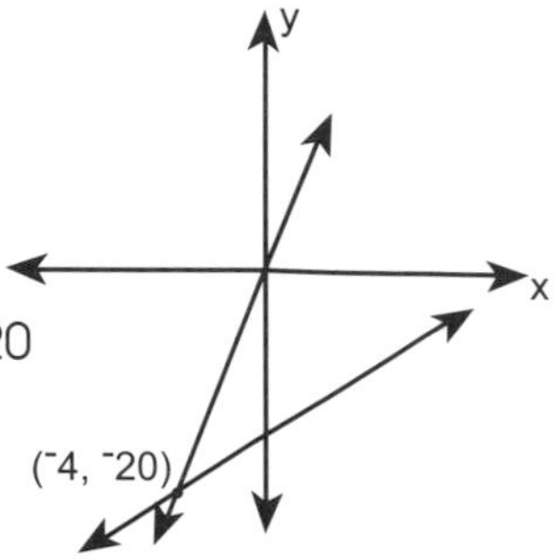

4. $28x - 35y = {}^-133$
$15x + 35y = 90$
$43x = 43$
$x = {}^-1$
${}^-3x + 7y = 18$
$7y = 21$
$y = 3$
$({}^-1, 3)$

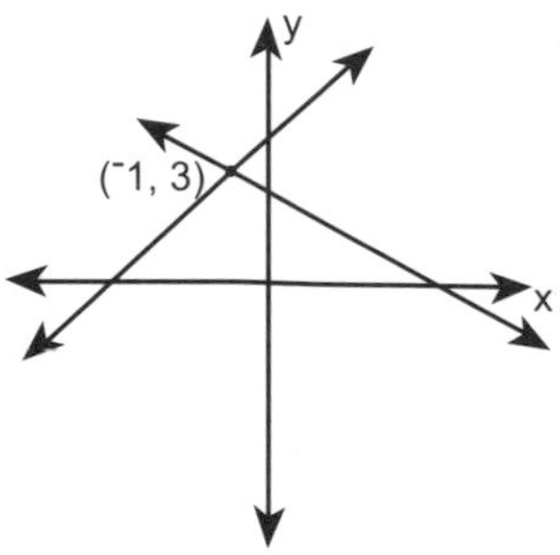

5. $5x - 6(4) = 11$
$5x = 35$
$x = 7$
$(7, 4)$

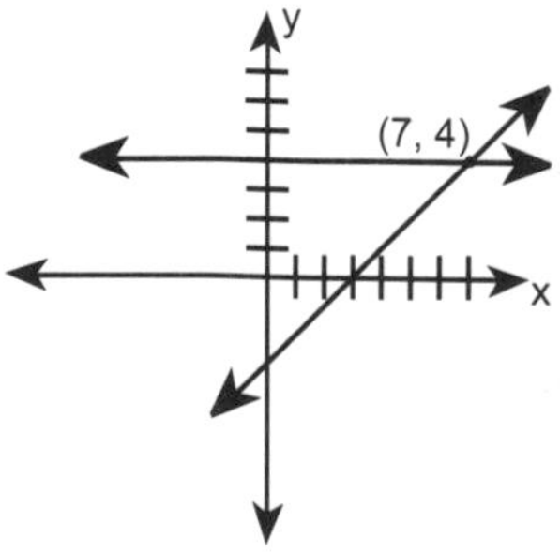

6. $2x - (x - 4) = \frac{{}^-5}{2}$
$2x - x + 4 = \frac{{}^-5}{2}$
$x = \frac{{}^-5}{2} - \frac{8}{2}$
$x = \frac{{}^-13}{2}$
$y = \frac{{}^-13}{2} - \frac{8}{2} = \frac{{}^-21}{2}$
$\left(\frac{{}^-13}{2}, \frac{{}^-21}{2}\right)$

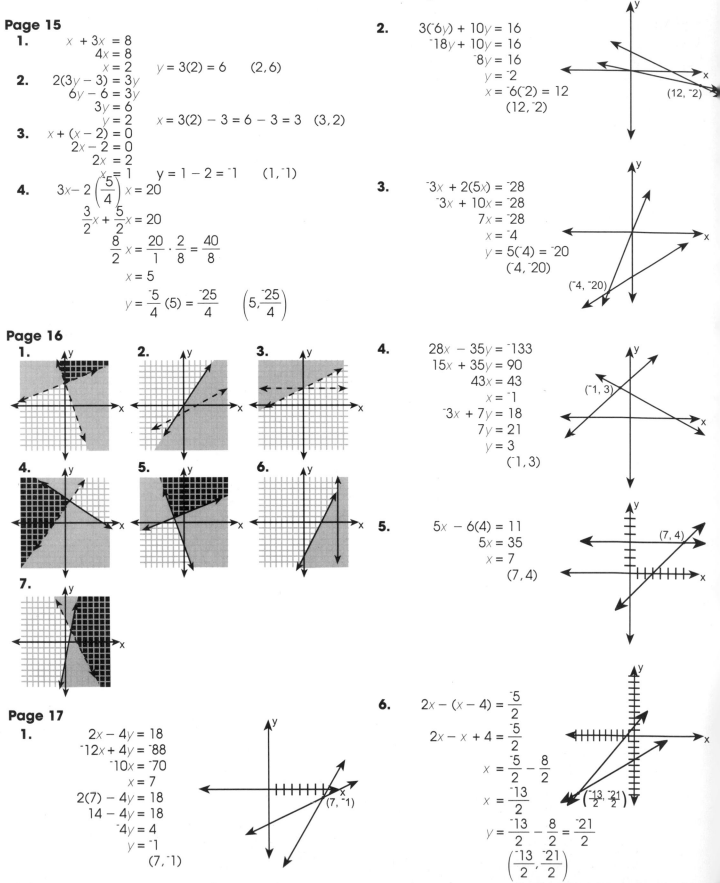

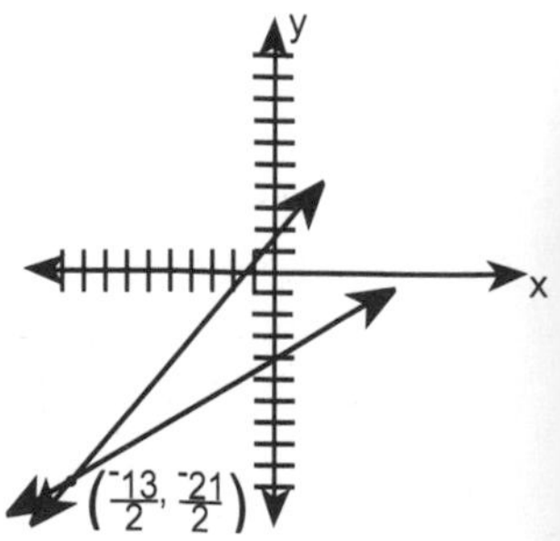

Answer Key

Page 18

1.

x	y
-2	8
-1	2
0	0
1	2
2	8

2.

x	y
-2	-4
-1	-1
0	0
1	-1
2	-4

3.

x	y
-2	-12
-1	-3
0	0
1	-3
2	-12

4.

x	y
-3	3
-1	1/3
0	0
1	1/3
3	3

5.

x	y
-4	-8
-2	-2
0	0
2	-2
4	-8

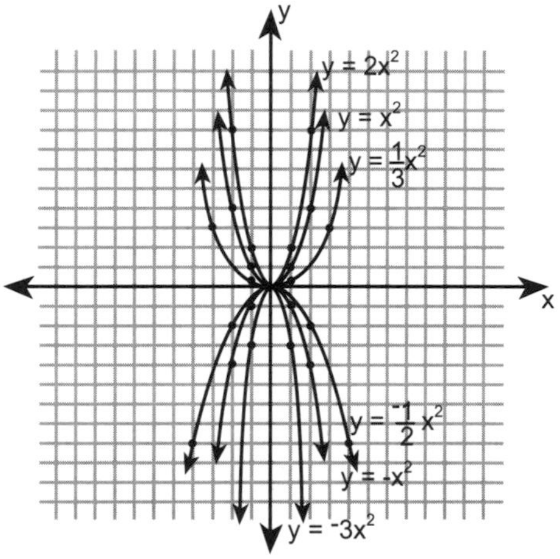

If $a > 1$, the graph narrows.
If $a < 1$, the graph widens.
$-a$ turns the graph upside down.

Page 19

1.

x	y
-2	2
-1	-1
0	-2
1	-1
2	2

2.

x	y
-2	8
-1	2
0	0
1	2
2	8

3.

x	y
-4	-1
-2	-7
0	-9
2	-7
4	-1

4.

x	y
-2	-6
-1	3
0	6
1	3
2	-6

5.

x	y
-3	3
-1	$-2\frac{1}{3}$
0	-3
1	$-2\frac{1}{3}$
3	3

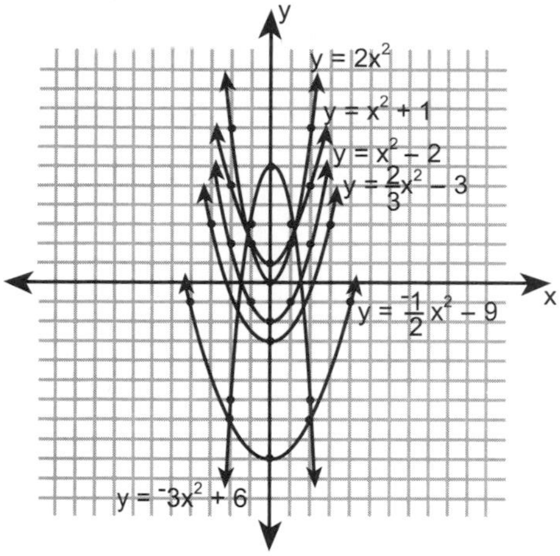

C moves the graph up C.
$-C$ moves the graph down C.

Page 20

1.

x	y
-5	8
-4	2
-3	0
-2	2
-1	8

2.

x	y
2	3
3	$1\frac{1}{3}$
5	0
7	$1\frac{1}{3}$
8	3

3.

x	y
5	-8
6	-2
7	0
8	-2
9	-8

4.

x	y
-5	1
-4	$-\frac{1}{2}$
-3	-1
-2	$-\frac{1}{2}$
-1	1

5.

x	y
-10	-3
-9	0
-8	1
-7	0
-6	-3

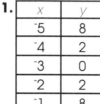

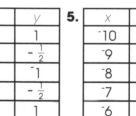

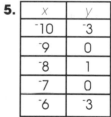

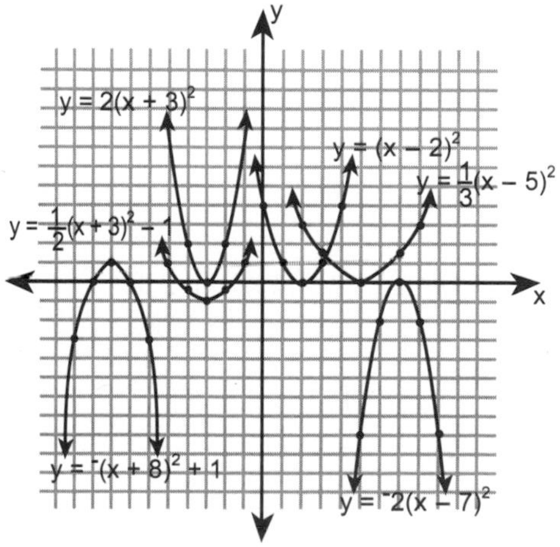

B moves the graph left b units.
$-B$ moves the graph right b units.

Answer Key

Page 21

1. $(2x + 1)(2x - 1)$
2. $(x - 3)(x + 3)$
3. $9(4x^2 - 1)$
$9(2x - 1)(2x + 1)$
4. $(10x - 9)(10x + 9)$
5. $(5x - 2)(5x + 2)$
6. $(9x - 11)(9x + 11)$
7. $(x - 4)(x + 4)$
8. $16(9x^2 - 1)$
$16(3x - 1)(3x + 1)$
9. $(x - 5)(x + 5)$
10. $(25 - 4x)(25 + 4x)$
11. $(10 - x)(10 + x)$
12. $(x - 6)(x + 6)$

$(x + 13)(x - 13)$ THE	~~$16(3x - 1)(3x + 1)$ SUM~~	~~$(x - 4)(x + 4)$ OFA~~	$(6x + 5)(6x - 5)$ PRO	~~$(25 - 4x)(25 + 4x)$ QUO~~	$(x + 1)(x - 1)$ DUC
$(9 + x)(9 - x)$ TOF	~~$9(2x - 1)(2x + 1)$ TIE~~	$(x + 7)(x - 7)$ THE	~~$(2x + 1)(2x - 1)$ NTA~~	$(9x + 1)(9x - 1)$ SUM	$(x + 2)(x - 2)$ AND
~~$(10 - x)(10 + x)$ WAS~~	$(5x + 3)(5x - 3)$ DIF	~~$(x - 5)(x + 5)$ HAS~~	$(8x + 1)(8x - 1)$ FER	~~$(11x - 7)(11x + 7)$ MAN~~	~~$(x - 6)(x + 6)$ NER~~
$(x + 18)(x - 18)$ ENC	~~$(10x - 9)(10x + 9)$ THA~~	~~$(x - 3)(x + 3)$ TIS~~	~~$(5x - 2)(5x + 2)$ MYP~~	$(7x + 11)(7x - 11)$ EOF	$(x + 8)(x - 8)$ THE
$(x + 15)(x - 15)$ SQU	~~$(9x - 11)(9x + 11)$ ROB~~	$(x + 9)(x - 9)$ ARE	$(3x + 2)(3x - 2)$ ROO	~~$(7x - 4)(7x + 4)$ LEM~~	$(x + 9)(x - 9)$ TS.

15. The factored form of the difference of the two squares is

T H E P R O D U C T O F T H E S U M A N D
D I F F E R E N C E O F T H E S Q U A R E
R O O T S .

Page 22

1. $(x - 6)(x - 6)$
2. $(x + 12)(x + 12)$
3. $(x - 18)(x + 2)$
4. $(x - 11)(x + 2)$
5. $(x + 16)(x + 2)$
6. $(x - 8)(x + 7)$
7. $(3x + 2)(2x + 1)$
8. $(3x + 8)(x - 2)$
9. $(3x - 4)(2x + 1)$
10. $(5x - 2)(3x + 1)$
11. $(6x + 1)(3x + 1)$
12. $(5x + 2)(4x + 1)$
13. $(5x - 1)(x - 5)$
14. $(x - 10)(x + 1)$

Page 23

1. $a = 1 \quad b = {}^-2 \quad c = 1$

$$\left(\frac{{}^-({}^-2)}{2(1)}, \frac{{}^-({}^-2)^2}{4(1)} + 1\right) = (1, 0)$$

2. $a = 8 \quad b = {}^-16 \quad c = 1$

$$\left(\frac{{}^-({}^-16)}{2(8)}, \frac{{}^-({}^-16)^2}{4(8)} + 1\right) = (1, {}^-7)$$

3. $a = {}^-3 \quad b = 6 \quad c = 1$

$$\left(\frac{{}^-(6)}{2({}^-3)}, \frac{{}^-(6)^2}{4({}^-3)} + {}^-1\right) = (1, 2)$$

4. $a = 1 \quad b = 0 \quad c = 9$

$$\left(\frac{{}^-0}{2(1)}, \frac{{}^-(0)^2}{4(1)} + {}^-9\right) = (0, {}^-9)$$

5. $a = 2 \quad b = 0 \quad c = 1$

$$\left(\frac{{}^-0}{4(2)}, \frac{{}^-(0)^2}{4(2)} + 1\right) = (0, 1)$$

6. $a = 1 \quad b = 0 \quad c = 0 \quad (0,0)$

7. $a = {}^-10 \quad b = 0 \quad c = 0 \quad (0,0)$

8. $a = 2 \quad b = 6 \quad c = 0$

$$\left(\frac{{}^-6}{2(2)}, \frac{{}^-(6)^2}{4(2)} + 0\right) = \left(\frac{{}^-3}{2}, \frac{{}^-9}{2}\right)$$

9. $a = {}^-4 \quad b = 0 \quad c = {}^-7$

$$\left(\frac{{}^-0}{2({}^-4)}, \frac{{}^-(0)^2}{4({}^-4)} + {}^-7\right) = (0, {}^-7)$$

Answer Key

Page 24

1. $\dfrac{^-(^-14) \pm \sqrt{(^-14)^2 - 4(3)(1)}}{2(3)} = \dfrac{14 \pm \sqrt{184}}{6}$

$= \dfrac{7 \pm \sqrt{46}}{3}$

2. $\dfrac{^-(^-1) \pm \sqrt{(^-1)^2 - 4(2)(^-1)}}{2(2)} = \dfrac{1 \pm \sqrt{9}}{4}$

$= \dfrac{1 \pm 3}{4} = 1 \text{ and } \dfrac{^-1}{2}$

3. $\dfrac{^-(^-6) \pm \sqrt{36 - 4(^-3)(1)}}{2(^-3)} = \dfrac{6 \pm \sqrt{48}}{^-6}$

$= \dfrac{6 \pm 4\sqrt{3}}{^-6} = \dfrac{3 \pm 2\sqrt{3}}{^-3}$

4. $\dfrac{^-1 \pm \sqrt{1 - 4(3)(0)}}{2(3)} = \dfrac{^-1 \pm 1}{6}$

$= 0 \text{ and } \dfrac{^-1}{3}$

5. $\dfrac{14 \pm \sqrt{(^-14)2 - 4(^-7)^0}}{^-14} = 14 \pm \sqrt{196 - 0}$

$= \dfrac{14 \pm 14}{^-14} = {^-2}, 0$

6. $\dfrac{^-0 \pm \sqrt{0^2 - 4(4)(^-9)}}{2(4)} = \dfrac{\pm\sqrt{144}}{8}$

$= \dfrac{\pm 12}{8} = \dfrac{3}{2} \text{ and } \dfrac{^-3}{2}$

7. $\dfrac{^-0 \pm \sqrt{0^2 - 4(1)(^-2)}}{2(1)} = \dfrac{\pm\sqrt{8}}{2}$

$= \dfrac{\pm 2\sqrt{2}}{2} = \sqrt{2} \text{ and } {^-\sqrt{2}}$

8. $x^2 - x = 6$

$= \dfrac{1 \pm \sqrt{1 - (4)(1)(^-6)}}{2} = \dfrac{1 \pm \sqrt{25}}{2}$

$= \dfrac{1 \pm 5}{2} = 3 \text{ and } {^-2}$

9. $2x^2 + 6x + 0 = \dfrac{^-6 \pm \sqrt{36}}{4}$

$= \dfrac{^-6 \pm 6}{4} = 0 \text{ and } {^-3}$

Page 25

1. $y = (x - 6)(x - 2)$
$x = 6, 2$

$v = \left(\dfrac{8}{2}, \dfrac{^-64}{4} + 12\right)$

$= (4, ^-4)$

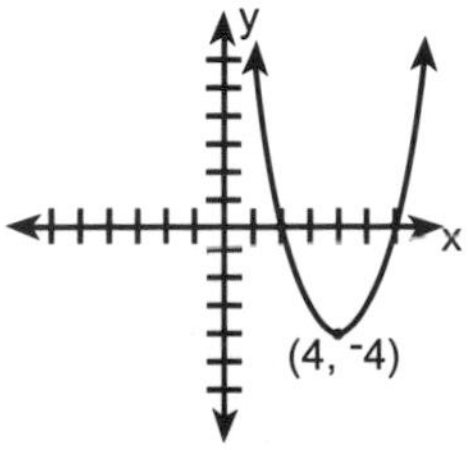

2. $y = (3x + 1)(2x - 4)$

$x = \dfrac{^-1}{3}, 2$

$v = \left(\dfrac{10}{12}, \dfrac{^-100}{24} - 4\right)$

$= \left(\dfrac{5}{6}, \dfrac{^-196}{24}\right) = \left(\dfrac{5}{6}, \dfrac{^-49}{6}\right)$

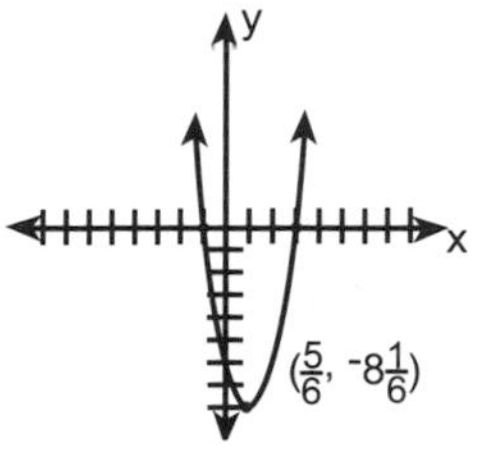

3. $y = (^-5x + 2)(3x + 1)$

$x = \dfrac{2}{5}, \dfrac{^-1}{3}$

$v = \left(\dfrac{1}{30}, \dfrac{121}{60}\right)$

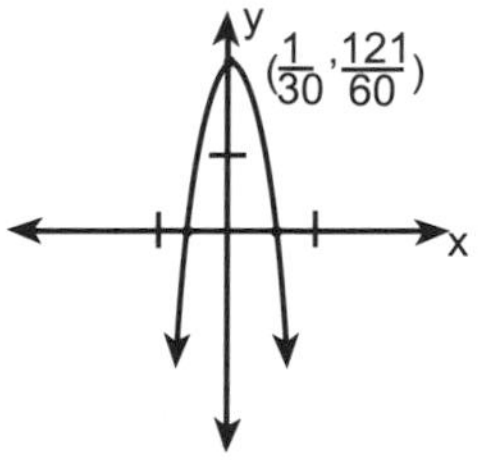

4. $x = {^-4}, 4$
$v = (0, ^-16)$

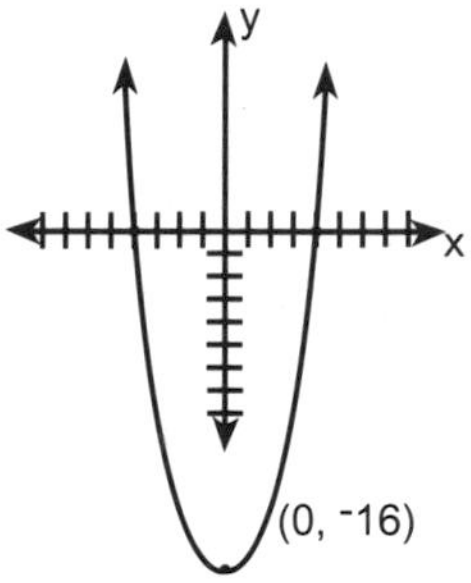

5. $y = x^2 + x - 6$
$x = 2, ^-3$

$v = \left(\dfrac{^-1}{2}, \dfrac{^-1}{4} - 6\right)$

$\left(\dfrac{^-1}{2}, \dfrac{^-25}{4}\right)$

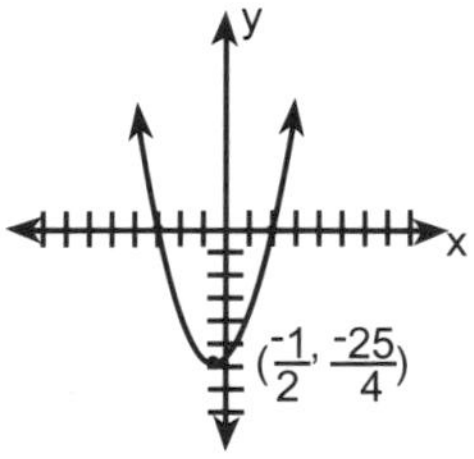

6. $y = x^2 - 25$
$x = \pm 25$
$v = (0, ^-25)$

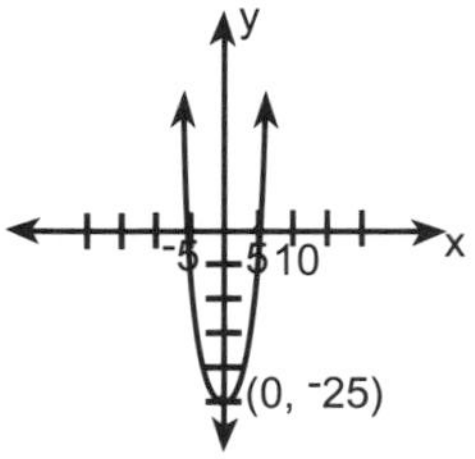

7. $y = (x + 3)(x + 2)$
$x = {^-3} \qquad x = {^-2}$

$v = \left(\dfrac{^-5}{2}, \dfrac{25}{4} - 6\right)$

$\left(\dfrac{^-5}{2}, \dfrac{1}{4}\right)$

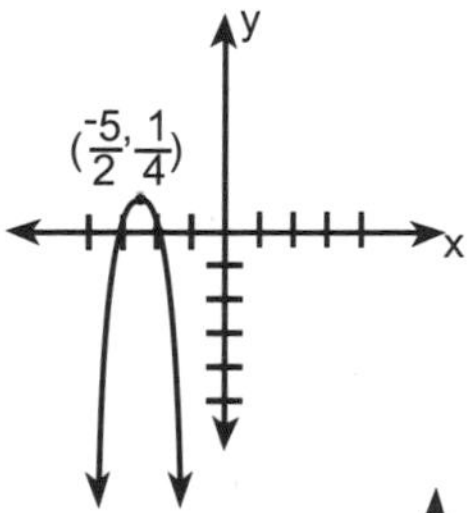

8. $x = \pm 0$
$v = (0, 0)$

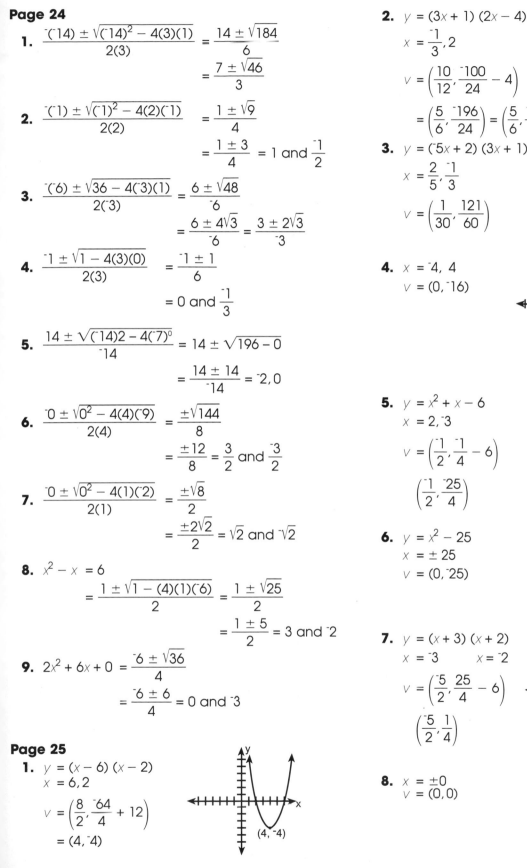

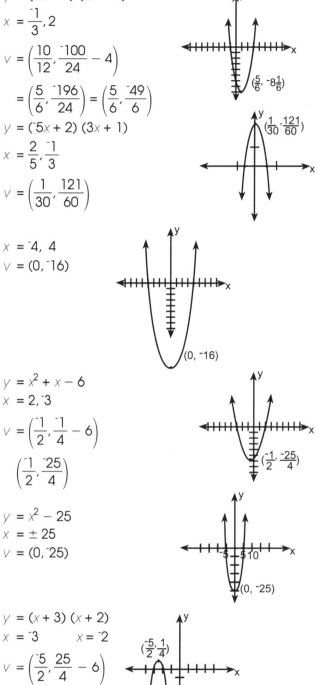

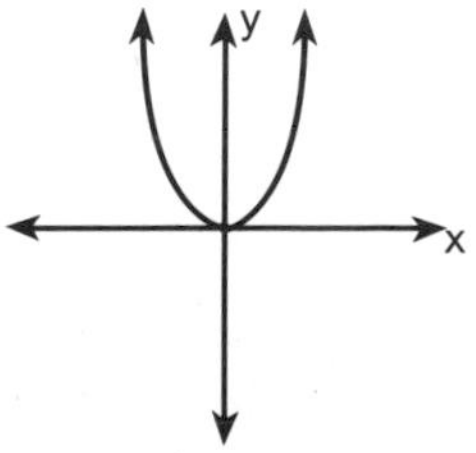

Answer Key

Page 26

1.

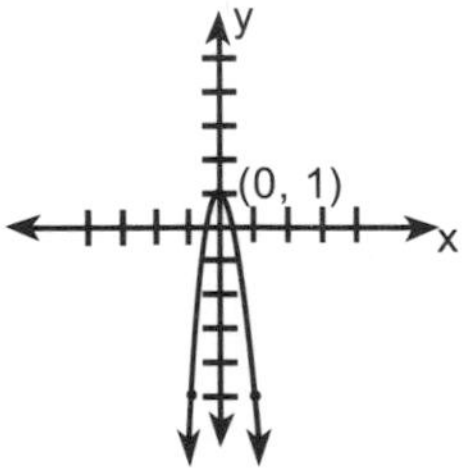

2.

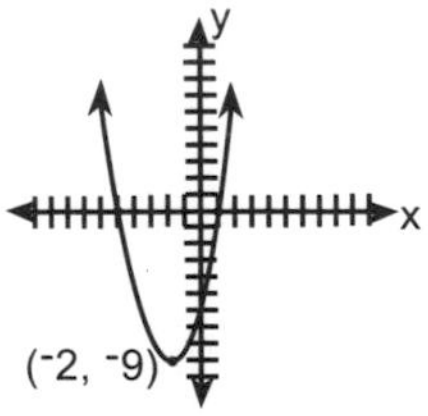

3.

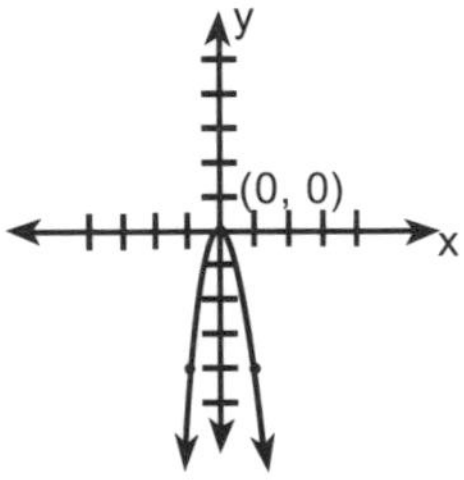

4.

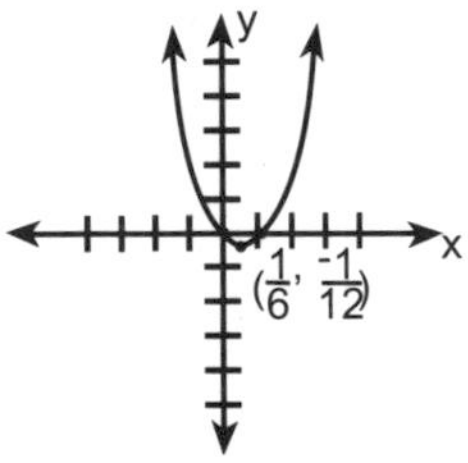

5.

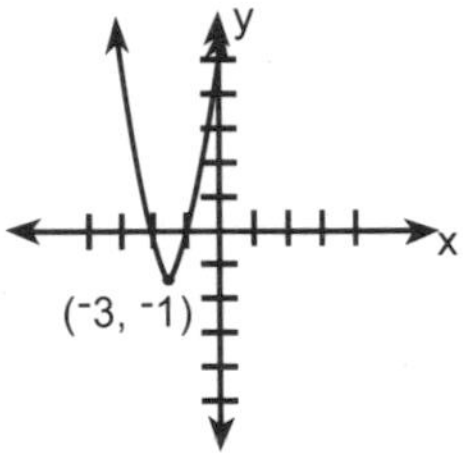

6.

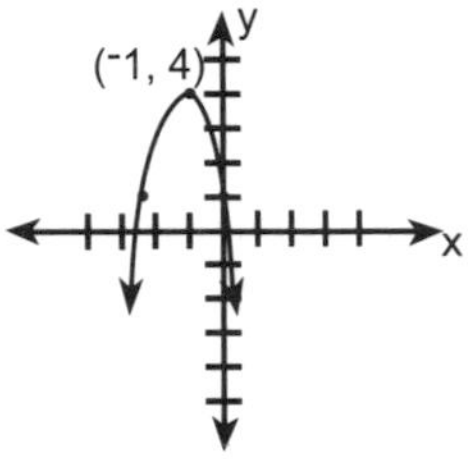

7.

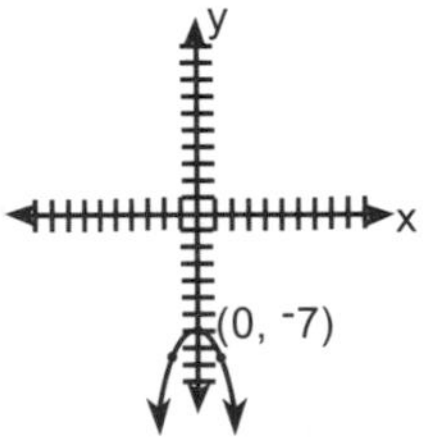

8.

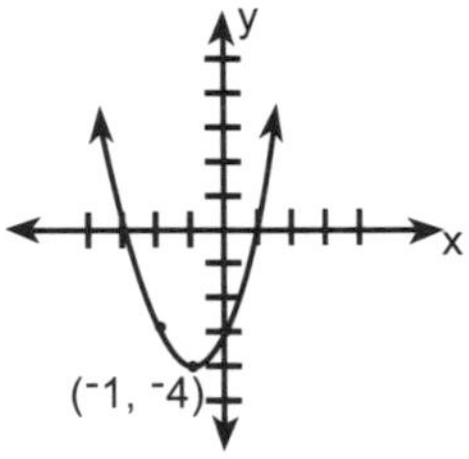

9.

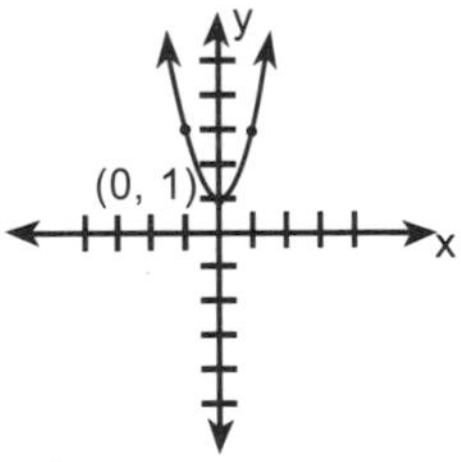

10.

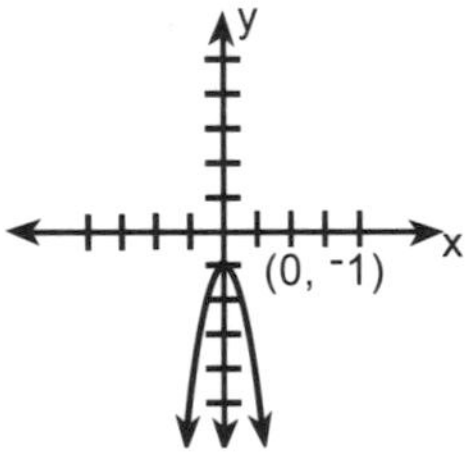

Page 27

1. yes; **2.** yes; **3.** no; **4.** no; **5.** yes;
6. yes; **7.** no; **8.** no

Page 28

1. $= {}^{-}2(x^2) + 7 = {}^{-}2x^2 + 7$

2. $= ({}^{-}2x + 7)^2 = {}^{+}4x^2 - 14x - 14x + 49 = 4x^2 - 28x + 49$

3. $= x^2 - 1$

4. $= {}^{-}2(x - 1) + 7 = {}^{-}2x + 2 + 7 = {}^{-}2x + 9$

5. $= ({}^{-}2x + 7) - 1 = {}^{-}2x + 6$

6. $= {}^{-}2(x^2 - 2x + 1) + 7 = {}^{-}2x^2 + 4x - 2 + 7 = {}^{-}2x^2 + 4x + 5$

7. $= (4x^2 - 28x + 49) - 1 = 4x^2 - 28x + 48$

8. $= {}^{-}2({}^{-}2x + 7) + 7 = {}^{+}4x - 14 + 7 = 4x - 7$

Page 29

1.

x	$f(x)$
$^{-}2$	$^{-}1$
0	3
2	$^{-}1$

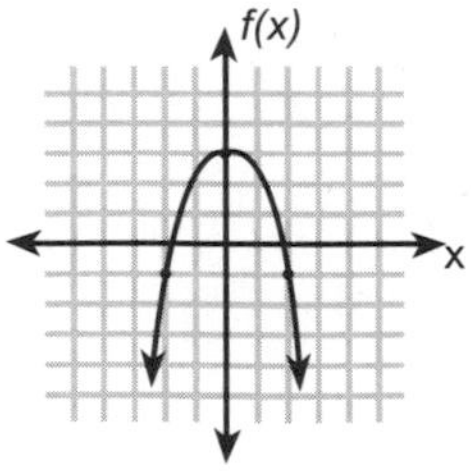

2.

x	$f(x)$
$^{-}2$	2
0	1
2	0

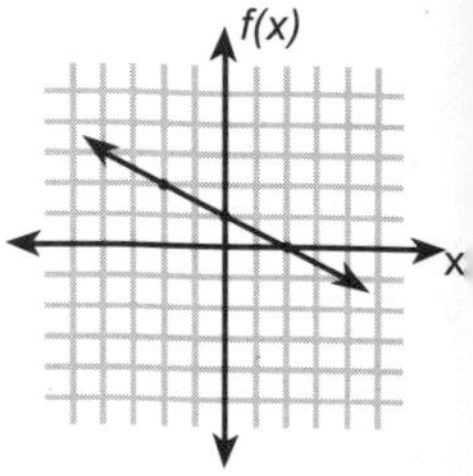

3.

x	$f(x)$
$^{-}1$	4
1	0
3	4

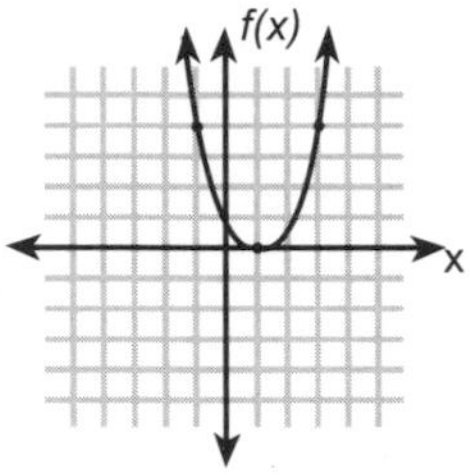

4.

x	$f(x)$
$^{-}1$	$^{-}2$
0	$^{-}4$
1	$^{-}2$

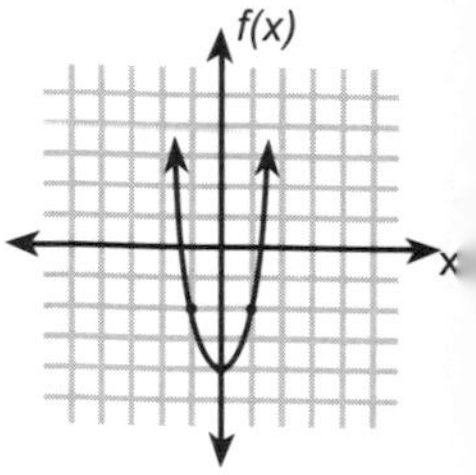

5.

x	$f(x)$
1	$^{-}3$
2	$^{-}1$
3	1

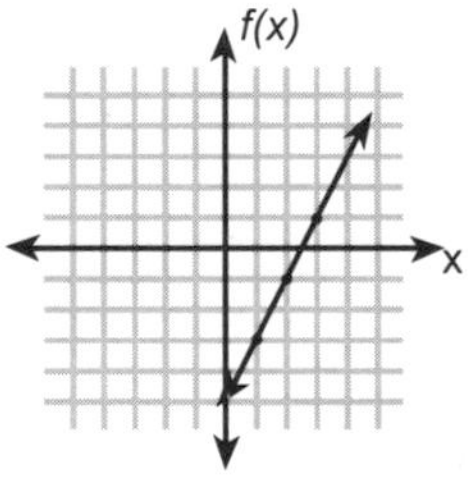

6.

x	$f(x)$
$^{-}2$	2
0	0
2	2

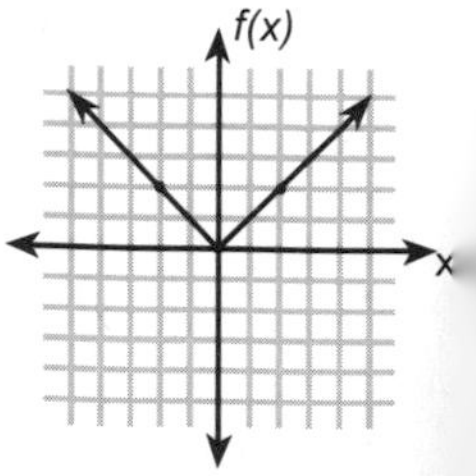

7.

x	$f(x)$
1	1
$^{-}1$	$^{-}1$
0	0

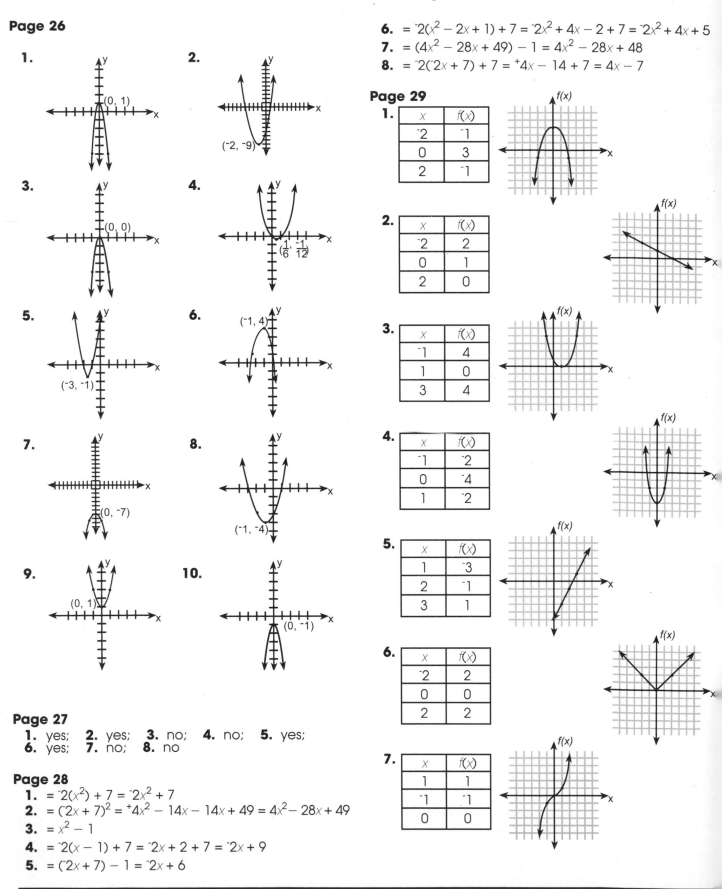

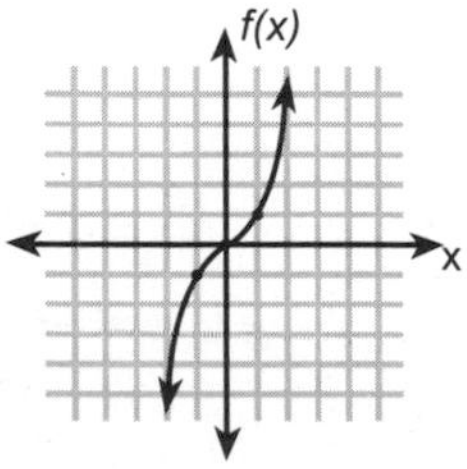

Answer Key

Page 30

1. inverse

x	$f(x)$
2	-2
1	-1
1/2	-1/2
0	0

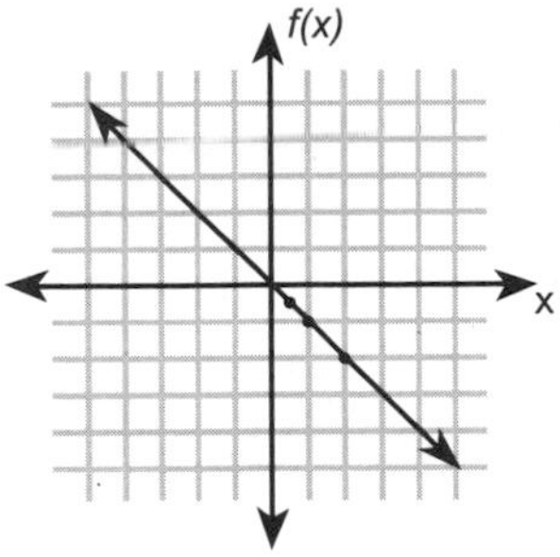

2. inverse

x	$f(x)$
-8	-2
-1	-1
-1/8	-1/2
0	0
1/8	1/2
1	1
8	2

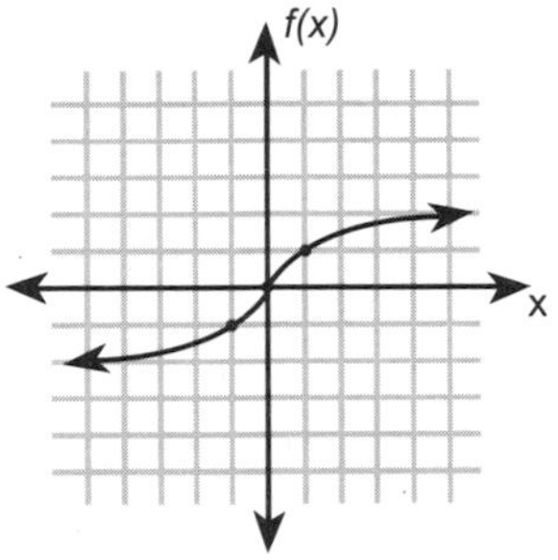

3. inverse

x	$f(x)$
-11	-3
-9	-2
-7	-1
-5	0
1	-3
-1	2
1	3

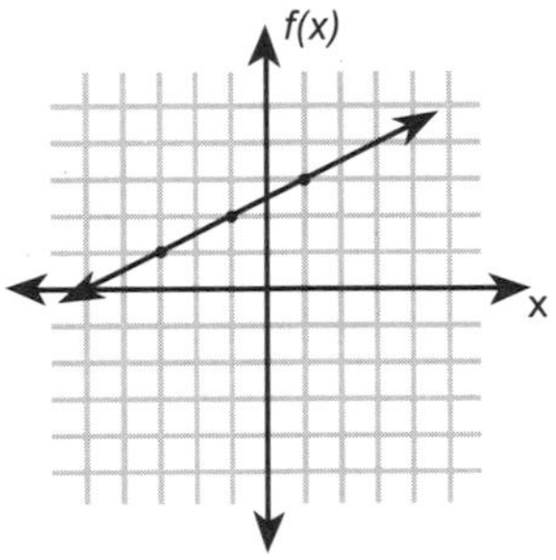

4. inverse

x	$f(x)$
-8	-2
-2	-1
-1/2	-1/2
0	0

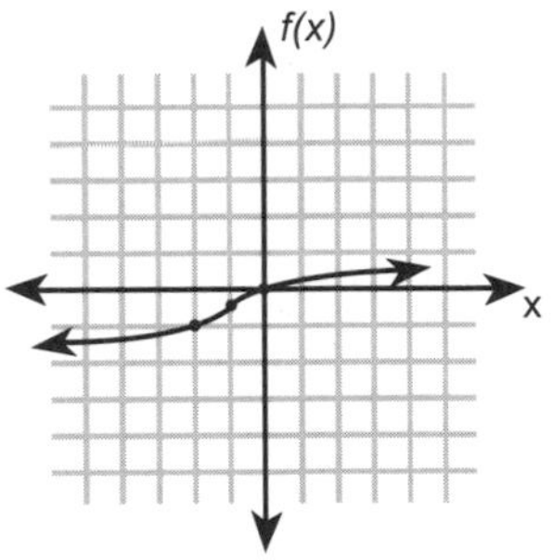

5. inverse

x	$f(x)$
8	-2
1	-1
1/8	-1/2
0	0
-1/8	1/2
-1	1
-8	2

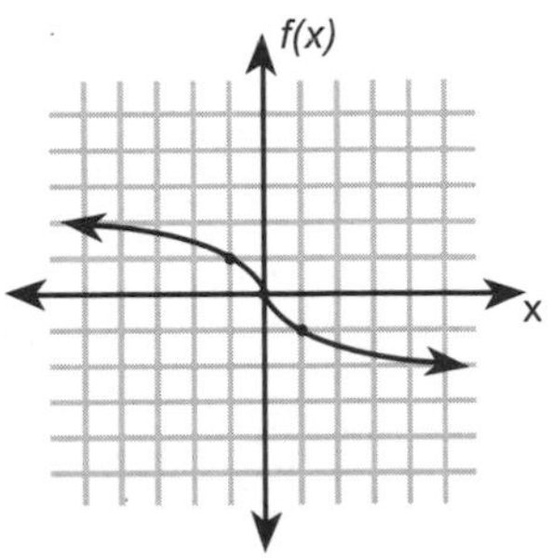

Page 31

1.
$x = 2y^2$
$\frac{x}{2} = y^2$
$y = \sqrt{\frac{x}{2}}$

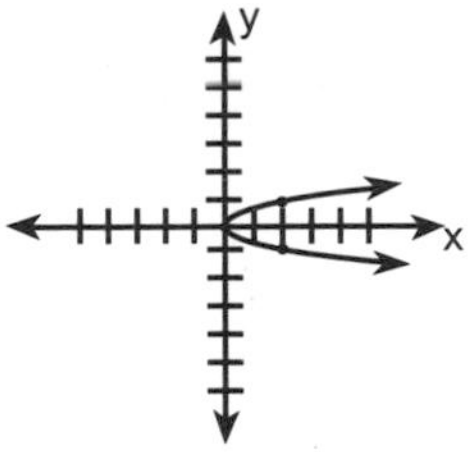

2. $x = |y| + 2$

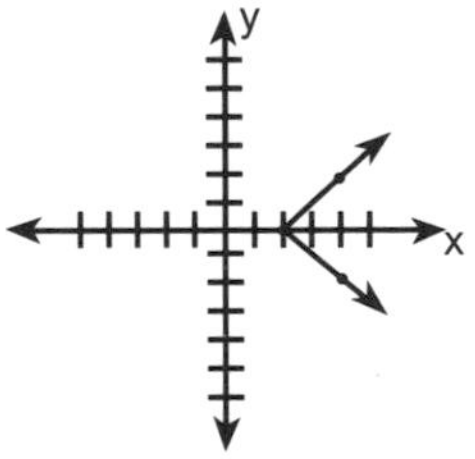

3.
$x = -y^2 + 1$
$x - 1 = -y^2$
$-x + 1 = y^2$
$y = \sqrt{-x + 1}$

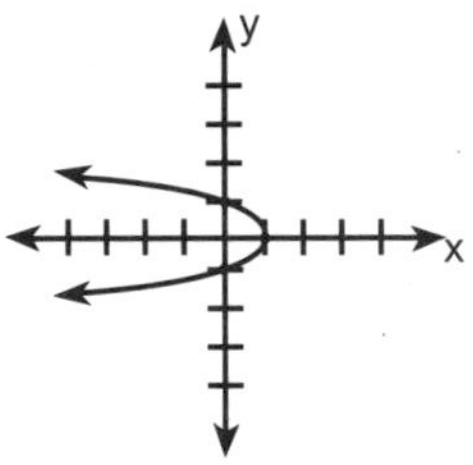

4.
$x = \frac{-1}{2} y^3$
$-2x = y^3$
$y = \sqrt[3]{-2x}$

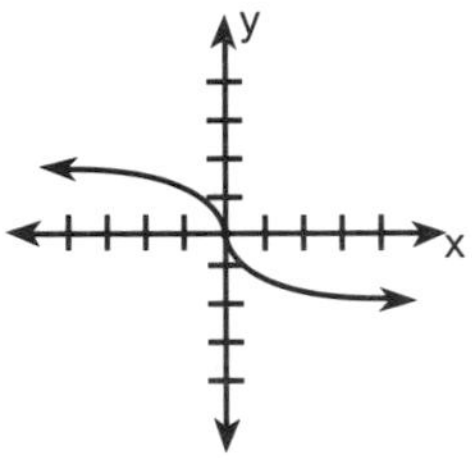

5. $x = |y - 1|$

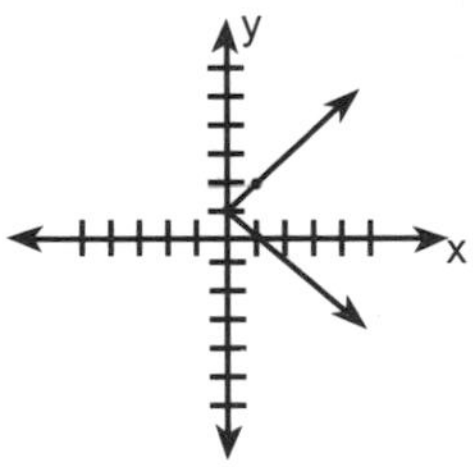

6.
$x = -4y + 7$
$x7 = -4y$
$y = x - \frac{7}{-4}$
$y = \frac{-1}{4} x + \frac{7}{4}$

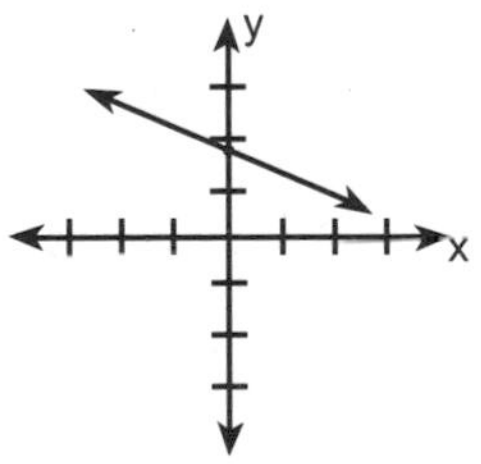

7.
$x = -y^2 + 5$
$x - 5 = -y^2$
$-x + 5 = y^2$
$y = -x + 5$

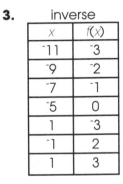

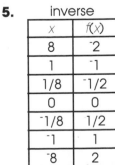

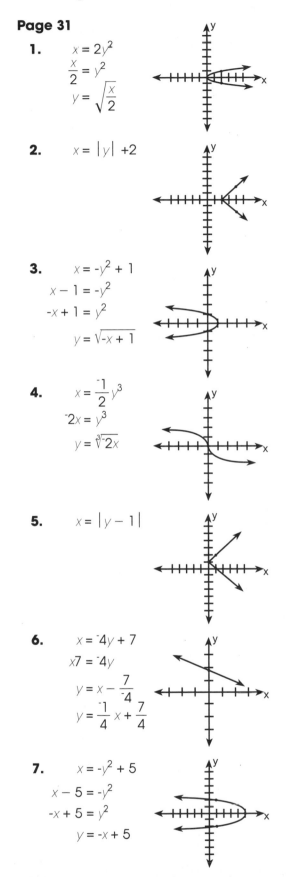

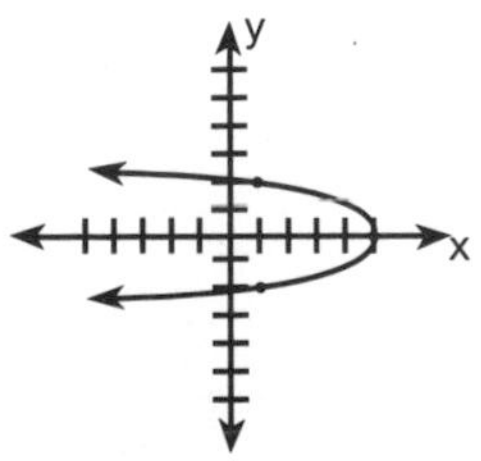

Answer Key

Page 32

1. Domain: $\mathbb{R}$; Range: $\mathbb{R}$
2. Domain: $\mathbb{R}$; Range: $y \leq 1$
3. Domain: $\mathbb{R}$; Range: $y = 1$
4. Domain: $\mathbb{R}$; Range: $\mathbb{R}$
5. Domain: $\mathbb{R}$; Range: $y \leq 0$
6. Domain: $\mathbb{R}$; Range: $\mathbb{R}$
7. Domain: $\mathbb{R}$; Range: $y \geq {}^-2$
8. Domain: $\mathbb{R}$; except 0; Range: $y > 0$
9. Domain: $\mathbb{R}$; except 0; Range: $\mathbb{R}$, except 0

Page 33

1. Domain: $^-7 \leq x \leq 7$; Range: $y = 3$
2. Domain: $^-6 \leq x \leq 6$; Range: $^-3 \leq y \leq 3$
3. Domain: $^-7 \leq x \leq 7$; Range: $^-5 \leq y \leq 4$
4. Domain: $^-6 \leq x \leq 6$; Range: $^-3 \leq y \leq 2$
5. Domain: $^-4 \leq x \leq 4$; Range: $^-7 \leq y \leq 7$
6. Domain: $^-4 \leq x \leq 4$; Range: $^-7 \leq y \leq 7$
7. Domain: $^-6 \leq x \leq 6$; Range: $^-3 \leq y \leq 2$
8. Domain: $^-3 \leq x \leq 3$; Range: $^-4 \leq y \leq 7$
9. Domain: $^-7 \leq x \leq 7$; Range: $^-3 \leq y \leq 3$

Page 34

1. $x^{4+2} = x^6$
2. $x^{8-6} = x^2$
3. x^6y^3
4. $\dfrac{x^5}{y^{15}}$
5. $\dfrac{1}{y^{15}}$
6. x^{15}
7. a^{-3} or $\dfrac{1}{a^3}$
8. 2^3c^6 or $8c^6$
9. $\dfrac{n^{10}}{n^{10}} = 1$
10. $12a^8$
11. $\dfrac{v^4}{3^4} \cdot \dfrac{5^2}{v^2} = \dfrac{25v^2}{81}$
12. x^{-4} or $\dfrac{1}{x^4}$
13. $\dfrac{x}{2}$

Page 35

14. x^6y^{-3} or $\dfrac{x^6}{y^3}$
15. $4x^{-2}$ or $\dfrac{4}{x^2}$
16. $\dfrac{8d}{90d^{-2}}$ or $\dfrac{4d^3}{45}$
17. $\dfrac{^-2}{x^2}$
18. $x^{\frac{3}{3}}$ or x^1
19. $\left(\dfrac{125}{8x}\right)^2 = \dfrac{125^2}{64x^2}$ or $\dfrac{15625}{64x^2}$
20. $\dfrac{a^{13}b^6}{b^{-2}} = a^{13}b^8$
21. $\dfrac{1}{x^6y^{11}z}$
22. $\left(\dfrac{(xz)^2}{x^2}\right)^2 = \dfrac{(x^2z^2)^2}{x^4} = \dfrac{x^4z^4}{x^4} = z^4$
23. $\dfrac{a^{12}}{x^6y^3z^3b^{21}}$
24. $x^{-4}y^{-4} \cdot x^4y^{19} = y^{15}$
25. $\dfrac{x^{-12}}{y^{18}} \cdot \left(\dfrac{y^4}{x^4}\right) = x^{-16}y^{-14}$ or $\dfrac{1}{x^{16}y^{14}}$
26. $a^{12}b^6c^{48} \cdot a^{-9}b^4x^1 = a^3b^{10}c^{48}x$
27. $\dfrac{x^{12}b^3}{4^{-3}} \cdot 2x^5 = 128x^{17}b^3$
28. $a^{-36}b^8c^{-4} \cdot \dfrac{a^3b^3}{x^3} = \dfrac{a^{-33}b^{11}c^{-4}}{x^3} = \dfrac{b^{11}}{a^{33}c^4x^3}$
29. $\dfrac{a^7b^9y^7}{c^{28}x^{22}z^{65}}$

Page 37

1. $7mt\sqrt{t}$
2. $3x$
3. $8ab^2$
4. $2x\sqrt[4]{xy^3}$
5. $3x^2y^3$
6. $xy^{10}\sqrt{1000x^2}$
7. $7a^2$
8. $^-2x - 1$
9. $(x + 1)^2$
10. $x + 1$
11. $2x - 3$

Page 38

1. $x = 343$
2. $x = 10$ or $^-10$
3. $x = 2$
4. $x = \pm 5$
5. $x = 125$
6. $x = 25$
7. $x = 10{,}000$
8. $x = 3$
9. $x = {}^-19{,}683$
10. $x = {}^-4$
11. $x = 43{,}046{,}721$

Non-real roots of an equation are the

I	M	A	G	I	N	A	R	Y		R	O	O	T	S
2	3	4	7	2	1	4	5	8		5	6	6	9	10

Page 36

1. $\dfrac{4}{9}$
2. $\dfrac{729}{64}$
3. $\dfrac{1}{8}$
4. $\dfrac{1}{5}$
5. $\dfrac{64}{125}$
6. $\dfrac{64}{27}$
7. $\dfrac{6}{11}$
8. $\dfrac{4}{9}$
9. $\dfrac{49}{81}$
10. $\dfrac{729}{8}$
11. $\dfrac{49}{16}$
12. $\dfrac{1{,}419{,}857}{759{,}375}$

As a check, for each problem number substitute the answer.

$$1 \cdot 2 \cdot 3 \div 4 \cdot 5 \cdot 6 \div 7 \div 8 \div 9 \div 10 \cdot 11 = \frac{22}{25}$$

$$\frac{4}{9} \cdot \frac{729}{64} \cdot \frac{1}{8} \div \frac{1}{5} \cdot \frac{64}{125} \cdot \frac{64}{27} \div \frac{6}{11} \div \frac{4}{9} \div \frac{49}{81} \div \frac{729}{8} \cdot \frac{49}{16} = \frac{22}{25}$$

Answer Key

Page 39

1. $(2x + 6)^5 = {}^-32$
$2x + 6 = {}^-2$
$2x = {}^-8$
$x = {}^-4$

2. $(2x + 1)^{\frac{1}{3}} = {}^-7$
$2x + 1 = {}^-343$
$2x = {}^-344$
$x = {}^-172$

3. $(x - 1)^2 = 144$
$x - 1 = 12$ or ${}^-12$
$x = 13$ or ${}^-11$

4. $(x - 2)^2 = 16$
$x - 2 = \pm 4$
$x = 6$ or ${}^-2$

5. $(2x - 5)^4 = 6561$
$2x - 5 = \pm 9$
$x = 7$ or ${}^-2$

6. $5x - 1 = 7$ or ${}^-7$
$x = \frac{8}{5}$ or $\frac{{}^-6}{5}$

7. $(10x - 18)^{\frac{1}{2}} = 49$
$10x - 18 = 2401$
$10x = 2419$
$x = 241.9$

8. $(12x - 1)^3 = 216$
$12x - 1 = 6$
$12x = 7$
$x = \frac{7}{12}$

9. $(4x + 3)^{\frac{1}{2}} = 81$
$4x + 3 = 6561$
$4x = 6558$
$x = 1639.5$

10. $(x - 15)^{\frac{3}{5}} = 343$
$x = 16{,}807$
$x = 16{,}822$

11. $x = 3$

Page 40

1. inverse

x	$f(x)$
${}^-1$	1/3
0	1
1	3
2	9

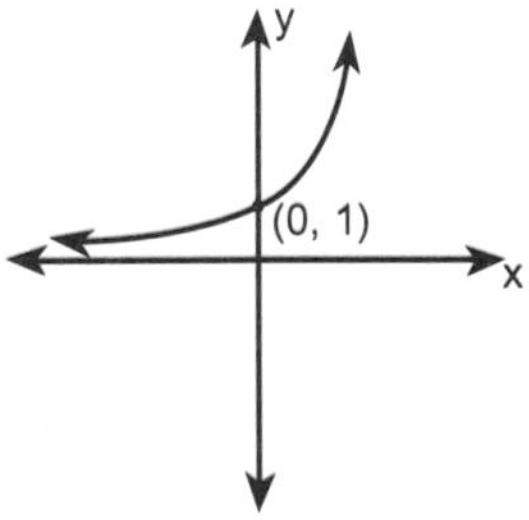

2. inverse

x	$f(x)$
${}^-1$	3 1/2
0	10
1	30
2	90

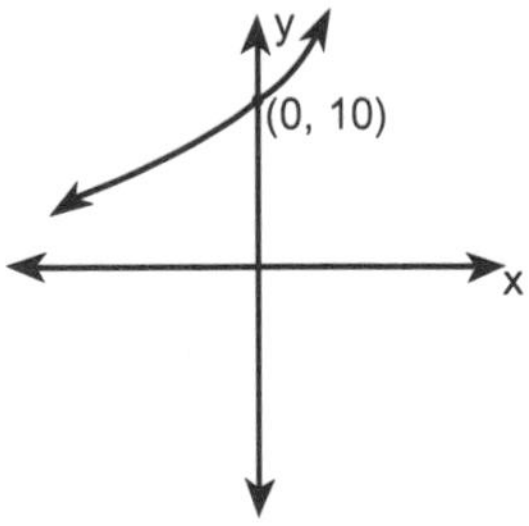

3. inverse

x	$f(x)$
${}^-1$	5
0	10
1	20
2	40

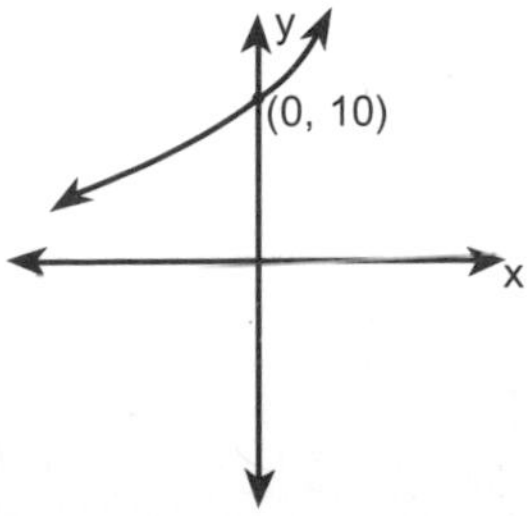

4. inverse

x	$f(x)$
${}^-1$	2
0	1
1	1/2
2	1/4

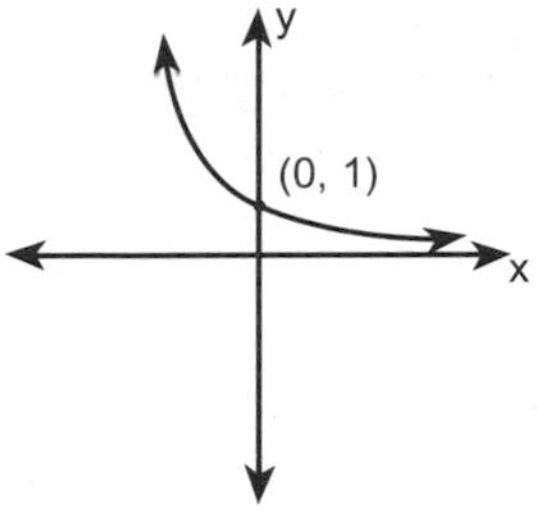

5. inverse

x	$f(x)$
${}^-1$	5
0	1
1	0.2
2	0.04

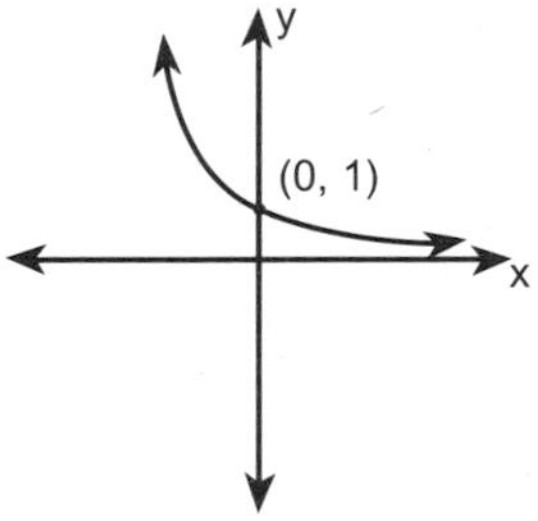

6. inverse

x	$f(x)$
${}^-1$	12.5
0	50
1	200
2	800

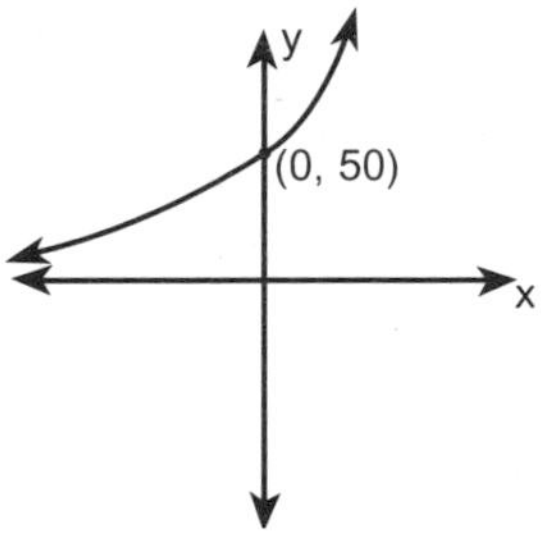

7. inverse

x	$f(x)$
${}^-1$	0.1
0	1
1	10
2	100

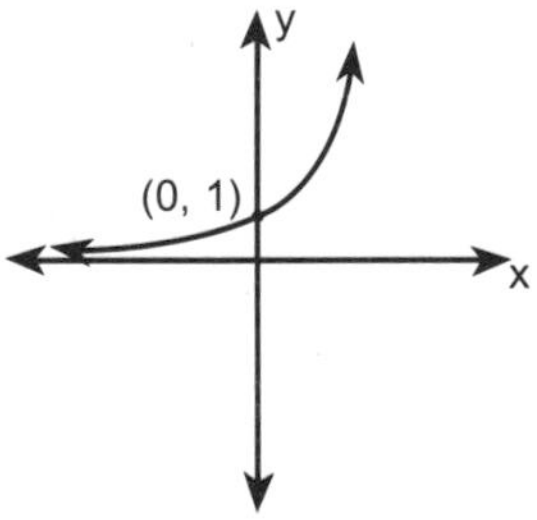

8. inverse

x	$f(x)$
${}^-1$	10
0	1
1	0.1
2	0.01

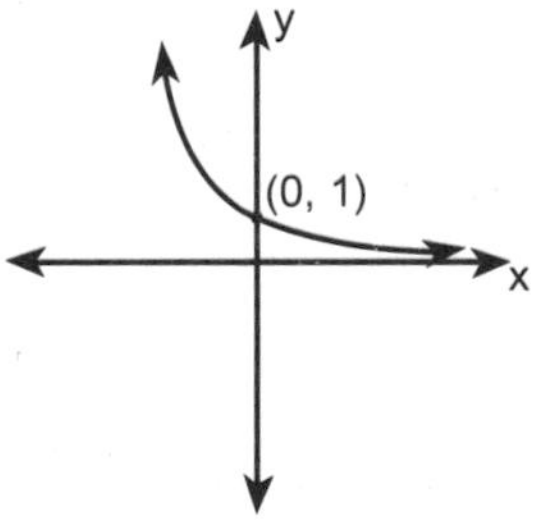

9. inverse

x	$f(x)$
${}^-1$	25
0	50
1	100
2	200

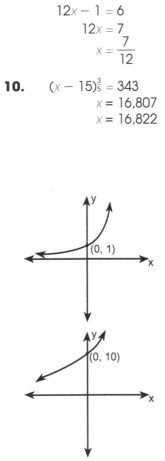

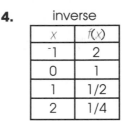

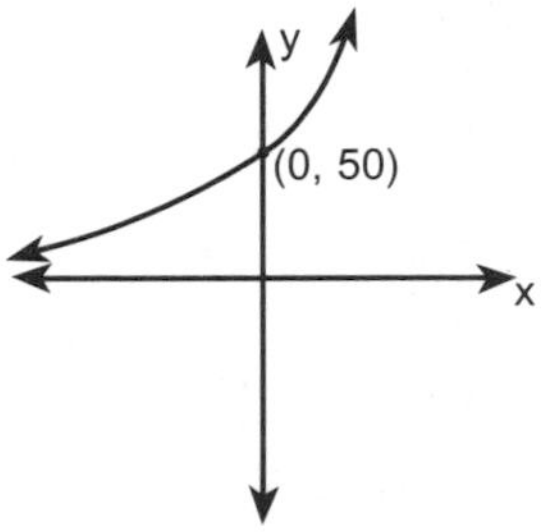

Problems 1, 4, 5, 7, and 8: The y-axis intersects at (0,1). Problems 4, 5, and 8: The y value decreases as the x value increases.

Answer Key

Page 41

1. $P = \$100.00$ $r = 3\%$ $n = 4$ $t = 3$ years
$A = \$109.38$

2. $P = \$1{,}500.00$ $r = 4\%$ $n = 12$ $t = 1$ year
$A = \$1{,}561.11$

3. $P = \$2500.00$ $r = 5\%$ $n = 4$ $t = 10$ years
$A = \$4{,}109.05$

4a. $P = \$7500.00$ $r = 6\%$ $n = 1$ $t = 1$ year
$A = \$7950.00$

4b. $P = \$7500.00$ $r = 6\%$ $n = 365$ $t = 1$ year
$A = \$7963.73$

4c. In answer b, Juan is earning interest on interest.

5. $P = \$5{,}000.00$ $r = 6\%$ $n = 12$ $t = 18.5$ years
$A = \$15{,}129.89$

Page 42

1. 0.625 grams **2.** 10 grams
3. 0.007 grams **4.** 1031.25 grams
5. 6.8×10^{-11} grams **6.** 22,920 years old

Page 43

1. $\log 1000 = y$, $10^y = 1000$, $y = 3$

2. $\log \sqrt[5]{10} = y$, $10^y = 10^{\frac{1}{5}}$, $y = \frac{1}{5}$

3. $\log \sqrt[3]{10^2} = y$, $10^y = 10^{\frac{2}{3}}$, $y = \frac{2}{3}$

4. $\log 0.1 = y$, $10^y = 0.1$, $y = {}^{-}1$

5. $\log 0.0001 = y$, $10^y = 0.0001$, $y = {}^{-}4$

6. $\log \sqrt[4]{10} = y$, $10^y = 10^{\frac{1}{4}}$, $y = \frac{1}{4}$

7. $\log \sqrt{10} = y$, $10^y = 10^{\frac{1}{2}}$, $y = \frac{1}{2}$

8. $\log 10^6 = y$, $10^y = 10^6$, $y = 6$

9. $\log 1 = y$, $10^y = 1$, $y = 0$

10. $\log 10{,}000 = y$, $10^y = 10{,}000$, $y = 4$

Page 44

1. $\log_5 125 = 3$
2. $\log_{10} 1{,}000{,}000 = 6$
3. $10^0 = 1$
4. $3^{-5} = \frac{1}{243}$
5. $\log_7 16{,}807 = 5$
6. $10^y = x$
7. $\log_{12} 87 = x$
8. $15^y = 30$
9. $Q^y = x$
10. $180^y = B$
11. $\log_{10} x = y$
12. $b^3 = 64$
13. $x^{10} = 5$
14. $\log_7 343 = x$

Page 45

1.

x	$f(x)$
1/9	$^{-}2$
1/3	$^{-}1$
1	0
3	1
9	2
27	3

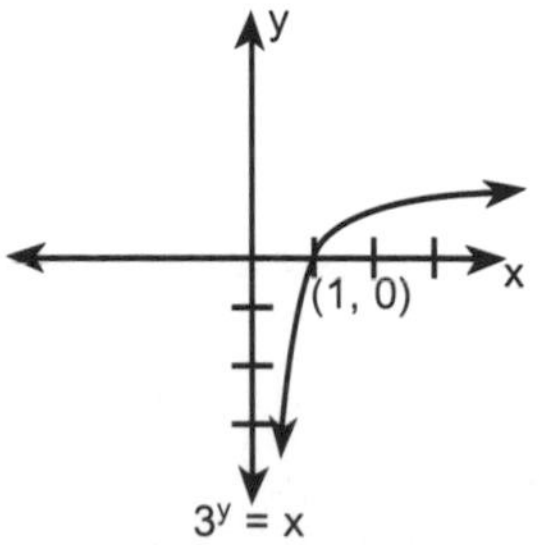

$3^y = x$

2.

x	$f(x)$
1/25	$^{-}2$
1/5	$^{-}1$
1	0
5	1
25	2
125	3

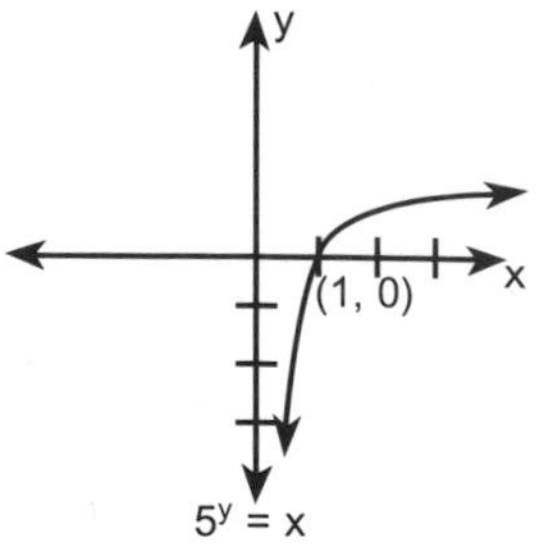

$5^y = x$

3.

x	$f(x)$
1/49	$^{-}2$
1/7	$^{-}1$
1	0
7	1
49	2
343	3

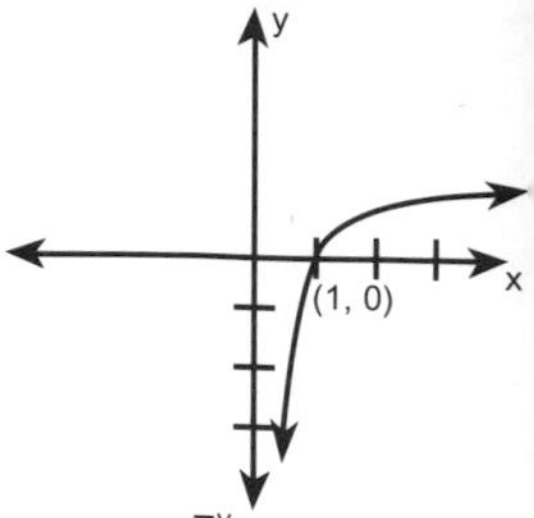

$7^y = x$

4.

x	$f(x)$
1/4	$^{-}2$
1/2	$^{-}1$
1	0
2	1
4	2
8	3

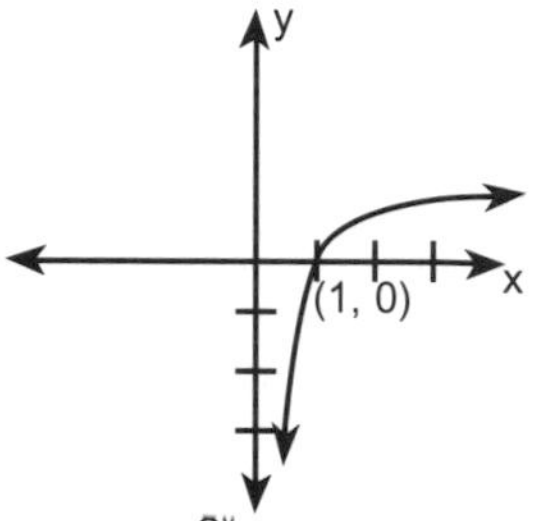

$2^y = x$

5.

x	$f(x)$
1/16	$^{-}2$
1/4	$^{-}1$
1	0
4	1
16	2
64	3

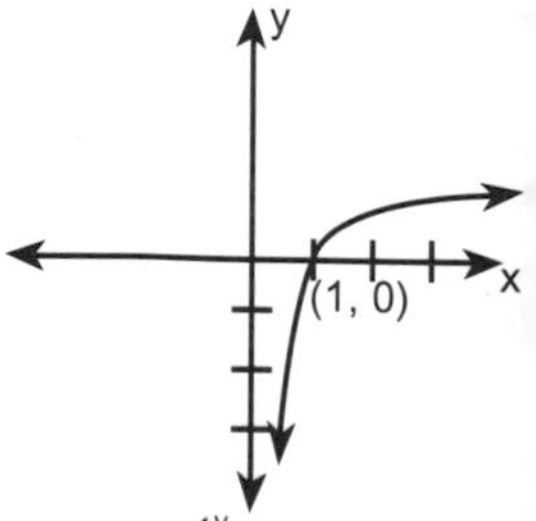

$4^y = x$

6.

x	$f(x)$
1/121	$^{-}2$
1/11	$^{-}1$
1	0
11	1
121	2
1331	3

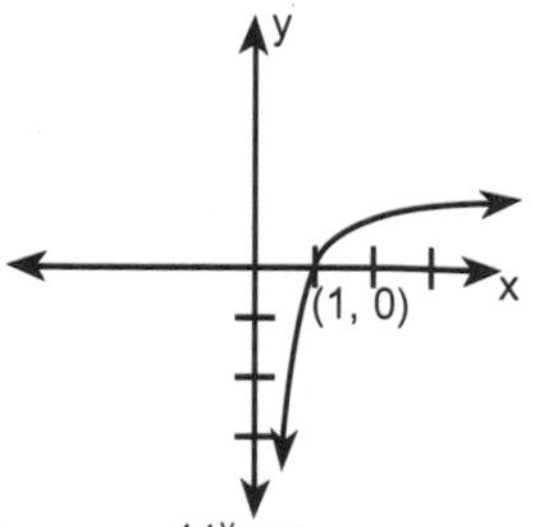

$11^y = x$

7.

x	$f(x)$
1/225	$^{-}2$
1/15	$^{-}1$
1	0
15	1
225	2
3375	3

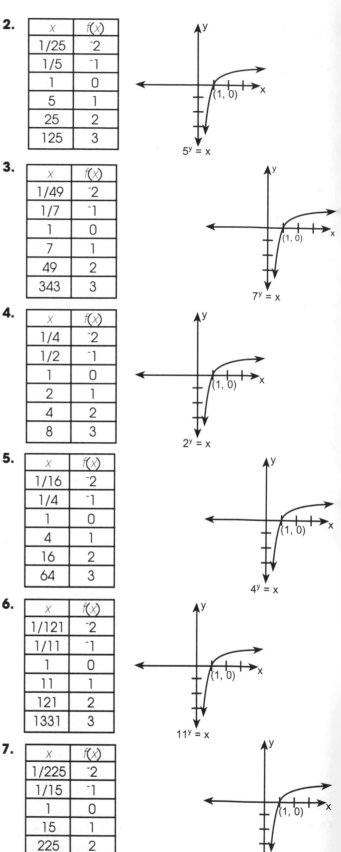

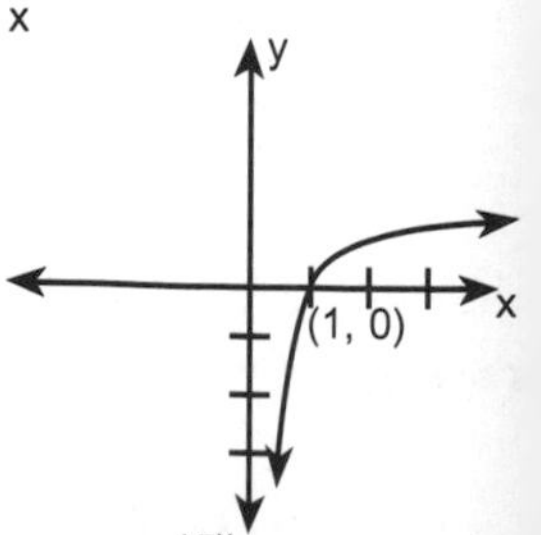

$15^y = x$

Answer Key

Page 46

1. $\log_9 24$ **2.** $\log_{12} 132$ **3.** $\log_{16} 3$

4. $\log\left(\frac{3}{2}\right)$ **5.** $6 \log 14$ **6.** $16 \log_{20} 10$

7. Cannot simplify because of different bases.

8. $\log 100$ **9.** $\log 5^3 = 3 \log 5$ **10.** $4\log_2 2$

Page 47

1. $\log_3 x - \log_3 2^2 = \log_3 3^3$

$\log_3\left(\frac{x}{4}\right) = \log_3 27$

$\frac{x}{4} = 27 \quad x = 108$

2. $2^9 = x$

$x = 512$

3. $2^x = 128$

$x = 7$

4. $x^{-2} = 144$

$\frac{1}{x^2} = 144$

$x = \frac{1}{12}$

5. $\log_2 x = \log_2 27^{\frac{1}{3}}$

$\log_2 x = \log 3$

$x = 3$

6. $\log_{16} 16 = x$

$16^x = 16$

$x = 1$

7. $\log 2^5 = \log x$

$x = 2^5 = 32$

8. $\log_2 \frac{x}{5} = \log_2 10$

$\frac{x}{5} = 10$

$x = 50$

A logarithm is an E X P O N E N T.
2 6 4 7 5 3 1 8

Page 48

1. 1.5 **2.** 3
3. No solution **4.** 2.7
5. 2.3 **6.** 3.1
7. 6.5 **8.** 4.5
9. 1.5 **10.** 2.1

Page 49

1. cubic binomial **2.** fifth degree binomial
3. tenth degree monomial **4.** sixth degree trinomial
5. sixth degree binomial **6.** 15th degree monomial
7. cubic trinomial **8.** fourth degree binomial
9. linear monomial **10.** seventh degree binomial
11. sixth degree binomial **12.** cubic trinomial
13. fourth degree trinomial **14.** linear binomial

Page 50

1. $7x^4 + x^3 + 0x^2 + x + 0$ **2.** $6x^3 + x^2 + 0x + 23$
3. $19x^6 + 0x^5 + 0x^4 + 0x^3 + 0x^2 + 0x + 1$
4. $14x^2 + 4x + 0$ **5.** $x^3 + 0x^2 + 0x + 0$
6. $3x^2 + 10x + 0$ **7.** $x^2 + 2x + 1$
8. $8x^3 + 0x^2 + 4x + 0$ **9.** $x + 1$
10. $3x^3 + 2x^2 + x + 0$ **11.** $x^4 + 0x^3 + 0x^2 + 20x + 18$
12. $25x^2 + 5x + 0$ **13.** $18x^3 + 0x^2 + x + 0$

Page 51

1. $= {}^{-}231$ **2.** $= {}^{-}314$ **3.** $= 14$
4. $= 65$ **5.** $= {}^{-}62$ **6.** $= 8$
7. $= 401$ **8.** $= 1082$ **9.** $= 785$
10. $= {}^{-}18$

Cross out the correct answers below. Use the remaining letters to complete a statement, then rewrite the statement as a common adage.

101 SIM	~~$^{-}231$ THE~~	$^{-}118$ ILA	5 RAV	~~65 LAS~~	17 IAR	~~401 TMA~~	41 YSP	~~$^{-}18$ NIS~~	37 ECI
~~$^{-}314$ STA~~	$^{-}14$ ESC	~~$^{-}62$ NDI~~	341 ONG	$^{-}894$ REG	~~1082 NG~~	$^{-}17$ ATE	~~14 IST~~	~~8 HEO~~	~~785 NE~~

S I M I L A R A V I A R Y S P E C I E S

C O N G R E G A T E.

Common adage: Birds of a feather flock together.

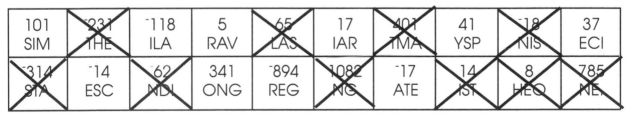

Answer Key

Page 52

1. $2x^4 - 3x^3$
$- 2x^3 + 3x^2$
$2x^4 - 5x^3 + 3x^2$

2. $= (x+1)(x+1)(x+1)$
$= (x+1)(x^2+2x+1)$
$x^3 + 2x^2 + x$
$+ x^2 + 2x + 1$
$x^3 + 3x^2 + 3x + 1$

3. $x^3 + 6x^2 + 10x$
$+ x^2 + 6x + 10$
$x^3 + 7x^2 + 16x + 10$

4. $2x^4 - 12x$
$+ x^3 - 6$
$2x^4 + x^3 - 12x - 6$

5. $x^4 - 1$

6. $54x^3 - 9x^2 + 9x$
$- 24x^2 + 4x - 4$
$54x^3 - 33x^2 + 13x - 4$

7. $5x^3 + x^2 - 8x$
$- 5x^2 - x + 8$
$5x^3 - 4x^2 - 9x + 8$

8. $6x^3 + 2x^2 + x$
$-24x^2 - 8x - 4$
$6x^3 - 22x^2 - 7x - 4$

9. $= (2x - 3)(2x - 3)(2x - 3)$
$= (2x - 3)(4x^2 - 12x + 9)$
$8x^3 - 24x^2 + 18x$
$- 12x^2 + 36x - 27$
$8x^3 - 36x^2 + 54x - 27$

10. $= (3x^2+1)(3x^2+1)(3x^2+1)$
$= (3x^2+1)(9x^4 + 6x^2 + 1)$
$27x^6 + 18x^4 + 3x^2$
$+ 9x^4 + 6x^2 + 1$
$27x^6 + 27x^4 + 9x^2 + 1$

11. $14x^4 + 14x^4 - 98x$
$+ x^3 + x^2 - 7$
$14x^4 + 15x^3 + x^2 - 98x - 7$

12. $^-6x^4 - 4x^2 - 2x$
$3x^3 + 2x + 1$
$6x^4 + 3x^3 - 4x^2 + 1$

13. $(11x^2 - 1)(11x^2 - 1)(11x^2 - 1)$
$(11x^2 - 1)(121x^4 - 22x^2 + 1)$
$1331x^6 - 242x^4 + 11x^2$
$- 121x^4 + 22x^2 - 1$
$1331x^6 - 363x^4 + 33x^2 - 1$

14. $(^-2x^2 + x)(4x^4 - 4x^3 + x^2)$
$^-8x^6 + 8x^5 - 2x^4$
$4x^5 - 4x^4 + x^3$
$^-8x^6 + 12x^5 - 6x^4 + x^3$

Page 53

1. $x(x^2 + 5x + 6)$
$= x(x + 2)(x + 3)$

2. $a = x \quad b = 1$
$(x + 1)(x^2 - x + 1)$

3. $a = 4x \quad b = 3$
$(4x - 3)(16x^2 + 12x + 9)$

4. $2x(x^2 - 4x + 4)$
$2x(x - 2)(x - 2)$

5. $(x - 4)(x + 2)$

6. $a = x \quad b = 6$
$x(x^3 + 216)$
$x(x + 6)(x^2 - 6x + 36)$

7. $(x + 1)(10x - 5)$

8. $x(2x^2 - 7x + 6)$
$x(2x - 3)(x - 2)$

9. $2x(125x^3 - 27)$
$2x(5x - 3)(25x^2 + 15x + 9)$

10. $10x^2(4x^2 - 1)$
$10x^2(2x - 1)(2x + 1)$

Page 54

1. $x^2 - 1 \overline{)\, x^3 - 1}$ (quotient x)
$-x^3 + x$
$x - 1$
$= x + \dfrac{x - 1}{x^2 - 1}$

2. $x - 3 \overline{)\, 2x^2 - 5x - 3}$ (quotient $2x + 1$)
$-2x^2 + 6x$
$x - 3$
$x - 3$
0
$= 2x + 1$

3. $x + 2 \overline{)\, x^2 - 3x - 7}$ (quotient $x - 5$)
$-x^2 + 2x$
$- 5x - 7$
$+ 5x + 10$
3
$= x - 5 + \dfrac{3}{x + 2}$

4. $x - 1 \overline{)\, x^2 - 6}$ (quotient $x^2 + x + 1$)
$-x^3 + x^2$
$x^2 - 6$
$- x^2 + x$
$x - 6$
$- x + 1$
$- 5$
$= x^2 + x + 1 + \dfrac{^-5}{x - 1}$

5. $x + 2 \overline{)\, x^3 - 6x^2 + 1}$ (quotient $x^2 - 8x + 16$)
$- x^3 - 2x^2 + 1$
$- 8x^2 + 1$
$+ 8x^2 + 16x$
$16x + 1$
$- 16x + 32$
$- 31$
$= x^2 - 8x + 16 + \dfrac{^-31}{x + 2}$

6. $x - 7 \overline{)\, 5x^2 - 34x - 7}$ (quotient $5x + 1$)
$-5x^2 + 35x$
$x - 7$
$x - 7$
0

7. $x + 2 \overline{)\, x^4 - 3x^3 - 5x - 6}$ (quotient $x^3 - 5x^2 + 10x - 25$)
$- x^4 - 2x^3$
$- 5x^3 - 5x$
$+ 5x^3 + 10x^2$
$+ 10x^2 - 5x$
$- 10x^2 - 20x$
$-25x - 6$
$25x + 50$
44
$= x^3 - 5x^2 + 10x - 25 + \dfrac{44}{x + 2}$

8. $2x + 1 \overline{)\, 6x^2 - x - 7}$ (quotient $2x - 1$)
$-6x^2 - 2x$
$- 3x - 7$
$+ 3x + 1$
$-$
$= 2x - 1 + \dfrac{^-6}{3x + 1}$

Answer Key

Page 56

1. $2x^3 - 7x^2 - 8x + 16$

$\underline{4|}$ 2 −7 −8 16
8 4 | −16
2 1 −4 | 0

$= 2x^2 + x - 4$

2. $2x^2 + 5x + 3$

$\underline{-1|}$ 2 5 3
−2 | −3
2 3 | 0

$= 2x + 3$

3. $x^2 + 3x - 18$

$\underline{-3|}$ 1 3 −18
−3 | 0
1 0 | −18

$= x + \frac{^{-}18}{x+3}$

4. $2x^2 + 4x + 3$

$\underline{3|}$ 2 −4 3
6 | 6
2 2 | 9

$= 2x + 2 + \frac{9}{x-3}$

5. $x^3 - x^2 + x + 8$

$\underline{1|}$ 1 −1 1 8
1 0 | 1
1 0 1 | 9

$= x^2 + 1 + \frac{9}{x-1}$

6. $3x^3 - x^2 + 2x - 4$

$\underline{2|}$ 3 −1 2 −4
6 10 | 24
3 5 12 | 20

$= 3x^2 + 5x + 12 + \frac{20}{x-2}$

Page 58

1. $(x - 2)(2x - 1)(x + 1)$
2. $(x - 1)(x + 1)(x - 1)$
3. $(x - 1)(x + 5)(x + 3)$
4. $(x + 2)(x - 4)(x + 1)$
5. $(x + 1)(2x - 3)(x - 1)$
6. $(x - 5)(x + 1)(3x - 1)$

Page 60

1. $x(2x^2 - 7x + 6)$
$x(2x - 3)(x - 2)$
$x = 0 = \frac{3}{2} = 2$

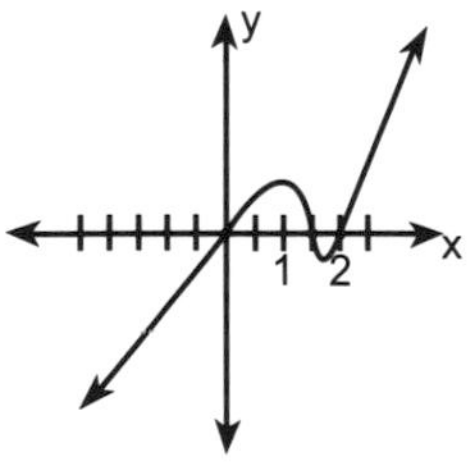

2. $-x(x^2 - 5x + 6)$
$-x(x - 3)(x - 2)$
$x = 0 = 3 = 2$

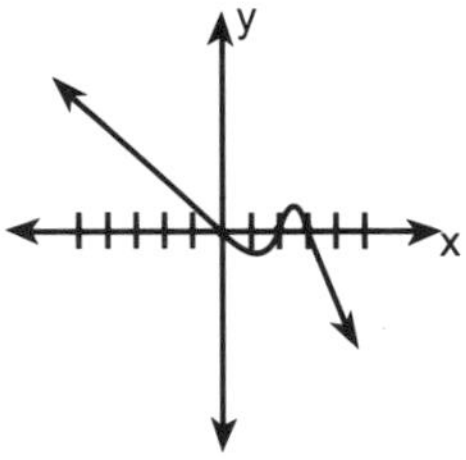

3. $^{-}4x^2(x + 3) + 1(x + 3)$
$(1 + 2x)(1 - 2x)(x + 3)$
$x = {^{-}3} = \pm\sqrt{\frac{3}{4}} \approx 0.86$

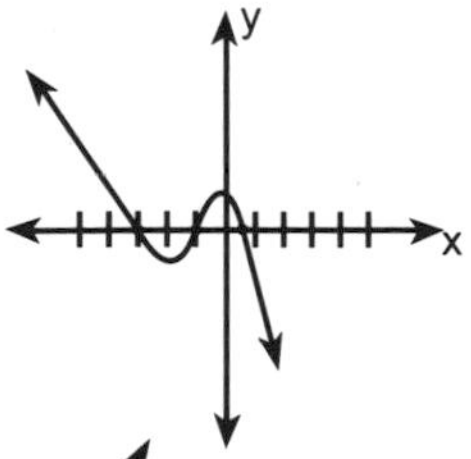

4. $(x + 1)(x^2 - 1)$
$(x + 1)(x + 1)(x - 1)$
$x = 1 = {^{-}1}$

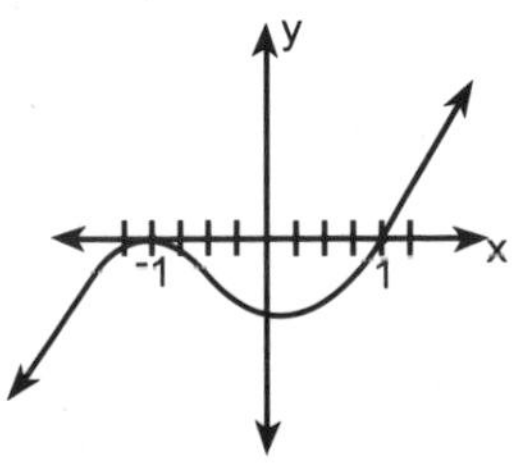

5. $10x^2(4x^2 - 1)$
$10x^2(2x - 1)(2x + 1)$
$x = 0 = \frac{^{-}1}{2} = \frac{1}{2}$

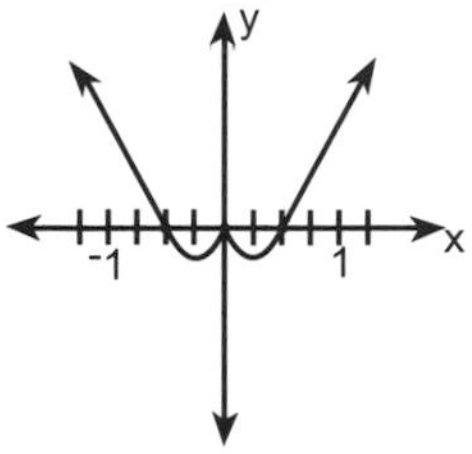

6. $x^2(x^2 - 9x + 20)$
$x^2(x - 5)(x - 4)$
$x = 0 = 5 = 4$

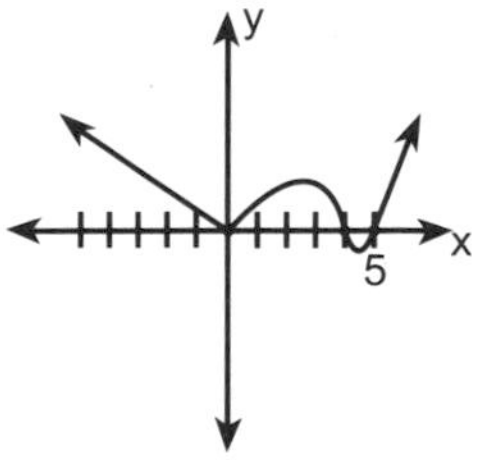

Page 61

1.

x	y
5	$^{-}1$
5	$^{-}3$

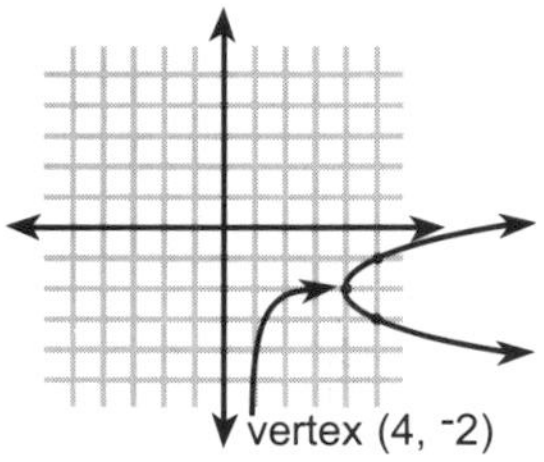

2.

x	y
$^{-}5$	4
$^{-}5$	0

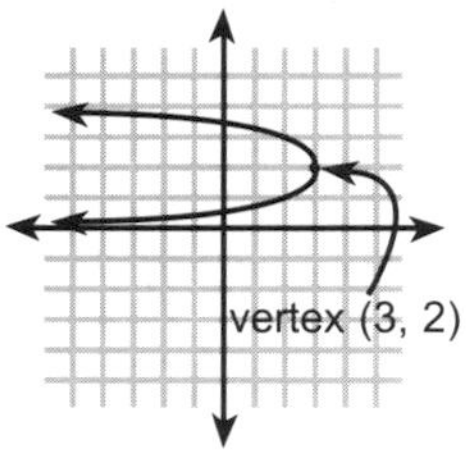

3.

x	y
$^{-}2$	$^{-}2$
$^{-}4$	$^{-}2$

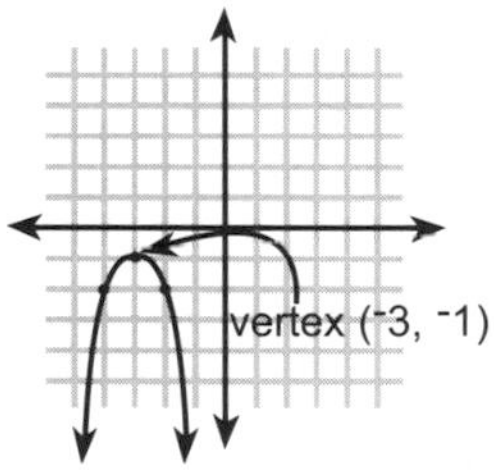

4.

x	y
$^{-}2$	3
$^{-}8$	3

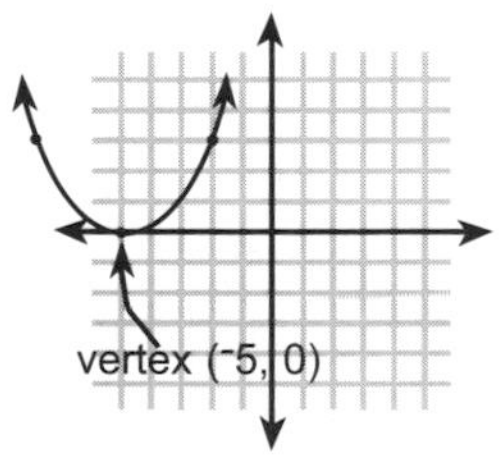

5.

x	y
$2\frac{1}{10}$	$^{-}3$
$2\frac{1}{10}$	$^{-}1$

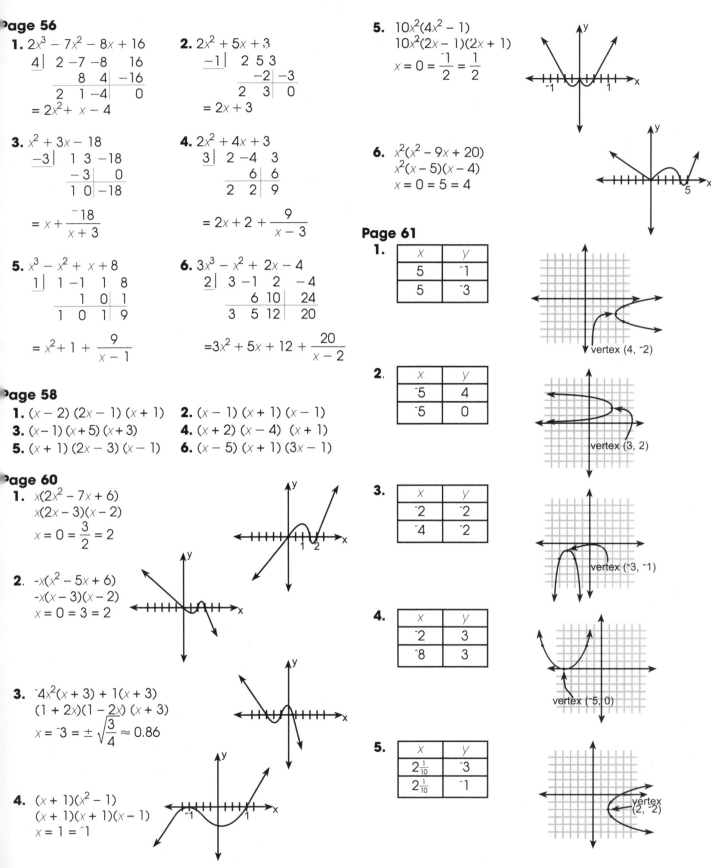

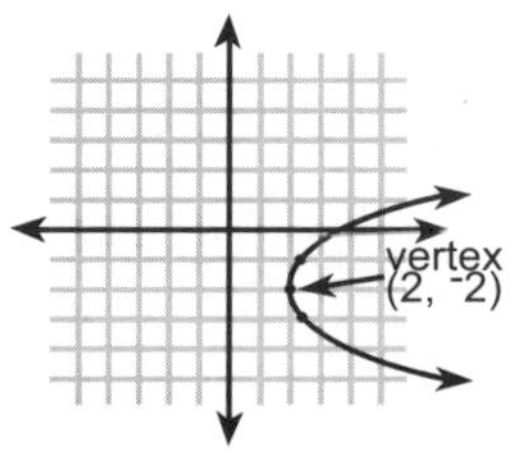

Answer Key

Page 62

1. $y = 2(x - 1)^2 + 6$
$v = (1, 6)$

2. $y = {}^-3(x + 2)^2 - 1$
$v = ({}^-2, {}^-1)$

3. $y = \frac{1}{3}(x - 3)^2$
$v = (3, 0)$

4. $y = \frac{1}{5}(x - 1)^2 + 2$
$v = (1, 2)$

5. $x = (y + 5)^2 - 31$
$v = ({}^-31, {}^-5)$

6. $x = (y - 5)^2 + 10$
$v = (10, 5)$

7. $x = 5(y + 4)^2 - 3$
$v = ({}^-3, {}^-4)$

8. $x = \frac{1}{2}\left(y - \frac{3}{2}\right) - \frac{11}{8}$
$v = \left(\frac{{}^-11}{8}, \frac{3}{2}\right)$

Page 63

1. center (4, -10)
radius = 12

2. center (0, 7)
radius = 7

3. center (0, 0)
radius = 1

4. center $({}^-3, {}^-11)$
radius = $\sqrt{15}$

5. center (15, 0)
radius = $\sqrt{10}$

1. $x^2 + y^2 = 64$
2. $(x + 2)^2 + (y - 3)^2 = 4$
3. $(x + 7)^2 + (y + 18)^2 = 196$
4. $(x - 12)^2 + (y - 9)^2 = 1$
5. $(x - 10)^2 + y^2 = 484$

Page 64

1. center (0, 3)
radius = 4

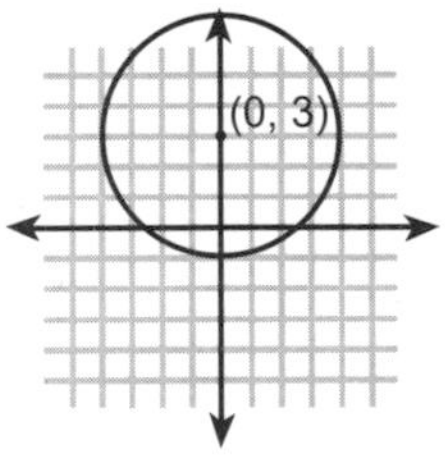

2. center (0, 0)
radius = 8

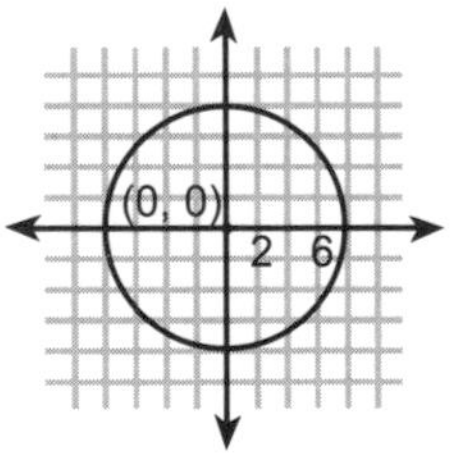

3. center (1, $^-1$)
radius = 1

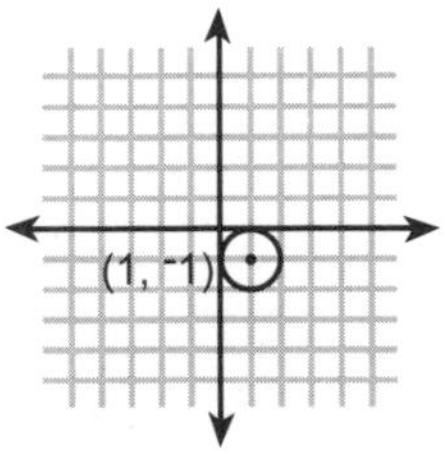

4. center (7, 2)
radius = 5

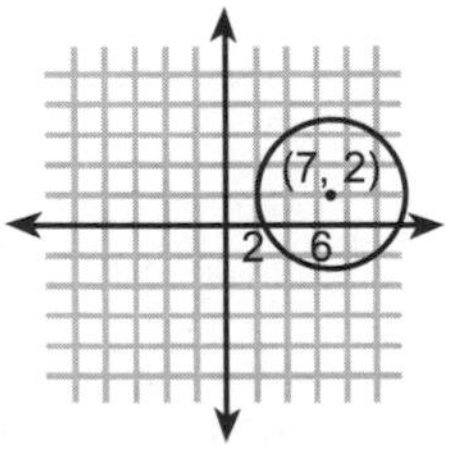

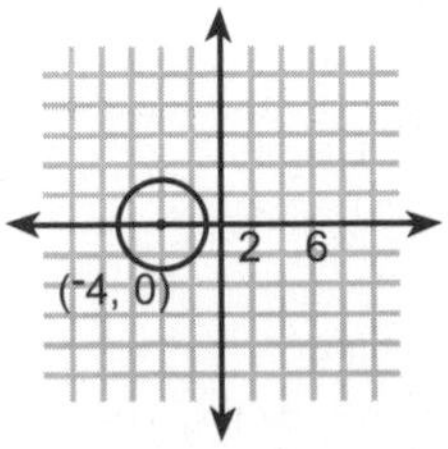

5. center $({}^-4, 0)$
radius = 3

6. center (0, 12)
radius = $\sqrt{20}$

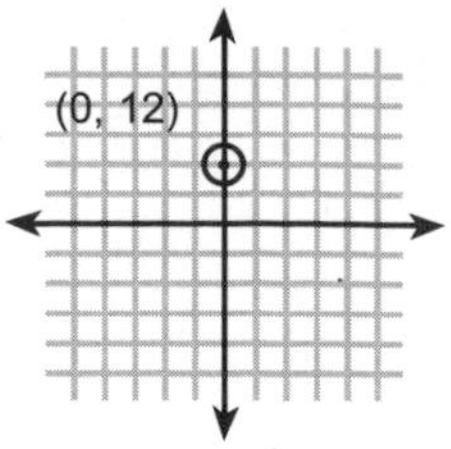

7. center $({}^-6, {}^-9)$
radius = $\sqrt{15}$

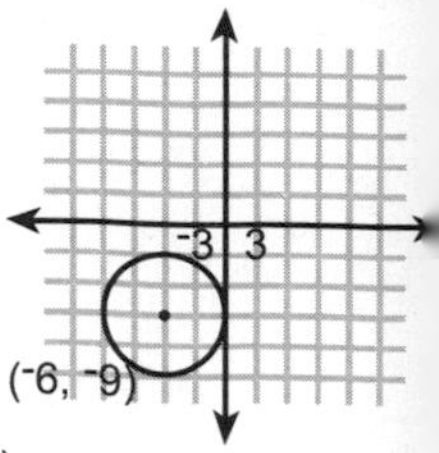

Page 66

1. $c = \sqrt{25 - 4} = \sqrt{21}$
$c \approx \pm 4.58$

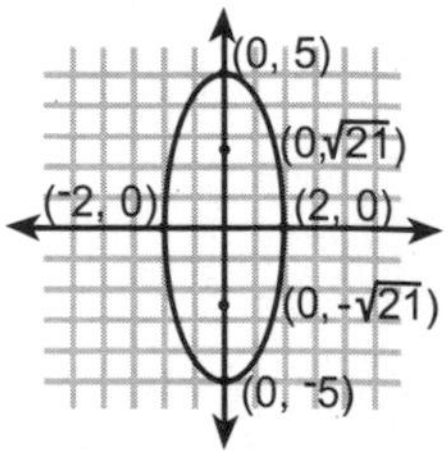

2. $c = \sqrt{64 - 1} = \sqrt{63}$
$c \approx \pm 7.93$

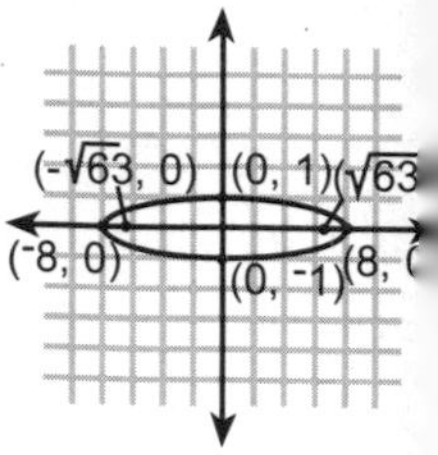

3. $c = \sqrt{64} = 8$

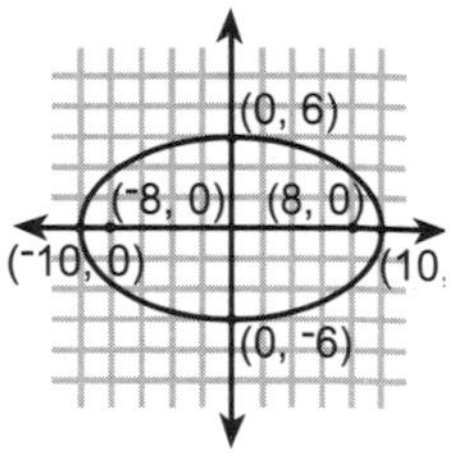

4. $c = \sqrt{95}$
$c \approx \pm 9.75$

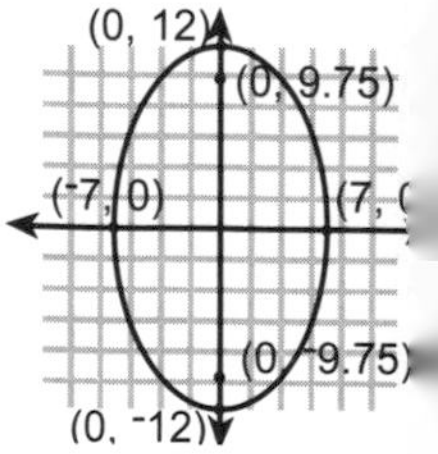

5. $c = \pm\sqrt{24}$
foci: (0, 24)
(0, -$\sqrt{24}$)

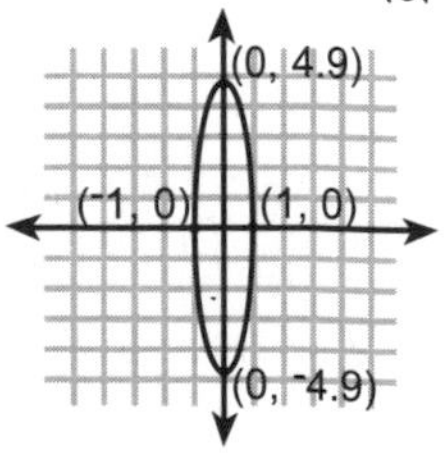

6. $c = \pm\sqrt{105}$
foci: (0, $\sqrt{105}$)
(0, -$\sqrt{105}$)

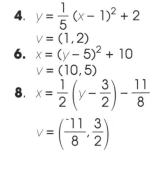

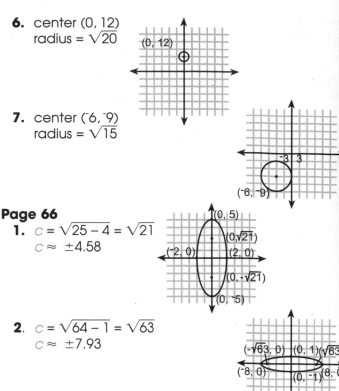

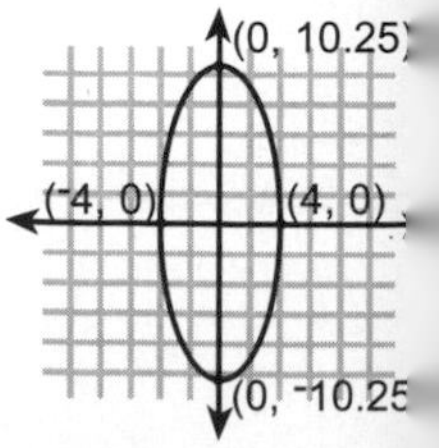

Answer Key

Page 67

1. center $(3, {}^-5)$

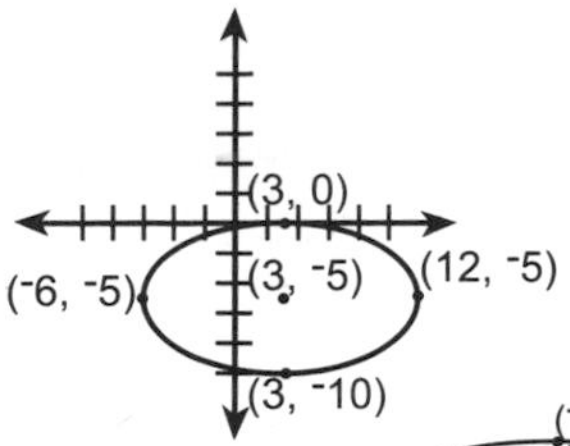

2. center $({}^-8, 6)$

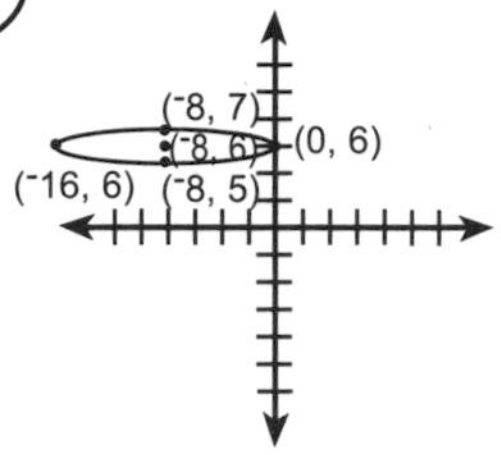

3. center $(0, 0)$

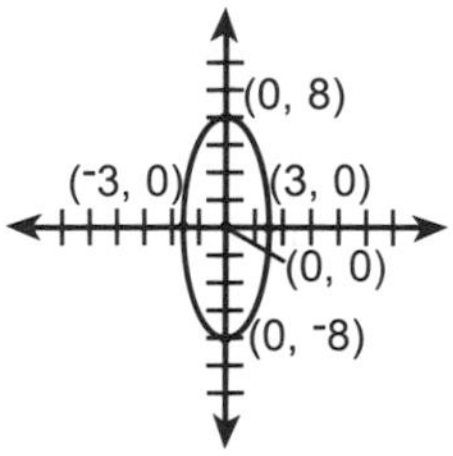

4. center $({}^-2, {}^-3)$

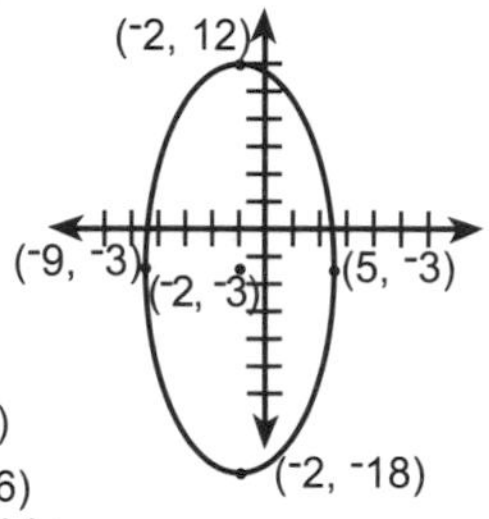

5. center $({}^-4, 16)$

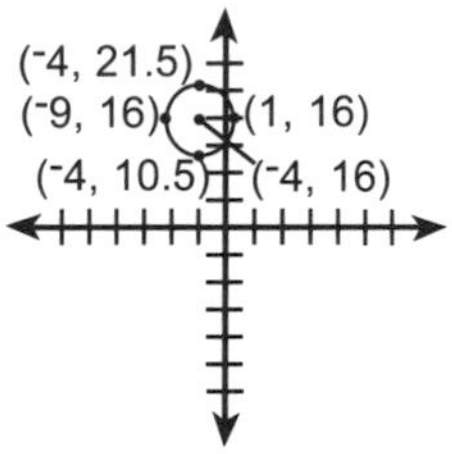

6. center $(5, 11)$

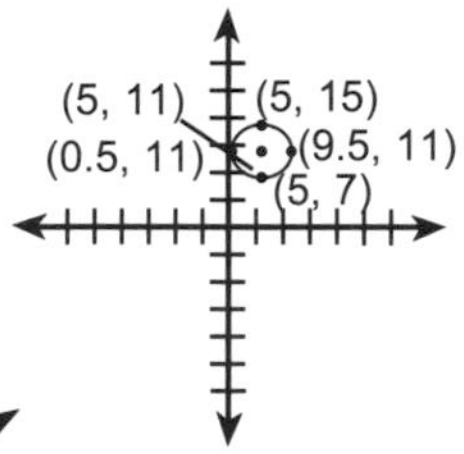

Page 69

1. foci $(\sqrt{74}, 0)$
$(-\sqrt{74}, 0)$

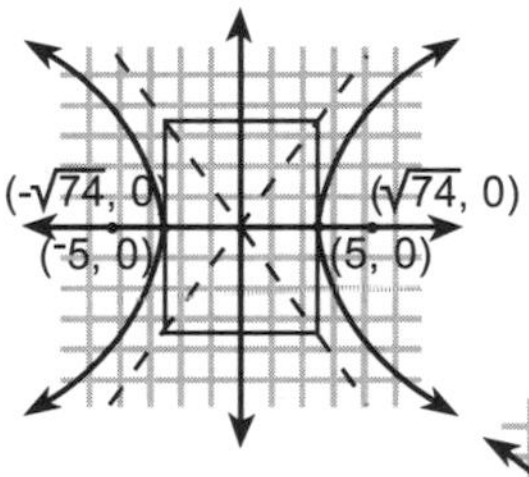

2. foci $(0, \sqrt{97})$
$(0, -\sqrt{97})$

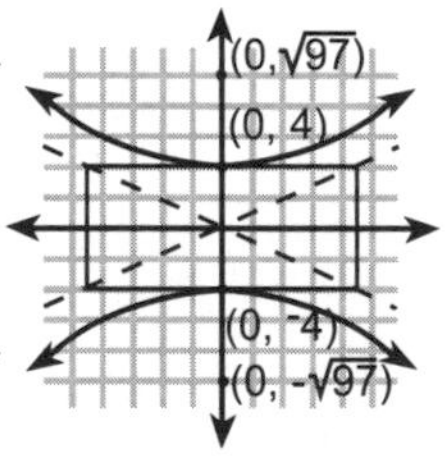

3. foci $(0, \sqrt{136})$
$(0, -\sqrt{136})$

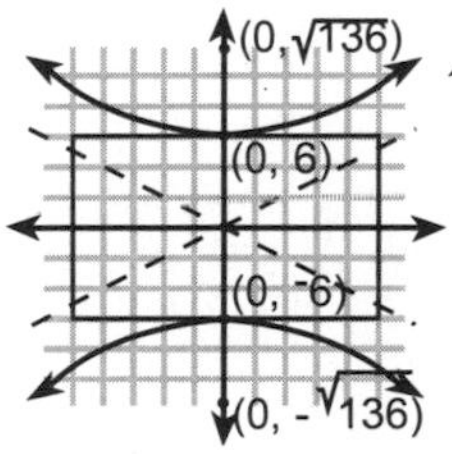

4. foci $(\sqrt{193}, 0)$
$(-\sqrt{193}, 0)$

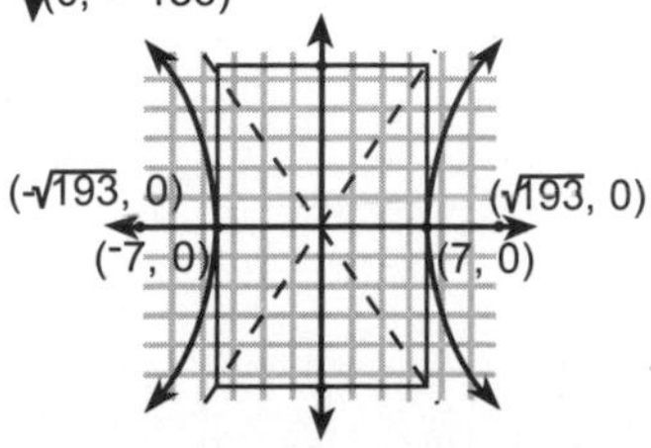

5. foci $(\sqrt{26}, 0)$
$(-\sqrt{26}, 0)$

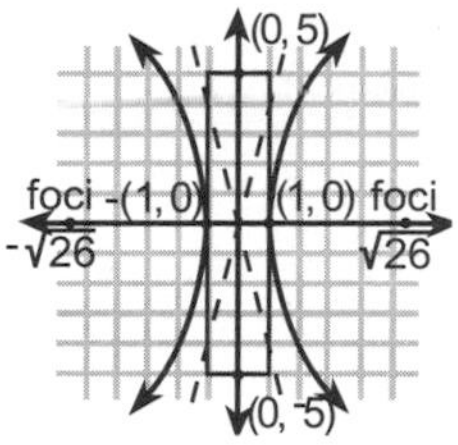

6. foci $(0, \sqrt{137})$
$(0, -\sqrt{137})$

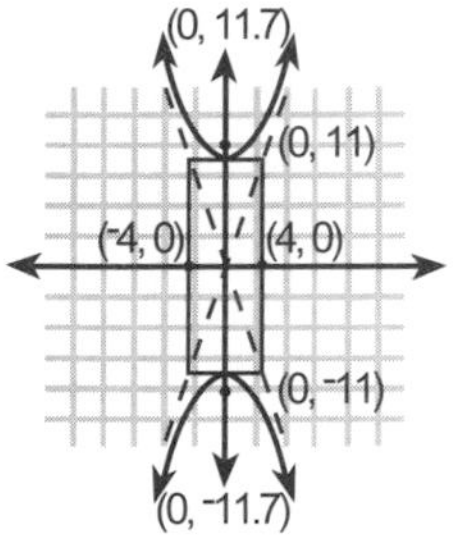

Page 70

1. center $(3, {}^-5)$

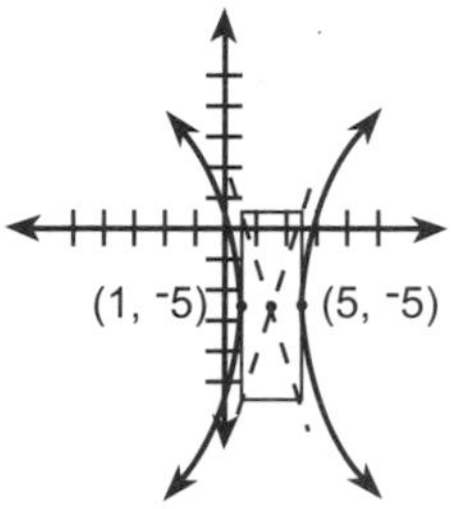

2. center $({}^-8, {}^-6)$

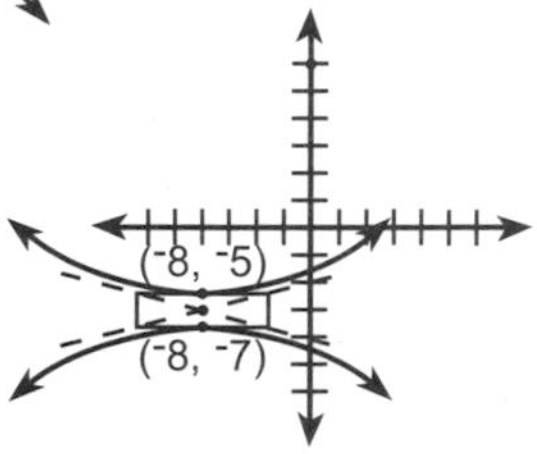

3. center $(0, 0)$

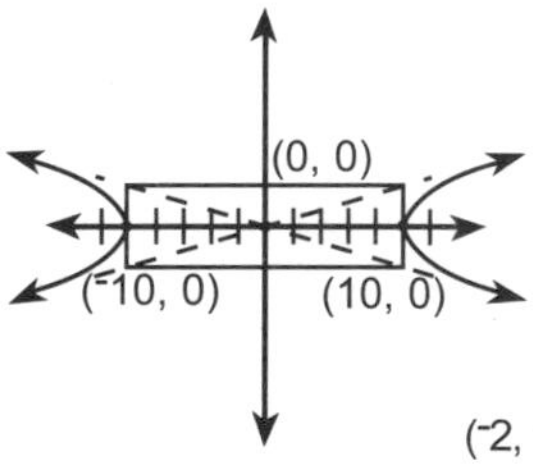

4. center $({}^-2, {}^-3)$

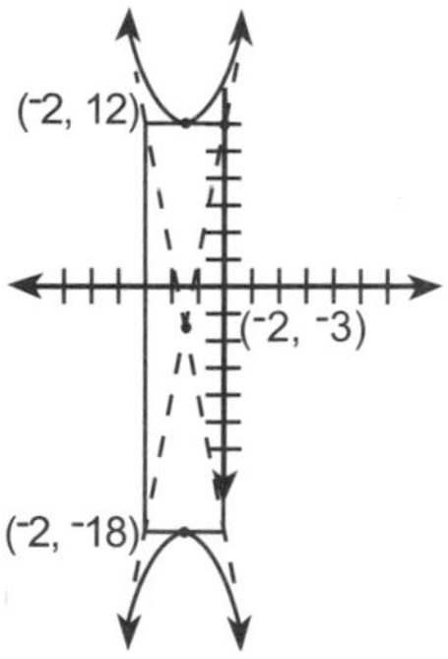

5. center $({}^-4, 16)$
vert: $({}^-4, 22)$
$({}^-4, 10)$

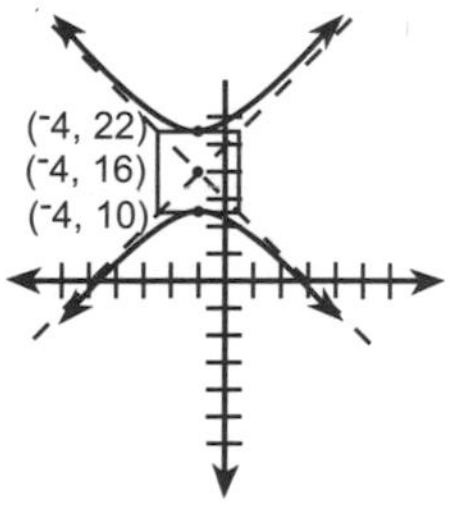

6. center $(5, 11)$
vert: $(9, 11)$
$(1, 11)$

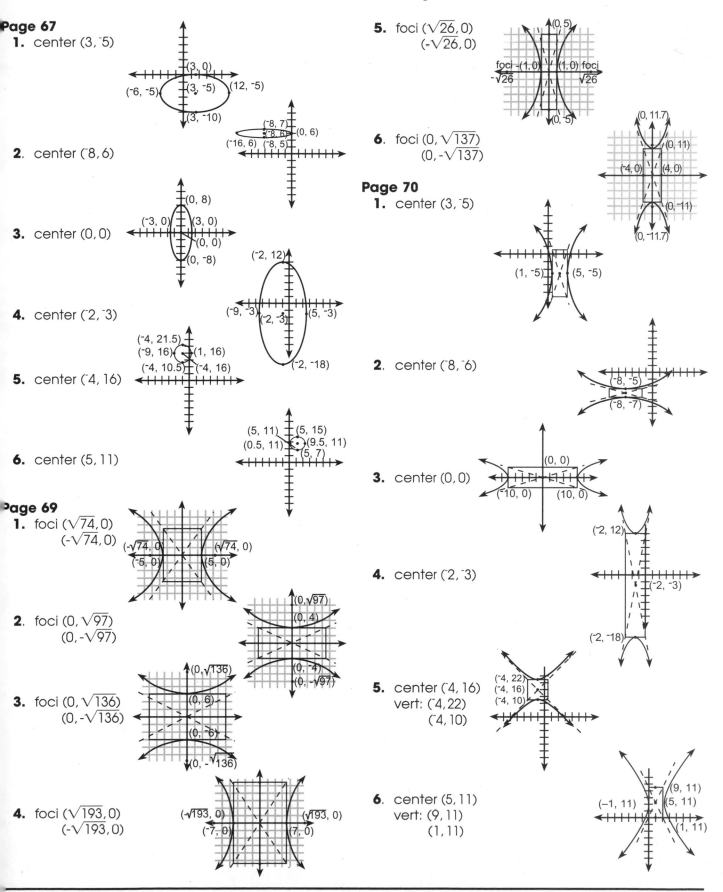

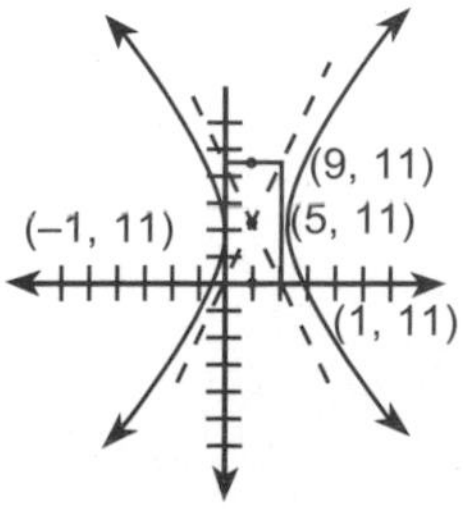

0-7424-1789-1 *Algebra II*

Answer Key

Page 71

1. $(x-2)^2 + (y+3)^2 = 9$

This is the equation of a circle with a center at (2, $^-3$).

2. $\dfrac{(x+3)^2}{4} + \dfrac{(y+1)^2}{9} = 1$

This is an ellipse with a center at ($^-3$, $^-1$).

3. $\dfrac{(x-6)^2}{1} + \dfrac{(y+4)^2}{25} = 1$

This is an ellipse with a center at (6, $^-4$).

4. $\dfrac{(x+3)^2}{1} - \dfrac{(y-4)^2}{16} = 1$

This is the equation of a hyperbola with a center at ($^-3$, 4).

5. $(x+4)^2 + (y+10)^2 = 4$

This is the equation of a circle with a center at ($^-4$, $^-10$).

Page 72

1. center (0, 2)

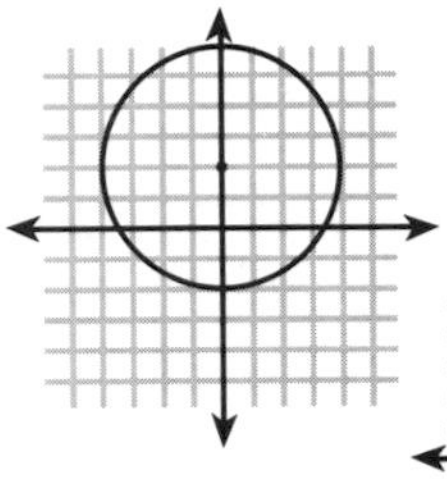

2. center (0, 3)

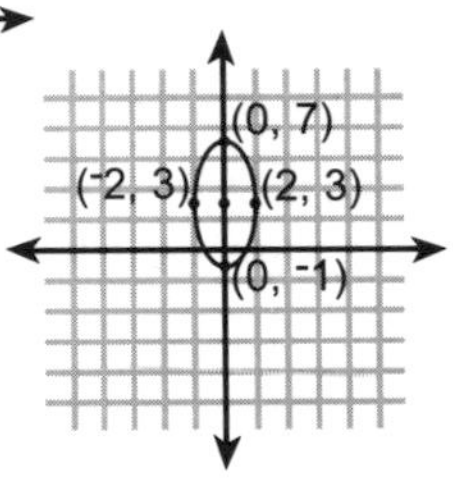

3. center (1, $^-5$)

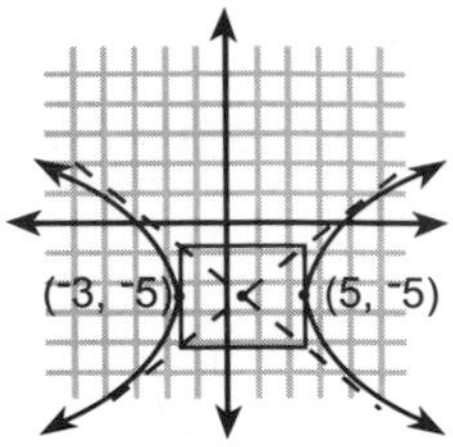

4. vertex ($^-2$, $^-3$)

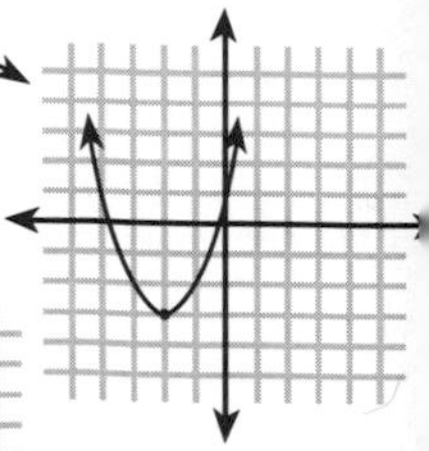

5. center ($^-3$, 1)

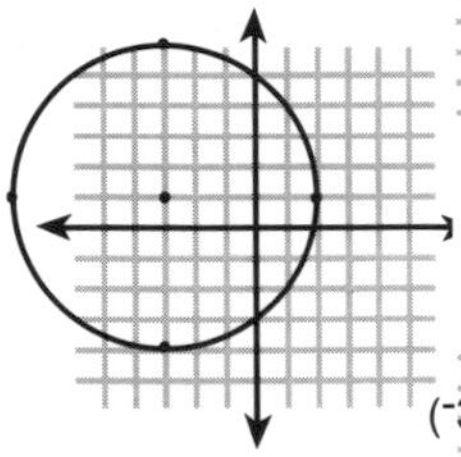

6. center ($^-1$, 3)

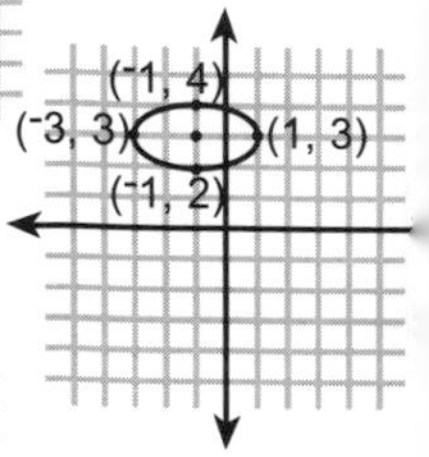

7. center ($^-2$, 1)

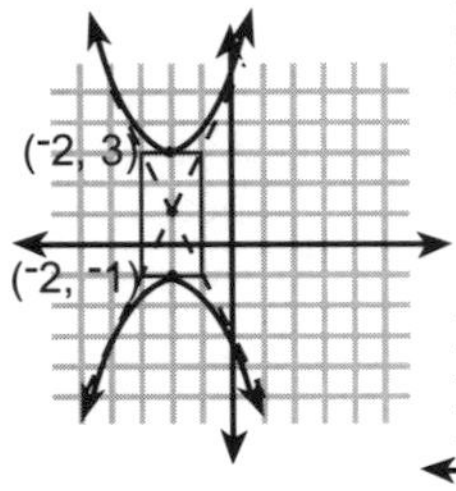

8. vertex ($^-4$, 4)

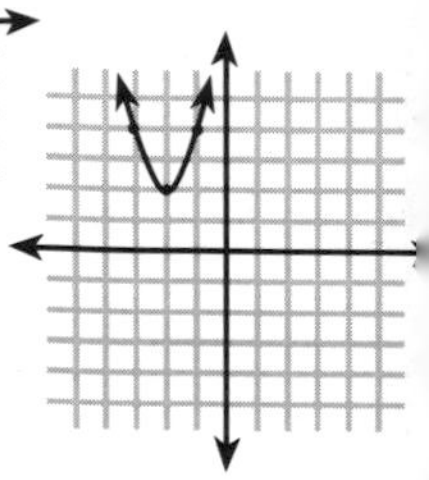

Page 73

1.

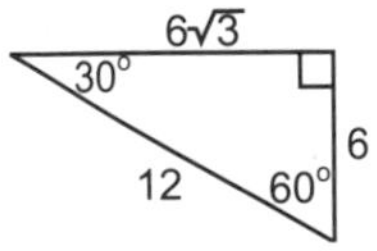

2.

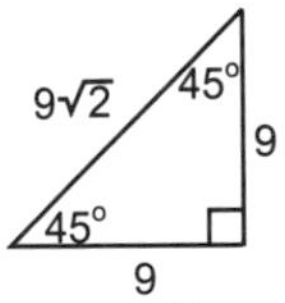

3.

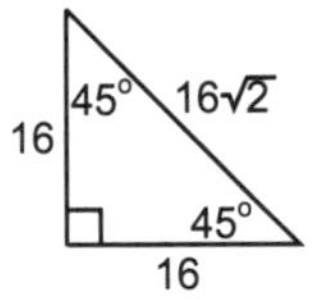

4.

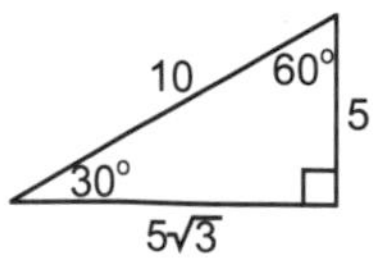

5.

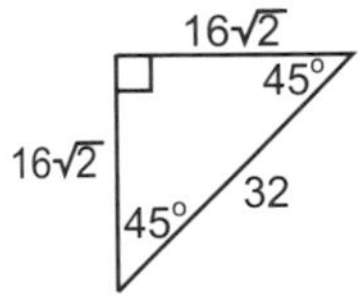

6.

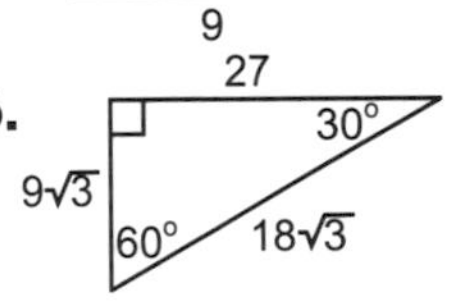

7.

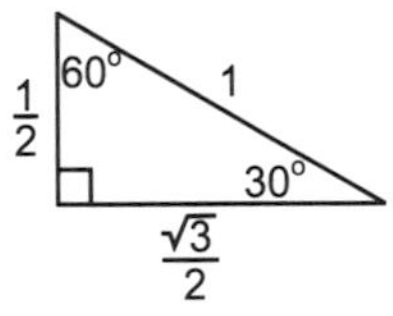

8.

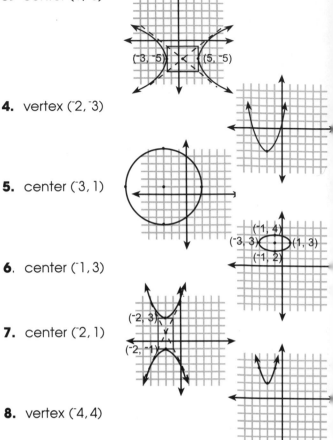

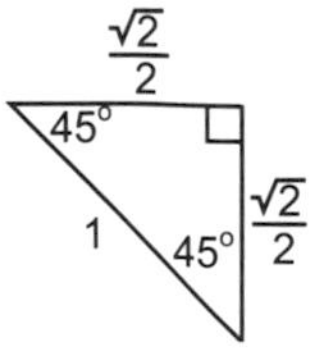

~~9 O~~	9/2 I	~~16√2 N~~	1/4 S	24 H	~~9√2 F~~	25 A	√2 L	~~16√2 O~~	√3 F	3 T	~~12 U~~
10 H	~~5 R~~	81 E	~~1/2 T~~	~~6√3 H~~	~~9√3 O~~	5/2 H	1/8 Y	7 P	~~16√2 F~~	7√2 O	~~√2/2 T~~
~~5√3 H~~	~~√2/2 E~~	11√2 T	11/2 E	15 N	25/2 U	~~16 L~~	~~√3/2 E~~	3/2 S	16√3 E	~~18√3 G~~	15/2 .

In a 30-60 right triangle, the side opposite the 30-degree angle <u>IS HALF THE HYPOTENUSE</u>.

Answer Key

Page 74

1. $\sin B = \frac{3}{5}$ $\cos B = \frac{4}{5}$ $\tan B = \frac{3}{4}$
2. $\sin A = \frac{15}{39}$ $\cos A = \frac{36}{39}$ $\tan A = \frac{15}{36}$

   $\sin B = \frac{36}{39}$ $\cos B = \frac{15}{39}$ $\tan B = \frac{36}{15}$
3. $\sin A = \frac{Y}{Z}$ $\cos A = \frac{X}{Z}$ $\tan A = \frac{Y}{X}$

   $\sin B = \frac{X}{Z}$ $\cos B = \frac{Y}{Z}$ $\tan B = \frac{X}{Y}$
4. $\sin A = \frac{12}{13}$ $\cos A = \frac{5}{13}$ $\tan A = \frac{12}{5}$

   $\sin B = \frac{5}{13}$ $\cos B = \frac{12}{13}$ $\tan B = \frac{5}{12}$

hey always have the same ratio.

Page 75

1. = 1 **2.** = 0.98 **3.** = $^-0.77$
4. = 0.98 **5.** = 0.39 **6.** = $^-1$
1. = 68° **2.** = 48° **3.** = 72°
4. = 54° **5.** = 75 **6.** = 5°

Page 76

1. $x = 11.3$, $y = 4.1$ **2.** $x = 38.6$, $y = 37.3$
3. $x = 9.1$, $y = 4.3$ **4.** $x = 14$, $y = 12.1$
5. $x = 21.9$, $y = 11.0$ **6.** $x = 19.1$, $y = 19.1$
7. $x = 8.6$, $y = 12.3$ **8.** $x = 4.9$, $y = 28.4$

Page 77

1. $x = 30°$, $y = 60°$ **2.** $x = 45°$, $y = 45°$
3. $x = 62°$, $y = 28°$ **4.** $x = 60°$, $y = 30°$
5. $x = 62°$, $y = 28°$ **6.** $x = 13°$, $y = 77°$
7. $x = 71°$, $y = 19°$ **8.** $x = 57°$, $y = 33°$

Page 78

1. $\cos x = \frac{3}{20}$, $x = 81.4°$

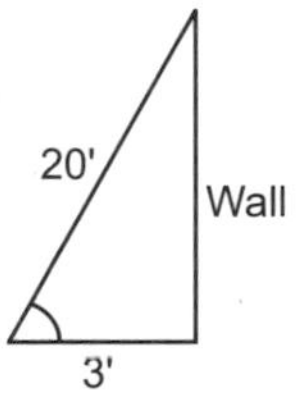

2. $\tan 30° = \frac{h}{100}$, $h = 57.7 + 6 = 63.7$ ft.

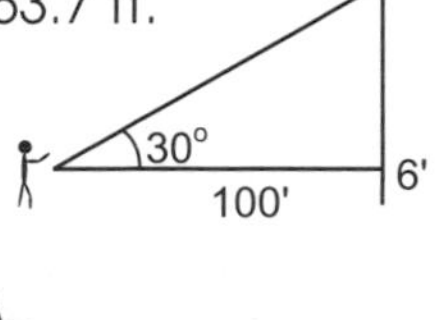

3. $\tan x = \frac{1500}{9000} = 9.5°$

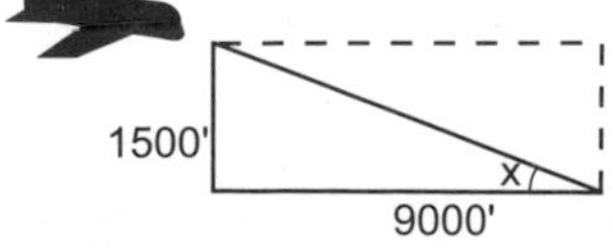

4. $\sin x = \frac{30}{150} = 12°$

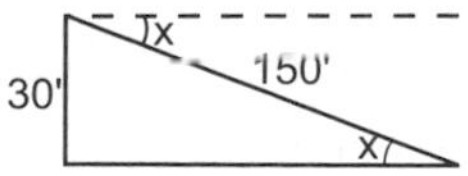

5. $\sin 30° = \frac{15}{x}$ $x = 30$ ft.

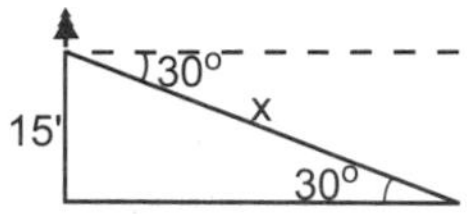

Page 80

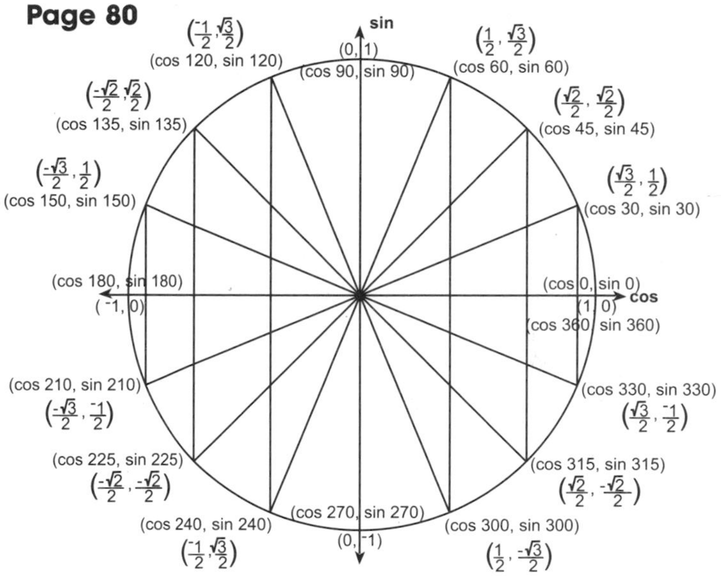

Page 81

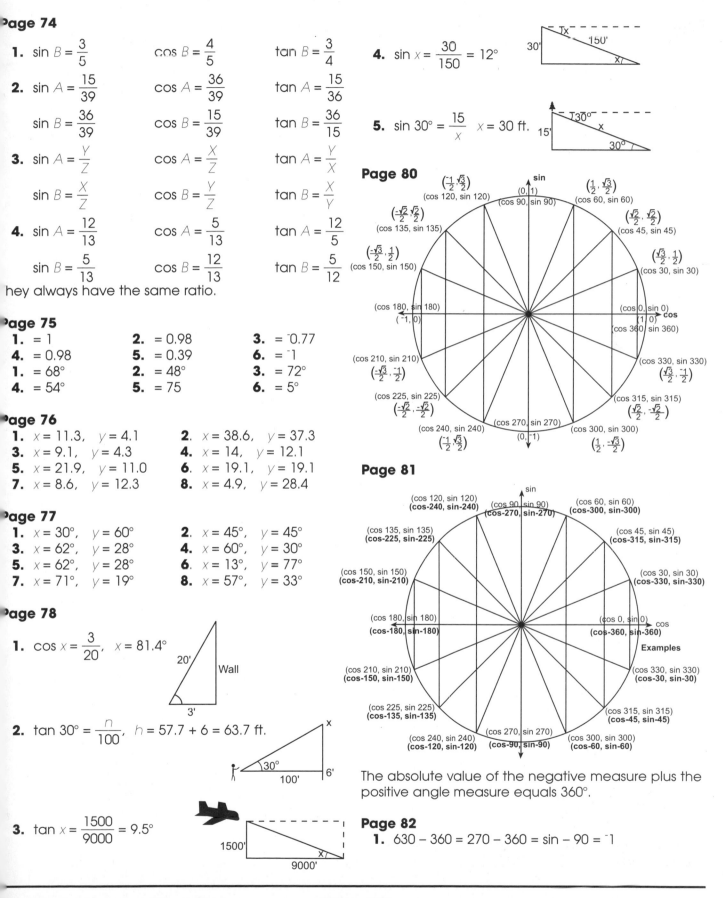

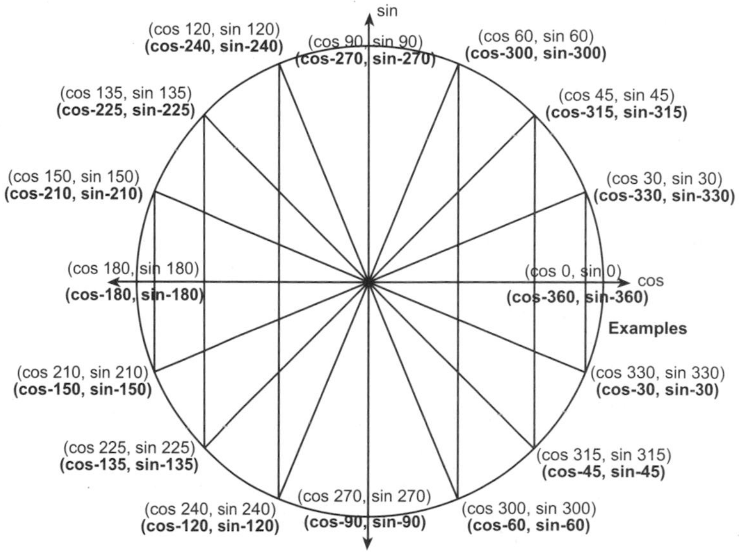

The absolute value of the negative measure plus the positive angle measure equals 360°.

Page 82

1. 630 – 360 = 270 – 360 = sin – 90 = $^-1$

Answer Key

2. $750 - 360 = 390 \cdot 360 = \sin - 30 = -\frac{1}{2}$

3. $480 - 360 = 120 - 360 = \cos - 240 = -\frac{1}{2}$

4. $420 - 360 = 60 - 360 = \sin - 300 = -\frac{\sqrt{3}}{2}$

5. $510 - 360 = 150 - 360 = \sin - 210 = \frac{1}{2}$

6. $1020 - 360 = 660 - 360 = \cos 300 = \frac{1}{2}$

7. $^{-}540 - 360 = 900 - 360 = 540 - 360 =$
$180 - 360 = {}^{-}180 = {}^{-}1$

8. $^{-}675 + 360 = 315 - 360 = -45 = \frac{\sqrt{2}}{2}$

9. $450 - 360 = 90 - 360 = {}^{-}270 - 360 = {}^{-}90 = 0$

10. $930 - 360 = 570 - 360 = 210 - 360 = {}^{-}150 = -\frac{\sqrt{3}}{2}$

11. $405 - 360 = 45 = \frac{\sqrt{2}}{2}$

12. $600 - 360 = 240 - 360 = {}^{-}120 + 300 = \frac{\sqrt{3}}{2}$

13. $3600 - 360 = 3240 - 360 = 2880 \times 10 = 0$

14. $^{-}1830 + 360 = 1470 - 360 = 1110 - 360 =$
$750 - 360 = 390 - 360 = 30 = \frac{\sqrt{3}}{2}$

List the pairs: 1 & 7; 2 & 3; 4 & 10; 5 & 6; 11 & 8; 12 & 14

In each pair, what is the relationship of the reference angles? The reference angles are complementary.

Page 83

1. $\frac{31}{18}\pi$ **2.** $\frac{5}{6}\pi$ **3.** $\frac{1}{6}\pi$

4. $\frac{7}{3}\pi$ **5.** $\frac{2}{3}\pi$ **6.** $\frac{35}{18}\pi$

1. 225° **2.** 720° **3.** 210°
4. 30° **5.** 315° **6.** 810°

Page 85. Answers may vary.

1. cos 30°, cos 330° **2.** cos 75°, cos 285°
3. cos $^{-}$90°, cos 450° **4.** cos 135°, cos 225°
5. cos 210°, cos 150°

Answers may vary.

1. sin 60°, sin 120° **2.** sin 150°, sin 30°
3. sin 0°, sin 180° **4.** sin 315°, sin $^{-}$225°
5. sin 40°, sin 140°

Page 84.

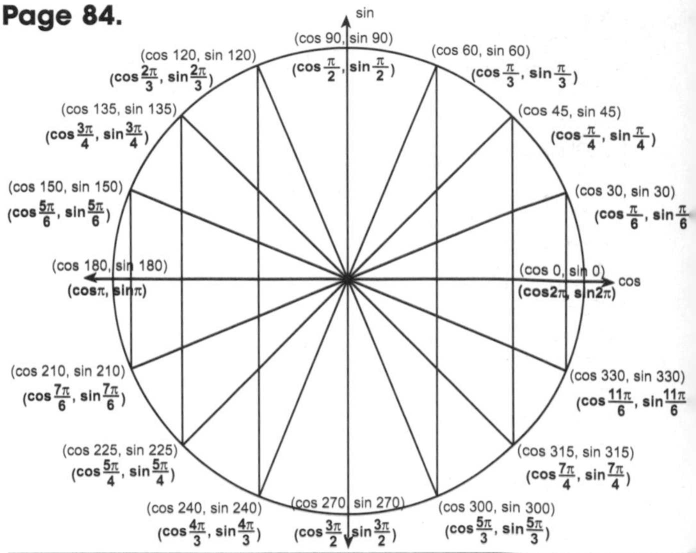

Page 86

1.

$x°$	y
0	1
30	0.86
45	7
60	1/2
90	0
135	$^{-}$0.7
180	$^{-}$1
270	0
360	1

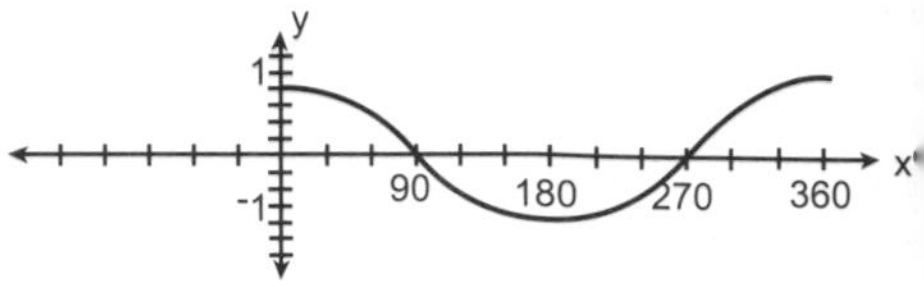

2.

$x°$	y
90	1
135	0.7
180	0
270	$^{-}$1
360	0
405	0.7
450	1

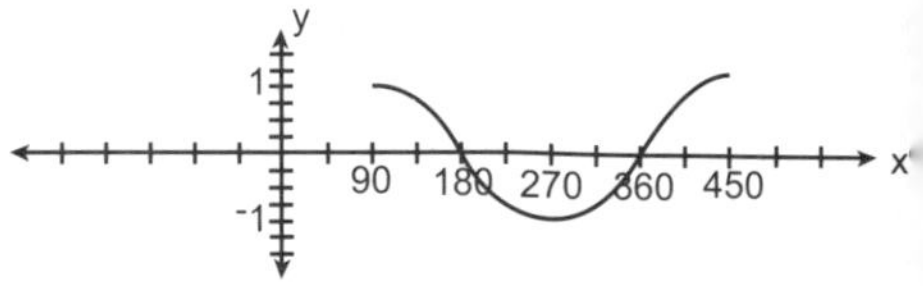

3.

$x°$	y
$^{-}$90	$^{-}$1
0	0
90	1
180	0
270	$^{-}$1

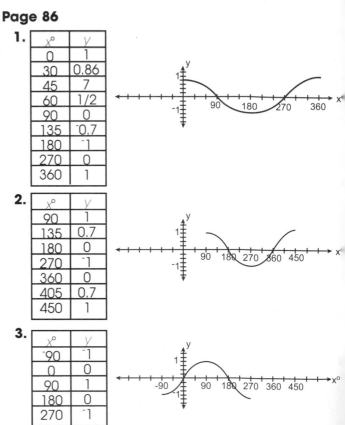

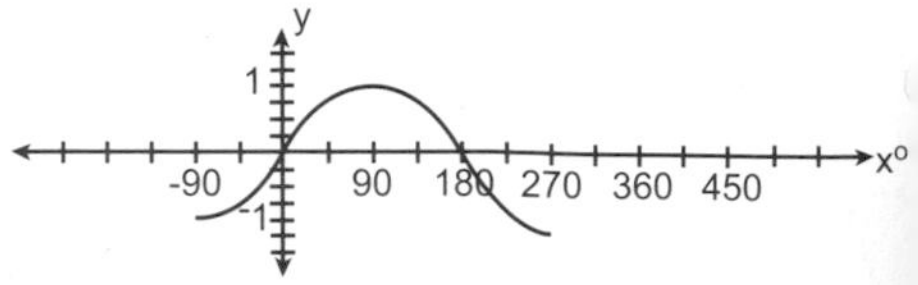

They look like the same graph shifted 90° to the right

Answer Key

Page 87

4.

x°	y
-360	0
-270	1
-180	0
-90	-1
0	0
90	1
180	0
270	-1
360	0

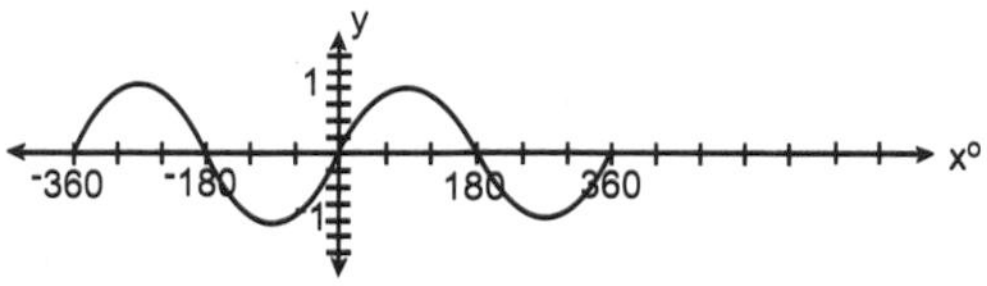

5.

x°	y
-360	1
-270	0
-180	-1
-90	0
0	1
90	0
180	-1
270	0
360	1

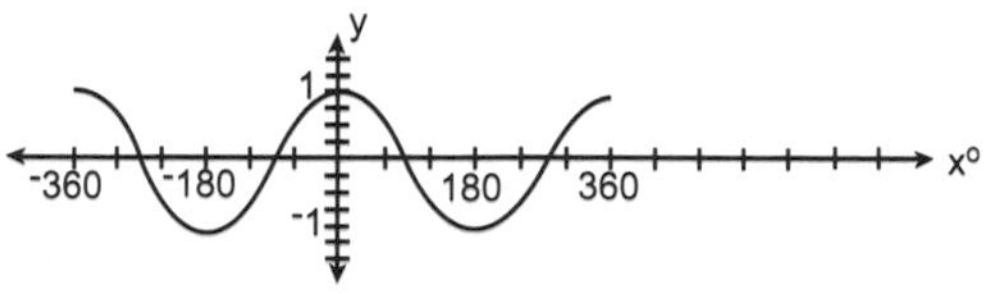

6.

x°	y
0	0
90	1
180	0
270	-1
360	0
450	1
540	0
630	-1
720	0

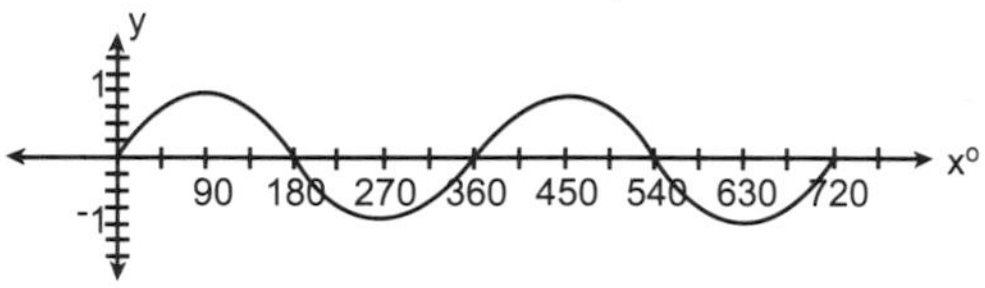

7.

x°	y
0	1
90	0
180	-1
270	0
360	1
450	0
540	-1
630	0
720	1

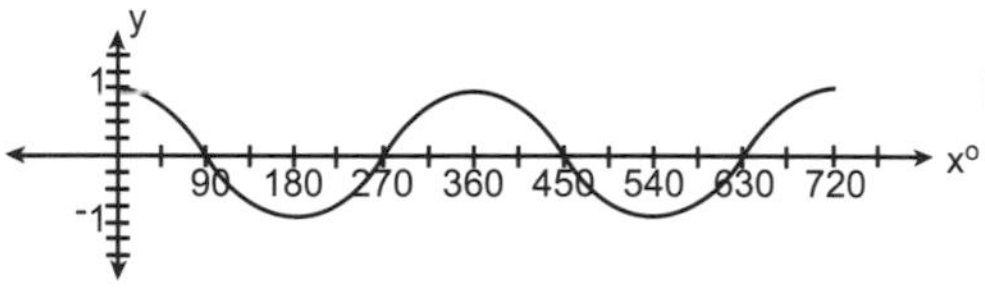

Page 88

1.

x°	y
0	4
90	0
180	-4
270	0
360	4

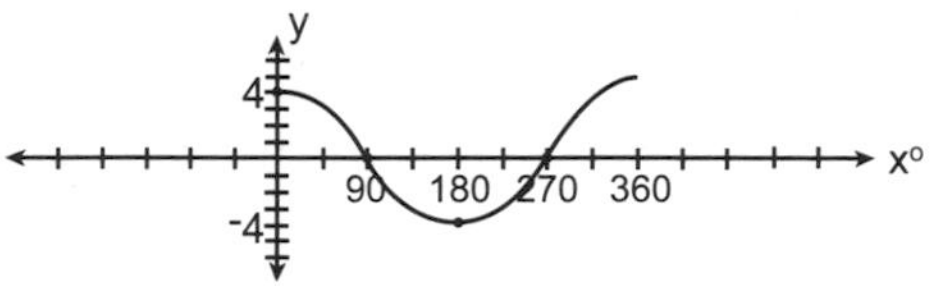

2.

x°	y
0	0
90	3/2
180	0
270	-3/2
360	0

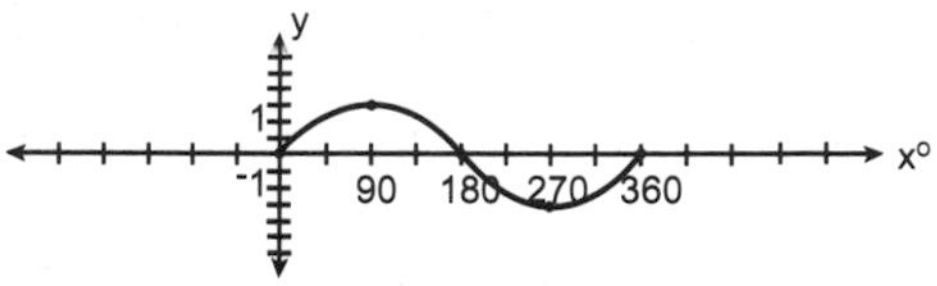

3.

x°	y
0	1/2
90	0
180	-1/2
270	0
360	1/2

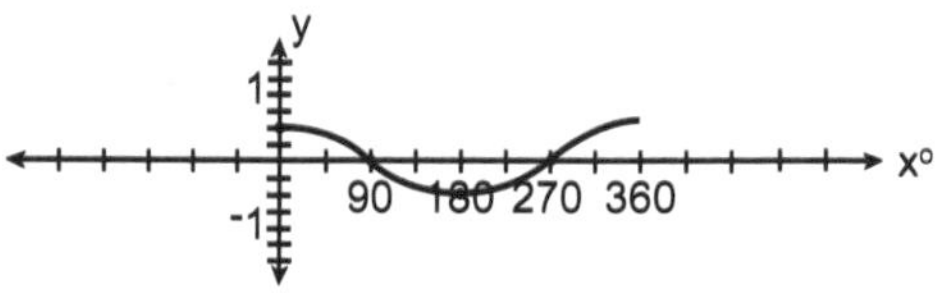

4.

x°	y
0	0
90	-3
180	0
270	3
360	0

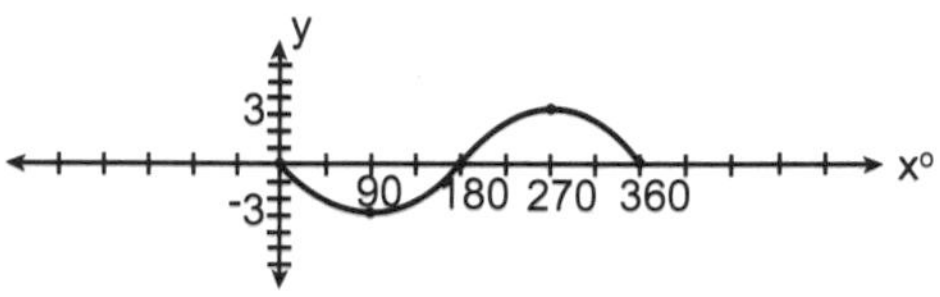

5.

x°	y
0	0
90	4
180	0
270	-4
360	0

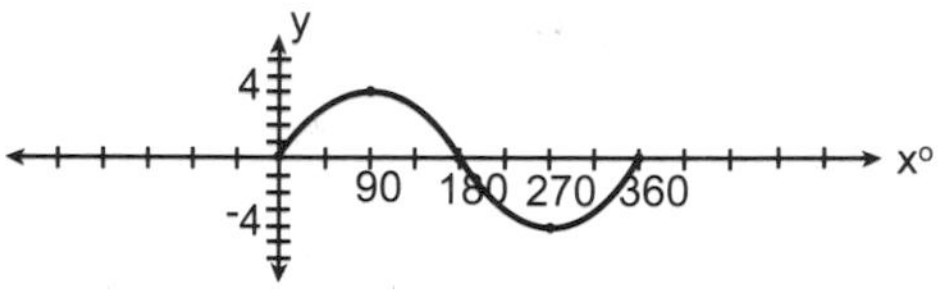

6.

x°	y
0	0
90	-1/3
180	0
270	1/3
360	0

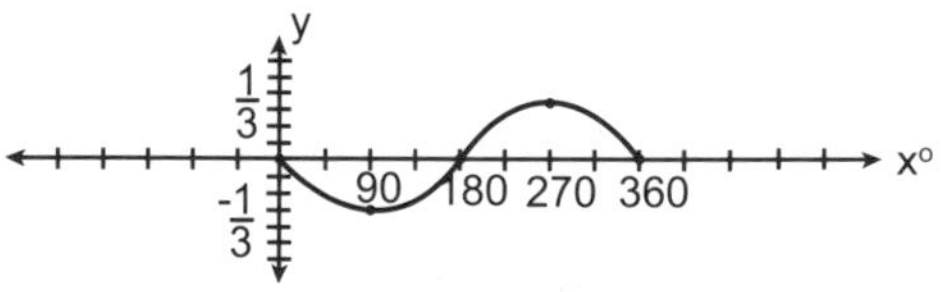

A increases the amplitude. -*A* inverts the graph.

Page 89

1.

x°	y
0	4
90	3
180	2
270	3
360	4

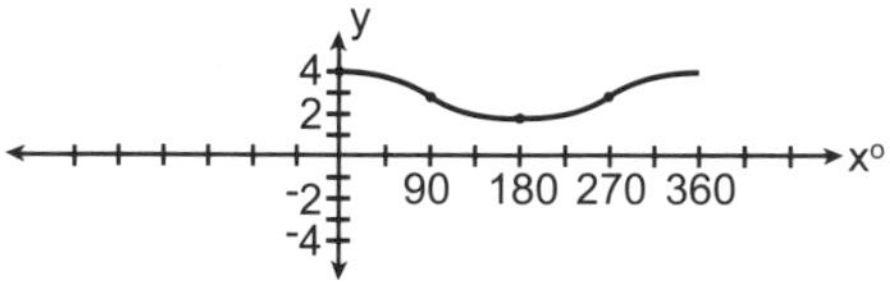

2.

x°	y
0	2
90	3
180	2
270	1
360	2

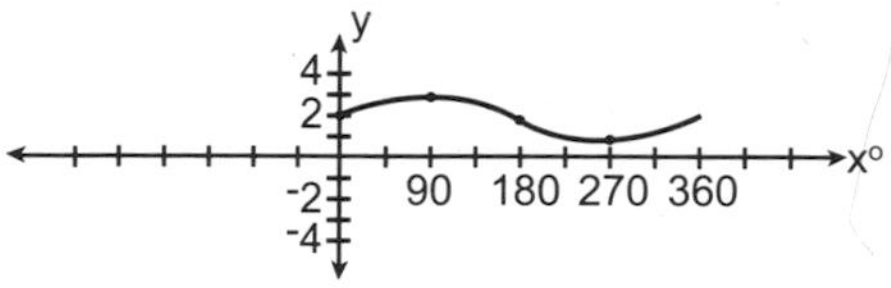

3.

x°	y
0	3/2
90	1/2
180	-1/2
270	1/2
360	3/2

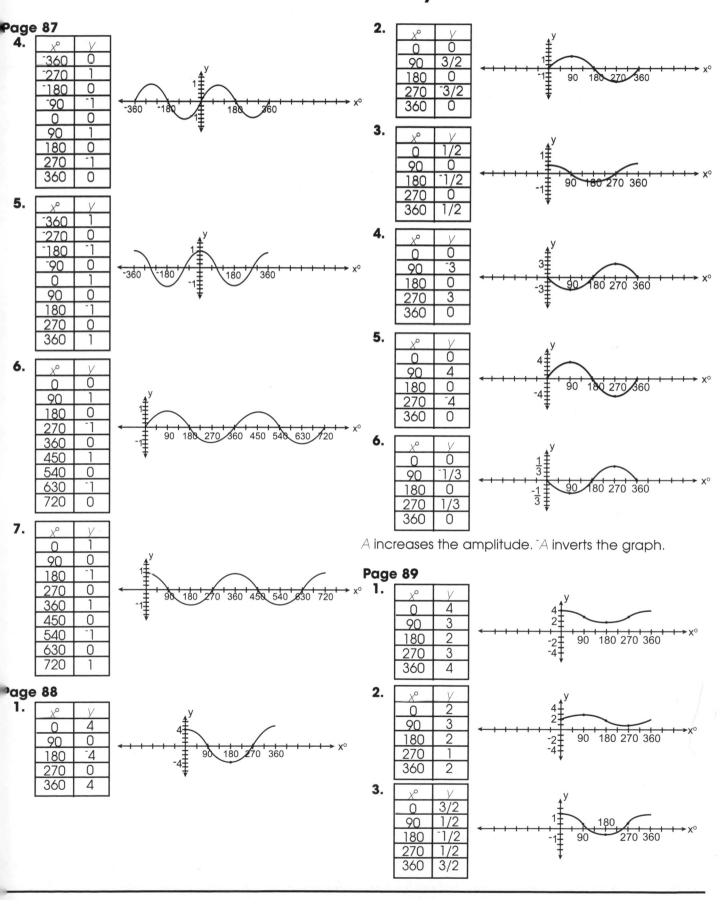

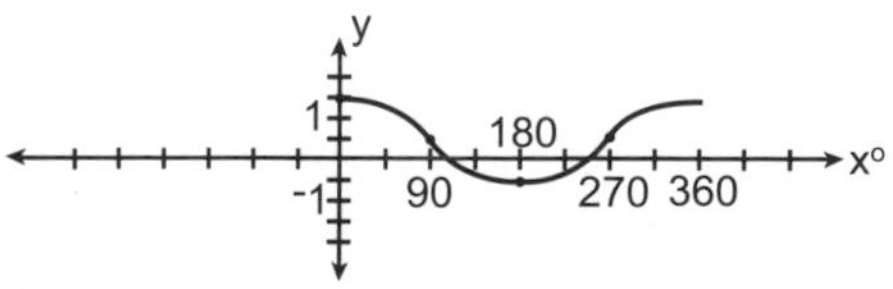

Answer Key

4.

x°	y
0	-3
90	-2
180	-3
270	-4
360	-3

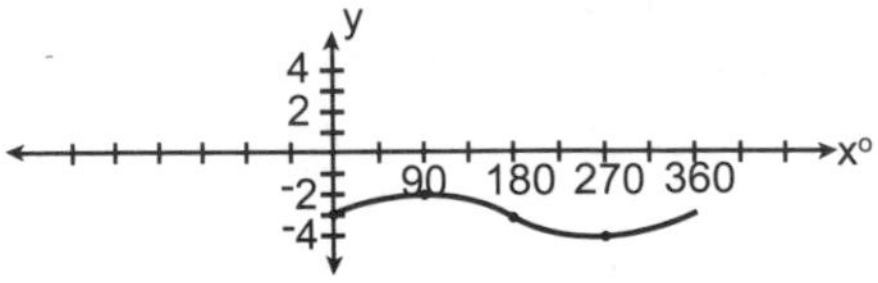

5.

x°	y
0	0
90	-1
180	-2
270	-1
360	0

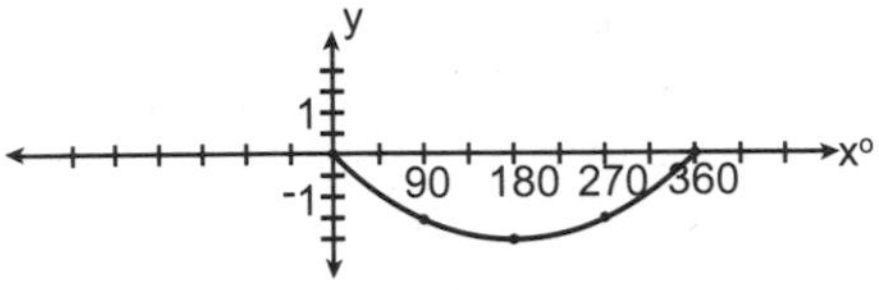

6.

x°	y
0	-1/3
90	2/3
180	-1/3
270	-4/3
360	-1/3

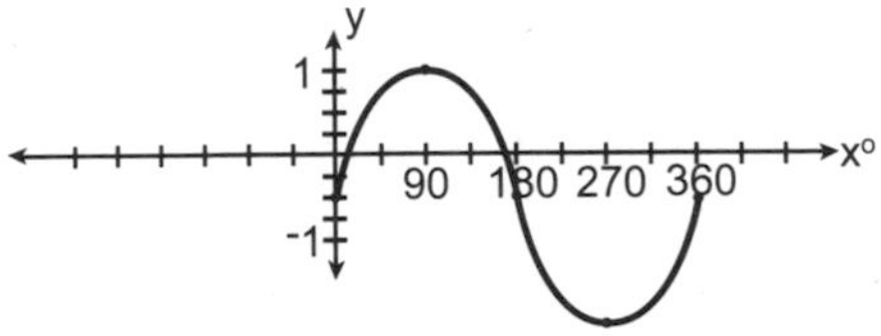

C moves the entire graph up. $-C$ moves the entire graph down.

Page 90

1.

x°	$4x$	y
0	0	1
22.5	90	0
45	180	-1
67.5	270	0
90	360	1

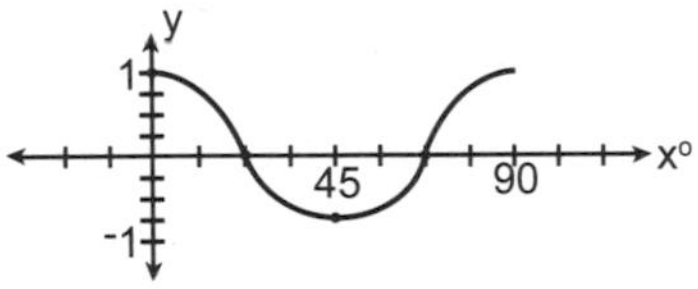

2.

x°	$3x$	y
0	0	0
30	90	1
60	180	0
90	270	-1
120	360	0

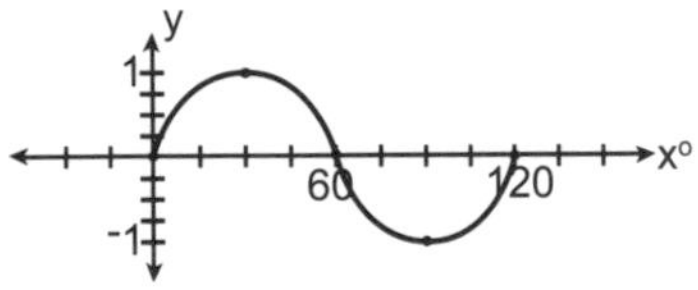

3.

x°	$1/2x$	y
0	0	0
180	90	1
360	180	0
540	270	-1
720	360	0

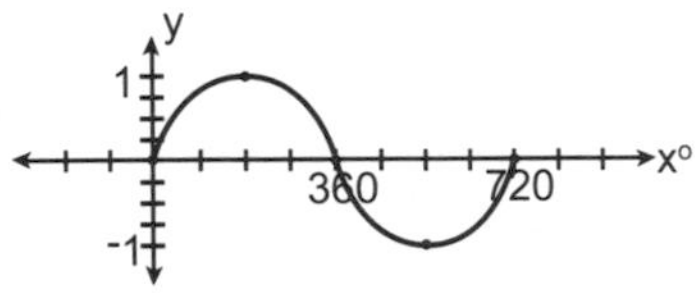

4.

x°	$1/3x$	y
0	0	1
270	90	0
540	180	-1
810	270	0
1080	360	1

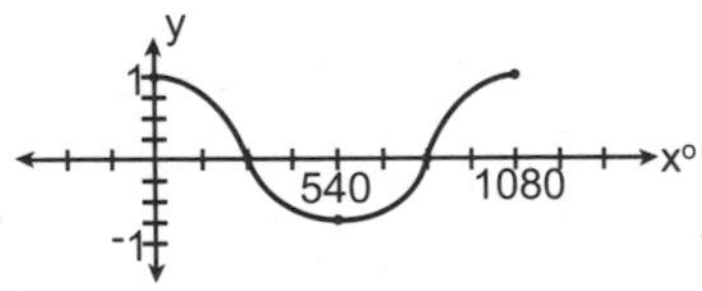

5.

x°	$1/4x$	y
0	0	0
360	90	1
720	180	0
1080	270	-1
1440	360	0

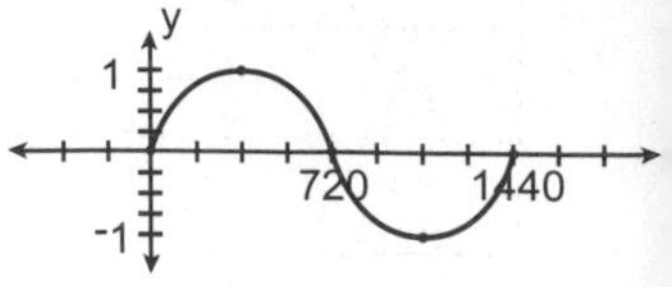

6.

x°	$2x$	y
0	0	1
45	90	0
90	180	-1
135	270	0
180	360	1

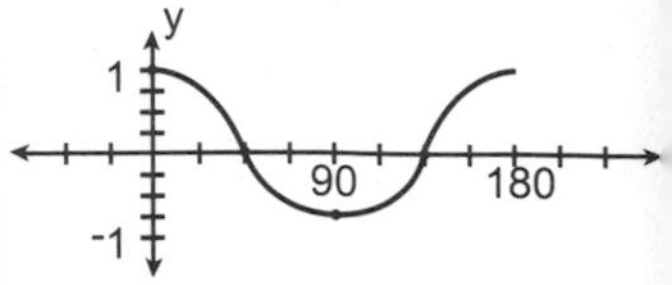

Page 91

1.

x°	$x - 90$	y
90	0	1
180	90	0
270	180	-1
360	270	0
450	360	1

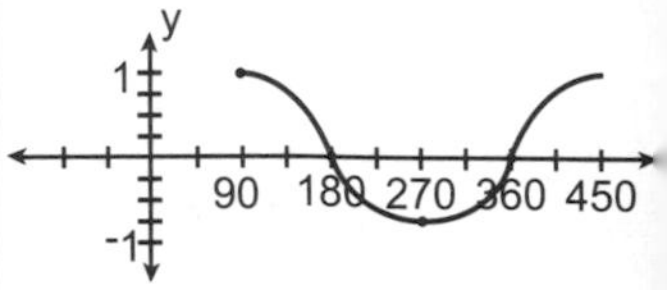

2.

x°	$x + 90$	y
-90	0	0
0	90	1
90	180	0
180	270	-1
270	360	0

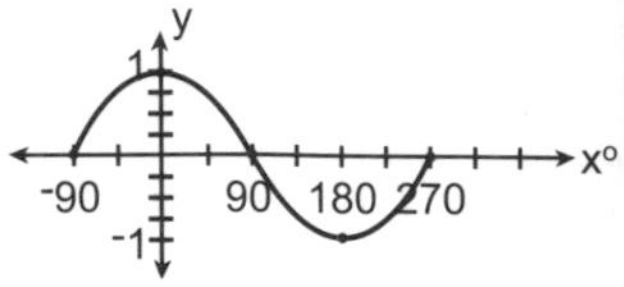

3.

x°	$x - 180$	y
180	0	0
270	90	1
360	180	0
450	270	-1
540	360	0

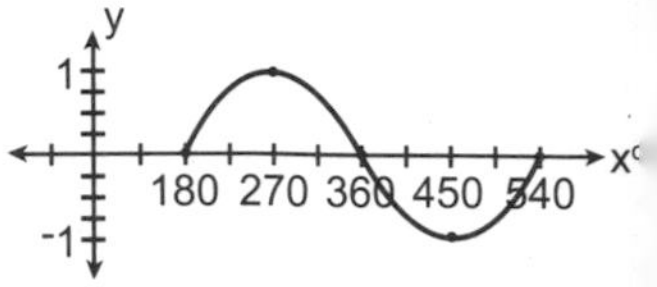

4.

x°	$x + 45$	y
-45	0	1
45	90	0
135	180	-1
225	270	0
315	360	1

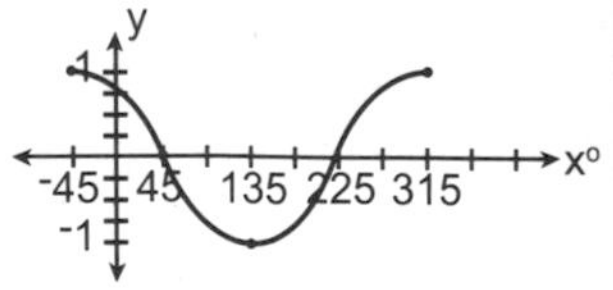

5.

x°	$x - 270$	y
270	0	0
360	90	1
450	180	0
540	270	-1
630	360	0

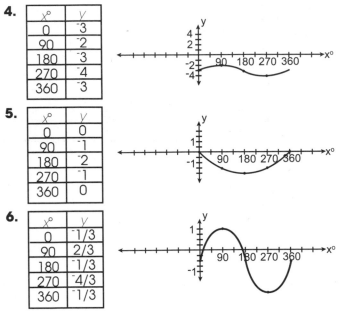

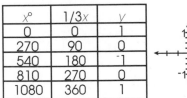

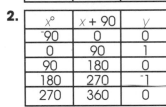

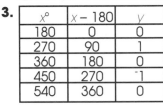

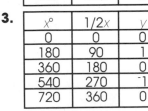

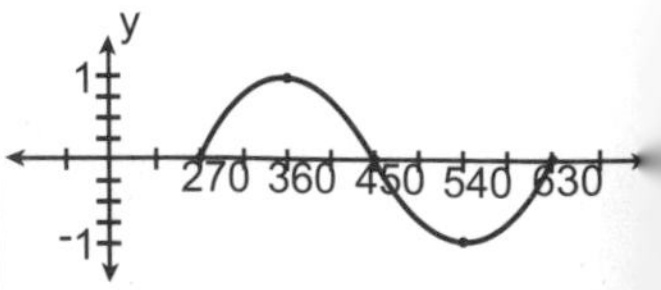

0-7424-1789-1 *Algeb*

Answer Key

6.

$x°$	$x + 30$	y
-30	0	1
60	90	0
150	180	-1
240	270	0
330	360	1

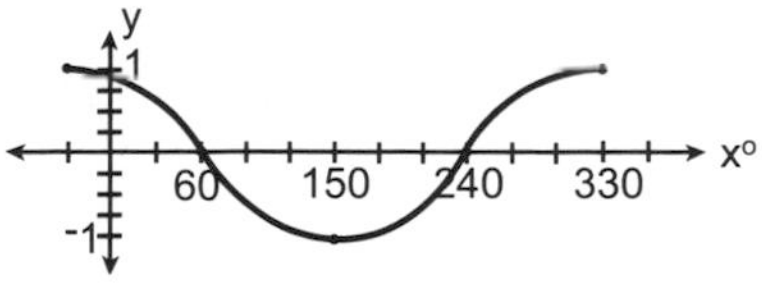

Page 92

1.

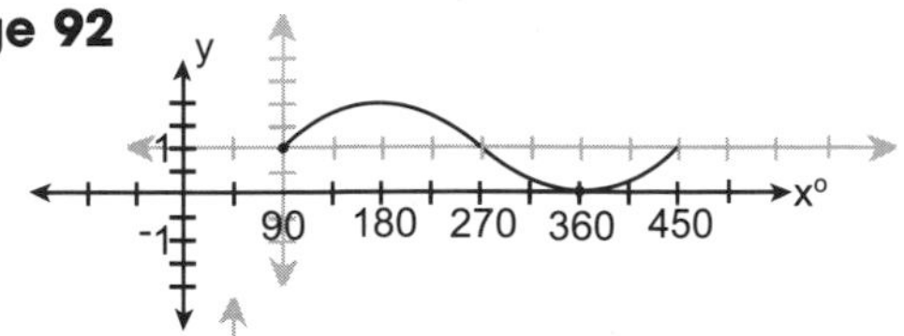

2.

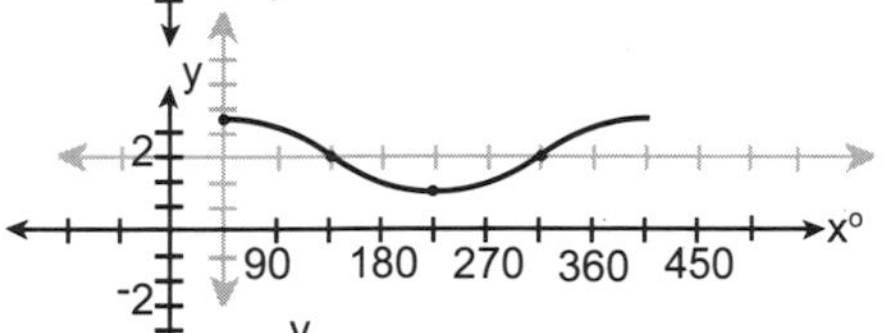

3.

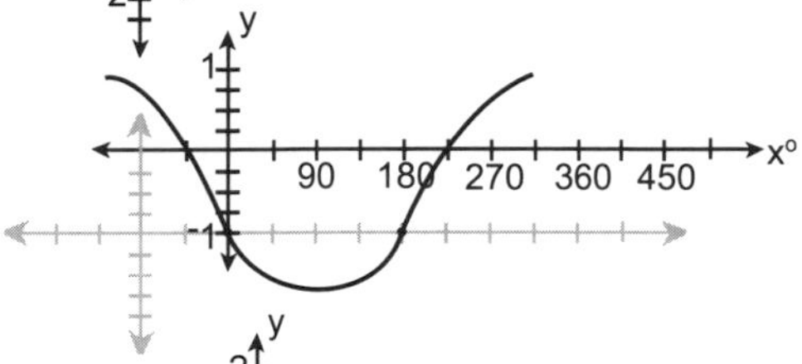

4.

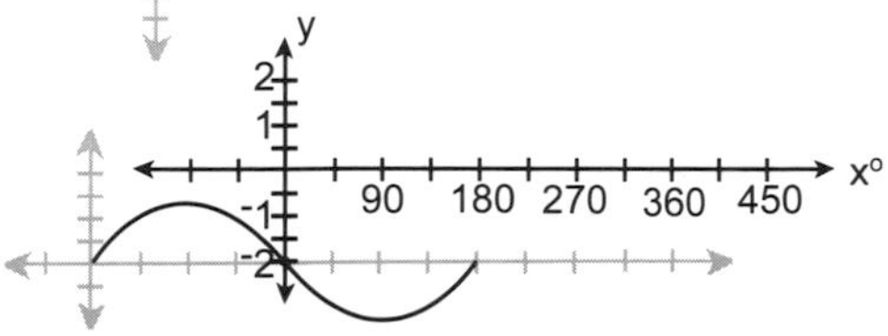

5.

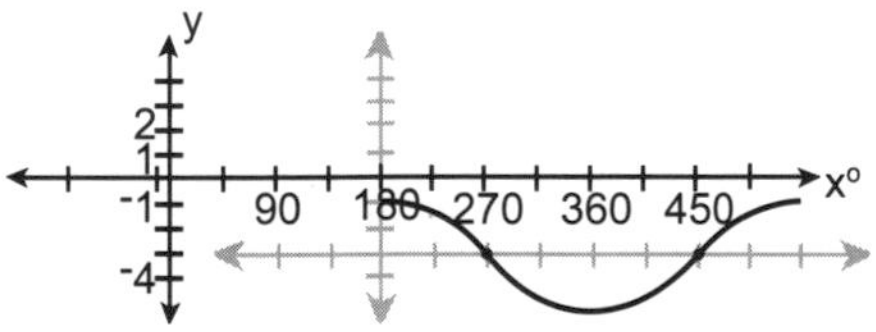

Page 94

1.

$x°$	$3x$	y
0	0	-1
30	90	0
60	180	1
90	270	0
120	360	-1

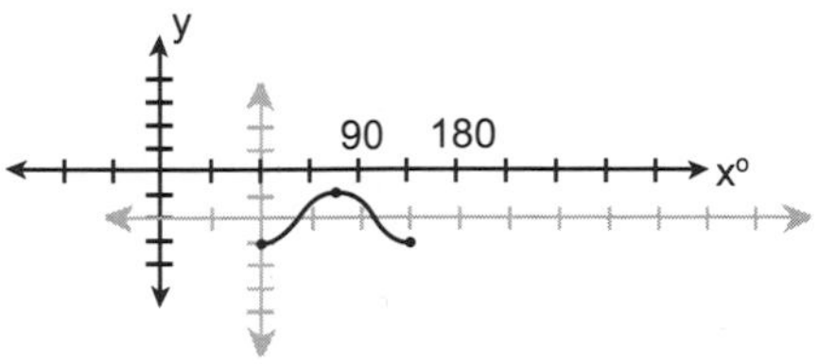

2.

$x°$	$2x$	y
0	0	1/2
45	90	0
90	180	-1/2
135	270	0
180	360	1/2

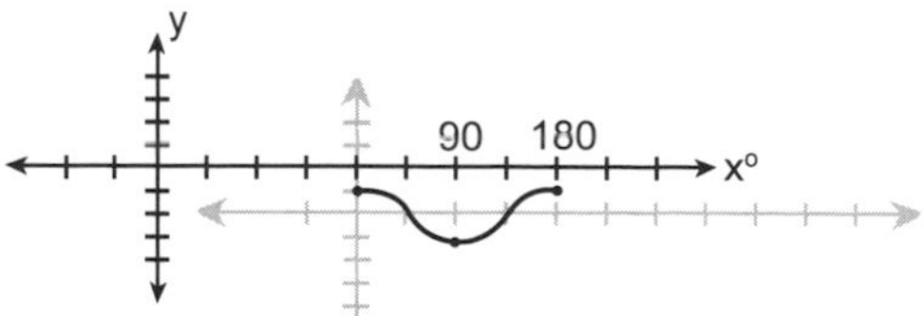

3.

$x°$	x	y
0	0	0
90	90	3
180	180	0
270	270	-3
360	360	0

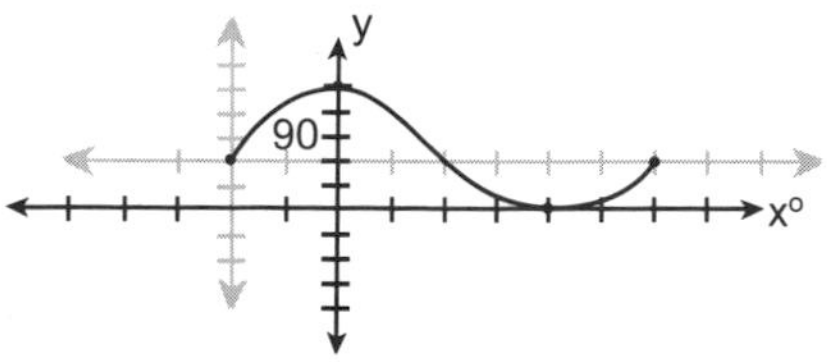

4.

$x°$	$1/2x$	y
0	0	0
180	90	-2
360	180	0
540	270	2
720	360	0

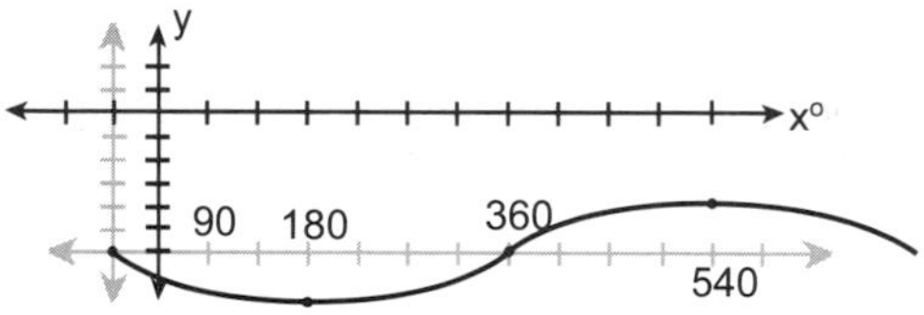

5.

$x°$	$4x$	y
0	0	3
22.5	90	0
45	180	-3
67.5	270	0
90	360	3

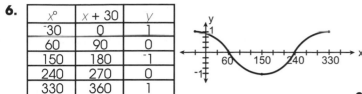

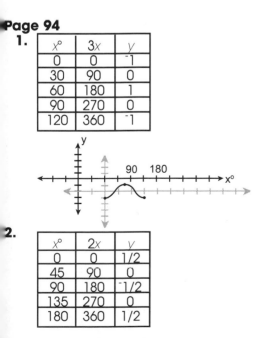

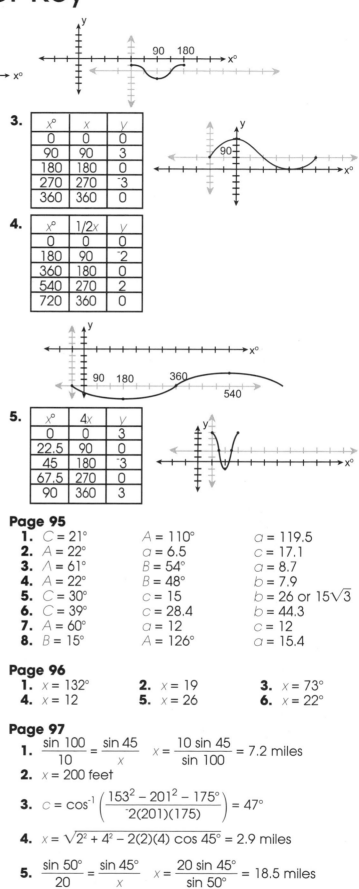

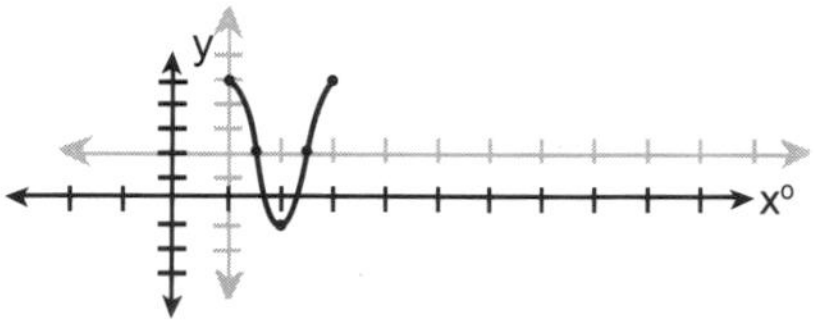

Page 95

1. $C = 21°$	$A = 110°$	$a = 119.5$
2. $A = 22°$	$a = 6.5$	$c = 17.1$
3. $A = 61°$	$B = 54°$	$a = 8.7$
4. $A = 22°$	$B = 48°$	$b = 7.9$
5. $C = 30°$	$c = 15$	$b = 26$ or $15\sqrt{3}$
6. $C = 39°$	$c = 28.4$	$b = 44.3$
7. $A = 60°$	$a = 12$	$c = 12$
8. $B = 15°$	$A = 126°$	$a = 15.4$

Page 96

1. $x = 132°$ **2.** $x = 19$ **3.** $x = 73°$
4. $x = 12$ **5.** $x = 26$ **6.** $x = 22°$

Page 97

1. $\frac{\sin 100}{10} = \frac{\sin 45}{x}$ $\quad x = \frac{10 \sin 45}{\sin 100} = 7.2$ miles

2. $x = 200$ feet

3. $c = \cos^{-1}\left(\frac{153^2 - 201^2 - 175°}{^-2(201)(175)}\right) = 47°$

4. $x = \sqrt{2^2 + 4^2 - 2(2)(4)\cos 45°} = 2.9$ miles

5. $\frac{\sin 50°}{20} = \frac{\sin 45°}{x}$ $\quad x = \frac{20 \sin 45°}{\sin 50°} = 18.5$ miles

Answer Key

Page 98

1. 11 meters at 49° west of north
2. 7 meters at 25° south of west
3. 12 meters at 65° north of east
4. 25 meters at 70° east of south
5. 14 meters at 55° west of south
6. 23 meters at 37° east of north

Page 99

1. 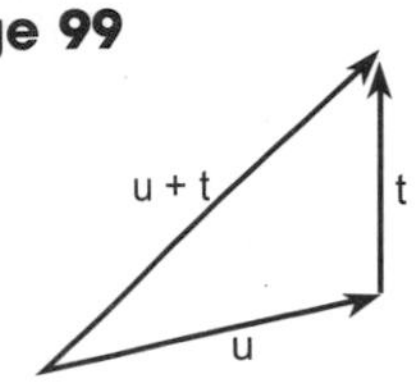

2. 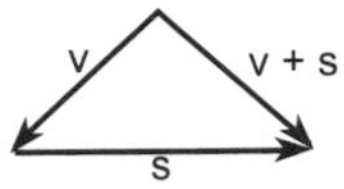

3. 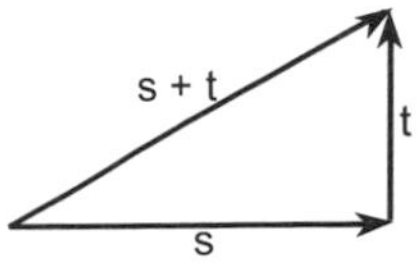

4. 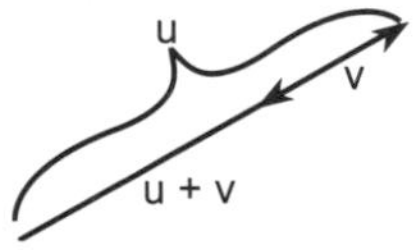

5. 

6. 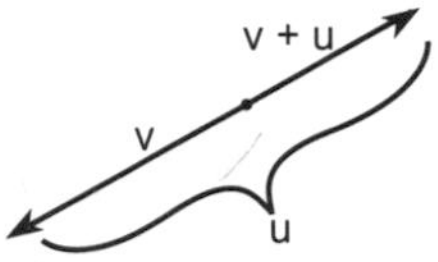

7. 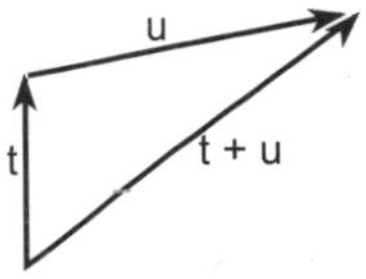

8. 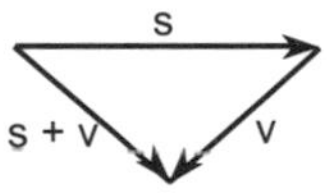

Yes, either way you add, the resulting vector is the same.

Page 100

1. 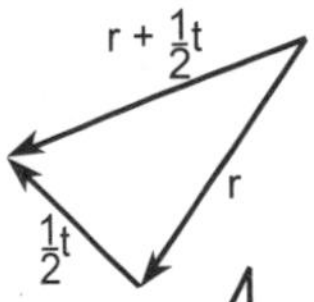

2. 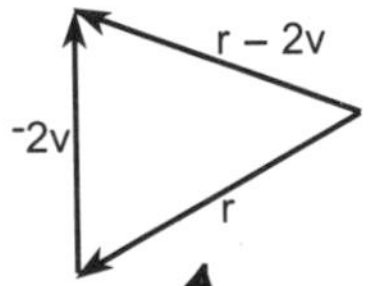

3. 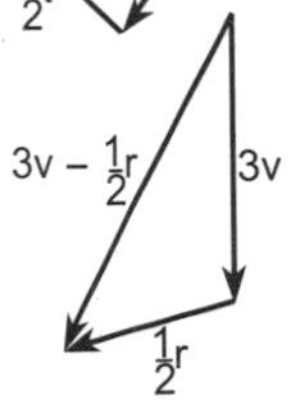

4. 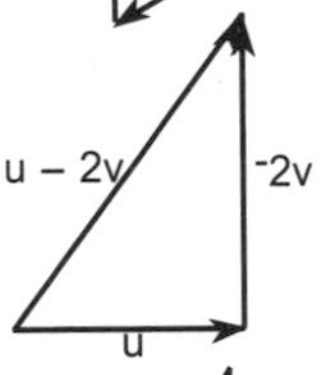

5. 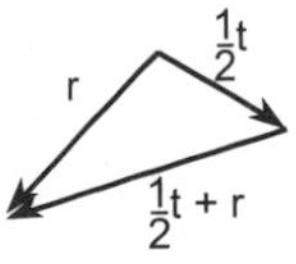

6. 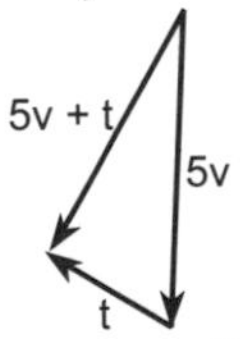

7. 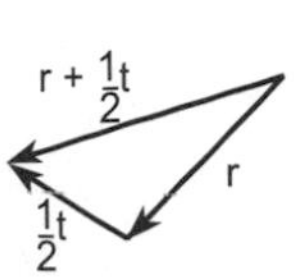

8. 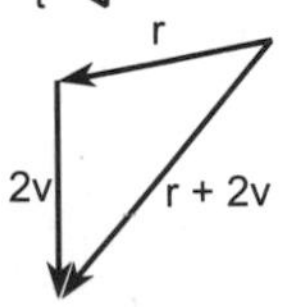

No, when you subtract the opposite vectors, you are changing the direction of the resulting vector.

Page 101

1. $x = -8.3$m $y = 7.2$m
2. $y = -6.3$m $x = -3.0$m
3. $x = 5.1$m $y = 10.9$m
4. $x = 23.5$m $y = -8.6$m
5. $x = -11.5$m $y = -8.0$m
6. $x = 13.8$m $y = 18.4$m

Page 102

1. 17.8 meters at 52° north of east
2. 16.6 meters at 65° south of west
3. 25.9 meters at 62° south of west
4. 40.6 meters at 52° north of west
5. 10.2 meters at 11° south of east
6. 4.1 meters at 76° south of west

Page 103

1. 30.4 mph at 9°
2. He must turn 8.5° east of south
3. 18.9 miles 58° north of west
4. 70 meters north; 70 meters west
5. 201 miles south

Page 104

1. 35 mph at 51° north of west
2. 9.4 mph at 67° north of west
3. 13.3 miles 78° north of west
4. 444.4 mph at 43° north of east
5. 3.2 mph at 2° south of east

Page 105

1. 35 mph at 51° north of west
2. 9.4 mph at 67° north of west
3. 13.3 miles 78° north of west
4. 444.4 mph at 43° north of east
5. 3.2 mph at 2° south of east